The Silvertown Kid

An Autobiographical Novel
By
Graham Mcglone

Front cover aerial photograph of Port Melbourne – by kind permission of Rueben Goossens – www.ssmaritime.com

ISBN – 13: 978-1475229752
ISBN – 10: 1475229755

I am indebted to the following persons for their willingness to lend a hand with photographs, research, anecdotes, documents and their precious time etc.

Sue Bonsor - for proof-reading, advice, and brilliant suggestions.
Petra Jelen - for research, encouragement, and steering me onto the right course.
Terry Willcox - for helping to bring back memories over the course of a few pints.
Ian Sharp - for supplying hop picking photographs.
Glynis Ryan - for providing family photos and for being a lovely sister.
Linda Parry - for passing on anecdotes.
Jim Lloyd - for donating Vindicatrix & Monty's Bar photo's.
David Hollis – for supplying anecdotes regarding Port Montreal
Bill Day – for family facts.
Lesley Sharp – for family photos and documents.
Tanya McDonald – archivist at Memorial University of Newfoundland, Canada, for supplying copies of ship's crew agreements and official log books.
Staff at the Caird Library, National Maritime Museum, Greenwich, for supply of further crew agreements and official log books.
Imelda Eastough – for jogging my fading memory.
Stan Dyson – After reading his excellent book "Silvertown Life – A Boy's Story" – for giving me the inspiration to tell my tale from a different angle.

Dedicated to those who go down to the sea in ships and occupy their business in great waters.

Extract from psalm 107

1: Silvertown

I was trouble even before I was born. My mum and dad had decided that mum wouldn't give birth to me in a hospital delivery room, but like a lot of women hardened by the harsh conditions of the war years, she chose to give birth at home. However, just at the last minute I was causing trouble inside her belly and she was having a difficult labour and needed the services of the local midwife. My parents and my sister Linda, who was just two years old, lived at No. 10 Eastwood Road in West Silvertown, London. Nurse Booth, the midwife lived just two streets away. It was gone past midnight when dad was asked to hurry to get her.

Nurse Booth answered the door in her nightgown. "What do you want at this time of the night, Mr Mcglone?" she demanded.

"You'll have tae be coming wae me, Nurse Booth," said my dad in his thick Glaswegian accent. "Me weef's just about tae give birth to our wee bairn."

"Sorry, I'm off-duty tonight," she said in her authoritarian voice. "You'll have to get the on-duty midwife out."

"But she lives two miles away in Canning Town. She'll nae be able tae get here in teem."

"That's not my problem," said the overworked Nurse Booth, who tried to close the door. My dad wedged his foot in the gap. He'd had enough, and wasn't willing to go in search of the deputy midwife. He spotted her leather bag of medical paraphernalia lying ready in the hallway. He stepped inside and shoved it into her arms. Whilst she stared at him with a mixture of surprise and annoyance, he grabbed her overcoat from the hook and draped it over her shoulders. "Let's be awey," he said, ignoring her complaints. He took her firmly by the arm and marched her through the dark streets back to our house.

Two hours later I had been born, and thanks to Nurse Booth's attendance, mum sailed through my delivery without a hitch. Now, after an initial noisy entrance into the world, and a bellyful of breast milk, I lay in my mum's arms sleeping peacefully. Nurse Booth sat at the foot of the bed drinking tea and happy that this had been a simple and straightforward birth. She was tired and ready to go back to her bed, but she always liked to spend a while with her new-born babies. Mum looked down at my tiny scrunched up purple face. Traces of blood from my birth still stuck in my hair. "He's very ugly, isn't he?" said my mum in her cheeky cockney accent. "Bloody hell, he looks as ugly as Winston Churchill."

"Oh don't say that, Mrs Mcglone. He'll turn out to be a lovely little boy, you'll see."

⚓

In the East End of London, there lies an area that was run-down for as long as I can remember. This is where I was born on Wednesday 26th June 1946. The Second World War had barely finished and the land was dotted with hundreds of bombed-out houses and acres of flattened buildings and factories. In some cases the German bombers had obliterated whole streets. As if this wasn't enough, London suffered from the most terrible smog. Due to the uncontrolled black smoke belched out by countless factory chimneys, shipping in the Thames often came to a standstill because they couldn't see where they were going. Another burden was the frequent

heavy flooding. Until 1984 when the Thames Flood Barrier was completed, numerous roads would be knee deep in flood-water, and untreated sewage and rubbish would gush out of the drains and into the streets. This was Silvertown.

The cost of the war had been astronomical, not only in the lives of those who had been fighting, but financially our little island was almost bankrupt. Money was so tight that very little rebuilding took place and the derelict buildings were an eyesore for many years after hostilities ended. In the shops there was little to buy, and food rationing continued well into the 1950s. During my early years the bomb-sites or 'debris' as we called them, became our playgrounds. Gangs of us kids would climb into derelict buildings to see what we could scavenge, or with a little bit of fertile imagination, they became our own make-believe world.

The Mcglone family comprised my father Hugh, who originally came from the Gorbals of Glasgow, and who now worked as a labourer in a cable-drum factory. My mum Dolly was a Londoner from the East End at

Poplar. My siblings were my elder sister Linda and younger sister Glynis. When I was born my parents agreed on my first name, but couldn't agree on a middle name. My father said quite firmly, "He doesn't need a middle name, because I'm only ever going to call him Graham" – and that was that!

We had many cousins from my mother's side of the family. In the days before the pill and contraception, families were generally quite large. She had ten other brothers and sisters! We had moved house from West Silvertown to East Silvertown – usually referred to simply as Silvertown. Owning your own home was quite unheard of in those austere days, and some of the houses or flats we lived in didn't even possess a bathroom. Bath-time was perhaps twice a week and was accomplished by using a tin bath that usually hung outside on the back wall. Later, when we had the money, we would go to the public bathhouse where one could soak in a proper bath for a whole hour – pure luxury.

Our neighbourhood ran from Canning Town in the west, through West Silvertown to North Woolwich, where the land once again juts out to meet the meandering River Thames. This vast area, three miles long by one mile wide, contained a huge assembly of industrial factories, manufacturing plants, sugar refineries, animal feed mills, ship-breaking yards, foundries, chemical plants and steel yards as well as hundreds of smaller workshops and businesses, all employing thousands of men and women. One of the major employers in the area was the Tate & Lyle sugar refinery, whose huge orange painted factory towered over the whole of Silvertown. Another equally large T&L factory, located at West Silvertown, was concerned with the production of syrup and molasses. They employed thousands. And right smack-bang in the middle of this industrial conglomeration was the biggest employer of all - The Royal Docks.

All these workers needed a place to eat and drink, and so hundreds of cafes and pubs dotted the area. For the men, the pub was an important part of their everyday routine. Very often they would have a pint of ale at lunchtime and repair to the pub again after work. It was the centre of his social life, and once a year the regulars would often go for a day at the seaside on a pub organised beano.

Thousands of people worked in the Silvertown area; ranging from the dockers, who did the cargo-handling, to ship's crews and factory workers. On any given day one could spot pigtailed Chinese sailors, Indian Lascar seamen, Philippino sailors, or black Africans from the ships that came from every corner of the planet. Mostly however, the crews were British merchant seaman, as a great majority of ships were British registered. From morning to night the place was buzzing with noise and energy. I loved it.

Great Britain had been a maritime nation for hundreds of years, and as our empire grew, so did overseas trade grow with it. In the mid-1800s the British Empire and her dependencies were at their greatest, but London never had enough quay space alongside the River Thames so as to load and discharge the millions of tons of cargo that was transported. Shipping was rapidly moving away from the wooden sailing ships and being replaced by larger ocean-going steel cargo vessels. Clearly more dock space and warehousing were required. And so between 1855 and 1921, three huge docks where constructed. These were the Royal Victoria, Royal Albert and King George V Docks; the largest enclosed docks in the world. Even more dock systems were constructed upstream nearer London, and yet another dock downstream at Tilbury. However, none were anywhere near the scale

of the Royal Docks. Shipbuilding and repair facilities and dry-docks sprang up, as did every kind of maritime and nautical offshoot; rope-makers and canvas-makers, shipwrights and victuallers. There was so much for a small boy to explore.

In the cut-and-thrust of today's fast paced society, no one seems to have time to chat to their neighbours. In many cases residents are even unaware of who is living next-door to them. Back in Silvertown's heyday it was very different. Strangely, bearing in mind that a huge diversity of different ethnic groups passed through the area, very few black or coloured families actually lived in the neighbourhood. But there existed such a close knit community, where everyone knew everyone else – and usually everyone else's business! This wasn't limited just to one's own street, and it wasn't unusual to be on friendly terms with families living some distance away. There also seemed to be a willingness to help out a neighbour. If say, a neighbour's husband died, there would very quickly be a door-to-door collection to raise some money for the unfortunate widow. It was similar to the Blitz Spirit that existed in wartime London, where residents knew that they were all in the same boat, and so all pulled together. There was a lot of community spirit and camaraderie in Silvertown.

Life was so much more relaxed in the 1950s compared with today's rat-race and peer pressure to own the latest electronic gadget. I cannot remember having many toys – "Sorry kids, Father Christmas can't afford expensive toys this year." My Christmas stocking perhaps consisted of a Cadbury's selection pack, an apple and orange, a toy car and a Beano Annual. There may also have been an item of clothing in my stocking somewhere, but it probably came from Santa's depot at Rathbone Street Market. Santa really was strapped for cash.

However, we had loads of fun hanging out with our friends, either in a camp or den that we boys had constructed on a bomb-site, or playing rounder's on street corners. Although we took up the whole road with our games, we didn't have to worry too much about traffic – hardly anyone could afford a motor car. For the boys a 'must have' toy was a barrow. These were always self-built using a set of old pram wheels, a thick plank, an orange box, and, if it were to be a really posh one, a padded seat. One also required a very good friend to push the damn thing whilst you steered. Usually we'd take turns. Another use for our barrow would be to load it up with bundles of firewood, that we'd scavenged from a bomb-site, and would go door-to-door selling kindling for a threepenny-bit (1.5p) per bundle.

We had to make money somehow, because come Saturday morning, it was the highlight of the week. Saturday morning pictures consisted of perhaps two cartoons, Pathe News, a short, and the main feature. The Imperial cinema was a bus ride away in Canning Town, but we preferred to walk through the foot tunnel under the River Thames to South Woolwich because there was a choice of two cinemas, the Granada and the Odeon. The ice-creams were fairly cheap and it was always good fun to take a seat upstairs in the balcony and lob dollops onto the unsuspecting kids underneath. Cries of, "You bastards" could be heard throughout the film. Usherettes wielding torches would patrol the upper level seats to catch the perpetrators of the dollops of ice-cream raining down, but no one suspected me with my innocent face and baby blue eyes.

I cannot say that I was particularly academic at school; in fact I was a bit of a slowcoach, and this would have a profound effect on my love of all things nautical. My primary education was at Drew Road School. The school overlooked the King George V Dock; and from my elevated position in the classroom I could gaze down upon the docks and watch the activity going on. Ships would be gently pushed into their berths by tugs whilst signalling with their steam horns. Cranes could be seen loading all manner of merchandise into the cargo hatches of the huge vessels and barges loaded with overseas freight would be manoeuvred alongside the ships. Lorries were offloading their goods into the warehouses, and fork-lift trucks, laden with export cargo, whizzed to and fro. The whole extraordinary scene had a hypnotic effect on me, and I must admit that all thoughts of education were forgotten as I stared out into this wonderfully busy sight. I knew even at that early age that I wanted to pursue a life at sea.

Dominion Monarch in KGV dry dock. Drew Road School on the right

On one particular day at Drew Road the hypnotic effect must have been working overtime because, due to my aforementioned daydreaming, I had completely forgotten to go to the toilet before school chucking out time. I was probably only about 6 years old, and like a lot of kids of that age, not yet in full control of my bowels. I only remembered my lack of toilet acumen as I walked home across the playground. Never mind I thought, our house in Wythes Road was only in the next street. If I clench my butt-cheeks together, I'll make it home alright. However, I'd not reckoned with a playmate who raced across the playground and shouted "Hi Gra, how are you?" and gave me a hefty slap on the shoulder. The hefty slap must have made me lose control of the aforementioned butt cheeks. Oh dear! What a sight. I was wearing short trousers, and the shit just let go and ran down my legs. The other kids laughed and I was mortified with shame. I'm sure that a pack of dogs followed me home. As my mum opened the door, so the tears ran down my cheeks. My mum wrinkled up her nose with the smell. She said "What happened to you, little man?"
"Oh Mum," I cried, "A big boy did it and ran away!"

Just a stone's throw from our school was where ships of the Glen & Shire Line berthed. These beautiful cargo vessels plied the Far East run, calling at Suez, Bombay, Ceylon, Hong Kong, China and Japan. The officers were British and the crew Chinese. Many years earlier, someone had come up with the wonderful idea of the school applying to the British Ship Adoption Society for our school to adopt one of the Glen Line ships, and the mv Glenorchy was chosen. Whenever she returned from a voyage to the Orient, we kids would be taken up to the flat roof of the school, where we would furiously wave the Glen Line house flag and the Union Jack and cheer for all we were worth. The crew regularly sent gifts from abroad, and one I particularly remember was a wooden model of a Chinese junk that went proudly on display outside the head-mistress' study.

Every time the ship berthed, an entire class of kids would be led into the docks and go aboard to explore the ship. We had to be on our very best behaviour. After an escorted tour we would be taken into the officers' saloon and treated to exotic oriental drinks and cakes, all served by uniformed Chinese waiters. We had never seen such luxury as aboard that ship, and to us cockney kids it equated to being taken to the Ritz Hotel for tea. Years later, Miss Green (headmistress) and Miss Lawler (deputy head) both retired at the same time. They had always had a yearning to visit Hong Kong, and so they took passage in the ship which for many years had been so close to their hearts – and a large part of their lives. What better way for them to travel than aboard the good ship Glenorchy?

Having a TV set in Silvertown during the 1950s was something of a rarity. Although funds were very tight, we were one of the first families in our street to have one. My grandad, Harry Billinge, was very good with electronics, and so built us a set. It had a tiny 9 inch cathode ray tube screen controlled by valves and the whole set was encased in a hand-made polished mahogany cabinet that grandad had built himself.

Holidays were a rarity for a majority of cockney kids, and our family was no exception. The adults would go on an annual coach trip to the seaside, usually organised by their factory or place of work. Copious amounts of beer were consumed as the coach stopped at the many fine pubs along the way, and even more beer would be consumed at the seaside. These were known as a beano, and they were generally either all male or all female affairs. Occasionally in the summer months we kids might be taken on a daytrip to Southend-on-Sea where we'd build sandcastles on the beach, eat whelks and jellied eels from a seafood stall, or your mum and dad may let you loose in the leisure park called The Kursaal.

Foreign holidays were not even on the horizon in those days, but there was one holiday that thousands of cockney kids spent the year looking forward to – and that was to go hop-picking. Hop-picking was a family working holiday toiling from morning to evening in the hop fields of Kent – the Garden of England. The hops are an important ingredient to the beer making process, and the addition of hops helps to give each beer its flavour. Thousands of families would descend onto hundreds of Kentish farms in August when the hop buds were ripe for picking. Row upon row of hop-bines covered many acres of hop gardens, and in each leafy row the thick hop-bines had been trained to intertwine around lengths of string and up onto 15 feet high wooden poles. Our job was to pull down the bine and separate the acorn shaped hops from the leaves. The hops were then placed into a wicker basket called a bushel. Picking the coarse leaves could make one's hands red and sore, making it hard manual work. Usually a family would go to the same farm year after year, and the farmer would send your parents an invitation to pick hops in this forthcoming year. Some families would often hire a furniture lorry and pile their meagre possessions onboard; and as the truck trundled out of London en-route to the hop fields, everyone would be singing their hearts out. We always went together with our Aunt Ethel and her three boys, Norman, Stephen and Ian, and so it was also a great time for re-cementing our close family ties.

On arrival, an entire family would be crammed into two small hop-pickers huts. These consisted simply of a black tarred shack with a window. Inside the hut, the spartan rooms were white-washed and contained just a wooden bed frame. The farmer would provide bales of hay with which you could stuff a mattress cover for your bedding. All cooking was done outside on a home-made griddle for which he would provide bundles of faggots for kindling. Toilet facilities were a hole in the ground covered over with a wooden latrine. Copious amounts of lime were thrown down the hole to keep it from smelling too much, and every now-and-then the farmer would drill a new hole and fill in the old one. Usually there would be a fresh water standpipe nearby. Life was very basic.

Our farm was Mr Bones hop farm at Boughton near Faversham in Kent. As we picked dozens of baskets or bushels of hops (no leaves allowed), Farmer Bones and his tallyman would make an entry into our tally-book to record what money was owed for our labours. In the 1950s the payment was about one shilling (5p) per bushel. Nevertheless, it brought in some much needed money, and at the same time we had ourselves a holiday in the lovely Kent countryside. Our hops would go into a circular building called an oast-house, where the hops would be dried in the kilns, packed into long sausage shaped sacks, and transported off to the brewery.

At this time, paid holidays were a rarity, so the men of the family often stayed at home and carried on with their everyday jobs, perhaps travelling down to the hop fields for the weekend.

Our parents quickly understood that children get bored with picking hops, and so they would be content that we just picked in the mornings. During the afternoons we were free to roam - and roam we most certainly did. After living alongside derelict buildings for most of the year, it was wonderful to have miles of hop-gardens, orchards and woodland right on the doorstep. We explored the Kent countryside for many miles around and filled our days with fishing, catching rabbits, mushrooming, or just go scrumping. Going scrumping is when you climb into a farmer's orchard and stuff your pockets with as many apples or plums as you can carry. Many's the time we were chased out of an orchard by a farmer, and on one memorable occasion we heard buckshot whizzing by as he fired his double-barrelled shotgun. Sometimes the grown-ups would go for a glass of stout at the village pub. But as we were underage and not allowed inside, we would sit outside on the warm evenings and sing songs and the girls would dance; and if we were lucky, our parents would send out a packet of crisps or a glass of lemonade and an arrowroot biscuit. Sitting around the campfire was another favourite pastime as we sang the latest songs. In the 1950s new singers were coming onto the scene. They weren't the boring and subdued artists that had been around for years and which were popular with our parents. These guys had slicked back hair and wore drainpipe trousers.

9

This was a new type of music which was exciting and had a great beat to it. It was called rock n roll! In the evenings we would sit around the campfire and lay large potatoes in the fires embers, a dozen at a time, and when they were cooked right through and the skins were almost black, we would retrieve them with a long toasting fork and slice them open. After putting on lots of thick butter we would eat them with our fingers, with the butter running down our chins. We were in heaven. Another very welcome fringe benefit was that the hop picking season overlapped the school holidays, well after the time when we would normally be due to return from our summer break, so that we kids got an extra week off school.

By and large I was a fairly honest and decent boy who mostly behaved myself and never got into too much trouble. Some dads would take off their leather belts and beat their child for the smallest misdemeanour, but my father never beat me for misbehaviour as some did in those days. He was a good dad. However, I'm sure that in some small way I feared what dad would do if I ever went over-the-top and did some serious mischief. Sure enough, we boys would climb into derelict factories or get into the docks to explore, but that was about the extent of it.

However, on one occasion, when I was ten years old, I fell by the wayside. One dark evening I had been playing 'dare' with a school-friend. We were hanging around the Constitutional Club when he dared me to lob a brick through a small window at the back of the club. Well a dare was a dare, and one couldn't lose face. I took careful aim and there was a loud crash of glass as the window disintegrated. My mate was off and running fast, but before I could follow, a hand grabbed me by the shoulder, and I looked up to find that I had been nabbed by the local police constable. He'd appeared out of nowhere. I had never been in trouble with the police before and I was somewhat terrified. To a small boy the policeman was enormous. He led me across the pavement so that the streetlight shone on my face. "Don't I know you?" he asked. "Aren't you Hughie Mcglone's boy?" I nodded my head miserably.

"Hhmm, your dad won't be very pleased if he finds out, will he?" We stood there quietly while he considered how he would tackle the problem. At last he made up his mind. "Right lad," he said decisively. "We can sort this out in three ways. Choice number one is that I can arrest you; take you back to the police station; make a report; and then you'll have a criminal record. You don't want to do that, do you?"

I shook my head. "No Sir."

"I know your dad quite well. I sometimes have a drink with him in this club here. Choice number two is that I could tell your dad, and he might give

you a bloody good hiding for being so stupid." He let this sink in. "You wouldn't like me to do that either, would you?" he asked sternly.
"No Sir I wouldn't."
"Okay young man. It's the third choice for you then." He guided me across to a darkened alley and held me tightly by the lapels of my jacket. He delivered three very hard and sharp slaps to the face which brought tears to my eyes. He handed me a handkerchief. "Right then, laddie, once you've calmed down just make your way home. We won't mention this again, will we?" And that was the way in which instant justice was meted out in Silvertown.

Lizzo

At eleven years of age I had moved schools to attend North Woolwich Secondary Modern School in Elizabeth Street, so we naturally called the school Lizzo. My first day at Lizzo is forever etched upon my brain. Our new intake of 11 years olds was from the easy-going Drew Road Primary or from Storey Street schools. Upon arrival in the school playground I immediately knew that we were in for a hard time. The playgrounds were not mixed. Girls and boys were kept apart. We new boys were milling around just inside the school entrance, not quite sure what to do or where to go. A schoolmaster was sat by the class entrance, but seemed unconcerned with telling us what to do. There was still ten minutes before the school bell would sound.

The expanse of black tarmac playground was devoid of pupils. However, at the far end was a sizeable shed with a corrugated iron roof and a bench seat which stretched the whole width of the shed. It was dark and shadowy under there, but I could see that every boy in the school was gathered under that roof. Soon, a low moan began which brought fear into our eyes, and we bunched together for safety in numbers, like a herd of wildebeest being stalked by lions. The moan became a nightmare chant, which was accompanied by them banging sticks against the tin sides of the shed. Their feet slammed onto the tarmac in time with the chant.
"We're gonna get ya – we're gonna get ya – we're gonna get ya."

The noise became deafening. One hundred-odd boys all grunted out the deadly chant. We new lads could only cower in abject terror as the chant got louder and they stamped their feet in unison. It crossed my mind that this was the terror that the British soldiers must have felt at the Battle of Rorke's Drift as 100,000 Zulu Impi warriors banged their war-shields as they gathered to decimate them. My eyes were like those of a rabbit caught in the headlights of an approaching car, and quite incapable to do anything about it.

"We're gonna get ya – we're gonna get ya – we're gonna get ya."

Suddenly they were off the benches and charging down the length of the playground straight at us. They let out blood-curdling screams as they bore down upon us, and we could only quiver in horror as we awaited the dreadful beating to come. We were bulldozed aside as the first wave hit us, and some boys were bowled over. But as quickly as it had begun, it was all over and the senior boys were laughing at what they thought was a great game of British Bulldog. Because of the close-knit community, many of the older lads knew the younger boys, and we were soon intermingled and laughing together. The school bell sounded and it was time to start lessons.

A year later, in early September, a new intake of pupils arrived at Lizzo. I sat in the shadows of the shed with the rest of the boys and we sang out our welcome –

"We're gonna get ya – we're gonna get ya – we're gonna get ya.

⚓

Time marched on. In 1959 my father died. The cancer caused by years of smoking non-filtered roll-your-own cigarettes brought his life to an early end. There were no savings, and life as a widow must have been tough. God knows how she could afford the simple funeral, but although mother somehow managed to feed us nutritious meals, our school uniforms, although clean, were looking decidedly threadbare. Certainly we never had any new clothes. They were mostly hand-me-downs from our cousins, or were purchased second-hand from a stall in Rathbone Market. We were as poor as the proverbial church mice.

This was resolved one Saturday morning when the whole family took the bus to a small department store in Canning Town. There, we were met by a kindly lady social worker from West Ham Council. She instructed the store's management to completely kit us three children out, not only with new school uniforms, but with everything else we might need, right down to our underwear. The council ratepayers picked up the bill. I shall never forget the sense of shame I felt when I overheard one of the store workers whisper to her colleague, "That lot don't look as if they need handouts. They're a bunch of scroungers."

Cunarder RMS Mauritania in KGV dock. Lizzo school is below it.

Soon afterwards, my younger sister Glynis, whose name had been entered on a list of needy children, was chosen to visit Norway on an exchange scheme for underprivileged kids. On arrival in Southern Norway she was met by a lovely couple, Barden and Edith Olson, who made her very welcome indeed. They had no children of their own, but what they did have was a gorgeous golden retriever dog, an ocean-going motor yacht, and a huge house near Stavanger. They were in fact millionaires. Coincidentally, they had made their fortune in the shipping industry. Glynis stayed with them for three whole months during the summer of 1960 and had a superb time. She was just 11 years old. Things were looking up.

Meanwhile, the man who lived across the street from us had recently lost his wife through ill health. His name was Albert Edwards – known far and wide as Soupy. He had a very busy job as the caretaker of the Tate Institute in Wythes Road. The Tate Institute had been built in 1887 by Sir Henry Tate for the social needs of his sugar workers. The company also provided a sports ground off Manor Way, and the workers had their own football and cricket teams. By all accounts Tate & Lyle were very good employers. They offered the best wages in the area, and there was a good social camaraderie and many workers stayed in their employment for the whole of their working lives.

Soupy Edwards would manage every aspect of the functions and dances held in the institute's bars and the dancehall; and if he wasn't working behind the bar, then he may be laying tables or cleaning. He was a non-stop workaholic. He had six children, only two of whom, both teenagers, were living at home. He lived in the caretaker's house which was attached to the Institute, which meant that he was better off than most, because his house came rent-free with the job, as well as Tate & Lyle paying for the council rates, gas, electricity, water rates and telephone. But best of all – he had an inside bathroom!

His life was so very busy that he asked my mum to help out as his paid housekeeper. This man would be up at 5am and work hard all day to 6pm; he was a bundle of nervous energy. He was also a union rep for the TGWU, and in the evening, members would stop by to pay their union fees, or he'd be seeing to other union matters. In addition, he organised coach trips to go see the latest musical or blockbuster film in London's theatreland. He never stopped working. Gradually the situation changed when he would take my mum out on a date aboard his motorbike and sidecar, and as the months passed, it was agreed that they would get married. This they eventually did when I was 14 years old. My sisters and I weren't invited to attend the simple registry office wedding, but just packed off to school as usual. They saved us kids some cakes and sandwiches from the small wedding meal. That's how it was in those days. We simply moved all our stuff across the street into his house and that was that. Many years later I asked my mother why she'd married him. I'll always remember her answer. She said, "We had no money and he needed a wife – so needs must." It was a marriage of convenience, but as she said years later, "He's not such a bad old stick, and I have grown to love him in my own particular way."

He asked me to help out doing odd-jobs around the dance hall. At one stage I was asked to clear out two huge storage sheds at the rear of the hall. I worked the weekends from early morning till night for several weeks - hardly taking a break. At the back of the shed were hundreds of tubular canvas-backed chairs. They all had to be taken apart, wire-brushed, and painted. It was back-breaking work. He was a hard taskmaster and expected everyone to work just as hard as he did. If I took as much as a ten-minute break he'd say, "Come on, Graham, keep going or you'll never ever finish it." However, he could also be very generous, as when he paid for me and my sisters to go away on several school trips to the Lake District and beyond.

When you looked at Albert he had an instantly recognisable face. Together with his short chubby body and his wide grin, he was the spitting image of the cartoon character Fred Flintstone. He had a great sense of humour. He needed to. One lazy Sunday afternoon, he was fast asleep in his favourite chair after eating a huge roast dinner. Some heavy snoring was underway, and so my sister Glynis and I decided that he would benefit from some make-up whilst he was in the Land of Nod. We plastered his face with foundation, bright red lip-gloss, mascara, eye shadow and some glitter for good measure. He slept right through it all. We then went upstairs to play and thought nothing more of it. Meanwhile, he woke up just as the front doorbell rang. It was a colleague from work who had come on union business. The poor chap said not a word, and kept a straight face, even when invited into the parlour. It was then that Albert caught sight of himself in the mirror. He yelled up the stairs "You little buggers", he chuckled. "Just wait till I catch up with you."

Sometimes Soupy could be somewhat overbearing. My mum and sister Glynis would often settle down to watch some "girlie" programme on TV. Then Soupy would come in and decide that he wanted to watch football. He took no account of what they wanted to watch. He would simply change channels and that was that. It really got on her nerves.

Months before, she had been prescribed Valium (or some similar tablets) by her doctor. She never found the need to take them, so she had built up quite a sizeable stockpile.

She would say to Soupy, "D'you wanna cuppa tea, love?" and off she went to the kitchen.

She would toss a Valium tablet into his cup, and ten minutes after drinking his tea he would fall fast asleep.

My mum would turn to Glynis and say, "Soppy bleeder ain't he? Switch over the TV Glyn."

Life at Lizzo wasn't so bad – mostly because I was hardly ever there! Usually when playing truant I would go and sit beside the river and watch the ships arriving and departing at the Royal Docks. Even more ships, tugs, barges, pleasure steamers, and every kind of vessel would pass by on their way to the West India, Millwall and Surrey Commercial docks which lay further upriver. It was much better than sitting in a classroom. It wasn't that I hated school, but basically I was one of life's daydreamers, and my days would pass by in a misty reverie, whereby I fantasised about sailing across clear blue seas. Although I wasn't academic, I had the capacity to stuff my head full of general knowledge and useless trivia. Someone bought me the Guinness Book of Records and I soaked the information up into my brain. Even today I'm good at quizzes and crosswords.

⚓

One day when I had played truant I had gone to the cinema in Bow High Street for an afternoon matinee. The movie was a sexy X-rated film, but the management didn't much care about underage kids getting in. As I sat in the darkened auditorium, I could see that there were only about half a dozen other customers. I sat in the centre of an empty row, where I could put my feet up and relax with no one nearby.

Gradually as my eyes adjusted to the darkness, I watched as a middle-aged man made his way along past the empty seats and sat down next to me. I'd never clapped eyes on him before.

"Hello," he said in a soft Welsh accent. "You seem a bit young to be watching an X-rated film, don't you?"

"So what?" I retorted. "No one else is bothered."

"Oh it's no problem to me," he said reassuringly, "but shouldn't you be at school?" Usually I was so shy I wouldn't say boo to a goose, but this man was upsetting me.

"You've got the whole cinema to sit in, yet you wanna sit next to me. Why's that?" I asked.

"I thought we could get acquainted," he whispered, and ran his hand along my thigh up towards my nether regions. That was it. I'd had enough of this dirty bugger. I jumped out of my seat; but instead of making a run for it, I shouted at the top of my lungs, "Will someone stop this dirty pervert from touching me?" Within seconds a bright torch was shone along the aisle and strong hands dragged him out of the cinema and threw him out onto the street.

My love affair with ships and all things nautical continued unabated, and instead of attending school, I'd bunk-off to the locks where the great ships entered the Royal Docks. I would watch them being assisted by powerful tugs as the cargo ships were manoeuvred into the lock from the River Thames. These vessels had voyaged thousands of miles from the other side of the world, and now their task was almost accomplished.

At weekends, when no loading or discharge work was going on, I would climb through a gap in the dock fence and would wander around the quaysides, rarely challenged by the docks police. Every facet of the ships -

16

what countries they were sailing to, what cargoes they carried and what ports they would visit, fascinated me.

.

At this stage of my life, I was fast becoming a painfully shy and introverted character. This I think had a knock-on effect with other lads at school. Because they perceived that I was a withdrawn and sensitive boy, I was sometimes picked upon by one or two boys in my class. It wasn't to last too long. Matters came to a head one afternoon when a boy called Roy, who was much bigger than me, scornfully asked me to fight him. "Sure," I said, attempting to sound unconcerned. "We'll fight on the debris right after school. I'll be there." I think I took the wind out of his sails by my blasé answer. Word quickly spread around the whole school, and a large crowd of boys, and even girls, gathered at the appointed hour on the debris. Roy was so much larger than I, that I was certain to be pulverised. I was worried as hell and trying not to show it. One lad called Peter, to whom I shall be eternally grateful, gave me some sound advice. "I've fought him before. He hates being hit in the face. Whatever you do - don't fight fair."

One boy took it upon himself to act as a referee. Whilst Roy and I faced each other, the boy prattled on about fighting fairly, no kicking, no

17

head-butting, etc; I remembered Peter's words, and without further ado, smacked Roy in the mouth. Down he went like a sack of spuds and it was all over. I looked around. "Anyone else fancy their chances?" I asked quietly. There were no takers, and my stock rose quite dramatically as the chancers realised that I wasn't a pushover

At 14 years old, most boys of my age had a girlfriend or mixed socially with girls. Although I was becoming interested in the opposite sex, I found that to strike up a conversation with a girl was beyond me. I just didn't know what to say. I was completely tongue-tied. I wasn't worried too much though, as I had the ships and the river to keep me occupied. However, on one of the rare days when I was at school, my sexual education took a new twist.

It was lunchtime, and most of the kids were out in the playground after lunch. I was walking past a classroom when the door suddenly opened and one of my classmates stuck his head out, quickly scanned the corridor and urgently whispered, "Graham, get yer arse in 'ere. But don't make a sound." I went inside. The curtains had been closed and the room was full of shadows. It was also full of other boys from my year-group, and there was a general air of expectancy with lots of whispering going on. I had no idea why I was there, so I asked my classmate.
"It's Francis," he whispered. "She'll be 'ere any minute. She's gonna show us her fanny." Francis was a rather chubby girl of our age-group who would sometimes let you feel her tits, and who one may kindly describe as, a 'good sport.'

A moment later the door opened and Francis stepped quickly inside. The room went deathly quiet. "Are you ready?" hissed Francis. We all nodded silently. One of the boys had the good sense to flick the lights on. In one fluid motion Francis slid her knickers down to her knees and raised the navy blue pleated skirt to above her waistline. No one said a word. We all silently stared at this rarely seen item of female erotica. Perhaps fifteen seconds passed. "Right that's yer lot," said Francis as she adjusted her uniform and swept out the door, leaving us boys with exclamations of, "Bloody hell" – "Did ya see how hairy it was?"

I went downstairs to the playground to ponder this new-found sexual information. A boy, who had not been present at the classroom striptease, raced up. "I just heard that Francis showed you her fanny", he said breathlessly. I nodded. "What did it look like," he enquired.
"Well," I said. "It's a sort of flat design and the crack of her bum comes all the way around to the front."

⚓

Some boys love playing sport, others have a stamp album, some collect bird's eggs, but my hobby was centred around my most enduring passion; I collected postcards of ships. This new found hobby opened up a whole new world for me; things I had never thought possible. I'm not sure who introduced me to ship postcards, because quite a few other local boys also collected them. Whoever it was, I'm eternally grateful. Our hobby involved an hour's journey by bus or train into the city centre of London; no mean feat for a 13 year old boy of a shy disposition. We would then trawl around the many shipping offices to ask for free photographs of their (usually) vast ocean-going fleets. Many of the old shipping companies are long gone and consigned into history, their ageing fleets overtaken by the advent of modern container ships and destined to be broken up and melted into razor blades and tin cans. Back in the 1950s and 60s, the companies numbered in their hundreds; their ships numbered thousands. Other companies, mostly cruise lines such as P & O or Cunard, survived the upheaval, and are still well known to this day. A great majority of company offices were centred on Leadenhall Street or Fenchurch Street in the city. There, they occupied vast ornate edifices built of granite and polished stone. Uniformed commissionaires would point visitors towards the right office, or alternatively keep the riff-raff out.

Very often in the front foyer there would be a scaled-down model ship housed within a polished wood and glass case. The hand- made models, perhaps 10 feet long, would be a perfect replica of one of the company's great liners. A brass plate on the wall outside in the street would indicate to the financial world that this was a company to be reckoned with; a company who could be trusted to deliver their goods. Dignified looking city gents dressed in the *de rigueur* gentleman's uniform of pin-stripe trousers, morning coat, bowler hat, rolled umbrella and brief case would shuttle between these offices on vital business. This was serious stuff! These offices were the centre of worldwide operations for each shipping company, and from these buildings, communications and signals would be sent to the fleet's ships to inform them of ports-of-call, cargo loading, fuelling arrangements, crew changes, etc. There was so much to organize.

In Leadenhall and Fenchurch Streets alone were the offices of, Cunard, Port Line, Royal Mail, Shaw Savill & Albion, Blue Star Line, Glen Line, Brocklebank's, Elder Dempster, Ben Line Steamers, Canadian Pacific, Ellerman Line, New Zealand Shipping Company, Federal Steamship Co, Blue Funnel Line, British India Steamship Co, The Peninsular & Orient Steam Navigation Company (I love that mouthful!), Clan Line and The Union Castle Line. Dozens more less well-known company offices were housed in the nearby side streets. They were companies who owned tramp steamers, oil tankers, tugs, pleasure craft, coasters, coal colliers. The list was infinite.

Although we lads were asking for free handouts of the company's ships, the office personnel manning the reception desks were usually only too happy to accommodate us and gave out thick wads of picture postcards of their vessels. It was after all just advertising literature. We soon accumulated quite a sizeable collection of these photographs, which would then be inserted into photo-albums. Many happy hours would be spent inspecting friend's albums and doing swaps for the ones we didn't have.

On one occasion I was mooching around the city centre quite alone. In the back streets I came across the small office of a Japanese shipping company; one that I had never heard of before. On the door was the company logo and its name, "Osaka Shosen Kaisha – OSK Line. I went inside. Two girls were manning the front desk, and I explained to the youngest that I was a collector of postcards and asked if they had any photographs of the OSK ships. I wasn't expecting too much. "Why, of course we have," she smiled. "You can have as many as you like." She brought out a great wad of top quality photographs. There must have been over fifty. Each ship looked to be a big sleek passenger/cargo liner with lovely graceful lines and an elegant colour scheme. I told them about the number of Silvertown kids who collected these postcards; and that I had never heard of OSK. "Our company's ships don't often come into London," she explained, "but we've got the Santos Maru docking at the West India Docks next week. Would you and some friends be interested in going onboard for a visit?" I said that I most certainly would, and that I could think of at least ten friends who would like to come along. They introduced themselves as Katie and Claire and said they would provide transport to the ship, and both would be accompanying us onboard. We made plans to get picked up next Saturday morning outside Canning Town railway station. That day I went home well pleased with my efforts.

I had no problem whatsoever filling my quota of ten places, and we duly awaited our transport on Saturday morning. When it turned up, we were gobsmacked. The youngest girl Katie, had a large chauffeur driven limousine, and the other girl, Claire, drove an Isetta bubble car. We scratched our heads as to how we would get everyone aboard. We were thirteen in total, so we loaded up the limo until it would take no more. That still left four to cram into the Isetta. We wedged ourselves in so tight that I'm sure I can still smell her perfume!

We arrived onboard the Santos Maru. She was big and sleek and modern with hardly a spot of rust upon her decks. As there was no cargo handling going on, the ship was quiet. There didn't appear to be any crew around, so the girls took us into the officers' saloon, made some coffee and suggested that we go have a look around the ship by ourselves.

We explored the whole ship from bow to stern. After inspecting the wheelhouse, we climbed down into the cargo holds. Some of the boys began sifting through the cargo to see if there was anything worth nicking. After climbing halfway up a mast, we clambered down into the massive engine room, looking into every nook and cranny. We continued along the propeller shaft tunnel at the very bottom of the ship, then up a vertical steel ladder through narrow ducting, back up into sunlight on the open deck. There were ropes and wires and bits of cargo gear everywhere, and it's a wonder that one of us didn't trip and injure ourselves. If this had happened in today's Health & Safety conscious society, with ten young boys running unsupervised around a ship, I have no doubt that OSK would have been banned from the London Docks – and then sued for millions of pounds!

The trip back to Silvertown was aboard an old steam train with separate passenger compartments. As the train set off, one of the boys brought a big fat Cuban cigar out of his jacket pocket. "Where did you get that?" I asked suspiciously. "Nicked it outta the cupboard in the officers' saloon," he openly admitted. With some difficulty, he set alight to the cigar and began puffing away. Another lad joined in, and they were both dragging the thick acrid smoke down into their lungs. The compartment stank.

I was rather upset about this turn of events, as Katie and Claire had been so good to us, and had gone out of their way to be nice to us all. They had even brought along a thick wad of postcards for the boys, and I didn't think that nicking stuff was a decent way to repay their generosity. We were nearing Silvertown station when the two lads went a funny grey colour. They just about made it to the drop-down window before they vomited in unison, but the forward speed of the train caused most of it to splash back all over their faces. Served them right!

Royal Albert (left) and King George V Docks. Royal Victoria is off-camera.

Over the years I collected many photographs of ships and I had one of the finest collections in the area. The albums of photos were categorized into their respective shipping companies and presented in chronological order. There were dozens of albums covering many great and historic, but now defunct shipping groups. They took up two whole shelves of a bookcase in my small bedroom, and I got much pleasure in occasionally leafing through them.

Many years later, probably thinking that I was far too old to possess such boyhood trifles, I presented the complete collection to a young cousin for safekeeping and in the hope that he would nurture and cherish them and get as much enjoyment from these historical postcards as I had done. He promptly lost them!

My bus journeys into London's city centre gave me much more confidence, and I started to venture further afield into the West End. The sleazy streets of Soho, with scantily clad girls trying to entice potential customers into strip clubs, were an eye-opener to any young boy. Later I gravitated to the museums in West London; the Natural History, the Science Museum, the V&A and many more. My innate interest in general knowledge got a shot-in-the-arm as I soaked up the wealth of information to be found there. At weekends I would walk for hours around the famous streets or through the royal parks with not a care in the world. Normally I would purchase a cheap Red Rover bus and train ticket which enabled me to go wherever I pleased. In those gentler times, parents felt that their children were much safer on the streets than in today's society, and my mum wouldn't be too concerned if I didn't re-appear until the evening.

⚓

I was now being more accepted at Lizzo, in the sense that my social skills must have improved slightly, and although I was still painfully shy in the girlfriend department, I now had a section of boys with whom I would hang out. The reason for this change of fortunes must be that I had unaccountably started to attend school more often. I now had lots of friends, some of whom would call me Ginge, on account of my reddish/brown hair, and over the years the nickname seemed to have stuck. My best friend at that time was Danny O' Sullivan, and we would often leave school during lunchbreak to watch the ships from the comfort of a riverside bench in Victoria Park. For lunch we would buy a fresh loaf of bread, rip out the middle, coat it with a copious spread of butter, and stuff it full with tasty hot chips with salt and vinegar – yummy. I took more interest in the lessons and remember especially looking forward to attending Mrs Gibbon's geography classes. I could name all the oceans and any capital city in the world. My studies of the Guinness Book of Records had brought their rewards. However, although I enjoyed the history lessons and Mr Martindale's woodwork class, the subject that brought me terror was mathematics. I could rattle off the times table – I wasn't that thick; but algebra, trig, fractions, angles, and division were a closed book as far as I was concerned.

The corporal punishment meted out by teachers in my schooldays would, in today's society, swiftly bring a criminal charge for GBH, job dismissal, or probably both. Back then it wasn't uncommon for a teacher to administer a caning for any slight infraction of rules or misbehaviour. Our teachers had a whole box of tricks when it came to punishment. Most teachers thought nothing of rapping any daydreamer across the knuckles with a wooden ruler to get his attention. Likewise, to throw a rubber or a stick of chalk, or even a chunky wooden blackboard eraser was common, and hardly worth a mention.

At Lizzo, Mr Clements, our muscular Welsh PE teacher, thought it great fun to send a heavy medicine ball crashing into you if one wasn't fast enough doing press-ups. Mr Hughes, another Welshman who taught maths, favoured a size 13 slipper to keep us on the straight-and-narrow. Every boy feared getting the cane from Mr Martindale, the woodwork and metalwork teacher, because he had a selection of five different width canes. The more serious the offence, the more slender was the cane. He would rock back on his heels, putting in much effort as the cane whistled through the air. It often left a red weal which took weeks to heal over. The lady teachers weren't averse to wielding the cane either, but would usually send you to the headmaster.

Last but not least was Mr Green our headmaster, who was nearing retirement. He was yet another Welshman, and could be a terror with regard to punishment. One day I had to go to his study to deliver a sick-note after a bout of impetigo. He shared his small office with his secretary, who informed me that he was out the office momentarily; please take a seat beside her desk and wait. She carried on typing a letter.

Moments later the door opened and a boy was propelled, at arm's length, into the office by Mr Green. He had a tight grip on the boy's throat. "I'm not taking any more of this shit from you, boyo," he shouted, and smacked the lad straight in the mouth. The boy shot across the room, and with a huge crash, collided with the steel filing cabinets, and ended up in an untidy heap. Blood trickled down his chin. "Now get back to your class. Get out of my sight." That was the end of that incident. The secretary hadn't even stopped typing!

⚓

One oddity of the area which I soon came to take in my stride was the number of poofters or homosexual sailors one would encounter on the streets. Every evening these characters would come ashore by the dozen dressed in 'drag' – and wearing enough cosmetics to sink a battleship. Their favourite haunts were The Round House, The Kent Arms and The California, all in North Woolwich. Another concentration of pubs were to be found in nearby Custom House where the bars catered for the stevedores and sailors working aboard ships berthed in the Royal Victoria Docks. The poofs would congregate there and get legless whilst trying to pick up stray drunken sailors. Their mannerisms, although attempting to emulate females, were completely over-the-top, and they ended up resembling a caricature of a normal woman. Where a lady may walk with a slight sway of her hips, the poofs would sashay across the room with exaggerated movements. It was all very strange. In the main I found that they were very sexually promiscuous – the AIDS virus was still well into the future.

Sometimes they'd get up onto the small stage and belt out a song or two, but I always found their faces sad and desperate, while at the same time attempting to put out the message, "Look at me. I'm so outrageous. What a great time were having." These 'Steam Queens' as they were known, would return to their respective ships, and during their workday have to conform to conventional standards as regards dress code and lack of warpaint. But come the night, they were out in force again, on the hunt for their next conquest. We'll hear more about the queens later on.

⚓

Just after lunch on a Friday in July 1961 we were given the afternoon off to go search for a job. There were so many jobs available in the early 60s, that by 4pm I had secured a job as an office boy at British Rail's Plumstead depot, and that was the end of my being a schoolboy. My wages as a 15 year old lad would be £3 15s 6d per week (£3:78 in today's money). In those days there was no end-of-school prom, no parties, and no fanfare. Simply goodbye, and you were out the school gate. The job didn't last too long. I was far too stupid!

On my first day at work, the office secretary gave me a thick wad of envelopes into which I was to insert a leaflet, seal them closed, and put them into the out-tray. Easy-peasy. An hour later, she looked aghast as I licked the last of the envelopes, thick globules of glue all around my mouth. It tasted dreadful. "What the hell are you doing, you twerp," she exclaimed." You're supposed to use the water-roller – not lick 'em." The next day, the depot manager, Mr Fuller, decided that my talents would be better employed working out on the delivery trucks as a van-drivers mate. This was wonderful news, as it got me out of the office, doubled my wages, and I was working with other lads my own age. I loved it.

The job entailed loading our ancient Scammel three-wheeled truck with boxes and parcels, rolls of carpet, etc. Most of the goods were mail-order catalogue items which we delivered in the suburbs of South East London.

My new post also introduced me to Jacko. Jacko was my driver, and it was my job to ensure that we went to each delivery address in proper sequence. Whilst Jacko sat in the truck, I'd quickly knock on the customer's door, hand over the item, get a signature and get on our way. Jacko was a handsome bugger. He was in his early thirties with dark good looks and great fun to work with. We were always laughing at something or other. But he would often go over-the-top, as when he would tell all and sundry how well-endowed he was. "Like a bloody donkey I am, son," he would chortle.

One sunny afternoon in Eltham, I knocked on a lady's door to deliver a parcel. She answered my knock wearing a revealing negligee. She wasn't wearing too much else except a lovely smile. I'd guess she was in her late twenties. I was now sixteen years old and looking fit and strong from the hard work of life out on the delivery vans. My face was devoid of any teenager's acne and I wasn't an unattractive young fellow. "Would you like to bring that parcel up to my bedroom, young man," she said in a husky voice. "Perhaps we could have a glass of wine together. You're not in any hurry, are you?" Although I got on well with my male colleagues, you will perhaps remember that I was still a very shy and retiring soul, and definitely not used to females sending carnal overtures in my direction. I blushed bright red. "Well, perhaps it would be okay," I stammered. My mind was racing with thoughts that at long last I was gonna get myself laid. Suddenly from out of nowhere Jacko laid a gentle hand on my shoulder and said, "You go sit in the van, Gra. I'll look after this customer," and without further ado he very firmly closed the front door and went upstairs with Her Ladyship. The lucky bugger didn't reappear for over an hour!

⚓

One week later one of my work colleagues, a lad of about my own age called Dave, invited me to accompany him to an evening social event at his local youth club at Abbey Wood in the south-eastern suburbs. Music was playing and some smoochy dancing was under way. I of course stood well back on the sidelines. A girl with long dark hair, whom I'd noticed looking in my direction, came over. She was very pretty with a lovely figure and innocent eyes. "Would you like to dance?" she asked softly. We had a couple of slow dances, during the course of which I was my usual tongue-tied self.

"It's rather hot in here. Would you like to go outside for a while?" she asked. Outside the building, she took my hand and led me underneath a nearby railway bridge. It was very dark. She made all the running and began kissing me. Suddenly her tongue was searching for mine, and her hips were grinding into my groin. I sensed rather than felt my nether regions growing fiercely like never before. She didn't need any coaching and extracted him from out of my trousers. She bent down and quickly fiddled with her clothes, and all of a sudden she was leaning back against the bridge and guiding him inside her, and unexpectedly, there was I having sex for the very first time. It was somewhat spoilt when a commuter train went rapidly by... clickety-clack...clickety-clack...clickety-clack. It had an almost nightmarish kaleidoscopic effect as it rushed by, and I was sure that I could see people on the train staring at us. I cannot truthfully say that having my first sexual encounter by way of a knee-trembler under a railway bridge constitutes a memorable moment. To be honest, I cannot even remember her name. Oh well..... *C'est la vie.* But hey, at least I'd lost my cherry!

But while I was fooling around under railway bridges, there was much more tom-foolery going on in central London and in the corridors of power at Westminster. A good-time girl called Christine Keeler had been having a steamy affair with Britain's Minister for War, John Profumo. She in turn had been having a sexual relationship with an alleged Russian spy, Yevgeny Ivanov, the senior naval attaché at the Soviet Embassy, and the stage was set for a political scandal that would bring down a prime minister.

Throw into the mix another call girl called Mandy Rice-Davies, a pair of West Indians, Lord Astor of Cliveden, a fashionable osteopath called Stephen Ward, a chiselling landlord called Peter Rachman, and the British secret service, and we had a cocktail with all the ingredients to keep Britain's citizens amused for months on end. The newspapers had a heyday, and the Prime Minister, Harold Macmillan, stepped down on the grounds of ill health. Another political dinosaur had bitten the dust.

⚓

Christmas was coming around and someone had organised the Plumstead Depot's Xmas Party. The event was held in the White Hart pub, and it was arranged that Dave, Jacko, an Irishman called Leo Cullen and I would arrive early to get the drinking underway. I had never had much experience with alcohol, but I surprised myself when the first pint of Courage Best Bitter slid easily down my throat. More followed in quick succession and the evening was livened up with a DJ and music. Some girls came in the bar and I recall having a dance, but I couldn't remember how many pints of bitter I'd had, and my legs wanted to go in different directions. It was certainly quite a few. By chucking out time I'd had far too much and I could hardly walk. The problem was, that I lived on the north side of the Thames, and Plumstead is on the south side. I took a taxi to the Woolwich foot tunnel and started to drag myself the quarter of a mile through the white tiled tunnel, deep under the River Thames. I must have been so pissed; I was bouncing off the walls. But happily a young chap, who I had never seen before, caught me just as I was just about to keel over. "Hey there, fella. Steady as she goes. Here, put your arm over my shoulder." He helped me through the tunnel to the North Woolwich side; I would have never made it otherwise. It was well after midnight when we exited the tunnel. The last bus had gone, but he very kindly assisted me for another mile or so to my house in Wythes Road. It was one-o-clock by this time, and the house was in darkness as he rang the bell. My mum answered the door in her dressing gown. Even though my brain was befuddled with drink, I shall never forget his words. He said to my mum, "Hey missus, does this belong to you?"

In early 1963, my sister Linda found that she was pregnant. There was never any thought of marrying the father of the child, and in that day-and-age, having a termination wasn't an option. As was usual in the early 1960s, young expectant mums went to a Home for Unmarried Mothers to learn how to care for a baby. The home was in Streatham, South London, where she stayed for about two months, before she would go to a regular hospital to have her baby.

I travelled over there one Saturday afternoon and took her out for the day. She told me that the rules and regulations in the home were very strict, and the mum's-to-be not only had cleaning tasks, but were required to be back behind locked doors at 8pm, and the lights were turned off at 9:30pm. She couldn't wait to get back home to Silvertown. On 18th September 1963 she gave birth to a baby daughter, and called her Toni Ann.

2: The Vindi

I was now 17 years old and the urge to travel the world was still strong. I applied to the Merchant Navy Training Board to attend a pre-sea training course. This would consist of a three month course, which would culminate in being allocated a first ship. I travelled into London to attend the interview, where I was shown into an office in which several people sat at desks looking busy.

My interviewer wore the uniform of a Merchant Navy Officer. As he finished off some important looking documentation, he indicated with a nod of his head that I should take a seat in the chair opposite. I made myself comfortable.

"WHO THE F**K TOLD YOU TO SIT DOWN?" he bellowed. His face was red with rage. *"DON'T YOU DARE SIT UNTIL I TELL YOU TO - GOT IT?"* I shot out of the chair confused and disorientated. "Yes sir," I mumbled. I stood awkwardly whilst he looked me up and down. As he grumbled and made some notes, I looked around the room. The other residents of the office hadn't batted an eyelid at the shouting and bad language, and I - quite rightly - guessed that the screaming fit was a regular occurrence, designed to highlight any boy who couldn't take the heat. After all, if any lad started crying for his mum whenever someone shouted at him, then he was hardly likely to be able to endure the rigors of a lifetime at sea, was he? As soon as I realised that, then I began to relax. "You can sit down now, son," he said. He handed me pen and paper and I was instructed to write - in my very best handwriting - how I had travelled to the interview, what trains or buses I'd taken, and how long was my journey. It was all very strange information. No questions at all were asked with regard to why I wanted a career at sea.   After half an hour I was handed a list of what clothes, wash gear, bath towels and pocket money etc that I must take to the sea school. Included was a list of the very strict rules that I would have to abide by. I was also handed a rail warrant and instructed to report in one month to the training ship Vindicatrix at Sharpness in Gloucestershire.

⚓

Onboard the train en-route to Sharpness, I met up with another lad called Chris Stafford, who would also be going to the Vindicatrix. It helped to pass the time as we played cards. On arrival at Berkeley railway station in Gloucestershire we linked up with dozens of boys from all over the country. Instructors from the training camp were there to meet us. We were quickly herded into two lines, and told that we would be marching to the camp - just three miles away.

The camp was a collection of a dozen or so Nissan type dormitory huts, all of which accommodated about 30-odd boys. There was also a quartermasters store, offices, recreation hut, guardroom, classrooms, sick-bay, games room, reading room, washrooms and smart bungalow accommodation for the Captain Superintendant and senior officers.

After being allocated a bunk-bed in a hut, we were marched through the camp to an offshoot of the Gloucester Canal, where sat the actual training ship. The Vindicatrix was a huge ex sailing ship built in 1893. She looked enormous. As a hulk, she now had her masts removed, and her former cargo holds had been reconstructed to provided messroom and classroom facilities. She had previously acted as accommodation ship, where the Vindi Boys had slept way down in the orlop deck at the bottom of the ship, but shortly before my arrival this was closed down due to serious infestations of rats and cockroaches. As we marched to the gangplank, boys lined the upper decks in their hundreds to greet us. "Hey Newboys - you'll be sorry you ever set eyes on the Vindi. You'll be crying for your mum within a week. You ain't ever going 'ome, Newboys." The situation didn't look good. What the hell had I signed up for? There were more ribald statements that we would starve to death within a week.

We were taken onboard, and at the ship's office our general information was recorded in the camp's register. Cash which we had been instructed to bring was taken from us and an account book started. These funds were to cover all manner of things, including paying for uniform and pocket-money at 5 shillings (25p) per week. Somewhere in amongst that sum, there was also the cash for a train ticket home, just in case the school decided that you were a liability if you stayed.

We were taken along to the messdeck and seated at long wooden trestle tables, where catering cadets would serve our meal as part of their training. Our instructor, who went by the name of Popeye, informed us that as we'd been travelling all day and would no doubt be very hungry, we would receive an extra large serving of dinner.

As a catering boy put my meal on the table, my worst fears were realised. On the plate was a dried up egg, half a chipolata sausage, a tired looking plum tomato, and a tablespoon of baked beans.
"What the hell is this shit?" I enquired from my server.
"Well if you don't want it Pal, then I'll have it," he said in a Scouse accent. He quickly crammed the lot into his mouth and was gone. Things went downhill from there.

The next day we new recruits - or Newboys - were taken to the quartermaster's store to be kitted out. My cousin Steve had been at the

Vindi six years previously and he had donated to me his old uniform. The induction papers had stated that the uniform would cost £4 15s 6d, and that this amount would be deducted from my cash account after our uniform was issued. My mum had washed and pressed Steve's old uniform and it was at this moment sat in my suitcase ready to be re-used. "That'll save us a few bob, Graham. Don't let anyone tell you the uniform's no good. It's perfect," she had said.

The quartermasters store was a sizeable Nissan hut with a linoleum topped counter running the length of the building. Behind the counter were wooden bins of clothing, footwear, headwear, bedding, cap badges, belts, socks, and miscellaneous items, all marked in their various sizes. Everything the Vindi Boy should need. The Quartermaster stood behind the counter with a clipboard ready to issue the kit. The boys gathered in a throng, eager to receive their new uniforms. As each of them was served, they signed for their gear and went out the door with heavy piles of clothing. My turn came. "What size trousers, son?"
"Er, well sir, I've already got trousers from my cousin who was here a few years ago. I've also got a battledress top, sir." The Quartermaster looked at me with suspicious eyes. He was a middle-aged Scotsman with a narrow angular face. "Well son, it looks like you're going to have another pair, doesn't it?" he said sarcastically. He reached into a bin behind him and threw a pair of serge trousers and a battledress jacket onto the counter. "What size boots?" he demanded. I remembered my mum's words. "Er... size 10 sir, but I've already got a good pair of boots. They were my cousins," I finished lamely.
"Here, you've got yourself another pair," he barked, and threw them noisily onto the counter. My new found friends sensed the atmosphere and moved away from me like a nasty smell. I was bad news. He laid another item on the counter-top. "Tie – black," said the QM testily, daring me to mention my cousin Steve. I didn't know what to say. I'd been here less than 24 hours, and here was I getting on the wrong side of a staff officer. My downcast eyes showed my lack of confidence. "I've got one of those, sir," I mumbled.
*"DON'T YOU TELL ME WHAT THE F**K YOU'VE GOT, BOY,"* he screamed. He went along the length of bins and extracted blue shirts, a trouser belt, cap badge, plimsolls, blue jersey, a beret and numerous other items. With a heavy finality, he slapped them all onto the counter.
"SIGN FOR THEM RIGHT HERE," he shouted. I signed where he'd indicated. "I'm sorry, sir," I said, not quite knowing what I should be sorry about. His voice mellowed. "Never mind, boy. You weren't to know. No

31

second-hand uniform's allowed. It's the rules and regulations. Understand?"

"Yes sir. I'm sorry, sir," I repeated.

"Yes, well you can bring your old stuff back here for disposal anytime, okay?" I had the distinct feeling that I had just been scammed. There was nothing wrong with cousin Steve's old uniform. I suspected that money was being made, and that I had unknowingly dropped a spanner in the financial works.

It quickly became apparent to me that, however tough I thought Londoners to be, some of the boys here were in a different league altogether. These streetwise guys from Liverpool, Sheffield, Leeds and Glasgow, made us London boys look like pussycats. In other respects I was beginning to question whether I had made the correct decision to come to the Vindicatrix. This was a twelve week course. Could I take the rigid discipline, or would I throw in the towel? Boys were disciplined for the slightest misdemeanour. If an instructor took a dislike to a boy, then that boy's life was made a misery, and there was nothing he could do about it. For any transgression, real or otherwise, he would be put on 'Jankers', which would often entail peeling bags of spuds or scrubbing decks on hands and knees.

Our training started on the second day, and we crammed every day thereafter with learning such important stuff as knowing port from starboard, how to steer a ship (very handy), and how to sail a lifeboat (just in case), knots and splices, cargo handling gear, anchor-work, signalling, rigging and navigation lights. There were of course, a thousand other items of nautical knowledge to learn, and our tuition continued apace. There were also physical exercises on the camp's parade ground. Come rain or shine, these commenced at 06:30 every morning, after being awoken by the sound of a very badly played bugle. Physical exercises included push-ups, sit-ups, knee-bends and running around the camp. Our flabby bodies were getting toned up. We never walked anywhere – we marched!

Whenever we marched we would sing a marching song as we swung our arms. My favourite concerned the Chief Deck Instructor, Mr John Agate.

Why did we join, why did we join
Why did we join old Agate's Navy?
Up at 6 o'clock, twice around the block
Bloody great icicles hanging from your c*ck

Why did we join, why did we join
Why did we join old Agate's Navy?
Five bob a week, F*ck-all to eat
Dirty great blisters hanging from your feet.

One rule that was strictly enforced was – *NO FIGHTING!* If any boys were caught fighting, then they were immediately sent home; which resulted in the premature ending of their Merchant Navy career. One way that any bad feeling could be overcome was to take part in an organised three-round fight in the boxing ring. Every Thursday evening Vindi boys would gather in the recreation hut where a full sized ring was set up. Most of the fights were grudge matches between two lads who simply wanted to knock seven bells of crap out of their opponent. The fights were overseen by the PE instructor and consisted of 3 x three minute rounds. There were seconds on hand in your corner to give advice, together with gloves, gum shields, towels, water and a loud bell.

One evening, I was in a quiet corner writing a letter home, when a young lad stopped me in mid-paragraph. "Excuse me for asking, but would you care to have a fight with me in the ring?" he asked candidly.
My eyes narrowed in suspicion. "What the hell have I done to make you wanna fight me?" I replied warily.

He had blonde hair with an open and honest face. "Oh, absolutely nothing. It's just that you're about the same height and weight as me and we'll be evenly matched." Sure enough, we were about the same size.

"Well I dunno," I answered cautiously. "Have you ever boxed before?"

"Yes I have – but not recently," he replied in a broad Bolton accent.

"Hhmm, well okay then. You go put our name on the fight list, and I'll finish off my letter."

We were issued shorts and gloves, and instructed to wait beside the boxing ring until our names were called. Meanwhile, some of the fights going on were real nasty grudge affairs, the two menacing fighters glaring at each other with hatful venom.

At last our names were called and we entered the ring. My challenger smiled as the referee gave us our instructions. The bell went for the opening round and I squared-up in a classic boxer's stance and danced around the ring – just as I'd seen Cassius Clay perform. The boy came within my range, and I was just about to attempt a left hook when..... Doof....Doof...Doof...Doof. I was down on the canvas and totally disorientated. I remember thinking, "Where the hell did that come from?"

The bell sounded and I returned to my corner. "Didn't see that coming, did ya?" said my second unhelpfully.

Round 2 didn't start well. My opponent was all over me, and landed several good hits around my eyes and stomach. He danced away like a gazelle and appeared to be confident, whilst I had legs like lead and was wheezing like an old man. He came in again and landed a haymaker around my left ear, and I went down. The next thing I knew, the bell had sounded, and through my puffed eyes I saw his arm being held aloft in victory by the referee. He'd stopped the fight.

Half an hour later, I was showered and dressed and getting some feeling back into my tired body. My opponent was nowhere to be seen. I bumped into Gary, one of the chaps who was a regular onlooker at the Thursday night fights. "Blimey Graham, he made mincemeat of you, didn't he?" he said with a grin.

"Jeez Gary, the little bastard told me he'd hardly ever boxed before," I moaned.

Gary threw back his head and laughed. "You've been stitched-up, mate. That young man is the North of England Schoolboy Boxing Champion."

Every Saturday morning was hut inspection. Our huts had 32 bunk beds with 32 steel lockers. The flooring was red painted linoleum, and at the end of each hut were the ablutions, or toilets. All this had to be cleaned and the floors buffed until you could see the reflection of your face. The toilets you should be able to drink from, and each item of your clothing had to be laid out onto your bunk in an exact square. Your uniform must have razor sharp creases, and your belt buckle and cap badge must be shiny. It was all very military. If the inspecting officer found just one speck of dust, or someone's shirt not laid out properly for inspection, then the whole hut would be denied shore leave. We fastidiously cleaned our hut to the highest standard. We strapped cloths onto our feet so as to buff up the floor as we walked. The tiles in the toilet were cleaned with an old toothbrush, and we double-checked that everything was tickety-boo.

At 11am every boy was stood to attention beside his bunk as the Chief Officer, Mr Poore, entered our hut followed by his entourage. Tension was high, as stories had circulated of terrible retribution for even the smallest infraction of hygienic standards.

Without a glance towards our gleaming bunks or lockers, the Chief Officer ignored the polished floor, and headed for the ablutions. There, he took off his uniform jacket, and handed it to his second-in-command. Rolling up his shirt-sleeve, he plunged his arm down the toilet so that his hand was right around the bend of the bowl. He scraped his fingernails against the porcelain as he extracted his hand. "That, I believe is shit," he said as he inspected his fingers. "It's not good enough. This hut is denied shore leave."

Cousin Steve had set me straight on the subject of cigarettes; so I'd saved up and purchased 400 Senior Service to bring with me. During my first week at the Vindi, a few old hands had tried to bum a cigarette. I quickly told them the score. "Cost you sixpence each. Pay me back next Thursday, okay?"
"Bloody hell, mate, that's outrageous. That's blackmail, that is."
"Take it or leave it. See you on Thursday." Thursday was when pocket-money was paid out. The word quickly spread that if one was short of money, but desperate for a fag, then you came to me. I became the Vindi's tobacco baron. I made a killing.

Twice a week we were marched to the shower block, where we were encouraged to practise cleanliness. Over the weeks, it had been noticed that one of our class had an aversion to taking a shower. He would take his time getting undressed, and loiter around the bath-house until boys getting out of the shower found him getting dressed again. Suspicions had been raised. His nickname was Spider - and he was fooling no one. The plan was, that if he didn't take a shower, then they would scrub his bare skin with a scrubbing brush.

On the appointed day, I got wind of what was planned, so as we were marched to the shower block, I slid up alongside him. "Spider, here's a bit of free advice," I whispered. "If you don't take a shower today, then the boys are gonna scrub you. If I were you, I'd definitely shower."

He spluttered denials, but I couldn't care less. Once in the shower-block I noticed that Spider hung back. I went about my business and jumped into the nearest shower stall. Suddenly, a loud scream rent the air as, sure enough, Spider was forcibly held down and scrubbed until his skin was red raw. Some people just cannot take good advice, can they?

Throughout our training we were never given enough food. We were forever hungry. So-much-so that I had seen boys hung over the ship's side by their ankles, so that catering boys working in the galley below decks, could surreptitiously slip them a few crusts of bread out of the porthole, which the dangling boys would then pass up to their mates. The food was awful. Invariably we'd be served something that had cheap ingredients; pot-mess, or a stew, or bread and butter pudding. Very often we would be served Sea-Pie, a glutinous mess of fish and potato. Frequently one would find cockroaches crawling in one's food. It did no good to complain – as it was explained that this was classed as extra protein. Each evening boys could have a mug of cocoa before bedtime. The cocoa was mixed up in steel vats by the duty galley boys. One had to be rather adventurous to drink it, as it wasn't unknown for stroppy galley staff to spit in it, or it may perhaps contain some snot. This concoction was also reputed to be dosed with bromide, which was said to curb the Vindi-boys sexual libido – we called it "Anti-Wank."

Some of us were lucky. My mum would regularly send me food parcels of chocolate, fruitcake and biscuits. I felt sorry for some of the boys. Some came from broken homes, and there was never going to be any food parcels with their name on the label. Whenever food parcels were given out at the mail call, you could always count upon someone trying to be your instant friend and wanting to share in your newly delivered bounty. One had to be hard-hearted and resist the blandishments of the have-nots. However, there was one small lad who occupied the bunk opposite mine. He never received any letters, food parcels, or mail of any kind, but would sit upon his bunk with sad brown eyes, and I wondered if he was an orphan. I regularly went over and shared a bar of chocolate and some Madeira cake with him. We never brought up the matter of his parentage.

Sometime in our third week our class was on the upper deck of the Vindi. It was smoko time. Walking along the towpath was a new intake of dozens of new Vindi boys. We all rushed to the ship's side so as to give them a rousing welcome. "Hey Newboys, you'll be sorry you ever came

36

here. You'd better go home while you can," we shouted. It sounded kind of familiar.

During week eight, specially picked boys were allocated a task around the camp. These tasks ranged from being responsible for the sailing boats and launches that were moored on the canal, working with a local farmer's dairy herd, or keeping the home fires burning by working as the camp's boiler boy. I was the latter, and a major part of my task involved keeping the boiler in tip-top condition, and forever moving sizeable quantities of coke with my trusty wheelbarrow. The rest of the week-eight lads were allocated maintenance tasks aboard the Vindicatrix. The plum job was to be promoted to Bosun's Mate or even Bosun. Boys promoted to Bosun were usually, not only bright in their classwork, but were physically big enough to ensure that their orders were listened too. For the remainder of their time at the Vindi, Bosuns wore a crossed anchor badge on both arms. All boys had a badge with the words "Merchant Navy" on the end of each shoulder. The deck department wore red badges and the catering ratings wore blue.

Codeine Annie!

If one were unfortunate enough to become ill whilst at the Vindi, then one would be sent to the camp's sick-bay. There, you would come under the care of the nurse, Sister Mimi Grey. However, she was also known by another name - Codeine Annie! One had to be very careful. Her first action when you entered her 5-bed sick-bay would be to thrust a thermometer into your mouth. If she didn't like what she saw - which was all too often - she would confine you to bed, and start a course of codeine tablets. There was a rumour that a boy went to visit his sick friend, and after having a thermometer shoved into his mouth, was then kept in bed until one of the training officers found him there. At first glance it may seem like heaven to be able to lie for days on end in a nice warm bed. However, one was brought back to earth when he remembered that each day spent in the sick-bay was added on to your total time at the Vindi. I heard of one boy who, instead of the usual 12 weeks, did 15 weeks there. That's definitely not funny.

In the week before our departure, one had to "stand watch" aboard the Vindicatrix. This entailed a night-time patrol of the decks in case of intruders (we were in the middle of nowhere!), and cleaning out the onboard officers' toilets. If not doing any of the above, I stood watch in a small cubicle amidships. In charge of the duty watch was an officer instructor.

On this particular night it was Mr Jackson, otherwise referred to (behind his back) as Squeezy Jackson, due to his inclination to awaken us

Vindi boys with a shot of cold water from an old Squeezy washing-up bottle. No kidding, he could hit the end of your nose from ten paces. He was also known for his favourite 06:30 wake-up call, "Okay boys, hands off cocks and on with socks. C'mon lads, it's time to get up."

I had cleaned the toilets and carried out my security rounds. All was quiet. Suddenly, the watchman's internal telephone rang. It was Mr Jackson. I was to report to him soonest in the officers' saloon.

Squeezy Jackson sat in a tall Dickensian chair looking down at me over his half-moon spectacles. "Don't be alarmed, boy," he said. "I just want to take a few details from you."

"Yes sir," I said, standing to attention.

"What's your name?" he asked.

"It's Graham Mcglone, sir." He wrote this information onto a pad.

"Have you ever been on a motorbike?" he asked.

"Yes sir, I have." I replied.

"Have you ever been over a hundred miles an hour?" he enquired. "Have you done a ton?"

"No sir, I haven't." I was wondering where this enquiry was leading as he was asking such strange questions. Meanwhile he wrote down my answer.

"Hhmm, that's a shame, isn't it?" He sounded almost sorry for me, but nevertheless carried on scribbling this information, and other important stuff onto his pad. He suddenly seemed to get bored with talk of motorbikes. "Are you hungry, lad? How would you like some fresh-baked bread with strawberry jam?" Was he kidding? I was starving! However I managed to contain myself. "That would be very nice, sir."

"Okay then, boy. Go along to the officers' pantry. There, you'll find a fresh loaf, some butter, a pot of strawberry jam and a bread-knife. Bring it all back here to me on a tray, got it?"

Sure enough there were all these wonderful items. The bread was so fresh, that I inhaled deeply, savouring the aroma. I carried them back to Squeezy, who by now appeared to be in a strange faraway mood. "Are you sure you're still hungry, boy?"

"Oh yes sir, I am," I said, hoping that he hadn't changed his mind. He carefully cut the loaf exactly in half, buttered both ends, and coated each side with a thick spread of strawberry jam. He jammed the two halves back together and handed the whole loaf down from his lofty perch. "There you are, boy, eat that."

"I won't be able to eat all of it sir," I said with alarm. "It's far too much."

"You told me you were hungry," he said testily. "Therefore you will eat the whole loaf." He said it in a manner that suggested he would tolerate no dissent. Of course I easily managed the middle section, but was struggling

38

by the time I had eaten a third of it. Squeezy glared down at me until I had consumed every last morsel. Then he said "I'm going to sleep now. Goodnight."

The 15th November 1963 was the end of week No. 12. It found us older, wiser and about to be let loose on the nautical fraternity. I was also the proud holder of a Merchant Seaman's discharge book, number R789181 and a red MN identity card. We were lined up outside the regulating hut or guardhouse. Our canvas kitbags, which we had hand-made ourselves, lay at our feet. My friend Chris Stafford, with whom I had joined the Vindi, grinned as he caught my eye. All of us were proud that, not only were we now ready to go forth and be merchant seaman, but that we had somehow survived this hell-hole. Everyone had exchanged addresses with heartfelt promises to keep in touch. We never did!

Mr Agate, the senior deck instructing officer, gave us a pep talk about putting our new-found knowledge to good use. Yes he agreed, it's been very hard for you here, because we instructors have deliberately made it so. But if you think the past twelve weeks have been hard, then God forbid that you ever serve in a ship with a rotten crew and intolerable working conditions. You'll think that this was a walk in the park. We were brought to attention and began to march out the camp gates towards the railway station. We would shortly be on our way home; and soon after that, we would be joining our first ships. I withheld the urge to throw my beret high into the air with a loud yippee. A boy had done that very thing some weeks back and Agate had ordered him straight back into camp for another week of hell!

We had been wearing our blue serge uniform for three whole months, so most of us quickly changed into civilian clothes the minute we boarded our trains, and then just as swiftly headed for the onboard bar. Soon, I was gulping down my first beer since leaving home.

That evening, my mum had served a delicious plate of home-made steak and kidney pie, roast potatoes, buttered Swede and fresh peas with thick gravy for dinner. "I hope that's good enough, Graham. I didn't know you'd be home today. It's all I could knock-up at such short notice." Was she kidding me?

3: The Port Pirie

Reggie the Rat

The next morning Chris Stafford and I reported to the Shipping Federation Office (commonly known as The Pool) in King George V Dock. There, behind the counter sat the Allocations Officer. It was his task to allocate seamen a ship from among the dozens of vessels in the Royal Docks that required crews. In reality, what transpired was that a seaman would glance up at the blackboard that took up the space of an entire wall. On the board were written requirements that every ship had for crew. It listed how many deckhands, stokers, or stewards were required for a particular ship. It also noted if the voyage was to be coastal UK or deep-sea (foreign going), and how long the voyage was expected to last. Importantly, it usually listed the final destination with sometimes ports-of-call. From this information any sailor could get a good idea of the type of ship he wanted to sail aboard, and ask that his name be put down for it. It was almost like choosing a holiday destination.

The Allocations Officer was a short man with thick pebble-dash spectacles and buck teeth who was known far and wide as Reggie the Rat. Years ago, he had sent a deckhand to join a vessel that was not only a hell-ship, but had gone on a two-year long voyage, instead of the three weeks that Reggie had promised. The man came back after two years and punched Reggie on the nose. After that incident Reggie the Rat's counter was protected by vertical steel bars.

I had no choice in what ship I would join. Reggie glanced at my Vindicatrix paperwork, consulted a file, and gave me a railway warrant. "There you are, lad. You're joining the Port Pirie in Hull as deck-boy. It's a one week voyage. Go up on the train on Monday."

⚓

I arrived at Hull Docks in the late afternoon. My first sight of the Port Pirie filled me with apprehension. She was high out of the water and no stevedores were onboard, as I rightly guessed that she had discharged most of her cargo. I took a few moments to look her over. She was a huge ship. I knew from my collection of postcards, that she was at least a 10,000 tonner. Her hull, as with all Port Line vessels, was painted a light grey, with red boot-topping around the waterline. The upperworks were white and she had a red funnel bisected by two black bands and a black top. I climbed the gangway with my suitcase and decided to have a quick look around.

The decks and cargo hatches were a jumble. Cargo derricks were topped up vertically with cargo runners, lifting gear, chain preventers and wire topping lifts (all terms that I would come to know intimately), laying in great coils. Resting on any spare piece of deck space were huge hatch-beams, weighing over a ton each. At each end of the cargo hatches were stacked 10-foot long heavy wooden hatch-boards. These were used to seal the hatch closed and make them watertight. They would have to be manoeuvred into place manually. Mountains of canvas tarpaulins, long steel battens and wooden wedges were littered across the decks in addition to the piles of timber and rubbish. It was a mess.

I made my way inside the accommodation and found the bosun's cabin. He was a soft spoken Yorkshireman in his mid-50s whose face was covered in grey stubble. I introduced myself and he told me where I would find the deck boy's cabin. "Once you've got into your working gear, get your dinner from the galley. Then I'll get you signed-on. We sail on the evening tide."

The deck boy's cabin was fitted with two bunk beds. There were also two clothes lockers, and two chests-of-drawers. A brass porthole looked out over the ship's side. My cabinmate was already in residence. Arthur Greenway was a dark haired lad who was also a first trip deck-boy. He came from St Mary's Cray, not too far from Eltham, where I had once delivered parcels for British Rail together with the redoubtable Jacko.

⚓

The Port Pirie had been built in 1947 by Swan Hunter & Wigham Richardson at Wallsend on the River Tyne. She was named after the town of Port Pirie in South Australia. She was some 10,535 gross tons and nearly 530 feet long. With six refrigerated cargo hatches and plenty of cargo equipment, she needed a sizeable crew to handle it all. She had a total crew of 62 from captain to deck-boy. The deck crew alone numbered twenty; Bosun, Carpenter, Bosun's Mate, Lamp Trimmer, eight Able Seamen, four Quartermasters (helmsmen), two Ordinary Seamen and two deckboys. The deck crew were mainly Scottish, a majority from the islands of the Outer Hebrides. They had a slow and indistinct way of talking which sometimes made them difficult to understand; but they were excellent seamen.

At last it was time to secure the ship for sea and batten-down everything so that she was shipshape. Arthur and I stood on the deck, not daring to touch any tackle or wires. The crew were clearly experienced from long years at sea. They knew what to do. The heavy hatch beams had been slotted into place and the ABs were now busy lifting the fifty or so cumbersome hatch-boards into their numbered positions. Two layers of green tarpaulin were then stretched across the entire length of the huge cargo hatch and secured into place with steel battens and wooden wedges. It all looked very watertight. The bosun called Arthur and I over. "You

41

boys stick close to me, okay? We're going to stow the cargo derricks any minute, and it can be a bit dangerous. Just watch and learn." He called for the ABs to secure the ship for sea, and they set-to with a will. It was pitch dark on this cold November evening and the crew were working with the aid of powerful arc lamps that cast an eerie glow over the open decks. The huge 50 foot long derricks, festooned with their multitude of wires and tackle were each gently lowered down into their stowage crutches so that they were horizontal fore and aft. The clutter of wires were coiled up, and slowly the decks began to look shipshape and tidy.

"Where's the ship bound for, Bosun?" I asked.

"We leave shortly, and sail to Antwerp in Belgium," he said. "We should arrive tomorrow evening. From Antwerp we sail to Bremerhaven in Germany. We offload the last of our cargo of butter, then head back to London." I nodded. It would be my first time abroad.

The crew steadily worked their way from hatch to hatch. The bosun let us coil up some guy-ropes and hammer in some hatch wedges. They were simple tasks, but it was the first time we had ever worked with a crew, and it felt good to be participating. Arthur caught my eye and gave me a huge grin. Finally we were ready for sea. The ship's giant twin Doxford diesels started up with a great chuff...chuff...chuff and red sparks shot out of the funnel as the engines were brought up to their working speed.

The river pilot came aboard. He was a certified Trinity House Corporation Pilot, and because of his local knowledge, he would guide the ship from the docks and communicate with the tugs. He would safely pilot the Port Pirie through the pitch dark; down past Grimsby, Immingham and Cleethorpes. After a two hour run down to Spurn Head at the mouth of the River Humber, he would disembark.

The bosun called us to harbour stations. My station was to be on the fo'castle head. Arthur would be back aft at the stern. I watched as we attached the tug's tow line and singled up our thick mooring lines. At last we let go the remaining mooring line and the tug took the strain. Up in the wheelhouse I could hear the ship's telegraph ring dead slow ahead on the engines, and we were finally underway. I felt a great elation. This would be the start of my travels around the world. This is what I had been born for.

⚓

The next morning found us rolling violently from side to side in the cold and grey North Sea. Because of the lack of cargo onboard, the rough seas were trying their best to send the ship reeling this way and that. There was nothing that could be done, and we would simply have to lump it. However, as day-workers, at least we didn't need to stand duty watches.

We were roused at 07:00 and the bosun explained our duties. We were to clean out the seaman's messroom, bosun's cabin, petty officer's messroom, toilets, showers, bulkheads, and deckheads. All of it was inside work. We would also scrub – on hands and knees – hundreds of yards of wooden alleyways, passageways, and ladders.

The crew came in from the deck, where they had been washing down with fire hoses. It was breakfast time. They ate a hearty meal of eggs, sausages, bacon, fried bread and baked beans. I couldn't face it. I just wanted to lie down on my bunk and die. But I knew that I couldn't. I needed to work. I didn't feel very well at all, and I'd almost lost the will to live. As the ship rolled and pitched incessantly, I mechanically scrubbed and mopped the decks - all the while wanting to be sick, but not able to manage it. I felt awful. I knew I'd feel better if only I could vomit. Even the pungent smell of Jeyes disinfectant did nothing to help.

One of the older Jocks came into the mess. He had a cheeky grin. "What's up, lad? Feeling a bit queasy, are we?" I could only nod my head miserably. He went off to the galley and returned shortly with a greasy piece of belly pork to which he'd attached a length of string. "This'll sort yae out, laddie" he laughed, and proceeded to lower it up and down his throat. That did it. I raced for the toilet followed by his raucous laughter. I count myself very lucky that in my entire sea-going career, I've been seasick only twice.

Later that afternoon the swells had calmed down and the ship tended not to roll so much. We picked up our pilot, and after a two hour run up the River Scheldt, the Port Pirie tied up in the Belgian port of Antwerp. The ship's young carpenter, known as 'Chippie,' decided that I would accompany him and a few lads ashore for drinks. We headed straight for Danny's Bar.

Danny's Bar was an eye-opener. It didn't appear to have any closing time – there wasn't any "Time gentlemen please." It was open all night and the place was buzzing. All booze was served by beautiful waitresses who expected, and received, a tip. They were dressed in frilly low-cut blouses – *sans brassiere*, with short black skirts and fishnet stockings which always managed to show an inordinate amount of their sexy thighs. Whenever they bent over – which was quite often – one either had a delicious eyeful of their lovely pert breasts or a pair of cheeky frilly knickers. The girls spoke excellent English and cracked jokes with the sailors in the bar. They seemed to be making a great fuss of me and nothing was too much trouble. It was wonderful; and as I sipped my Stella Artois, I was in seventh heaven. The music was loud and the girls were swaying their hips and singing along with The Chiffons "He's so fine. (do lang-do lang-do lang)"

A strange sight in the toilets was the cleaning lady – an old crone – who kept the place clean and tidy. She stationed herself at a small table upon which were tablets of soap and hand-towels for the use of her patrons. For this service one was expected to drop a few centimes into her collection plate. When I used the toilets, this elderly lady was mopping the floors. We chaps carried on having a slash as if she wasn't there. Not to be done out of her simple pleasures in life, she blatantly stared into each urinal to size up the men's wedding tackle!

As we weaved our way back to the ship in the wee hours of the morning, the chippie asked me if I'd enjoyed myself. How could I answer that one? What an experience. It had been a wonderful evening.
He said, "What did you think of the girls?"
"They were fabulous. Some of the most beautiful girls I've ever seen."
"I'm glad you think so," he said laughing. "Every last one of them was a man!"

⚓

Just a few hours after getting back onboard, the ship sailed for Bremerhaven. Once out in the open North Sea, the weather conditions were misty with a rough sea with a heavy swell. That same evening brought awful news. The ship was en-route northwards along the coast of Holland towards the Frisian Islands when our radio-officer tuned in to the BBC long wave broadcast. The news he heard on the radio was devastating.

Captain Edward Dingle made the announcement over the ship's internal speaker system. "I regret to tell you," he said sombrely, "that President John F Kennedy has been assassinated earlier today in Dallas, Texas. He and Texas Governor John Connelly were both shot whilst riding in the presidential motorcade. President Kennedy died later from his wounds." The Captain said he would keep us abreast of events when more news was known. It was Friday 22nd November 1963.

We entered the River Weser and picked up our river pilot, and two hours later the ship docked at the port of Bremerhaven. The German stevedores piled aboard and immediately began to unload our cargo. That would not have happened in London, due to the docker's routine of not working at night, and only rarely at weekends. All too soon the London stevedores would live to regret that they insisted upon working to such a rigid unionised doctrine. They could never be as competitive as their opposite numbers in Europe, and they would later suffer huge job losses as the modernisation of the transport industry surged ahead.

I went for a brief walk around the town to stretch my legs. On the Georgestrasse, near the post office, I looked into a department shop window to pass the time. Suddenly I had the strangest feeling. My whole body began to sway as if I was still aboard ship in the rough North Sea. Some German folk strolled by and I was certain that I must have seemed very strange to them as my body attempted to compensate for a non-existent pitching and rolling. But of course it was all in my mind. Back onboard, the lads told me that it could be quite a common occurrence for first trippers, and I shouldn't worry too much. It wouldn't last.

Two days later the Port Pirie sailed up the River Thames and into the King George V Dock. We glided sedately along the dock to the Port Line berths, where tugs gently pushed us alongside. Within the hour we had been paid-off. This meant an ending of our contract with the shipping company. Some of the present crew left the ship, and we would require fresh crew nearer to the time of departure (no doubt via Reggie the Rat). The ship was due to sail for Australia on the 19th December 1963. I had been asked to rejoin the vessel for the deep-sea voyage, and so I would work-by the ship until she sailed.

⚓

My house was only half a mile along Dock Road, so I was back home within the hour. My mum and Albert were at home and my sisters were out at work. I told them of my overseas travels, even though I had been away for only a week. They hung onto every word as I recounted the story of my skirmish with the rough North Sea and the strip of belly pork and I kept them laughing as I described the counterfeit waitresses in Danny's Bar who all turned out to be fellas!

During the three weeks that the ship was in the Royal Docks, I was able to go home every night and be with my family. A new deck boy reported onboard who would be my cabinmate for the foreseeable future. Chris Morling was a blonde headed boy a year younger than I, who came from Ramsgate. He was also fresh from a sea-training school, The Prince of Wales School, Dover, and like me it would be his first deep-sea trip. When he was much younger, Chris had suffered a bout of polio, which had resulted in his left arm, from the elbow downwards, appearing to be rather limp. However, I was to find that it didn't prevent him from doing the same activities as his shipmates. I liked him immediately.

During the days prior to sailing, there was frenetic activity aboard our ship as she was loaded down with every kind of general cargo. The stevedores stowed away huge packing cases, engines, cars, pipework, boilers, castings, ingots, chemicals and all types of heavy manufactured goods. The list was endless. As freight was loaded into the holds and the ship sank deeper into the water, her fully laden state would increase the ship's stability, and make her much more comfortable and easier to handle in rough seas. As sailing day came closer, the ship's officers would check her draft marks to see how deep the vessel was in the water, so that she wasn't overloaded. Usually the ship would be loaded to capacity; right down to its Plimsoll marks. The ship also took onboard diesel fuel for her long voyage; over a thousand tons of it. Tons of food, both tinned and frozen would be required, together with ship's stores, spare mooring ropes, engine spares, paint, shackles, light bulbs and hundreds of other necessary items. We would also pump aboard hundreds of tons of drinking water.

Some unusual cargo that came onboard at this time was 'Tulip's Baggage.' Tulip was an effeminate steward with soft skin and very feminine features. I wasn't to discover her real name for some time, but everyone called her Tulip and referred to her as "she." Even the Captain called her Tulip. Her unofficial job title was The Captains Tiger – which meant that she was exclusively the captain's personal steward, and kept his suite of rooms clean and tidy. She was an Australian from the state of Victoria. These effeminate and clearly homosexual crew members were known throughout the Merchant Navy as 'steam queens.' When Tulip stepped onboard, she had one suitcase containing working uniforms, which was quite normal. But down on the dockside she also had several suitcases and trunks of her female attire - her 'Drag.' She had sat upon this great pile of luggage, all the while being bombarded with saucy remarks from the dockers - and she loved it. She was the centre of attention. Eventually us deckies rescued her and brought her gear aboard.

When Tulip got dragged-up in her full regalia and warpaint, one would be hard pressed to tell the difference between her and a regular female. Possibly the only dissimilarity was that she would sometimes be dressed in clothes that the ordinary woman couldn't hope to afford, or one may occasionally find her mincing around the accommodation dressed to the nines in expensive finery.

⚓

On the 18th December we again signed-on. This was known as Signing Articles of Agreement. All the crew were gathered in the officers' saloon, where the captain and a Marine Superintendent from the Board of Trade were present to witness the crew's signatures. The Articles were large A2 size documents which detailed all the crews vital information, including name, address, date of birth, date of signing-on, pay rates, and in what capacity a crewmember was employed. It also showed particulars of the ship itself; vessels name, port of registry, official number, nett tonnage and rated horsepower. The document was signed by both parties and was legally binding. This was a contract that bound crews to serve aboard a ship for a period of up to two-years! It was not unknown for a crew to sign-on for a voyage of three weeks, only to find later that the ship's cargo contracts had changed, and the voyage time increased to 18-months or more. New crew were joining the ship on a daily basis, and a lot of the Scotsmen who had sailed on the coastal trip, now rejoined after a spot of leave. A new bosun, who came from the Outer Hebrides, also joined the ship at this time.

Port Pirie (Port Line Ltd) 10,561 gross tons

On my first short voyage to Europe, I had largely been confined to working below decks, and so I hadn't seen many of the officers. Today was the first time I had seen the ship's master. Captain Harry Conby was a magnificent looking officer. He was tall with a weather-beaten face, and looked resplendent in a navy-blue uniform with the four gold stripes of his rank on the arm. My first impression was that Captain Conby was a man in whom his crew would have the utmost confidence as regards to their safety.

Eventually sailing day arrived and the ship was a hive of last-minute activity. In the messroom I got chatting to a steward by the name of Noel. He was a tall skinny soft-spoken chap who had the strangest eyebrows I'd ever encountered. Each of them seemed to be shaped like an arrow and joined together above his nose. Apart from that, he seemed like a nice enough bloke. He was, he said, an assistant steward – whose duties included serving meals to the officers and passengers in the saloon and keeping their cabins and staterooms tidy.

The crews of most cargo ships are made up of deck, catering and engine room departments; and although each department is important to the smooth running of the vessel, I much preferred working out on deck rather than inside the accommodation or down in the depths of the noisy machinery spaces.

As the final pieces of cargo were loaded, the deckies sealed up the cargo hatches and lowered the derricks into their stowage crutches. At last we were ready to sail. Once again my harbour station was forward on the fo'castle head. It was dark as we let go the last of our mooring lines and the tugs gently nudged us towards the lock entrance. We would briefly need to tie up inside the lock until the water level equalised and the ship could back out into the River Thames.

However, there was a problem. Another inbound ship was already in the lock and so we would need to loiter for half an hour until we could enter.

The chief officer called me over. "Peggy, go down to the messroom and make a brew of tea. Bring it all back here to the fo'castle."

"Yes sir," I said and made my way aft.

The Port Pirie's crew mess arrangements were a little old fashioned; in that there were separate, but interconnected open plan mess-rooms for each department. I quickly busied myself making a brew.

I heard whispered voices coming from the steward's mess on the starboard side. Then I saw the strangest sight. A girl who was dressed in the most outlandish clothes and make-up was perched upon the edge of the mess-room table. I had no idea who she could be, as we certainly didn't carry any female crew members. She had long dark hair and wore skin tight jeans with a flowery blouse and a floppy polka dot bow-tie.

Suddenly, from behind a wooden partition, came a huge swarthy chap who looked as if he may have been a hairy-arsed dock worker. He was attired in navy blue overalls and wore a flat cap upon his head. Without delay he crushed the girl in his arms and proceeded to give her a long and lingering kiss. I could see his rough hands feverishly wandering across her body and down her legs. From his alcoholic demeanour and glazed eyes I guessed that he was as drunk as a skunk. She must have been enjoying his attentions because she was moaning with pleasure. Things began to ratchet up when he bent her across the table and began to undo her jeans. I'd never seen anything quite like it within my - as yet - shy and innocent years and I couldn't take my eyes off the scene. I was mesmerised.

48

They were so intent on what they were doing that they were unaware of my presence. I studied her face and things swiftly began to click into place. There was no mistaking those strangely shaped eyebrows. To say that I was shocked would be an understatement. Having had a brief chat with Noel earlier, I had no inkling that he was queer. By this time the bloke was running his hands across the bare flesh of her bottom.

In a booming voice I shouted, "Hey fella. The ship's about to come into King George locks. Unless you wanna sail to Australia, you'd best jump off."

The pair had no idea I was there and they panicked. Whilst he scrabbled to readjust his clothing, she fell off the table and hit the deck with a loud thump.

As the Port Pirie gracefully exited from the locks, I could see the pier where, as a schoolboy, I had watched the great ships arrive and depart. And now here was I, about to embark on a five month voyage to the other side of the world. Who could have foretold that this first-trip deck-boy would one day in the distant future be commanding his own ship, and bring it up the River Thames, under Tower Bridge, and into the very heart of the City of London?

Later that day, the ship was off the south coast of England as she steadily steamed westwards. I popped out on deck to see what the crew were doing. My cleaning duties were keeping me inside the accommodation, but I was eager to muck-in with the boys and work out on deck as a team.

They were tidying up the decks and washing off the multitude of detritus that had accumulated in three weeks of being in London. Other deck crew were throwing long planks of wood over the side and into the sea.

In 1963 it came to be the norm that anything that was not wanted onboard was ditched into the sea. There were heavy bundles of this surplus wood – called dunnage – that had been used to trim the cargo down in the holds. No thought whatsoever was given to the damage that these timbers could do to small boats or the environment. It simply became another pile of driftwood along the English Channel. All the waste food went into the sea. All human waste from toilets went into the sea. Black bags of paper, plastic, and beer cans all went into the sea. When tankers washed out their oily tanks, it went into the sea.

Twenty four hours later, the ship was off the Ile de Ushant, and we entered the notorious Bay of Biscay. The Bay was famous for the long oceanic swells that would cause big ships to roll violently. This was to be no different. As The Port Pirie turned southbound, she rolled from side to side and from end to end in a nightmare corkscrew motion. The whole ship groaned in protest as the heavy seas put massive strains on her steelwork and rivets. As the huge swells hit the ship, and she rolled in a violent protest, I could see why we had to stow every last item onboard so that it couldn't break loose and do some damage. Even the crew's tea mugs in the messroom were stowed in cup-holders, so they couldn't slide off, and end up on the deck in little pieces. The captain briefly allowed the ABs to go out onto the sea-swept decks to rig rope lifelines, just in case of emergency. Otherwise all outside work was prohibited and the crew kept inside for their own safety.

A little over a day later we had passed through the Bay of Biscay and drew abeam of Cape Finisterre in northern Spain. The swells begun to ease off and I could feel the temperature slowly rising as we began our 28-hour run parallel to the coast of Spain and Portugal. Later, as the voyage progressed, we would steam the entire length of the Mediterranean to the Suez Canal, through the Red Sea, and out across the vast Indian Ocean to Australia. There was still a very long way to go.

Peggy!

A strange expression which took some getting used to, was the name the crew used when addressing the deck-boy. He was called 'Peggy.' The name didn't apply just to me and to Chris Morling, but to any deck-boy on any British ship. We were all Peggys!

It was explained that the name was a throwback to the ancient times of sailing ships, when an aged sailor who had lost a leg in a shipboard accident (a common occurrence), would be fitted with a false peg-leg and put onto light duties below decks. Over the years the name had been handed down.

There were other strange job titles to be found amongst most British ship's crews. Apart from the captain's tiger, these included the donkeyman (he originally looked after the donkey boiler, but nowadays is the engine room department's storekeeper.) The lamp-trimmer (before ships had electric lamps, the lamp-trimmer ensured that all the oil lamps, especially the navigation lamps, were burning brightly.) Nowadays he is the bosun's right-hand man and usually does the wire splicing and is deck storekeeper. The ship's carpenter was the senior petty officer. He would take his orders directly from the chief officer and was responsible for taking daily soundings of the ship's ballast and cofferdam spaces and repair any domestic faults within the accommodation. Many ships also carried a surgeon (he was actually a general practitioner, but was always signed on

50

ship's articles as a surgeon). The Blocker was an alternative way of referring to the bosun and the captain was commonly known as 'The Old Man.' The job title that always made me grin was The Farmer. Normally the duty deck watches are made up of three deckhands per 4-hour watch and they steer the ship and carry out look-out duties. Basically, whilst The Farmer did the middle two hours look-out, his two watch-mates took care of everything else. Obviously, the duty watches rotated so that we all did an equal share of the work or there would be complaints, but it's a system that worked very well indeed. It's rumoured that the name of 'The Farmer' comes from the days when live animals were carried aboard ship, and it was the duty watch's job to feed the livestock. Therefore the guy who did that task was called The Farmer.

The Port Pirie had no washing machine of any kind, but just an old fashioned washboard. All one's washing was done by hand in a sink and then hung in a drying room. Jeans would normally be laid on the tiled deck and were scrubbed with a stiff scrubbing brush, but it was something I soon got used to, and it became normal to hand wash ones 'smalls' in the sink. Another way to clean one's jeans was to pass a rope down through the legs and toss them over the ship's stern. We would tow our jeans in the ship's wake for an hour or so and they would come out looking nice n' clean. Job done! Doing one's laundry was known as dhobying. This is a word of Indian origin, when officers in the British army would employ dhobi wallahs to clean their uniforms.

We didn't have a TV set onboard, but we would be shown a movie perhaps once a week whilst sailing across the oceans. The only other form of entertainment available to the crew was a ping-pong table and a dart board, or perhaps a deck of cards with which to play cribbage. All these pieces of kit could be found in the cheerless and dingy crew's recreation room. The officers had a comfortably furnished saloon with a bar and leather sofas, but the lower deck crew were allowed none of these things. It was either the rec room or nothing.

⚓

That evening of the 22nd December, our Radio-Officer picked up an S-O-S distress signal from a passenger liner that was on fire some 200-odd nautical miles to the west of us. The 20,000 ton Lakonia had been built in 1929 for Dutch owners, and had been purchased just this year by the Greek Line. She had sailed from Southampton on the same day that we had left London. She was bound for Madeira and a Christmas cruise around the Canary Islands. And now, unaccountably, she was ablaze from stem to stern.

Captain Conby was in communications with the US airbase at Lajes in the Azores, who were coordinating the rescue mission. He offered the services of the Port Pirie to assist with the search and rescue, but was advised that our ship would not be required, as there were presently six ships and four USAF C-54 aircraft on scene. In any case it would have taken at least 12-hours for us to arrive at the location.

Greek shipping in 1963 didn't have a very good track record as regards safety, and this was highlighted at the subsequent Board of Inquiry. Many shortcomings were found. The captain had left it far too late in ordering abandon ship. Crew didn't give enough assistance to passengers, and in one case, they were angered when the ship's radio-operator, in company with a nurse and two musicians, had left the ship in a launch. They didn't bother coming back to help. Others claimed that crewmen took advantage of the chaos to loot passenger staterooms. Lifeboats were rusted into their davits, and others were not launched correctly, causing them to be swamped.

Of course I didn't know any of these facts as we continued on our southerly course, but it did cross my mind that life in the Merchant Navy could be a dangerous occupation. We continued on our way, and shortly came abeam of the lighthouse at Cape St Vincent on the southerly tip of Portugal, and we made our left turn towards the Straits of Gibraltar. That night, 128 people died aboard the Lakonia.

⚓

Christmas Day found us off Cap De Fer in Algeria. The weather was reasonable for this time of year, with a moderate north-westerly sea, and slightly misty conditions. No work would be required from the deck crew except for steering duties (the Port Pirie was not fitted with automatic steering), and for look-out duties. However, one department that was working at full blast were the galley staff. Our chef and his team, had been working their socks off from early morning, preparing the slap-up Xmas lunch that was due to be served at about 13:00. Some of the crew had told me that our ship's food, especially in relation to the quantity we received, wasn't very good compared with other shipping companies. The opinion from the older hands was that the Port Pirie wasn't a 'good feeder.' However, to someone like me, who had recently spent three months on Vindi food, this was luxury.

In one of the seaman's cabins, the Jocks were having a party. It was only 09:00, but they were getting well sloshed. It was the captain's belief that sailors and beer didn't mix very well together. Therefore, it was his policy that each seaman was allowed to purchase only two cans of beer per day from the ship's 'slop chest.' The Jocks easily got around this problem by saving up their daily allocation since leaving London, and they were rapidly getting drunk. At about 10:30, one of the seamen, a highlander called Willie Mackay, had somehow gone into a sad and maudlin mood and had announced to his friends, "Ah f**k it. I think I'll throw myself over the side." His chums really thought it was a joke, and said, "Yeah okay, Willie. We'll see yae later. Yae have yourself a nice wee swim." Willie went out the door and we never saw him again.

The alarm was raised an hour later when Willie failed to return. A full bow to stern rummage was instituted and the captain was informed. He turned the ship around, posted a lookout in the crow's nest, doubled up the bridge look-outs and we went to search down our track on an opposite course. He also sent out radio signals requesting any ships in the area to render help. By midday we had ten other ships carrying out box-pattern searches – but to no avail. After five hours, all ships dispersed and we carried on our way towards Port Said.

After a much delayed Christmas lunch, Captain Conby and the other senior officers came to our messdeck. The captain thanked us for our efforts and said that he was sorry we had lost a shipmate in such tragic circumstances. We nodded sadly in agreement.

"As you may know," he said. "It is usually traditional for the captain to bring a bottle of rum to the messdeck on Christmas Day to help you celebrate the festivities. But after these tragic events, I didn't think it would be in good taste, or indeed appropriate to do so." I could hear some of the Jocks harrumph under their breaths. Captain Conby wished us all a happy Christmas and went back to the bridge-deck. One of the Jocks summed up what he thought of their departed shipmate Willie. "He's cost us a whole frikken bottle of rum, he has."

⚓

The next day was work as normal, and as the Port Pirie sliced through the blue waters of the Mediterranean, the bosun took Chris and I to one side. "How would you lads like to work out on deck with the crew?" My eyes lit up. We had been working inside on cleaning duties ever since we had left London six days ago, and I wasn't enjoying it. I longed to be outside.

"Okay, lads," he said in his soft voice. "There's still cleaning to be done, so you work inside in the mornings, and out on deck in the afternoons." This was great news.

After lunch Chris and I joined the boys out on deck. The bosun put us with two experienced seamen, a dark haired Hebridean with the unlikely name of Murdo Macleod and a fellow islander; Billy MacIver from Stornoway. They showed us how to carry out maintenance on the ship's lifting gear. Every block and tackle had to be greased, and ensure that their sheaves and swivel pins were freed up. Billy would get hauled up the mast in a bosun's chair, quickly disconnect another cargo block, and send it down to us via a wire-rope. Each cargo wire had to be oiled to stop it going rusty, and every piece of equipment that should be greased – got greased. It was heavy work, and would take the best part of the next ten days to complete. Murdo and Billy taught us little nuggets of seamanship that we would remember forever. The rest of the deck crew were also working in gangs, and as the days went by, we worked our way from hatch to hatch until the task was complete.

In early morning mist we arrived at Port Said in Egypt, at the northern end of the Suez Canal. As the sun came up, it burned off the mist and promised to be a nice day. We tied-up to a mooring buoy to await the departure of our southbound convoy later that afternoon. There were perhaps forty other cargo vessels, passenger vessels and tankers awaiting transit of the canal and all ships would have to wait whilst the convoy was assembled and the northbound convoy came through.

A number of Arabs came onboard. Firstly was the canal pilot who would guide the ship safely through the 105-mile long waterway. With him came the searchlight crew. These four men rigged a massive one-ton searchlight up on the ship's bow so that it would illuminate ahead as we steamed along at night. Another squad had their boat slung over the ship's side ready to drop into the water and moor up the ship when we entered a cutting called the Bitter Lakes. We would be tying-up in the cut for an hour or so whilst another northbound convoy moved safely down the main channel. There were other oddball characters who were allowed onboard. An Arab who went by the name of MacGregor was a barber who, whilst cutting your hair, would talk to you in whatever accent you happened to have, whether it be Cockney, Scotsman, Geordie, Scouse, Welsh, or Brummie. He addressed everyone as Macgregor. Another was the Gilly-Gilly Man. He was a magician who would perform for the crew for a small fee. He could usually be counted upon to do something magical which involved day-old baby chicks. Alongside the ship a fleet of bumboats assembled. They were loaded down with trinkets and tourist crap which they would attempt to sell us. Amongst the brightly painted bumboats, the Arab boatmen were some of the most colourful characters afloat. They mostly had anglicised names and were known by many of the sailors who regularly went through the Suez Canal.

On this particular day we also had an Arab who had sneaked aboard and was trying to sell smutty postcards. It was after lunch, and this man, dressed in a traditional flowing Arab jalaba, was going from door-to-door in the crew's accommodation to sell his wares. I was in my cabin alone when he knocked.

"Pssst. You wanna buy filthy postcard from me please." He held up a dozen faded and rather old fashioned sepia postcards. The women in the photos were being bonked by men in the most unromantic of positions. "Not for me, thank you," I said and closed the door.

He was persistent. "You buy from me and I go away. You no buy – then I stay."

I cracked open the door. "I don't want any photographs; you keep 'em."

"You filthy English – you buy from me." The words were spat out with anger. From his robes he brought out a long bladed stiletto knife and made a lunge at me. I slammed the door closed and threw the bolt, just as the blade came straight through the thin plywood door panel, and missed me by inches. I screamed blue murder, and within a minute I could hear the crew outside as they came to my aid. I gingerly cracked opened the door. They had the Arab by his arms and legs as they carried him out onto the deck and threw him straight over the ship's side. They didn't enquire if he could swim.

In the afternoon, we slipped our mooring and proceeded in convoy into the canal. The distance between ships was kept at a half mile, and at a stately seven knots we crept southwards. With the nice weather our passengers came out on deck. I had not seen much of them since leaving London as, apart from a short stroll around the decks, they had kept mostly inside their staterooms. The majority of our passengers were a far cry from the regular cruise ship variety that enjoyed exotic ports of call and nightly entertainment aboard the giant P & O or Cunard liners.

We carried a maximum of 12 passengers, and mostly they would be elderly well-off couples who enjoyed a more leisurely voyage to Australia. They would be very discerning, as passage aboard cargo liners didn't come cheap. It was equal to sailing first-class on a cruise ship, as one had a large stateroom and one's very own steward. These gentlefolk, especially the ladies, were invariably of the "upper classes" and wouldn't have looked out of place at The Cheltenham Ladies College or at Ascot Races. On this voyage we had four elderly couples, some of the blue-rinsed variety, who tended to keep very much to themselves, and mostly played bridge or deck quoits or read a book from the ship's small library.

Aboard the passenger liners you could always differentiate the first class passengers who were regular cruisers from those who were sailing on their first voyage. The regulars would demand a cabin on the shady side of the ship, so that the hot sun beat down on the opposite side. In the northern hemisphere the sun is always to the south, therefore on an outward bound voyage towards the east, the cool shady cabins are to be found on the port side of the ship. This gave rise to the term POSH (port out – starboard home).

We also had onboard a doctor and his young family, who were immigrating to Australia. Doctors could get free passage by serving in a medical capacity whilst en-route. This gave the shipping company peace of mind that a doctor was onboard if required; and the doctor was able to ship all the family household furniture in the ship's hold at no cost. Usually the doctor would be signed-on articles as a bona-fide crew member at the rate of one shilling (5p) per month. Our doctor and his wife were in their late thirties and had a daughter Susan of 15 years old, and a boy called Douglas of 9 years old. We shall hear more about them later.

As Port Pirie progressed through the 105-mile canal transit, there was not an awful lot to see that one would normally associate with Egypt. There were no camel trains, but just a few young boys with donkeys loaded high with bales of esparto grass. There were also hundreds of goats; they were everywhere. One was disappointed if expecting to see Egyptian temples or pyramids. The nearest were the Great Pyramids of Giza outside Cairo, some 80 miles away. We made our way slowly past Ismailia and Qantaran and left the main channel as we awaited the northbound convoy to pass by. It was such a strange sight. As the northbound convoy made their way past us, their hulls were hidden from our view by high sand dunes. As the fifty-odd cargo ships, oil tankers and passenger liners went by in the opposite direction, we could see only their upperworks and funnel and masts. It gave a whole new meaning to the term, 'Ships of the Desert.'

In the evening the powerful searchlight was switched on. It illuminated the narrow canal as we steamed along in the pitch dark. At last in the small hours of the morning we reached Port Suez in the Red Sea and our canal transit was complete. Pilot, searchlight, and various Arab workers were quickly offloaded and we increased speed to 16 knots. Our run down the Red Sea would be 1650 nautical miles and would take four days.

⚓

By now the weather was clammy and humid and we wore just shorts and a hat in the hot sunshine. The heavy cargo gear work was now complete and the deck crew set about painting the Port Pirie from top to bottom. The more experienced ABs were sent up to the very top of the mast in a bosun's chair (a small wooden seat attached to the mast via a block and gantline.) The seaman would have a pot of paint slung below his chair, and after being hoisted up to the top, he would paint the mast as he descended. There was plenty to keep us busy. Rust spots had to be treated before applying primer, and every part of the steelwork was painted. Vast areas of steel decks were painted green, and the older more experienced hands varnished the teak woodwork on the upper-decks.

One job that was universally hated by the deckies was holy-stoning. On the accommodation levels, ships normally had their decks inlaid with teak; and whilst they looked superb when they were clean, they needed constant attention. The best way to achieve this was to liberally sprinkle water, soda, and grit, and then use a device called a holy-stone. This consisted of a heavy slab of sandstone within a metal frame attached to a long wooden handle. The stone would be dragged back and forth in a standing position and the decks would be scoured and whitened. To keep them clean, the decks would be holystoned on a regular basis.. The term holystone is believed to stem from the days of sail, when sailors sand-stoned the decks upon their knees as if in prayer. Even today we would refer to holy-stoning as 'morning prayers.'

The seas were now generally calm with cloudless blue skies. The Red Sea is known for its abundance of exotic fish and marine life; and as we cut through the smooth waters, we could see the dorsal fins of sharks, or flying fish frantically flapping their wing-like fins to skim across the water for a hundred yards or more. Very often pods of bottle-nosed dolphins would suddenly appear and they would leap far out of the water in displays of pure exhibitionism, twisting in mid-air as they went. They would surface and dive in unison as they played around the ship's pressure wave at the bow. It was wonderful to see the dolphins and one couldn't fail to be impressed.

In the evenings I would go up to the bridge-deck to steer the ship. It was a requirement that I should take a turn on the helm as part of my training and I would usually steer for two hours per night. It wasn't too difficult; and I soon learnt the nautical steering terms. After completing 28-hours steering time I was given a steering certificate signed by the captain. I was learning my trade.

Apart from Tulip there was one other steam queen onboard. Our second resident queen was Christine. She was a chubby good-natured dining room steward whose cabin on the starboard side of the lower deck was open house and always seemed to have a ready supply of drink. She was also the proud owner of a Dansette record player, so there was always some music playing. Some of these steam queens acted and dressed in such a feminine manner that they were always referred to as 'she.'

Christine suffered from a heavy '5 o'clock shadow' that grew upon her face in such profusion that it made her appear swarthy and definitely not feminine. It was a relentless battle for her to keep the stubble down. However, she was always good for a laugh and had a great sense of humour.

She had given her cabin the womanly touch by adding flowery curtains, a shag-pile rug and some velvet cushions. The place always smelt of pot pourri. Christine was a mine of information. She could not only be relied upon to impart the latest navigational updates on when we would arrive here or there, but she had all the latest gossip on every facet of life aboard the Port Pirie at her fingertips. She loved to gossip. There wasn't much she didn't know; and if she didn't – then it probably wasn't worth knowing.

On the second day out from Suez the bosun ordered me to assist the crew in building the swimming pool. I looked at him blankly - a swimming pool? Was he joking? However, our new bosun was not known for his humour. But sure enough, from the aft deck store we brought out neat stacks of heavy timbers, a canvas pool liner and some pool steps. The timbers were nearly fifteen feet long and it crossed my mind that this would be a fair size pool. Within two hours it had all been assembled next to No.4 cargo hatch on the after deck by simply slotting numbered timbers into steel frames and bolting it all down securely. A hose-line from the ship's fire-main was plugged into the canvas liner and it was filled with sea water within ten minutes. We had ourselves a swimming pool. However, with 62 crew and 12 passengers onboard, some sort of organisation was required, and so it was ordered that officers and passengers could use it during the day and crew in the evening. That seemed fair enough.

But one type of swimming that wasn't to be recommended was to swim in the ocean when the ship was underway. On hot sultry nights, when one came out on deck to escape the non-air-conditioned accommodation, it was natural to lean on the guardrail and watch the sea go by. However, I sometimes noticed that the sea could appear oily smooth and possessed a warm phosphorescent quality as it appeared to twinkle with millions of weak lights. It also had a magnetic attraction which made one, just for a brief moment, want to jump in and immerse oneself in the warm, smooth water.

I looked into this phenomenon and discovered that it is in fact bioluminescence caused by millions of living creatures in the ocean called dinoflagellates. These creatures, such as plankton and micro-organisms, emit a light much like the firefly does on land. We were discussing this one night in the messroom, and my shipmates agreed that it does indeed have a magnetic quality. One of our elderly quartermasters told us that many years ago he had succumbed to the magnetism and had jumped into the sea when the ship was underway in mid-ocean at 16 knots. He was damn lucky. He told us that someone had seen him go over the side, and the ship was turned around to rescue him.

⚓

As we sailed southwards down the Red Sea, the officers changed their uniform from the navy blue worn in northern climes, into tropical whites. Instead of the blue uniform and tie, they now wore white open-neck shirt with gold shoulder epaulettes and white shorts, white socks, and white blancoed shoes. On their heads they wore white caps with a polished cap badge. The captain normally sported laurel leaves, or 'scrambled egg' on the peak of his cap. In the evenings it was obligatory for the officers to dress formally for dinner. This would consist of a white cutaway waistcoat style jacket with white trousers. I thought they looked magnificent.

Each day on the forenoon watch the captain and deck officers would gather on the bridge-deck with their sextants ready to take a midday sunsight. After getting a reading in degrees of the sun's position in relation to the horizon, they would apply the exact Greenwich Mean Time (GMT) and numerous mathematical formulae, and the ship's latitude could be determined. This was called "shooting the sun." Later, another fix for longitude would be taken and the ship's position would be fixed on the chart. Usually all deck officers would take the midday position and compare their results. They would then draw a circle around the positions all closest together. It wasn't an exact science, especially if the sun was not visible for days on end; and results that had several nautical miles of error would be quite acceptable. In today's high-tech world, navigators simply take a reading at any time of the day or night from a GPS – a Global Positioning System, with its satellite technology. Usually they are accurate to within 5 metres.

Normally, in the day-to-day scheme of things, one hardly ever saw the captain. When the ship was on passage at sea he usually remained in his cabin with a multitude of paperwork, or he would be seen on the bridge, especially for the midday fix. The captain didn't stand a navigational watch. That was the job of the Chief Officer, 2nd Officer and 3rd Officer. He would obviously be present whenever the ship arrived or departed from port, and he would also be required to see all manner of officials that came onboard. These ranged from the ship's agent to customs, immigration, police, harbour masters and consular officials, but he mostly kept himself remote and distant from us - the lower deck crew. However, with the authority vested in him via the Merchant Shipping Act 1894, a ship's master had powers only slightly lower down the scale than God!

One occasion when we may see the captain was on master's inspection. Once per week, usually on a Saturday morning, the crew would be required to clean their cabins, which were to be kept tidy to a high standard. The captain, together with his entourage of chief officer, chief engineer and chief steward, would tour the accommodation going from cabin to cabin; and if any were found to be in a messy state, then the occupant would have to explain himself and get it cleaned up. The required standard wasn't over-the-top as it was at the Vindicatrix, but woe betide any crew-member who presented his cabin for inspection looking as if it were a train smash. A dirty and unhygienic cabin was a logging offence, and was definite grounds for the captain to impose a fine on the filthy inhabitant of the aforesaid cabin. I knew of several occasions when a crewman, after having being warned, hadn't bothered to clean his accommodation, and been logged. Fortunately Chris and I always kept our cabin neat and tidy and highly polished, but there is no quicker way to fall out when sharing with a cabin-mate, than if that person was an untidy git.

⚓

Tulip was in love. She had fallen madly for a middle aged engine room stoker from Bridlington called Bob Braithwaite. I knew Bob slightly when I had met him around at one of Christine's soirees. He was a tall muscular guy with a broad Yorkshire accent. He didn't talk an awful lot, but when he did, it was instantly apparent that he was somewhat lacking in the brains department. One could almost mentally visualise the cogs inside his brain turning – ever so slowly! He didn't strike me as being that way inclined with steam queens, but I suppose it took all sorts. Hey, what the hell did I know? I was only seventeen and a half years old.

It was arranged that they would get married on New Year's Eve, and there would be a honeymoon when Bob was off-duty. Invited guests would be only from the lower decks – no officers allowed. Tulip wasn't about to ask the captain if he would perform the ceremony. Obviously it wouldn't be a real marriage because Tulip was a man, and presumably it would last only until the ship returned to London, and quite clearly Bob Braithwaite was lacking a full set of marbles. But it would be close enough. There was to be an open-house party afterwards and Christine had been put in charge of providing canapés and booze. She loved it. She was in her element.

The marriage would be performed by an oddball character called Bernie Schwartz. For the ceremony Bernie needed a bible. He didn't possess a real bible, but what he did have was a 'Port Said Bible.' This also wasn't a real bible, but just a pornographic book whose notoriety was based upon the fact that it is so poorly written as to be laughable. You will perhaps remember my run-in with the Arab in Port Said just recently who tried to sell me shoddy and substandard pornography? Well, it was along those lines. The Port Said Bible was published by an outfit called Olympia Press in Paris, and the grammar was atrociously comical. A typical passage might read "He fugged her and he fugged her until the spug ran down her thig and she was in Exeter."

The big night arrived. The ceremony was to take place in the stewards' messroom at 19:00. All afternoon other stewards had hung streamers and tinsel and generally made it look akin to a chapel. Christine had arranged with chef for vol-au-vents and fancy pastries, and the 2nd Steward did some creative accountancy and lots of booze was suddenly available for the festivities. No one had a copy of the "Wedding March" so, as the happy couple entered the messroom, it was to the dulcet tones of Mark Wynter singing 'Venus in Blue Jeans.' Tulip was of course dressed in a genuine virginal white wedding dress with a long train. Call me cynical if you like, but she probably had several of them secreted away amongst the many suitcases and trunks that she possessed. She looked very demure as the marriage took place. But hey, perhaps she got married every trip? Bernie was magnificent and carried out the nuptials to perfection. He produced an authentic looking marriage certificate which detailed their names in copperplate writing, together with the latitude and longitude of where the ceremony had taken place. He then blessed everyone in the room and tried to kiss the bride.

At least the wedding was a harmless affair and caused no one any problems. This is unlike the queer marriage that almost caused an 'international incident.' Back in the mid-1950s there was a cargo/emigrant ship called the Captain Cook whose regular run was UK – Auckland. In New Zealand the ship already had a bad name with drunken crews causing mayhem ashore, or even deserting.

On one unforgettable occasion, two queer stewards decided to get married ashore, and chose Auckland Town Hall for their venue. Somehow or other, the city's mayor and other high dignitaries were invited and duly attended the ceremony dressed in their mayoral regalia. In that part of the ceremony when the reverend asks, "If any person present can show just cause why these two people may not be lawfully married, then let him speak now," that's when the trouble started. Someone said in a loud voice that they were a couple of queers and ripped the wig off the 'brides' head. The wedding broke up in confusion and the mayor and his wife went off in high dudgeon, claiming that, as he represented the City of Auckland, then these two queer-boys from the Captain Cook had embarrassed Auckland and the whole of New Zealand. There were rumours that plans were afoot to ban the ship from New Zealand waters, but it never came to anything.

⚓

The Port Pirie reduced speed as she sailed into the harbour at Aden and made her way towards the fuel facility at Steamer Point. As she did so, four huge manta rays majestically glided down our starboard side. We were here to top up our fuel tanks with diesel. We secured onto a mooring buoy and a fuel barge came alongside to pump hundreds of tons of fuel bunkers onboard.

The Aden Protectorate could be a very dangerous place to visit. In what would later become the South Yemeni Republic, the local Arab population wanted rid of the British who, as always, tended to overstay their welcome. Therefore the British armed forces, with units mostly of Royal Marines, had to keep a very fragile peace. Due to the instability of the area, Captain Conby allowed no shore leave. In any event we stayed for only a matter of hours. On a later trip to Aden some eight months later, our crew had been allowed ashore for a short spell to stretch our legs. Myself and three others had gone into the British Sailors Mission, and twenty minutes after we had left the building, some terrorists had lobbed several grenades inside.

By the evening of the next day the ship had arrived off Cape Gaurdafui on the Horn of Africa. We set our course towards the south east at a speed of 16 knots. We had 4604 nautical miles to run until we rounded Cape Leeuwin on the extreme southern tip of Western Australia. It would take us twelve days. The smooth swells had a glassy appearance, and the sun's rays were a joy to feel on one's face as we sped towards the Equator. The swimming pool began to get used by everyone onboard. Everyone that is, except the blue-rinsed ladies, who wouldn't dream of letting anyone see their scrawny cellulited legs. On most afternoons and evenings the pool was full to overflowing and there was much laughter and splashing going on.

A few days later, I was painting No. 4 hatch-coaming on the opposite side to the pool. I had my head down and keeping out of the hot blistering sun. One of the ordinary seamen, Terry Bentham, was also painting nearby. He called over in an urgent whisper, "Graham. Get an eyeful of that." I followed his eyes and looked towards the pool. Jeezus! Standing next to the pool ladder was the doctor's young daughter Susan. She was dressed in a skimpy bikini that left little to the imagination. I had never taken much notice of her before, but now it was obvious to see that, although she was only 15 years old, she had a beautiful woman's body. She was an absolute knockout. She had apparently made an impression upon quite a few other crew-members as well, because they were lingering around the pool area on the most flimsiest of pretexts. There was no doubt that this young lady sensed the interest being shown in her, and saw the carnal longing in their eyes, and she loved it. Every afternoon thereafter, she would show up at the pool and bask in the inordinate amount of lecherous looks that came her way. Later, she would lie on the hatch tarpaulin to sunbathe and 'accidentally' let a delicious breast slip out of her bikini. This became a regular occurrence. This girl, who looked as if butter wouldn't melt in her mouth, was a consummate prick-teaser. Not only that, but she was an under-age prick-teaser. We shall hear more about her later.

One warm and balmy evening, a movie was shown on-deck. The 8mm projector was set up on the engineer's deck adjacent to No. 4 cargo hatch, and the large white screen was placed atop the winch-house. Although the movie was to be for the benefit of everyone onboard, the officers and passengers were kept very firmly apart from us lowly crew. We settled down sitting cross-legged on the hatch-top to watch the film, whilst on the deck above, the officers were in tropical rig and the ladies sat in wicker chairs with their legs covered by tartan blankets against the evening chill.

The credits rolled and we found that the film tonight was to be 'Room at the Top' starring Lawrence Harvey, Simone Signoret and Heather Sears. It followed the story of a go-getting Yorkshireman called Joe Lampton who has a sexual *ménage a trios* with Signoret and Sears. At one point in the movie, Lampton returns late at night to the woman he had previously dumped (Sears). She decides that she can bolster their flagging relationship if she goes down upon her knees and performs fellatio upon him right there and then. As the camera angle follows her head disappearing southwards towards Lampton's tackle, it didn't take much imagination to realise what was about to happen, and the lower elements (i.e. the deck crew) went wild. There were great whoop-whoops and a huge cheer, with some ribald remarks concerning Sears not talking with her mouth full. After all, this was quite risqué stuff back in 1964!

From the blue-rinsed ladies and their docile husbands, there was the silence of utter disbelief. Not disbelief that such a movie had ever been made; but the disbelief that someone aboard the Port Pirie had been so stupid as to show it in their presence. Apparently questions were asked in the higher echelons, and the poor chump in-charge of movies (i.e. the 3rd Mate), was instructed to ensure that, henceforth any movies were suitable viewing for the ladies.

Crossing the Line

Two and a half days after departing the Horn of Africa, the Port Pirie had steamed some 950 miles, and according to the officer of the watch, we would cross the Equator into the southern hemisphere about mid-afternoon. There was much excitement, and word spread about the ship that

63

King Neptune and his entourage would come aboard this very afternoon to exact revenge on the Pollywogs who dared to enter his kingdom uninvited. There was much trepidation from us first-trippers because we had obviously heard the stories of the 'Crossing the Line' initiation ceremonies, and the punishments meted out. Our crewmates gave us evil grins as they knew what was in store for us.

By mid-afternoon the Port Pirie had reached the Equator, and the 2nd Mate sounded the ship's horn jubilantly for some minutes. Some of our shipmates appeared and Chris Morling and I were grabbed and bound by the wrists so that there was no escape. Other first trippers who had never crossed the equator were corralled with us and included the galley boy, a junior engineer, an officer cadet and an engine room rating.

From up on the fo'castle appeared King Neptune carrying his trident. He wore a long white robe and a bushy beard made of strands of rope and his hair seemed to be a mop head. He also looked suspiciously like our ship's carpenter. He and his entourage of his Royal Barber and Royal Doctor joined the procession as they made their way back aft to where he would hold his court at No. 4 cargo hatch. There were loud shouts of, "Where are these Pollywogs who have dared to enter my kingdom?" The whole crew and passengers were gathered and the atmosphere was of good-natured anticipation. Some of the catering staff rounded off the festivities by dressing as women, and they looked quite fetching with their faces made-up in garish colours.

At last, Neptune's Court was convened. We Pollywogs were accused by the Shellbacks of entering King Neptune's domain uninvited. I wanted to be difficult and plead not guilty, but I had been told that it would do no good whatsoever. You will always be found guilty. Oh well – here goes!

Firstly we had to go onto our knees to beg forgiveness from King Neptune. Then the verdict was handed down - guilty! Now it was time for our punishment. As 'medicine', a spoonful of a harmless but noxious looking green liquid was ladled down our throats by Neptune's doctor until we gagged. Our bodies were then covered in galley waste slops and our faces covered in a mixture of foam, flour and water which had been dyed red. After being shaved by the barber with an oversized wooden cut-throat razor and hosed down with a fire hose, our penance had been paid and we were fully fledged members of King Neptune's Domain. Captain Conby stepped down onto the deck to shake each of our hands and to give out signed certificates verifying that we now belonged to The Grand Order of the Deep. What a day!

One morning we made a sharp alteration of course to starboard when another Port Line vessel was sighted on the horizon. The two vessels closed the distance at a combined speed of 34 knots, and paralleled each other to pass a half mile distant. The other vessel was the Port Brisbane, and she was homeward bound after having loaded dairy and meat products in Australia. She was a more modern ship and had a rounded aerodynamic forepart of her bridge-deck and sleek swept-back lines, whereas our ship was older and had been built with not much thought to what looked aesthetically pleasing. As the two vessels came abeam of each other, their horns were sounded for some minutes, and both the crews lined the rails and waved for all we were worth. I had been instructed to go aft, and on a signal from the bridge, I dipped our Red Ensign in salutation and as a matter of courtesy.

Each shipping company had a strict seniority list for all captains and other officers. They also had a company flagship, and this was normally the newest or largest in the company fleet. Usually the most senior captain got to command the flagship, and lesser masters got the smaller or older ships, right down to the rust-buckets that were almost ready for scrapping. There was a rigid pecking order, and senior masters also expected to be in the forefront when new cutting-edge equipment was supplied.

Back in the mid-1950s, the new fangled radar sets were starting to be seen fitted to merchant ships. Of course, radar had been around during the war, but they were large ungainly affairs that involved several aerials and required specialist operators. But now the new breed of radar set was mounted upon a single mast and could be operated by the officer-of-the-watch. Every senior captain wanted one.

The story goes that an elderly Blue Star Line cargo vessel, commanded by a very junior captain, was bound for Sydney, Australia. It was of course not fitted with a radar set. Neither yet was the company's flagship, but it was due to be fitted in the very near future. The master of the Sydney bound vessel was aware that the flagship would be in harbour on arrival, so he decided to fit his own radar set. As the ship steamed across the oceans weeks before arrival, he ordered the ship's carpenter to manufacture a radar mast and scanner out of scrap timber and any spare material they had onboard. The Chippie excelled himself. He not only built a tall radar mast, but built-in a winding mechanism, so that the scanner could be turned by hand. Imagine the scene as the senior officers aboard the flagship watched through their binoculars as their lowly colleague sailed into Sydney with a radar scanner whizzing around. They were green with envy. Happy days.

⚓

I went into the sailors' messroom and sat down at the table. Billy MacIver and another able seaman, Barry Townsend, had been talking. The conversation stopped dead. There had been an atmosphere of whispering and shared secrets. "Am I interrupting something?" I asked.

Barry said, "Well you're gonna know about it sooner or later, so you may as well know about it now." I looked from one to the other wondering who was going to share this snippet with me.

"It's Andy Roberts," whispered Barry. "He's been caught red-handed by the 4th Mate with that girl Susan in his cabin. Apparently they were in bed together." Andy Roberts was a good looking dining room steward who I thought wouldn't have any problem chatting up the ladies.

"Aye," said Billy. "I saw the doctor and his wife and the wee daughter going into the skipper's cabin this morning. They dinnae look none too cheery. Then later Andy and the 4th Mate also went to see the skipper. It dinnae look too good for Andy." I certainly had to agree with him.

Later that evening I bumped into Christine. She had all the latest gossip at her fingertips. She knew everything. "Well, darling," she gushed (she called everyone darling!). "Andy has told me...in the strictest confidence mind you....that he's being sent back home as soon as we get to Melbourne." She looked pleased that she had this morsel of information to share. "Apparently," she continued, "the 4th Mate was suspicious and he followed the girl to Andy's cabin." Christine momentarily paused as she dragged out the suspense. "He waited for twenty minutes and walked right into the cabin, and there they were darling; going at it hammer and tongs."

I nodded. I was sure there was more to come. If Christine knew something, then she had to tell someone. If you wanted to keep a secret; don't tell Christine. "The skipper's told Andy that he doesn't want the doctor's family embarrassed, so he's to keep all these details to himself; so Andy's only told me about it."

On our eighth day out from Aden we saw a sight that took one's breath away. The weather was fine with long smooth undulating swells and the sun was hot on our backs. It started with just a few bottle-nosed dolphins playing around the ship's bow. Then more dolphins joined in. It was a wonderful sight to see them weave in and around the dozen or so others in their pod. They would all surface in unison, then expel their breath in a great whoosh, and take a lungful of air for their next dive.

Suddenly, almost unannounced, hundreds more dolphins came from a mile out on both sides of the ship. They were homing in on the Port Pirie. Some of the crew and many of the passengers went up onto the fo'castle head where they could get a better view. Within minutes this huge pod of mammals were alongside; easily keeping pace with our cruising speed of 16 knots. They had tremendous fun playing in our bow-wave, whilst others were leaping high into the air and turning somersaults. But it wasn't to last, and something must have spooked them, because within minutes they had all disappeared again.

However, soon afterwards, another sight awaited us. Out on the starboard bow someone sighted water spouts from the blow-holes of a pair of whales. The 2nd Mate altered course to converge with the last sighting, but the whales had disappeared. Everyone was keeping a sharp lookout. Just as we got near their last known location, someone shouted, "Look – Over there," and two huge sperm whales that appeared joined together, leapt majestically out of the water and flopped back into the sea, their massive 50 tons bulk causing an enormous splash. What a marvellous sight. Sometime later, I read that the sperm whale mates by diving down deep, then joining together in copulation as they ascend. They then break apart as they come to the surface. This appears to be just what we had seen, and apparently it's a very rare sight.

A few days later our ship rounded Cape Leeuwin on the southern tip of Western Australia. My first sight of the coast were some rocky outcrops which, as they were hit by the long oceanic swells, sent columns of white spray high into the air. A red and white painted lighthouse stood someway inland. Cape Leeuwin was visible only for an hour or two, for as we rounded the cape and turned eastbound, we entered the Great Australian Bight, and the land curved out of sight as it meandered northwards. We wouldn't see the land again until almost arriving at Melbourne in the Australian state of Victoria. I was later to discover via the 3rd Mate that we still had a huge distance to travel. There were still 1700 miles to run. Therefore, our journey across The Bight at 16 knots, would take us four and a half days. That really brought it home to me how immense this country truly is. In fact, the whole of Europe can comfortably fit into the vastness that is Australia.

As I stood on deck and watched the sea slip rapidly by, I was excited and eager to discover Australia's pleasures for myself. I had read of the wonderful scenery and different cultures there were to be seen, and I wanted to take in all of its delights. It crossed my mind that with my poor wages of only £16 per month, I would not be able to afford very much in the way of delights. However, the crew had told us tales of wonderful parties and booze-ups they had been to – so perhaps things wouldn't be so grim after all.

It was mid-January 1964, and the wind was warm across my body. It felt good to feel the hot sun on my face and to see almost cloudless blue skies. This was the antipodean summer, and I thought of my ex school-friends and ex work colleagues who were battling against the cold biting winds and icy pavements back home in England. It brought a smile to my lips. They were struggling to get to their factories and offices, whereas I on the other hand, needed only to fall out of bed and I was at my place of work. Whilst my friends back home were shivering, my body was getting nicely tanned, and my thick reddish brown hair, which had last had a Vindi style short-back-and-sides four months ago, was over my ears and neck. Another advantage of shipboard life was that I had almost no outgoings from my wages. Apart from the £4 per month that was sent to my mum as an allotment, all my heat, light, and rent were free, and I was served four meals per day with snacks in between. In addition, almost everyone in that day-and-age were smokers, and I was no different. The exception was that my friends were paying shoreside prices, whereas I was paying the duty-free price of 7/6d (41p) for a carton of 200 Senior Service. Yes, I thought, all things considered, life wasn't too bad at all.

A large Albatross went by, skimming the waves with its wingtip as it rode the thermals. These huge majestic birds can have a wingspan of up to eleven feet, and they had been known to follow a ship the entire way across the ocean. On the oceans, Albert Ross rarely landed to take a rest. They usually stayed aloft for thousands of miles. The only time they ceased flying was to land upon the sea to feed on the food scraps that were dumped overboard via the galley trashcan.

Four nights later I bumped into Christine. "You'll never guess what's happened," she said excitedly.
"What?" I said.
"It's the 4th Mate," she said. "The dirty bugger's been caught shagging the doctor's daughter. It all happened this evening."
"Bloody hell," I said in complete surprise. "But it was the 4th Mate who stitched up Andy Roberts, wasn't it? And now he's been caught doing the same thing," I laughed. "It serves him bloody right. How was he caught?"
"The chief officer went to his cabin to ask about a navigation chart," she informed me eagerly, "and he had that 15 year old girl in bed with him."
"Jeezus", I said, "the shit's gonna hit the fan big-time."
"It already has," she said. "According to Tulip, she overheard the captain shouting at the 4th Mate in his cabin. He's being sent off the ship when we get to Melbourne tomorrow as well as Andy," she laughed. "That's sweet justice for him, isn't it?" Christine remembered another snippet of hot gossip. "Also," she continued, "the skipper's banned the daughter from

leaving her cabin. She's got to have all her meals there and she's not to come out before the ship arrives in Melbourne tomorrow."

For the 4th Mate it would probably be the end of his sea-going career. Andy Roberts would also find it difficult to secure another job at sea. Each seaman's discharge book contained a section that reported on one's ability and general conduct. For having sexual relations with an underage girl whilst that person was under the responsibility of the vessel's captain, both would probably receive a discharge that read "Decline to Report" – know as a DR. Such an entry, even though it was non-committal, was the worst possible report that any seafarer could receive.

The next morning The Port Pirie entered Port Phillip Bay and picked up our harbour pilot. Within the hour the ship was alongside a pier lined with warehouses, and her engines were shut down. The ship's agent brought aboard mail that had arrived for the crew. I had one blue airmail letter from my mum with a short note to say that the family all missed me, and had I yet got a tan? Back in those days there was no prospect at all of a phone call back to England. Firstly, one would have to go to the post office to book a call with the international operator, as one couldn't simply direct-dial-like in this day-and-age. Secondly, the call was so expensive as to be prohibitive.

The ship's agent was an important cog in the smooth running of any shipping company's business. The agency would arrange for gangs of wharfies to work the cargo, order fresh food, organise fresh water to be pumped onboard, or even a crewmembers trip to see a doctor if necessary. In short, he made the vessels stay in harbour run faultlessly. Prior to arrival, the ship would radio the crew's currency requirements, and the agent would deliver hundreds of Australian pounds onboard (this was pre-decimal Australia). The crew could then draw on this money as a "sub" against their wages.

The wharfies were opening up the cargo hatches ready to start discharging. Meanwhile the crew quickly topped-up the cargo derricks and rigged them in a union purchase, so that cargo came out of the hatch and straight onto the quayside. Time was money. The deckies managed to get an early knock-off and so Terry Bentham and I hit the streets and headed for - according to Terry - the best bar in town.

Chloe's Bar at the Young & Jackson Hotel on the corner of Flinders Street was a fabulous place to get seriously drunk. The bar was heavin' with sweating wharfies dressed in shorts and singlet. It was standing room only. More of our crew piled in the door as we ordered our beer. This was in the days when, by law, all the hotel bars closed at 6pm, and every strong drinking man in town thought it was his God-given duty to get himself legless before the bar closed. This was known as "The 6-o-clock swill."

Other Australian states, notably Tasmania and NSW, had changed to 10pm closing years ago, but Victoria wouldn't alter their laws for another two years. South Australia would be even later in 1967. One couldn't get a drink at all if it was a Sunday. All the bars were closed. However, if you knew which bars were still doing business, then you could knock on the side door and they would probably let you in for some Sunday boozing. Mind you, because one could only legally drink if one was a traveller, you normally had to sign-in and be seen to have a meal. Just in case the police decided to raid the place, the landlord would sometimes lay out some dirty plates as evidence that you had eaten. It was known as "Sly-Groggin."

As 6pm drew closer, the men would line their jugs along the bar, and instead of the barman taking each to a pump to refill them, he simply walked along the bar with an extending hose fitted with a gun and pulled the trigger – magic!

Chloe herself is a magnificent life-size full-frontal nude painting of a 19 year old model by the French artist Jules Lefebvre, and has graced the back wall of the bar since 1908. In the early 1960s these bars were strictly all male affairs – no women allowed. Chloe was the only exception.

The combination of the hot weather and ice cold beer and my lecherous looks at Chloe had an intoxicating effect, and Terry and I were rapidly getting legless. However, we were not the only ones. A loudmouthed wharfie staggered over in our direction. "You'se guys off the Port Line boat, are ya?" We nodded. "Yeah, well let me tell ya summat," he said, breathing beer fumes in my face. "You bloody Pommies, ya come over here and ya drink all our beer, and ya fuck all our women," he said - his legs quite wobbly. "We don't mind that so much, but we've gotta bloody marry 'em." Having delivered this titbit of human philosophy, he weaved his way back to his mates looking mighty pleased with himself.

As we staggered back aboard the Port Pirie we could hear that a party was underway in the officers' quarters. However, it was one to which we would not be invited. The officers and engineers normally didn't mix with crew from the lower decks. It was a class distinction thing. They usually phoned the local nurses home on arrival and arranged for any off-duty nurses to come aboard in the evening, thereby cornering the market in the medical profession. The nurses, always eager for a good party, came in droves.

Terry and I had a late dinner and wandered around to Christine's. She cracked me a beer. "What's been occurring, Christine? What's the latest gossip?" I asked.

"Andy Roberts has gone," she said sadly. "He packed his bags and was off the ship by this afternoon. He's flying back to England tomorrow."

"What about the 4th Mate?"

"He's gone as well. I don't know when he's flying back. He'd better not be on the same flight as Andy, or they'll be some blood spilt, won't there?"

"And what about the prick-teaser who made all of this happen?" I asked.

"The whole family were picked up this morning by a guy driving a utility. Apparently the doctor's taking over a practice up-country, near Ballarat."

"Well", I said, "that might keep his little girl out of trouble. God bless the citizens of Ballarat." We bummed another beer and I turned-in for the night.

⚓

I was walking down the gangway in the late afternoon on my way ashore. On the quayside were a middle-aged couple who definitely didn't look like city folk. The man was aged about fifty and dressed in tough-wearing denim overalls, a thick leather belt, and some sturdy polished boots. On his deeply tanned head he wore a bush hat with the brim turned up on one side. He resembled the stereotype of an Australian sheep farmer. His wife wore a flowery dress and a pleasant smile. They were stood beside a rough-terrain utility vehicle with bull-bars welded across the front end and enough spot lights to illuminate a theatre.

"G'day, mate," he said in a gravelly voice. "Can ya tell us if our son's aboard? We'd kinda like to see 'im."

"What's your son's name?" I asked.

"It's Malcolm."

"I'm afraid I don't know anyone called Malcolm. Is he an engineer or a deck officer perhaps?"

"No mate. He's a steward," he said with a hint of embarrassment.

"Are you sure you've got the right ship?" I queried. "I know all the stewards, and we don't have anyone onboard called Malcolm."

He screwed up his deeply lined face and his mind seemed in torment. He appeared to make a decision. "Yeah well, ya might know the stupid bugger as Tulip," he said, his lip curling downwards.

"Oh Tulip," I said. "Yeah shhh...He's onboard. Hold on mate. I'll just go get him." I ran back aboard and found her cleaning the captain's cabin.

"Your mum and dad's here to see you, Tulip. They're on the quayside."

"Ooh thanks ever so much, Graham," she lisped. "The chief steward's given me a few days leave." Her face creased in consternation. "Does my Dad look as if he's in a good mood?" she enquired.

"I'm sure he'll be okay," I said. "Go on. Don't keep them waiting." I followed as she sashayed down the gangway. I'll never forget the look upon her father's face as she minced across the quayside. It seemed to say, "Where the hell did we go wrong with you?"

Our stay in Melbourne lasted for eleven days. Mostly we would drink at Chloe's Bar, or at weekends go out to the seaside suburb of St. Kilda, which had a great beach and some fabulous bars. Usually when the pubs closed, someone would know where there was a party going-on.

A strange phenomenon, at least for an Englishmen, was the sight of Australian city businessmen walking to their offices. They wore a normal jacket and tie, but instead of trousers they wore shorts and long socks. There were many knobbly and hairy knees on display and it seemed very odd when compared to the bowler-hatted city gents of London back in my teenage years.

I had such high hopes of seeing more of the scenic or cultural side of Australia, but when it was time to leave Melbourne, the sum total of my look at Australia's delights had I fear, been a long list of bars - and the bottom of empty beer-glasses.

⚓

Two days later we sailed through the entrance to Sydney Harbour, which claims to be the largest natural harbour in the world. We picked up our pilot and continued westwards, and as the harbour opened out; it revealed a beautiful panoramic sight. We steamed past small bays with beautiful houses lining the foreshore. Everywhere were yachts and small motor boats which seemed as if they were there just to welcome our ship. And in the distance was the city of Sydney and the giant Sydney Harbour

Bridge. We passed Fort Denison, an old convict prison island in the centre of the harbour. At last we slowed down as we approached Circular Quay where the cruise ships were berthed and we could make out the tall buildings of the city. As the Port Pirie passed beneath the huge spans of the world famous Sydney Harbour Bridge or "The Giant Coat-Hanger," as it was locally known, I stared in wonder at the sheer size of it. I knew from my studies of the Guinness Book of Records that the bridge was designed and built by Dorman Long & Co Ltd of Middlesbrough in 1932, but I wondered how such a huge amount of steel, some 30,000 tons of it, could possibly have been shipped out from England and assembled into such an iconic masterpiece. It must have been like assembling a gigantic Meccano kit. Shortly afterwards, the ship berthed at Pyrmont in Darling Harbour and we put out the thick mooring ropes. As was usual, we topped-up the cargo derricks in readiness for the wharfies starting to work the cargo, and very soon the ship was a hive of industry as cargo was being discharged from all six hatches.

In the evening, myself and several crew went to Monty's Bar. It was handily located right at the end of our pier. Gratefully we didn't have to endure the 6-o-clock swill – it was 10pm closing in New South Wales.

Monty's had a circular bar with a single shoulder height shelf running all around the walls of the pub. There were no seating arrangements - that, I was told, was for cissies - so the shelf was for parking one's glass of beer upon. Wooden doors, made up of small panes of glass, ran down one whole side of the bar and exited onto Union Street. These could all be opened - as they were on this evening - to let in lots of cool air. The two remaining walls were covered from floor to ceiling in white tiles. These I was told somewhat tongue-in-cheek by a crew-mate, made it easier to wash the blood off from the numerous fights that took place. I think he was exaggerating.

The no-females rule didn't apply in NSW; and certainly not in Monty's Bar. On this night there were several girls and a dozen or so sailors from various ships. It was noisy and smoky and the music was playing loudly. The sort of women that tended to inhabit Monty's Bar were perhaps not the type of girl one would take home to meet one's mother. But then again, they were mostly pretty and had a great sense of humour. We were always laughing in Monty's. Sometimes one would see the odd Aborigine female in the bars, but not too often. They tended to keep to themselves.

Monty's Bar. Pyrmont, Sydney

Many Australian women were drawn towards British men rather than the home-grown Aussie male. There were numerous reasons for this; namely, the Australian man's world was very macho orientated; in that he would rather talk to his mates than to his wife or girlfriend. At an Aussie party, one would see all the men down one end of the room talking beer, footie, and big cars; whilst at the other end, women were expected to chat about girlie stuff; and never the twain shall meet. Also most Australian men didn't have a clue when it came to fashionable clothes. In the early 1960s, they were dressed in bib & braces and a lumberjack shirt and looked as if they had just stepped off an outback cattle station.

It wasn't just the girls in the bars that preferred Englishmen. Hordes of nurses and office girls would turn up at a party onboard ship or to a shoreside party if they knew that the English lads were going to be there. I was to find out later that the same applied to New Zealand girls. They much preferred the English sailors.

Another strange quirk was that The Beatles and The Rolling Stones were presently taking the world by storm and fashions trends were being set with long hair. The latest craze was Beatles jackets with cutaway collars and Afghan coats, but the macho locals would have none of it, and the typical Aussie male took no notice at all - and in fact thought that any man with long hair was sure to be "a woofter."

74

One evening I saw a weird event at The Bunch of Grapes, another dockside seamen's watering hole. One of our engine room stokers, an ex SAS Territorial soldier from Clitheroe called Stan, was sat at the bar nursing a beer and minding his own business. Stan had hair almost down to his shoulders as per the latest fashion. Nearby were some Australian lads bent on causing trouble, and one came over to push his luck. He flicked Stan's hair, "What's the long hair for mate. Are ya some kinda poofter?" Stan sipped his beer and ignored him. "Well ya gotta be a poofter with hair like that, ain't ya?" said Macho-man as he gave Stan's hair another flick. Stan stared ahead and said not a word. Suddenly the Australian superman grabbed a thick hank of Stan's hair. "Come on Goldie-locks, ain't ya got no bloody fight in ya?"

Without a word Stan's hand shot out and grabbed Macho-man by his jaw. His huge hands, with fingers like machine tools, grasped the man's face and gave it a twist. There was a wrenching sound and a look of utter disbelief as the Aussie realised that Stan had dislocated his jawbone from the rest of his face. His lower mandible hung down separately from his upper jaw. As he and his mates went out the door, presumably heading for some urgent hospital treatment, he had to physically hold the two halves of his jaw together. That'll teach him to be a prize twat!

For the remaining days we spent in harbour, I have to admit to using my spare time mostly in the bars. My high hopes and good intentions of seeing the culture of Australia had fallen by the wayside.

Valentina

Eventually it was time to depart Sydney and make our way south. The Port Pirie sailed in the evening for the 640 nautical mile run down to Hobart, Tasmania. The two day voyage took us southwards down the Tasman Sea, across the Bass Strait and into Hobart Harbour. The imposing 4200 foot Mount Wellington looked out over the city, and as we tied up in the port, a heavy rain shower gave us a Tasmanian welcome. The temperature in Hobart was vastly different from the high 90's that we had experienced in sunny Sydney, and it was far cooler by at least 15 degrees, but for all that, it was a handsome looking city.

Later that evening I had been for a walk around Hobart to stretch my legs. It had been a particularly hard day and I felt ready for my bed. I came back aboard and could hear a party going on in Christine's cabin, so I popped my head around the door. There were a few deckies and stokers and about five girls from shoreside who had somehow been lured onboard. Music was playing and everyone had a drink in their hand. There were about ten people all trying to cram into the small cabin space and some were sat up upon the top bunk-bed. Others were sat on the shag-pile. I was offered a beer and squeezed myself quietly into the corner. I didn't intend staying for too long – I was feeling sleepy. The women seemed the usual mix of ladies who like English sailors, but it was hard to tell. Christine liked to keep the lighting down low, so as to not only enhance the party atmosphere, but to move the focus away from her swarthy chin. Two of the girls were sending looks in my direction which seemed to indicate that they were interested; but although they were quite pretty, I was so tired that I simply wanted to go off to my bunk.

I noticed one particular girl, dressed in a smart black suit, who appeared to be on her own. She was a slim girl with long dark hair, and from what I could see, she had beautiful brown eyes with dark curly lashes. I caught her eye and she gave a secretive smile and looked away. A few minutes later I noticed one of the stokers was trying to chat her up. It was time for me to go turn in. I drained my beer and said a general goodnight to everyone.

Chris Morling was fast asleep in the top bunk and snoring soundly as I got undressed and turned-in. I lay there in the pitch dark, and was in that half-world, when one's breathing slows down just before sleep takes over. Some five minutes later the door noiselessly opened, and for a full fifteen seconds she was framed in the light from the passageway as she stood stock still, waiting for her eyes to adjust to the darkness. It was the girl from Christine's party. She was tall and slender and her figure seemed like perfection. I lay prone in my bed staying quiet, my eyes just slits – watching and waiting. She seemed satisfied that she had chosen the correct cabin and just as noiselessly stepped inside and closed the door. The cabin became black once again. I still played possum. She knelt beside my bunk, her knees on the carpeted deck. She seemed unsure what to do next. I could smell her perfume and took a long breath of the fragrance. I began to stroke her hair and she knew that I was awake.
"I'm sorry if I am disturbing you," she whispered. "I wasn't sure which was being your cabin." Her accent appeared to be foreign.
"Sshhh. No need to apologise. I'm glad that you decided to come see me."
She seemed comforted by my words and snuggled up closer. "The bunk's not very wide but you can get in alongside me if you want to."
"Alright then," she murmured demurely. She removed her shoes and her short jacket and I pulled the blue counterpane back so as to make room for her to get in. At last we got comfortable. "How did you know which cabin was mine?" I whispered. I was aware that Chris was asleep in the top bunk.

"The lady called Christine. She tells me where you live. Is okay?" It was hard to place her accent, but she later told me that her parents had emigrated from Yugoslavia when she was six years old.

I took her into my arms and squeezed her tightly. Our lips met and I felt her tongue searching for mine as they sought out the other and writhed in unison, like a pair of snakes making carnal love. I ran my hand across the exquisite curves of her hips and across the flawless curvature of her bottom. "What's your name?" I asked her.

"It is Valentina. You are liking my name?" I told her that I liked her name very much indeed and then introduced myself. She experimented with the pronunciation, "Gray-hom" and started to giggle. We kissed again, this time our tongues intermingling in a fiery passion. Her arm slipped across my back to pull me closer. There was a sudden sharp intake of breath. "But you haven't got any clothes on, Gray-hom," she whispered urgently. "Is being very naughty. Is not correct. I don't know what to be doing."

Inwardly I smiled. I'm quite sure that she knew exactly what she was doing, but I wasn't about to make an argument of it. My hand traversed across her flat stomach and sought out her left breast. She slid over onto her side so that her back was to me, and we lay silently for some minutes as I gently kissed the back of her neck and stroked her hair. Her hair smelt of pine, and I found myself taking in deep breaths of air so as to savour the wonderful aroma of her womanliness. Silently and without any action on her part, I removed her clothes. She turned onto her back and I kissed her again, her breath coming in great rasping gulps. I could hear the church clock strike 10pm as we made slow love in the pitch darkness of the narrow bunk. Afterwards, before we fell asleep, I held a thick hank of her hair and breathed in deeply. The smell was intoxicating. Shortly afterwards, we both fell into a deep slumber.

We were up by 6am the next morning and I escorted her ashore to catch a taxi home. In the morning light I could see that she was even more beautiful than I had imagined. Her dark brown eyes were liquid pools of sable and she had laughter lines that made her face light up and gave it character. Her thick black hair spilled over her shoulders and came to a stop halfway down her back. She told me that she was 24 years old – some six and a half years older than me. But it didn't really matter. I was smitten! As we waited for the cab, she told me that she worked as a junior solicitor in a firm of lawyers that mostly did house conveyance work and family law. Wow - A beauty with brains! All too soon the cab arrived. She gave me a quick kiss and slid into the back seat. The cab driver took off and she was gone. It was only after the cab had departed that I realised I hadn't asked to see her again and I had no idea whatsoever how to find her, other than to phone every firm of solicitors in the city.

That next day, a Friday, the crew were asking me every sort of question, both rude and downright filthy. Of course Christine had spilled the beans concerning Valentina asking where my cabin was to be found ("Darling, I didn't know you wanted it kept a secret"), and the gangway watchman had reported to all and sundry that I'd taken a glamorous young lady ashore as the dawn was breaking.

At 5pm that afternoon I was in the messroom when the quartermaster came to tell me that a young lady was waiting on the dockside for me. That brought instant whoop-whoops and ribald remarks from my shipmates. I ran down the gangway to find Valentina waiting patiently. I scooped her into my arms and kissed her. Her lips felt as soft and yielding as they had just last evening and she buried her face into my shoulder.

"I wasn't sure if I should come. You didn't ask me to be seeing you again after you are loving me last night. Did I do the right thing? Is correct?"

"But of course you did the right thing. We were in such a hurry this morning that we both forgot."

"That is good, Gray-hom. Anyway, do you have the weekend off-duty?"

I told her that it shouldn't be a problem. I'd be free for Saturday afternoon and Sunday. What did she have in mind?

"I thought that maybe we go to my house and I cook you some good food. Then perhaps we walk along the seashore. It is lovely sandy beach." She giggled deliciously, "Then maybe we go home for some more loving. Is okay?" I laughed out loud at her crazy fractured English, but said that would be very acceptable.

And that's the way in which we spent the next ten days. In the evenings and at weekends, whenever I could get off the ship, I would walk to her rented house a mile out around the headland. Her house was a typical clapboard design with a veranda that went around three sides. We would walk for miles, sometimes taking her neighbour's dog with us. At other times we would simply put our feet up and sit out on the veranda and she would tell me how her day had progressed, or I would tell her of my, as yet, limited travels across the seas. And every evening we would sleep together in the double bed in the room with the harbour view.

Those two weeks were not only idyllic in a romantic sense, but they were a foretaste of my sexual education. I came to be familiar with her beautiful body, because she thought nothing of walking around the house stark naked. At first, due to my typical staid English upbringing, I would avert my gaze, but later, as I got used to seeing her perfectly formed figure, I would openly stare in wonder at her beauty. She would laugh at my embarrassment when she caught me studying her small perfect breasts, her curvaceousness, or the forbidden black triangle. Valentina, because she was older and more experienced, showed me every way in which two people could enjoy each other's bodies. Nothing was prohibited, nothing was taboo. Our frequent lovemaking sessions even extended to outside on the beach or in the forest to the north of the city. Sometimes our lovemaking was gentle and sensual, and at others she wanted to be mounted roughly and urgently in a noisy animal passion.

Meanwhile the Port Pirie had unloaded the last of the general cargo that had been brought from England and it was rapidly re-loading with a cargo of apples for export to the UK. Each day she sank deeper into the water and each day got closer to our day of departure. Our next port of call was a return to Sydney, to load butter and meat. We had spoken almost with reluctance about when we would see each other again. She had told me that she loved me, and I had reciprocated; but it made no difference to the fact that we would soon be apart for a very long time. There was nothing to be done but to have beautiful memories.

The fateful day came. It was a Tuesday morning. We had just spent a lovely weekend together, and now here we were with the ship's engines ticking over and about to depart. She stood on the quayside and the tears rolled down her cheeks as the ship slowly slid out of the berth. As I looked down from my harbour station upon the fo'castle head, I was helpless to do anything. As we sailed down the harbour, the lonely figure standing on the quayside got smaller and smaller, until at last I could see her no more. I shall always remember that smell of fresh pine.

⚓

Our arrival back in Sydney was an anti-climax and I had no interest whatsoever in enjoying myself. For days on end I would see her face as she had stood on the dockside as the ship had departed. I could see her face crumple into tears and it made me so miserable.

My shipmates had tried to cheer me up, but to no avail. I had discussed my feelings with Christine, even though it was taking a risk that she might be a blabbermouth and tell all. Christine had told me that the type of girls that regularly came aboard the British ships were "Good-time girls." They liked to party, and they liked English sailors. However, the truth was that very often, when their current boyfriend's ship sailed out of the harbour on its way back to England, they simply walked across the quay to another British ship and found a fresh boyfriend – just like that!

In fact Valentina had told me how she came to be onboard the Port Pirie on the night we had met. A girl who worked in her office building had invited her to a party and she'd found herself in Christine's cabin with a

79

drink in her hand. Chris went on to say that she didn't for one minute think that Valentina was in the same mould as the others. Your regular ship's party girl, she'd argued, wasn't a high-flying career woman – and a solicitor to boot.

In the scorching heat the ship continued to load more cargo, and now she was almost fully laden. There was room for just a few hundred tons more cargo to be stowed at our next destination. In the morning we let go our ropes and headed out of the harbour to begin the two and a half day voyage to our last port in Australia – Adelaide.

Our arrival in Adelaide coincided with evensong; and as we berthed, the church bells all over the city were ringing out for all they were worth. Adelaide, founded in 1836, is the state capital of South Australia and was named in honour of Queen Adelaide, the German consort to King William IV. It has more places of worship per head of population than many big cities of the world, but certainly more than any other place in Australia. It's known as The City of Churches.

Work started the next morning to finish loading the last few hundred tons of lamb carcasses which would be stowed in the refrigerated tween-deck spaces. Once that was completed, we would then load a deck cargo of hundreds of bales of wool.

After lunch on Sunday I was free to do as I pleased, and so I strode out to explore the city. I walked down Victoria Street and stared in the shop windows. The goods on display seemed a bit dated, especially in the clothes shops. It didn't matter to me; with only £12 per month to spend, I had only enough for the necessities in life – beer!

My mind wandered to the letter I had received from Valentina via our ship's agent when we'd docked. She had said how much she missed me, and how much she loved me, and so wished things could have been different in our lives. She so wished there would never be a need for me to leave her again. She wondered if she would ever see me again. She asked how long it would be? When would I return to Hobart? These were questions I couldn't answer. I would firstly have to finish this voyage; which would take at least another two months before the ship returned to London. Then I would have to be lucky enough to get a berth on a vessel bound for Hobart. Even if that could be arranged - what then? At some stage I would just have to leave her all over again. It didn't bear thinking about.

I strolled along King William Street, once again lazily window shopping. On the pavement outside the Ambassadors Hotel, I came upon a pair of fat middle-aged American tourists, presumably a husband and wife, who were attempting to get a drink of beer. They weren't having much luck, because clearly it was a Sunday and the bar was closed, and quite obviously bars in South Australia didn't open on Sundays. The Americans weren't to be put off. They were giving a hard time to a local innocent passer-by who had been unfortunate enough to have been standing near the bar entrance. But all the same it was a strange conversation. I pretended to look in a nearby shop window, but my ears were flapping.

"Well, this just ain't good enough," said the Yank. "You'd think a guy and his wife, after coming all this goddam way from the States, would be able to get a drink in this town, wouldn't ya?"

"Hard luck, mate," said the passer-by. "But if ya wanna come back tomorra, you'll get a drink, no probs."

"We don't wanna drink yesterday or tomorrow. We want a drink today. What's wrong with this goddam country? Man should be able to get what he wants, can't he?"

Mr Innocent Bystander didn't quite know what to say. "You come back tomorra – she'll be right," he repeated.

Mister loud-mouth's wife - whose complete ensemble was in nipple pink, waded right in. "Another thang. Those Aborigines," she said in a rasping voice. "They're so goddam ugly. They just stand about on street corners all the time. Whose idea was it to let them into this country?"

Hank, or whatever his name was, wanted everyone to know he was from the Good Ol' USA because he wore a ten-gallon hat, a bolo bootlace tie, a leather belt with cow-horns for a belt buckle, and alligator shoes. I'll bet he'd never been west of New York City.

He spotted me lingering nearby and brought me into his argument regarding Australia's shortcomings. "What do you think?" he said pointing a finger. "Am I right or am I goddam right?"

I tried to be a bit diplomatic. "Listen to me shit-for-brains," I said. "Why don't you and that fuck-ugly wife of yours, get the hell back to wherever you came from?" I didn't actually say that, but just shook my head in despair at how some people can be complete arseholes.

I continued my walk along the wide boulevards, and in the numerous open spaces and parkland. At the end of Victoria Street was the magnificent General Post Office and The Treasury, just two of the many old colonial buildings that looked as if someone cared for them. Old tramcars, looking very much like their namesakes in San Francisco, made a noisy but stately progress. And everywhere I went across the city, I was so very pleased to see just how clean the streets were. Adelaide, I decided, was an okay place to live – as long as you were a churchgoer – and you didn't want to buy a beer on a Sunday!

The next day we sailed on our way homeward bound. The passage home clearly didn't have the same aura of discovery to look forward to as on our outward voyage. Our route took us in exactly the opposite track, the only thing different was that we had no passengers, and we now had a new 4th Mate and a replacement steward in place of Andy Roberts. I think we were missing a few other crew members, as several had decided to jump ship and make a new life in Australia. The other great difference was that we were heading for Antwerp in Belgium, and not the Royal Docks in London. Some of our crew would be paying-off and leaving the ship there and replacements would be flown out from England.

From Antwerp the ship would sail on a three-week voyage into the Baltic Sea to unload at Scandinavian ports. The ship would call at Hamburg, Gothenburg, Stockholm, Helsinki, then back to England. Like most of the crew, I would be remaining with the ship until it eventually arrived back in London. The weather was good and we made excellent time ploughing our way across the Indian Ocean and for the run up the Red Sea.

Scandinavian Beauties

Just over one month later, on 26th April 1964, the Port Pirie docked at Antwerp. A hired coach awaited on the dockside with our partial crew change who had flown in via Southend Airport. Captain Conby departed on leave and our new skipper was Captain Richard Bettess.

They brought mail with them from the London office. I had two letters, and I read the one from mum firstly. She didn't have an awful lot of news, but just family chat and a funny story about Albert aka Fred Flintstone. I would have plenty of stories to tell my family when I got home. I could tell them tales of man-overboard, of sailing through stormy seas, of going through the Suez Canal, and sailing across the oceans to faraway places, during the course of which I had been seasick, lovesick, and homesick!

From the Australian stamp I knew that the second letter was from Valentina. I had been so much looking forward to hearing from her that I clutched the letter to my chest, almost not wanting to burst the bubble by opening it. At last I opened the envelope, and inside was a two-page letter and three photographs of her standing on the veranda and on the beach. She looked so beautiful, and I would have gladly given a year's wages to have her in my arms at that very moment. Her handwriting was small and neat. She said how much she missed me, of how she thought her life had changed now that I wasn't there anymore. She said that she loved me very much, but found herself constantly sad by my going. And then she got to the core of our problem. Valentina said that, even if I managed to come back to her;

unless I could somehow become an Australian citizen and remain in Hobart, then I would have to leave her all over again. This of course, was something I had already thought of, and she was absolutely correct. She said that she couldn't ask me to give up my love of the sea. Therefore, she was releasing me from any promise to return, and I would henceforth be free to pursue whatever course my life would take. That part sounded like legal jargon from a legal mind, but I knew what she meant. She brought the letter to a close by saying that she would always love me and would never forget me, but that we must both get on with our lives. I silently agreed with her reasoning. It would do no good to wonder what might have been, and I needed to shake myself out of this self-imposed gloominess..

⚓

Meanwhile, as life went on, we tasted the delights of Danny's Bar again. That evening seven of us from the deck crew went to Danny's for a wonderful booze-up that finished somewhere in the early hours of the next morning. A new galley boy, Terry Willcox, had just joined the ship and coincidently came from Faversham, which is close by where our family for years went hop picking. Terry had come straight from training at the Vindicatrix, so we dragged the 16 year old ashore to teach him some bad habits and get him drunk. In this we were highly successful, in that he not only got roaring drunk, but tried to chat-up one of the Danny's Bar resident 'waitresses' – thankfully without any success.

We sailed the next morning and steamed northwards to Hamburg, where we stayed for six days. Terry Bentham and I sampled the delights of the red-light district and drank in the bars of the Reeperbahn. We sailed at midday and the weather was good as we steamed into the Baltic Sea. The evenings stretched themselves out until it was 9pm before the light faded. At last Port Pirie arrived at Gothenburg in Sweden to discharge wool, butter and lamb.

In the evening Terry and I went ashore to stretch our legs and find a decent bar. As if by magnetism we were drawn towards the Liseborg Amusement Park, where nearby we found a suitable bar. The beer, like everything else in Scandinavia was expensive, but we nevertheless put glasses of pilsner quickly down our throats so as to get into the party spirit. Terry went into philosophic mode and decided to put my life into perspective and give me the benefit of his unsolicited advice. It was extremely simple. "Ever since we left Hobart," he said, "you've been the most miserable git on God's earth. So snap out of it."

I had to agree and told him about Valentina's letter. "There you go, mate," said Terry. "She's given you your freedom. You both knew that it was never going to work. Not unless you emigrated out to Tasmania and became an Aussie. Am I right or am I right?" He gave me a great hearty slap on the back. "Come on, Gra, let's go see if there's any decent crumpet around here."

We went into the amusement park and skylarked on the waltzer and the haunted house. Later we were having a coffee at the open-air cafeteria when two pretty girls sat down at the next table. The place was almost deserted. Terry whispered, "Hey, Gra, we're onto a winner here. There's dozens of empty tables, but they've chosen to sit next to us. Let's go."

I was I fear, still a relatively shy individual and deficient in the chatting-up department, but Terry had the gift of the gab. I'm sure he must have had some Irish blood in his veins because he sure as hell had some blarney. "Good evening ladies," he grinned as he pulled a chair out at their table. "Mind if we come and join you?" I did likewise. "I hope you girls speak English because we don't speak one word of Swedish." The girls were gorgeous in that clean, fresh, sparkly blue-eyed, Scandinavian way. They had stunning figures with tanned arms and legs.
"I am good with the English," said the brunette. "My name is Lisle." She indicated her blonde friend. "This is Birgitta. She is speaking a little of the English also." Birgitta gave me the most wonderful sensual smile. Her teeth were perfect and she had the loveliest snub nose. We chatted for a while and found that both girls were 18 years old and were students studying hotel catering at the local college. They shared an apartment together near the college campus not far away. It quickly became apparent that Lisle was attracted to Terry, which suited me just fine because Birgitta looked absolutely gorgeous. I chatted to her about her studies and how long was the course – just small talk. Suddenly a chill wind swept across the cafeteria and she shivered in her thin jacket. I put my arm around her to warm her up and she snuggled closer into my chest. That settled matters. I tilted her chin upwards so that her lips were inches from mine and kissed her passionately. My tongue was searching for hers, and it didn't take long to feel her reciprocate with her hands running across my body and through my hair. I peered sideways at Terry. He had taken my cue and was kissing Lisle rather enthusiastically and his hand, I noticed, was up inside her sweater and feeling her breasts. The two girls had a quick chat between themselves in Swedish. Birgitta said, "Lisle and I are thinking that perhaps you would like to come to our apartment for some wine? You would like to come, ya?" Was she kidding?

Their two-bedroom apartment was Spartan but cosy; but it didn't really matter because I immediately asked which was her bedroom and led her through the door. Within minutes we had our clothes off and were making love in the surprisingly comfortable double bed. Outside in the diner, we could hear Lisle and Terry making love rather enthusiastically on the kitchen table. The next morning, Terry and I were up early and headed back to the ship for a quick shower before starting work at 7am. We made arrangements to meet the girls at their apartment that evening.

The bosun was up and about when we stepped aboard. "I hope you boys have still got some life in those poor bodies," he chuckled in his soft Highland voice, "because we've got a lot of heavy work today lads." He went off smiling and shaking his head in wonderment at how we two could manage to pick up girls when the ship had been in port for just a few hours.

In the meantime, Frank our chief cook, who had been suffering from chest pains since we sailed from Hamburg, had been taken into hospital with a blood clot on the heart and we sadly left him behind when we sailed onwards around the Baltic. Our baker John Stevens was promoted to chief cook to replace him.

That evening we took a dozen beers to the girls flat and sat around chatting. We gave the girls the option of what to do tonight, hoping that they wouldn't choose anything too expensive. They had a chat in Swedish. "We will go to shop for pizza and fries, ya?" We nodded. "Then we spend time in apartment, and you can love us again. Is good?" Terry threw back his head and laughed. "That sounds perfect to me sweetie." The next three nights were spent much like that one, and we had a wonderful time.

However, there was a small price to pay for my sexual licentiousness, and it came in the form of guilt. These two sensual girls from 'The Land of Free Love' had freely given us pleasure with their beautiful bodies. I asked myself how things would have been if Valentina hadn't given me my freedom. Would I have been strong enough to resist the temptations of the beautiful Birgitta? Even though we were 10,000 miles apart, I felt as if I had somehow been unfaithful. And with these unsavoury feelings running around inside my head, the Port Pirie let go and sailed for Stockholm.

⚓

On our second night in the capital of Sweden, there was to be a cocktail party held onboard to which the Mayor of Stockholm and other civic dignitaries were invited. During the afternoon the deck crew washed and scrubbed to ensure that everything was ship-shape and tidy, and that the guests wouldn't be getting any grease or dirt on their hands as they stepped onboard. A striped canvas awning was stretched across the deck adjacent to No. 3 cargo hatch and coloured lights were hung from the gangway. The quartermasters, looking smart in their Port Line sailor suit uniforms and round hats, were stationed at the gangway to assist the guests aboard, and the captain and ship's officers looked resplendent in their white mess

85

uniforms. All was ready. The deck crew were warned to keep a low-profile, and so we watched proceedings from the distance of No.4 cargo hatch back aft. As limousines disgorged their passengers by the ship's gangway, they were met by an officer and escorted onboard. The men mostly wore tuxedo suits and the ladies wore cocktail dresses. There was an awful lot of handshaking and obsequious bowing and fawning going on, and some of the officers' voices miraculously took on an upper class accent as they tried to impress the guests.

Halfway through the party, Christine, who had been on-duty serving canapés and cocktails, came racing down the ladder onto the after deck where we were congregated. She had the look of someone with secrets to tell. "You'll never guess what's happened?" she said breathlessly. "Ooh my God. It's Bella. The silly cow must have been pissed or high as a kite on something." Christine stopped talking long enough to get her breath back under control. Bella was another of the queer stewards who had joined in Antwerp. She could be quite temperamental, and nothing about her would surprise me. "She was supposed to be serving the guests cocktails," continued Christine, "and she's gone and turned up for duty dressed in drag. Ooh my God, you should have seen her. She was dressed in her Sunday best and with full warpaint on her face."

"Calm down, Christine," I said as the rest of the crew gathered around to hear the news. "What exactly happened?"

"Well, she came into the officers' saloon dressed in her finest and tried to serve the Mayor of Stockholm some canapés. The captain went spare. He ordered the chief steward to get her out of the saloon and to be detained in the ship's sick bay until a doctor can examine her." She didn't have much else to tell and had to get back on duty serving the guests. Later we heard that Bella had indeed been examined by a doctor and kept in the sick bay overnight. After that episode everything returned to normal, but Bella wasn't invited to return for the next voyage aboard the Port Pirie. Mind you, she did make life interesting and spiced up our lives a bit.

I'm afraid I don't have very much to tell about Stockholm itself. Sweden can be quite expensive, especially to a lowly paid deck boy, so only once in our three day stay did I venture ashore. Chris Morling and I caught a tram into the city centre to walk around the streets. The city was stunningly beautiful and very clean with a cared-for look about it. Stockholm is not called The Venice of the North for nothing. Over a third of the city is made up of waterways, canals and islands; and another third is given over to parkland. We had a long walk around the city, had a beer in a pavement cafe and returned back onboard.

⚓

Helsinki was a fabulous city; mostly because of the fact that Terry Bentham and I got picked up by two pretty girls within an hour of arrival. Someone had told us about a fabulous swimming complex, so we hopped aboard a tram and made our way there. Terry and I were soon in our swimming costumes and having great fun on water slides, white water rapid rides, water fountains and a regular swimming pool. The place was heaving with swimmers and families on a day out. We'd seen nothing like it; certainly not in London. At the cafeteria, the two girls approached and asked if we had a light for their cigarettes. Motor-mouth Bentham of course not only had a lighter, but invited them to sit at our table. They were both pretty girls of 20 years old who spoke excellent English, and it didn't take very long for us to get paired off. Within minutes Terry had his arm around Anna, and I was hand-in-hand with the tall blonde, Jenni. Both girls were stewardesses with Finnair and due to fly abroad in two days time; but tonight they were free as birds. We spent another two hours poolside, then were invited back to their apartment in the suburbs. Very soon Anna was casually rolling up 'reefers' for us all. Although I smoked cigarettes, I had never had any marijuana. This would be a first for me. We all sat around in a circle and sucked the smoke down into our lungs, and I must admit to being stoned within minutes. My head was full of beautiful thoughts and wonderful kaleidoscopic images, but mostly I had a fit of the giggles. But one other effect was that the stuff made me as randy as hell. Without thinking, I took Jenni's hand in mine and led her into her bedroom where we made love, none too quietly, for what seemed, within my slow-motion world, simply ages.

⚓

Terry Willcox the new galley boy was serving up lunch. One had to wait in line at the serving hatch, where Terry would dish up your selection from several tureens. Ahead of me was Paddy from County Cork, a stoker of indeterminate intelligence. He was so thick that he gave the Bog Irish a bad name. To make matters worse he also had a speech impediment in the shape of a nasty lisp and a slight stutter. His turn came, and Terry grabbed a plate and waited for Paddy to choose what to have.

"Er...giveth a pieth of beef, will ya?" said Paddy. Terry laid two slices of beef on the plate.

"An...an...a thpoonful of thwede, pleath." A large dollop of swede was placed beside the beef.

"Er...an...an...a pieth of that thavoy cabbage, pleath," said Paddy pointing to the greens.

"Umm...an...an...an thome thpud. Giveth a pieth of thpud." Terry gave him roast potatoes.

And so it went on. Try as he might Paddy couldn't pronounce the word piece and it always came out as pieth. He'd always ask for a pieth of this or a pieth of that. One squally day, after Terry had endured another bout of sea-sickness, Paddy stood at the serving hatch and tried to decide what to select. It was all too much for his pea-sized intellect. Terry stood poised with a clean plate in hand, expectantly waiting for Paddy to make his choice. "Err.. giveth...um...giveth...er giveth a pieth of...er....plate," said Paddy unexpectedly. The few choices had completely defeated him.

Without looking up, Terry smashed the plate against the steel hotplate and handed Paddy the remaining fragment. "There you go, Paddy, enjoy your dinner – Next!"

⚓

On the 19th May 1964 - five months and three days after setting out from London, the Port Pirie sailed again into the King George V dock and secured at the Port Line berth. For days prior to arrival there was much excitement as suitcases were packed in readiness to go home. Clothing was dhobied and pressed and the whole ship was tidied up. Most of the crew were walking around with permanent smiles stitched upon their faces. This was known as 'Getting the Channels' and no one was exempt from the feeling of anticipation and euphoria at once again going home on leave.

The Chief Steward's store-room, or slop-chest, contained almost everything us sailors should need on a voyage. Cigarettes, cases of beer, washing powder (dhobi dust), toothpaste, tea shirts, underwear, shoe polish, or even an aerial photo postcard of the ship, could all be purchased from the ship's stocks. However, as the ship neared London the favourite item to spend our money on was a 'docking bottle.' Usually spirits were not available to us lowly deck crew, but most captains would allow us to purchase a litre bottle to take home on leave. This was known as your docking bottle.

Some of the Hebridean crew wouldn't be rejoining the ship for her next voyage, but would seek employment on another vessel. One of the highlanders would sadly never be going home again. Christine would be rejoining for our next voyage, but Tulip said she would look for something else (and presumably get married on her next trip). Most of the crew would seek other employment and we would also have a new bosun.

Even though we made many friends and shipmates during the course of a five-month voyage, it was a strange fact-of-life in the Merchant Navy that we rarely stayed in touch. That's why such friends were known as 'Board of Trade Acquaintances,' so named after the government body that oversees all maritime matters.

Two hours after docking, the crew gathered in the officers' saloon to pay-off. This was a reverse procedure to the signing-on of articles when joining the ship, and it signified the ending of the contract between the seaman and the shipping company. Once signed-off, the seaman received his wages in a small brown envelope. All wages were kept in an account and the usual tax and insurance deductions were made. He would also receive a statement of deductions for items purchased from the slop chest, and this usually meant how much of his wages he had squandered on beer and on subs to spend ashore. I was quite pleasantly surprised to find that, even allowing for the £4 per month allotment that was sent to my mum, I still had £57 6s 9d to pay-off with - which I was quite pleased with. Once signed-off, the crew now had to be on their way home. In some cases this took almost two days when, for example, the Hebridean guys needed to take a train journey from London to northern Scotland, then by inter-island ferry to whatever Outer Hebridean island that they happened to live upon.

One sad figure signing-off was Paddy, the lisping engine room stoker from County Cork. As previously stated, Paddy wasn't the brightest star in the sky, and one could sometimes visualise the cogs turning inside his head. Paddy possessed just the one suit of clothes to travel home in, and prior to arrival in London he thought it would be a good idea to wash it. Of course the whole thing shrank, and I shall never forget the Chaplinesque sight of Paddy, with suitcase in hand shuffling down the Dock Road with the legs and arms of his suit at half-mast.

A half hour after signing-off, I was back home in Silvertown and my mum cooked me a lovely fried breakfast while we talked. There were big hugs and lots of news to tell, but first I held the new addition to our family, Linda's baby Toni. It seemed strange holding a new-born; but within the hour I was getting quite adept at nappy changing as well.

I told them of my travels and the tales of rough seas in the Bay of Biscay; of Willie the highlander going overboard on Christmas Day; about our passage through the Suez Canal and the Red Sea, and across the wide Indian Ocean. There was so much to tell, that even I began to doubt that all this had taken place within the space of just five months. I told them of the friends I had made - Chris and Terry and Billie MacIver and many others. I told them the lurid details regarding the doctor's teenage nymphomaniac daughter and Bob Braithwaite and Paddy the stuttering stoker. I made them laugh all afternoon about Christine and Tulip. And lastly I explained about Valentina. My mum could sense that my poor heart had been broken and she gave me a huge hug. Over the next few days I would have so much more to tell them, but for now I would let the stories came out gradually.

4: Return to Port Pirie

I had been asked by the chief officer if I wished to sail on the next deep-sea trip which was due to depart in early June. If so, then I would be promoted to junior ordinary seaman (JOS) and I wouldn't be the peggy any longer. I would also get a pay rise. The Port Pirie was a happy ship, and so I immediately said yes. Chris Morling would also be promoted and would once again be sharing a cabin with me. The ship was due to sail again to Australia and also to New Zealand, but would not I noted, be calling at Hobart.

Whilst the ship was loading her general cargo I would be on stand-by, which meant I would be earning wages and be at home in the evenings, so life wasn't too bad. There were not many crew onboard, so there wasn't too much for me to do. I filled my days tidying up and checking out the ship's lifeboats, and painting out my new cabin with a fresh coat of white paint. I cleaned up the porthole brass and re-varnished the woodwork and cleaned the carpet. All was neat and tidy.

One morning I walked aboard and found a strange fellow unpacking his suitcase in my cabin. He was a good looking guy of about my own age with light brown hair and deep clefts under his eyes.
"What the hell do you think you're doing?" I said testily. "This is my cabin."
"It ain't your cabin, mister," he replied bluntly. "The bosun told me to park my stuff in here, so this is where I'm living."
I looked at him quizzically. "This is the ordinary seaman's cabin. What rank are you?"
"I'm a DHU – and the sign over the door says DHU - so this must be my cabin." He was sounding more confident by the second. He jerked his thumb towards the other cabin. "The ordinary seaman's cabin's next door."
The term DHU means Deck Hand Uncertificated. This is a rank assigned to a crewmember that has some sea-going experience, but is too old to join the Merchant Navy via the sea-school route.
I stepped outside the cabin and looked above the door. Sure enough, the brass plate above the door-frame said 2 x DHU's. A brass plate on the cabin opposite said 2 x Ordinary Seamen. I said to him, "You listen to me, sunshine. I know that this is my cabin – not the one next door. I was aboard this ship last trip, and it was me that painted out this cabin just last week. So sling your hook."

His shoulders slumped in defeat. He knew he'd been caught out, but he still tried to redeem the situation. "Well, someone must have switched the signs over. It wasn't me."

I was starting to get mad at this joker. "You must think I came along on the last wave. It was you that switched those plates over. Now get your stuff outta my cabin and move it next door."

He put his hands up in surrender. "Yeah okay – you're right. It was me that switched 'em. I thought I'd get away with it. Sorry." Later that afternoon he came to my cabin looking sheepish. "Hey look, I'm sorry that we got off on the wrong foot today. I didn't mean any harm by it."

"No problem," I said rather curtly. "You tried and you lost. Forget about it."

"Do you fancy coming ashore for a pint this evening?" he asked uncertainly. "Sure, why not? My cabin mate, Chris Morling, and I were gonna have a drink in the Round House," I told him. "You're welcome to join us if you want to."

He held out his hand in friendship. "I'd like that very much. By the way, my name's John Sheppard. What's yours?" I took his hand and introduced myself; and so started an on/off friendship that was to have far-reaching and life-changing implications for many decades to come. Over the course of the following years we each served as 'best man' at our respective weddings and I was godfather to his children and he to mine. Our families were close-knit and our children played together and we even went on holiday together.

That night we went to the Round House pub in North Woolwich. The place was packed to the rafters and heaving with steam queens and regular sailors of every shape and size. The beer was flowing and the room was a fog of cigarette smoke and the music was thumpin' out of the juke box. Over in the corner Christine gave me a girlie wave then went back to chattering with her coterie of homosexual friends, some of whom, in the way they dressed and plastered on their make-up, wouldn't have looked out of place in a fairground horror show. I could never understand their reasoning. On the one hand, they wanted to closely resemble a female, but then they would apply enough gaudy cosmetics to sink a battleship. Their cheeks, coated with bright red rouge, made them look like a pantomime dame. Their mouths, with a bright slash of crimson lipstick and eyes coated in varieties of mascara, only helped to increase their resemblance to one of the ugly sisters! Furthermore, they looked less like a female of the species whichever way they dressed and walked. Whereas a normal woman will be attired in simple everyday clothes, the queens would dress in the most bizarre bright clothing; and that old saying, "mutton dressed as lamb" would spring to mind. The queens didn't just walk; they sashayed across the floor with exaggerated movements of the hips that no sane woman would ever consider doing.

Their flamboyant style of talking was a mixture of British gay slang and Yiddish. This followed Kenneth Horne's radio show "Round the Horne", with Kenneth Williams, and Hugh Paddick in which the camp pair, playing Julian and Sandy, started off a whole new gay language. It was known as Polari.

Some Polari words still survive today. Bona means good. Camp implies effeminate. Cottaging is looking for sex in a public toilet, and drag is women's clothes. Omi-palone is an effeminate or homosexual man and fantabulosa means wonderful. If you mince it is to walk effeminately, and naff can mean drab or bad, whilst slap is a girls' makeup. Very often, onboard ship, you would hear two queers talking in this language, and it sounded so very strange that one hardly knew what they were saying.

The Round House: The author aged 17 – John Sheppard- Chris Morling

It wasn't just the homosexuals from the ships who frequented the gay pubs. Some of the old queens who lived – and presumably worked – locally also hung around the dockside bars. They were often known by outrageous names. I remember Scouse Cath and Gilda Gash. One in particular that springs to mind was an infamous queen by the name of Stella Minge (in vulgar slang, Minge is a woman's pubic hair or genitals). Stella lived in Silvertown and would regularly frequent the Kent Arms. After chucking-out time, a crowd of sailors, both straight and queer, would often go back to Stella's house and a party would ensue which could sometimes continue into the weekend and beyond. Stella's house was known by the police as a bawdy establishment where her legendary parties were frequent and loud. Police officers often stopped by because of the noise complaints, but individually would come back when off duty to join in the fun. Sometimes it was raided. One day when Stella was going to be away for a while, she went to the local police station to ask them to keep a eye on her house. The constable replied: "Stella, we've been keeping an eye on your house for donkeys' years".

Port Pirie had been back in London for a week when I decided to catch up with a guy I had been to the Vindicatrix with - Chris Stafford. After leaving the Vindi, we had reported to the Shipping Federation on the same day and Reggie the Rat had allocated me the Port Pirie, and had given Chris a New Zealand Shipping Company vessel – the Huranui. He had sailed off to New Zealand, and should be home soon. I called his home number in Chislehurst in Kent. His mum answered the call. I introduced myself and asked when Chris's ship would be getting back home. There was a prolonged silence. Then she said, "I'm sorry to tell you this, but I'm afraid that Christopher is dead."
"Oh my God," I said. "I'm so terribly sorry. How did it happen?"
There was a long pause whilst she collected her composure. "He's been reported missing overboard and presumed drowned." I said I was sorry to hear of her sad loss and offered my condolences. There was not much else I could say. I said my goodbyes and rang off.

Two days later the Huranui sailed into the Royal Docks from New Zealand and I scrounged an hour off work so as to meet the ship on arrival. As soon as the vessel was tied-up I went aboard and saw the deck crew. They told me the circumstances of his death. Chris, they said, had fallen madly in love with one of the good-time girls in New Zealand; the type who one can always find aboard the British ships. He was smitten by this girl and promised to come back to New Zealand next trip. The Huranui then departed to sail across the Pacific Ocean and back to the UK. On arrival at Panama he had received a "Dear John" letter from the girl, and poor Chris went to pieces. It broke his inexperienced heart. As the ship was steaming through the Caribbean Sea at night, Chris had gone missing, never to be seen again. He was only seventeen years old.

It brought home the message that I should not get too involved with the ladies. By all means have loads of fun, but don't fall in love again. But that would be easier said than done.

Once again Port Pirie was loaded down with every kind of general cargo, and as sailing day approached, she sank deeper into the water. New crew began to join the vessel in dribs and drabs. Our new Bosun was Sammy Logan from Northern Ireland, a short no-nonsense man who was a very competent seaman. There was a sprinkling of Jocks from Stornoway in the Outer Hebrides, and more from mainland Scotland, including the two Smith brothers, James and Bill from Lossiemouth. A blonde guy called Kevin and his younger cousin Finn came from the very tough city of Belfast, and I noted with some trepidation that Kevin spoke in a rapid-fire dismissive manner that certainly didn't endear himself to us southerners, especially to me and John Sheppard. I thought that we may have some trouble with Kevin in the future, and that proved to be correct.

Other deck crew coming aboard included a first-trip DHU called Dave Knight, who was to share John Sheppard's cabin. Dave hadn't a clue about being on a ship, and with his sincere and innocent demeanour, he seemed quite green and naive. Others, especially the nasty Kevin, took advantage of his inexperience, and would send Dave on wild goose chases to the engine room to ask for a bucket of steam or a left-handed screwdriver. Another able seaman was a tall half-caste lad called Dave Moorcroft from Lewisham in South London who had a great sense of humour and with whom John and I immediately hit it off. Likewise was a bespectacled able seaman whose name I never did find out, but whom everyone called The Professor. There was also a 19 year old seaman called Clive Hunt who came from Southsea, near Portsmouth. A tall bearded laid-back young Cornishman called Phil Trevelyan who forever had a grin on his face, rounded off the deck crew. However, before we had even sailed, the Belfast lads, led by Kevin, and the Jocks had grouped together. Somehow, lines seemed to have been drawn. They ate together in the messroom, they went ashore together, and they had cabin parties together. This left us southerners confused and expecting a flare up at any time.

By this time, John Sheppard and I, who had met under such inauspicious circumstances, found that we enjoyed each other's company to such an extent, that we were inseparable. We toured the pubs together on most nights, and I had also taken him home to meet my family. My sister Linda thought that he was far too free and easy with his compliments and didn't quite trust him, but my mum thought that he was Mister Wonderful and would load his plate with bacon and eggs whenever he came around home.

Back to the Land of Oz

On 3rd June 1964 we again signed-on articles. The voyage was expected to take five months and the Port Pirie would be calling at some Mediterranean ports, then through the Suez Canal to Melbourne, Sydney, Brisbane, Auckland, Gisborne, Napier, and Wellington. I was glad to see that Captain Harry Conby would once again be our ship's master. With the departure to new pastures of his tiger, Tulip, another steam queen had been signed-on in her place. She was called Lily – so she was obviously known as Tiger Lily.

Two days later, after fond farewells to my family, we slid out of the King George V Dock on a balmy summer day, and sailed down the River Thames towards the open sea. Our passengers were the usual mix of the well-to-do and affluent brigade. We also had a doctor with his emigrating family, but thankfully, *sans* nymphomaniac daughter. After dropping our river pilot at North Foreland, we steamed down channel as we headed towards Dover, Dungeness and Beachy Head, then set course towards the coast of Brittany and the Ile de Ushant. In the afternoon all crew members and passengers were gathered on deck for lifeboat drill. The passengers were instructed in how to put on the bulky lifejackets and get wrapped up in warm clothing in case of abandon-ship. This is what we called Board of Trade Sports, and these musters, by law, must be held at regular intervals. All the lifeboats were lowered out ready to be boarded as if it was a real emergency.

The ship's passage across the Bay of Biscay was uneventful, as was the voyage through the blue waters of the Mediterranean. The big difference on this trip was that, as Chris and I were no longer peggys, we spent all of our time working out on deck, and not inside the accommodation. Meanwhile, the heavy work of greasing and maintaining the cargo lifting gear carried on apace, just as it had done on the previous voyage. As the days flew by, and I worked upon the decks with the experienced crew, I was gaining more and more skills and competence that would enable me to become a fully-fledged able seaman.

Every morning, and again mid-afternoon, the deck crew would have a tea-break known as smoko. If it was a warm sunny day we would have smoko out on the decks, usually sitting atop a cargo hatch. The peggy would bring a tray with teapot, mugs, sugar and milk, out onto the deck and the lads would drink and chat and smoke their cigarettes. During the afternoon smoko we would have an extra treat. The assistant cook would usually make up a tray of fancy cakes or sticky buns for the boys. They were called "Tab-Nabs."

95

The Port Pirie called at the Italian port of Genoa to load a cargo of porcelain goods including baths and lavatories. I'm not sure why, but I didn't much like Genoa. I'd had a preconceived idea that Italy would be a romantic country with ancient buildings and great food. It has all these things I'm sure, but I found Genoa very industrialised and just plain noisy and dirty. I couldn't wait to depart.

We docked at the Greek port of Piraeus in the early morning, and very soon the stevedores were loading cargo for Australia. It was a brilliantly sunny day and the chief officer gave the deck crew a "job-and-knock" to wash down the funnel. We had finished by midday, so by the early afternoon John Sheppard, Dave Knight, Chris Morling and I were walking the streets of Piraeus. As we strode along the narrow lanes, we noticed that whole lots of people turned to stare at us. These were ordinary citizens that gawped as if we had grown a second head or just stepped off an alien space-ship. This happened in every street – everyone stared. It was most disconcerting and an argument started amongst us as to who they were looking at.

"It's you, Graham," accused John. "It's your long hair they're staring at. It's got to be."

"Nothing to do with me," I said, shaking my head.

"Tell you what," said John. "You stay here, and we'll walk on the other side of the street. That'll sort it out," and with that, the three of them crossed the road.

He was absolutely right. The residents of Piraeus continued to stare at my hair. They gawped openly. With my hair hanging just over my collar, I didn't think it was overly long, but obviously the Greeks did.

We sat at a table in the Black Cat Bar and were having a few beers when I got accosted. The lady who was doing the accosting was in her late twenties and quite attractive. She sat up close to me, and without being invited, put her hand over my trousers in the region of my penis. She then whispered in my ear that she thought that we ought to go to bed. The rest of the guys thought it was hilarious and were egging me on to take her up on her offer. It was quite obvious that she was on the game - that was crystal clear. But I was very hesitant. At the tender age of seventeen, I had never been with a prostitute and I didn't want to start now. However, I also didn't want to hurt her feelings. Under the tablecloth she was sensuously rubbing my Old Chap lightly up and down. I asked her how much she charged, thinking that I could wriggle out of this by claiming I was broke. The guys were listening intently when she looked me straight in the eye and said, "I would not charge you anything. You are beautiful. This is for free." I didn't know what to say. The fellas were going wild and punching the air.

"What a result, Gra. Go on - give her one." What was I to do? She took my hand. "Come – we go now to my house." I was in a panic. The boys were going crazy. I did the only thing that my brain could think of. I told her that I couldn't go with her because I had a dose of the clap. Her face suddenly changed to one of anger, and with a crash, she swept beer glasses off the table and stormed out of the bar. A quick end to what could have been a beautiful relationship.

Two days later we arrived at Famagusta on the island of Cyprus. As the Port Pirie glided into the harbour approaches, I looked over the ship's side and had never seen such clear blue waters. The water was so translucent that one could see the sea bed some 50 feet below. Fish were scurrying to get away from the giant steel monster that was above them.
In the evening, John, Dave Moorcroft, Dave Knight and I went ashore to sample the local beer. All around the town were army vehicles, land-rovers, half tracks, and light armoured cars. All were wearing the blue insignia of NATO peacekeeping forces and the soldiers wore blue berets. For some time Greek and Turkish Cypriots had been at each other's throats, and the island had been divided along secular lines. NATO was there to keep the two warring factions apart. It was nothing to do with us, and so we found a suitable hostelry and proceeded to throw beer down our throats and get roaring drunk.
Around midnight, as we were staggering back to the ship, we came upon a drunken Irish sailor who was even more plastered than we were. He could hardly walk, so we dragged him along with us, unaware of the location of his ship. We realised that we were lost when we could see the good ship Port Pirie just 50 yards away – but a high barbed wire fence stood between us, and there seemed no way around it. "Never mind," we thought, and started to climb the fence.
Suddenly the whole area was flooded by a powerful searchlight and we could hear the sounds of heavy calibre guns being cocked. Oh shit! From out of nowhere land-rovers skidded to a halt beside us. *"STOP RIGHT WHERE YOU ARE. DO NOT MOVE. YOU'RE UNDER ARREST."* Soldiers surrounded us, their rifles levelled at our chests. The sergeant looked at me. *"WHO'S THE SENIOR MAN HERE?"* he demanded. I pointed at the Irishman. They grabbed him, but couldn't get any sense out of the man whatsoever. Within moments they realised that we were just a bunch of drunken sailors. Mumbling and shaking their heads in resignation, they opened up a gate in the fence and let us through. We never did find out what happened to the Irishman.

On arrival at Port Said in Egypt, the Port Pirie secured to a mooring buoy and awaited the departure of the southbound convoy to transit through the Suez Canal. Once again the searchlight crew readied the big heavy searchlight in the bows of the ship, and the mooring party made their boat ready to go at a moment's notice. Over the side of the ship, several wooden bum boats were attempting to sell their wares. Most of the items were cheap tourist junk; brass pyramids, shoddy camels, tatty models of the sphinx, rugs and masks of Cleopatra. Usually the bumboatman would pass up a thin rope that was attached to a wicker basket. The crewman could then pull up on the string to bring onboard whatever he was buying, and the boatman could pull down on the string to retrieve his payment for whatever the crewman had bought. It was a simple method.

John Sheppard had been hanging out of his porthole and trying to do a deal with one of the boatmen with regard to buying some crap or other. He decided that he would rip-off the poor boatman instead by taking the goods, but not paying for them. He simply took the goods out of the bag, stuck two fingers up and closed the cabin porthole. There was nothing the poverty-stricken bumboatman could do about it. I didn't agree with it, and I told him so. The poor guy had a living to make. Why rip him off?

Sometime later, Dave Knight, who shared the cabin with John, opened the same porthole, and quite oblivious to the rip-off that had occurred earlier, started to haggle with the same boatman for some brass pyramids. There wasn't a cash sum involved, but some trading took place. They eventually settled on Dave sending down 200 cigarettes and the boatman would send up the pyramids. Of course, with Dave being very naive, he did as he was told. But as soon as the boatman got his hands on the cigarettes, he refused to keep his side of the bargain and said that he's keeping them because he'd just been ripped-off earlier. Dave of course was angry, and told us what had transpired, and he wanted to know what he could do about being cheated.

John Sheppard had a plan. He suggested that Dave go get a heavy shackle from the deck store. Dave carried the shackle back to the cabin and leaned out of the porthole. He shouted down to the boatman, "Hey, are you gonna give me back my cigarettes?" The boatman looked up and shook his head. "Alright," said Dave, "well cop this then," and threw the steel shackle straight down through the bottom of the wooden boat. There was utter chaos and pandemonium as the bumboat quickly filled with water and started to sink. The boatman was still frantically trying to salvage his wares by transferring his goods onto his colleague's boat as his boat sank under him.

The score: England 1: Egypt nil

Our convoy moved into the canal and headed south at a sedate seven knots. Later in the day we pulled into the cutting that leads to the Bitter Lakes in order to allow the northbound convoy to pass by. Our Arab mooring gang, whose boat was suspended from a wire hung over the ship's side, were lowered away and they were quickly ashore and pulling Port Pirie's mooring ropes onto shoreside bollards. Within minutes the main engines were stopped and we would remain here for some hours whilst the convoy went by.

It was just after lunch and the sun shone down unmercifully. Some of the crew decided to have a swim in the canal. The braver ones were jumping from the bridge deck and making a huge splash as they hit the water 40 feet below. John and I decided to swim the 150 yards to the opposite bank so as to actually set foot on Egyptian soil. We began a fast overhand stroke as we raced each other for the far bank, but within 50 yards we had to slow down due to the heavy meal we had just eaten and I took up a more sedate breast stroke. We were nearly three quarters of the way across when I began to get acute pains in my abdomen. I had got the side stitch and I felt cramps in my belly. I was in a great deal of pain, but we were more than three quarters of the way across, and past the point of no return, so I could only carry-on, rather than return to the ship.

Just then, from behind a sand dune, a soldier in the uniform of the Egyptian army appeared and began shouting at us. "What's he saying?" asked John. I was by this time in so much pain that I could only shake my head and keep making for the bank. We were now only 10 yards away. The soldier began screaming at us and waving his arms frantically in a way that indicated we should turn around and not to attempt to come ashore. However, I was in no position to turn around. My poor body needed time to rest and for the cramps to subside. We kept swimming inexorably towards the shore. The soldier unslung his rifle and pointed it directly at us. His chatter became demonic as he shouted and waved us away with arms flailing like windmills. As my feet touched the sand I looked up and found myself staring down the business end of a rifle barrel. Just then, he pulled back the bolt and fed a bullet into the chamber. My mouth went dry, and I raised my hands in surrender. Quickly John did likewise.

Then, another soldier, an older man, came over the brow of the sand dune, and the two of them began to jabber away in Arabic. The older man was shaking his head and pointing at our ship. He seemed to be telling his colleague that we were simply sailors from the English ship who were having a swim – not Israeli saboteurs here to cause mayhem. The younger gung-ho soldier nodded his head miserably and his shoulders sagged in defeat. With the age-old help of hand signals the older soldier indicated that we should not attempt to come ashore, but to make our way back when we were ready. We gratefully nodded, and they walked away. Staring down the end of a gun-barrel put me right off swimming for a while.

The score: England nil: Egypt 1

⚓

Our voyage through the Red Sea continued uneventfully, although it was stiflingly hot. One had to take care with the sun's rays and ensure we put on skin protection. Some of the deck crew used a mixture of boiled linseed oil, the same lubricant that we soaked ship's steel wires in to keep them supple. It seemed to work and I got very brown. However, one soppy steward decided to sunbathe atop a cargo hatch during his off-duty time, but foolishly fell asleep for two hours. He almost died from dehydration and burns to his body, and he needed to lay in the ship's sick-bay for three days whilst his body mended itself. He was in a very bad state. When he returned to duty, the captain logged him three days pay for causing a self-inflicted injury.

Four days later, during the late afternoon, we called into Aden and immediately began to load fuel bunkers. I was rather surprised that the captain allowed the crew shore leave, due to the civil unrest from terrorists and nationalists. After all, the British Royal Marines had been having some problems keeping the peace, because the locals' idea of keeping the Brits on their toes was to lob the occasional bomb or sow a few mines. These days the city of Aden is now part of the lawless Yemeni Arab Republic. However, whilst the engineers oversaw the loading of many hundreds of tons of diesel fuel, us silly sailors - John, Dave Knight, Dave Moorcroft and myself, hailed a water taxi and were soon ashore.

The mission was located on the waterfront, just across the street from a leper colony. We went across to look. The place seemed to contain some brick huts set inside a steel barred fence on all four sides and across the roof of what was basically a prison. Because leprosy is a communicable disease, then these people were being kept in forced quarantine, and there was to be no escape for them. A dozen desperate and ill-fed inmates of both sexes put their hands through the bars, seemingly pleading for money. Their fingers and toes were shortened and deformed, and deep skin lesions and nodules covered the bodies of some of the older inmates due to being eaten away by this awful disease. It was such a shocking sight that it made us delve into our pockets and throw some English money through the bars, and the inmates scrabbled desperately to pick up the coins from the dry earth.

We headed inside the Mission to Seamen. Because of its winged angel logo, it was otherwise known as the Flying Angel – or even the Flying Tab-Nab! We could buy only soft drinks in this strictly Muslim country, so after just a half-hour in the Mission, John Sheppard had a bright idea which, I must say, was not one of his best. "Hey, I've heard that you can have a great time here in a place called Crater City – Let's go!" We all squeezed into a cab for the short ride up the hill to Crater.

After paying our cab fare, we were dumped in a dirty looking market or *Souk*. Wherever we looked, the Arabs stared at us with barely concealed hostility. Within ten minutes the sun had disappeared, and as it became dark, the stalls of the markets traders were lit up with strings of bare electric lamps. The locals didn't appear too friendly because they began hissing oaths at us, and I got the distinct impression that we were not welcome. I must admit to being somewhat frightened. "So Mister Sheppard, do tell us what the hell is so great about this place, and where we can have this good time you were telling us about?" I asked. "Dunno, mate," said John nonchalantly. "If you ask me I think we ought to bugger off outta here and get back to the ship." The words were no sooner out of his mouth when suddenly the power supply was cut off and the whole area was in darkness. It may have just been a routine power cut, but in my mental state I was sure it had been arranged with me in mind. All around us, unfriendly Arabs swore obscenities at us from the blackness, and I must now admit to almost shitting myself. Dave Moorcroft had the great idea of all linking arms so as not to be split up in the stygian blackness as we slowly made our way towards the road, and out of this hell hole. Eventually, after twenty minutes we found a cab and leapt aboard.

As the cab dropped us back on the waterfront near the Missions to Seaman, we could see smoke coming from the building and several British military vehicles parked outside. A tall muscular Royal Marine sergeant with a bristling moustache came bustling over.

"WHO THE F**K ARE YOU LOT?" he barked. We told him we were sailors from the Port Pirie and he calmed down somewhat when he found that we were English. "You must be off your bloody trolley coming ashore in Aden. Don't you know there's a war going on?" When Dave asked him what had happened at the mission, the sergeant informed us that a terrorist had lobbed several grenades inside just a half hour ago. Just to think; if we had not gone to Crater City, then we would have still been inside having a leisurely drink when the bombs went off. Dave told him about our visit to Crater City and the power cut. The sergeant looked aghast. "Who the hell suggested you go up to Crater City? Jeezus, that place is a death trap. Even us Royal Marines, who are armed to the teeth,

101

keep well away from there." We all looked daggers at John, but said nothing. Talk about Mad Dogs and Englishmen. Two hours later the Port Pirie set off on her marathon voyage across the Indian Ocean.

⚓

John Sheppard and I were working on the foredeck when along came Kevin and Jimmy, one of the Jocks. We were behind a winch-house, out of sight of the bridge. Kevin was straight in John's face and confrontational. "I hear that you told Angus that ya dinnae wanna have a drink with me. Is that right?" His strong Belfast accent came out fast; like bullets from a Maxim gun. John had earlier said something to Angus along the lines that Kevin wouldn't be his most favourite drinking partner to go ashore with.

"Well," said John diplomatically. "If we meet up in a pub when we're ashore, then you can ask me if I want a pint, can't you?"

"I'll tell you now, so I will. I don't like you Sheppard. I don't like ya one bit and if I see you ashore I'll smack ya in the mouth, so I will."

John looked back at him steadily and sneered. "Why wait until then? Why don't you do it now?" Kevin was taken aback. It wasn't the answer he was expecting, and he realised that some action on his part was required. He began to make his move, but it was too late. With the full weight of his body, John's arm shot out and whacked him square on his jaw, and down he went. He was groggy and on all fours. He tried to get up, but John leaned over him and said, "If you get up, Kevin, I'll hit you again - so stay where you are, okay?" Meanwhile Jimmy thought he should do something and started to square-up. I said "Back down, Jimmy, and you won't get hurt. Anyway it's not your fight." He lowered his fists. John reached down and helped Kevin to his feet. "Listen Kevin. I didn't start this. You did. If you come at me again, I'll put you back down on the deck. Do you understand?" Kevin nodded. John offered him a way out - a face-saver. "But, if you want to take me for a drink in Sydney, then just knock on my door, okay?" John extended his hand with goodwill, and Kevin shook it. Kevin and Jimmy went uncertainly off back to the accommodation. We never had any more problems after that.

The next day we crossed the Equator, and although the ceremony was slightly different from last trip, at least I wasn't on the receiving end of the bucket of galley slops, the medicine or the hosing down. John Sheppard had previously been on a voyage to South America so he had already paid his penance, but Dave Knight, Finn the Peggy and several others had to endure the initiation ceremony. Once again our ship's carpenter acted the part of King Neptune. This time his costume was far better prepared as

Christine had bought a long white beard in London and donated one of her old wigs.

Two days later, on the 26th June, it was my 18th birthday. I had forgotten about it – but not Christine. Oblivious to what day it was, I had worked out on deck all day painting the decks and the ship's handrails – a particularly dirty job – but under the warm sun I didn't mind. Christine had asked the cook to knock up a cake and it was topped-off with candles. As we sat down for our evening meal, the cake was brought out. I was gobsmacked. No one - other than my mum - had ever done that for me before.

It crossed my mind that I had been drinking in pubs and getting drunk ever since that night long ago when I had got rat-arsed at the White Hart pub in Plumstead; and I had been barely seventeen. And now it was official – I was old enough to legally have a beer.

The Nullabor

We passed Cape Leeuwin during the night watches, so didn't see anything of Western Australia. The Port Pirie turned eastbound and entered The Great Australian Bight. The next morning the seas started to pile up into huge white-topped swells. This was the antipodean winter, and The Bight, which was a part of the Southern Ocean, was infamous for its hostile weather at this time of year. For days on end we endured the ship's structure groaning and creaking in protest as she ploughed through the mountainous seas.

Several years earlier, far to the north in the parched desert of Western Australia, my cousin Steve had almost died. He had jumped ship in Fremantle (the port for Perth), but wanted to make his way to Adelaide where he had a girlfriend. He had no money, so decided that he would hitchhike the 1700 miles to go see her. Most of this distance is through the Nullabor Plain.

He was such a scatterbrain and never planned anything. He had no food, but did have the sense to carry a water bottle. He got a lift as far as some God-forsaken hamlet on the road that runs beside the dead-straight railway line on the southern edge of the Nullabor. He then unwisely decided he would try strolling along the road to get in some extra mileage. But as nightfall came, he turned off the road and sought shelter for the night just a few hundred yards away. When he awoke the next morning, he became disorientated and set off in the wrong direction – away from the road and further into the desert. For three days he wandered around in circles. His water ran out and he was delirious with the heat and starving hungry, but was lucky enough to stun a rabbit with a rock. He skinned it with his penknife and ate it raw.

Fortunately, he regained the road and eventually he got a lift out of danger and all the way to the girlfriend in Adelaide. But by then of course, she had found someone else!

⚓

Five days later the ship docked at Melbourne and secured at one of the many wharfs in the city centre. We got the ship ready for the wharfies to work cargo and headed ashore. The chief officer had given the deck crew a job-and-knock, so John, Dave, Chris and I were away ashore for a pint. They had never been to Melbourne before, so I introduced them to the delights of Chloe's delightful body at the Young & Jackson Hotel.

Ever so gradually my lack of self-assurance, especially in the female chatting-up department began to change, and I found myself talking to girls and not being a bundle of nerves in the process. I wasn't a bad looking chap, or at least some ladies had found me attractive enough, and this had bolstered my self-confidence and I was becoming more outgoing.

Work on unloading our cargo continued day-after-day, and ever so slowly the Port Pirie rose out of the water as thousands of tons of heavy cargo was discharged. The wharfies, who were very strongly unionised, would occasionally stop work for the most inexplicable of reasons. One day they all came out on strike because they wanted 'embarrassment money' for the cargo they were in the process of unloading. These hard-drinking, profane, macho-men all milled around on the quayside until their union convener had extracted extra money for discharging – porcelain toilet bowls!

One evening John and I, who had been to a pub on Flinders Street, came back onboard and were about to go to the messroom, when two girls came down the ladder from the direction of the officers' quarters. They were quite attractive and appeared not to be accompanied, so we asked them where they were going. They said they were just having a look around the ship, so I asked if they would like to look around my cabin. John gave me a queer look. Hijacking officers' women was strictly taboo; even if they were willing accomplices. They introduced themselves. The taller of the two was Heather, who linked her arm into mine, and the younger girl was called Noelene. We went below to my cabin. "Would you ladies like a beer? It's all we've got, I'm afraid."

I poured the beer into glasses. "John," I said, "Why don't you show Noelene your cabin?" Noelene didn't object and followed him next-door. That left Heather and I alone.

"Wasn't the officers' party very good?" I asked her. "No it was boring," she moaned.

"Were you with anyone in particular?"

"There was no one that I wanted to be with – until now," she said. Well if that wasn't a green light, I didn't know what was. I put my arms around her slim waist and pulled her in closely. She didn't resist. Her blonde hair spilled over her eyes, and together with her cheeky grin, she gave off an impression of a girl who would be a lot of fun. I lifted her chin and gave her a long kiss. She kissed me back and her tongue searched out my own. I turned the cabin light off except for the dim bunk-light. She undressed and slid under the sheets, and I did likewise. I knew that next door John - never one to hang around where females were concerned - would be getting Noelene into his bunk.

Sometime later, as Heather and I lay entwined in a deep sleep, the door opened and Chris Morling came in, quietly undressed, and climbed into his top bunk and tried to melt into the woodwork. That was the name of the game when you shared a cabin. If one wanted to entertain young ladies, you couldn't expect your cabinmate to disappear for the night. Next door, I guessed that Dave Knight was also doing his impression of The Invisible Man. We took the girls ashore before the sun came up and put them into a taxi.

The next day was a Saturday, and in the late afternoon I went for a walk around the city. John wasn't the type of guy who enjoyed seeing the cultural delights of a city, so I went alone. There was much to be impressed with, and much to be saddened by. I walked along Flinders Street, and at a kiosk picked up a free street map which included a history of the city. As old tramcars clattered down the street, I sat on a park bench to read the brochure.

During the mid 19th century, it said, Melbourne had doubled its population and size due to the discovery of gold at the towns of Ballarat and Bendigo in 1851. To get to the up-country goldfields, everything and everyone came through the city of Melbourne. The enormous wealth of the gold-rush fuelled a boom that lasted for forty years and this led to the construction of many fine buildings. Libraries, art galleries, churches, a cathedral, hotels, a railway station, museums, theatres, a treasury and wide boulevards were all built with gold rush-money. The list was endless. All these buildings were solidly built in the Victorian tradition and many were embellished with ornate wrought iron verandas and mouldings.

I walked across to Collins Street and bought some damper bread from a stall. It was sweet and tasted delicious. Collins Street is the main thoroughfare of Melbourne, and with its profusion of offices, shops and hotels, it's at least a mile long. As I strode along the wide avenue, I unaccountably came across several old Victorian buildings in various states of demolition. Their beautifully ornate columns and bowed windows and coppered rooftops were in the process of being ripped apart. On nearly every demolition site a billboard proclaimed the name of the demolition company, "Whelan the Wrecker" in large letters, as if the bulldozing of these fine old buildings was an achievement to be proud of.

At a pavement cafe I had a coffee and again read my brochure. Melbourne city centre, it boasted, was undergoing a period of urban renewal, whereby old Victorian edifices would be demolished to make way for modern structures, and especially any buildings with wrought iron balustrades or verandas would be pulled down. I looked across to the far side of Collins Street. There on a building site, a new office block was taking shape as it rose vertically into the sky. It consisted of just sheets of glass and concrete slabs. I was barely eighteen years old, but even I could see that a huge mistake was being perpetrated in the name of progress.

That night John and I, who had now become inseparable, met up with Noelene and Heather at a soda bar/disco in St Kilda. The evening went well and we laughed and danced to slow smoochy music on the small dance floor. The place was strictly non-alcoholic, so the girls bought glasses of coke and we surreptitiously topped them up from a hidden flask of Bacardi. They shared an apartment on the outskirts of St Kilda, and we knew without being invited that we would be staying the night and sharing their respective beds. The next day, Port Pirie let go her mooring ropes and headed for Sydney.

⚓

The ship glided under the Sydney Harbour Bridge and made for the docks at Pyrmont. As soon as the ship was moored, we topped up the derricks and opened the cargo hatches.

Later that evening we met a couple of girls outside Monty's bar and took them inside for a drink. Their names were Rhonda and Rachel. They had been in the bar before, so we didn't need to warn them about the bad language.

Most shipping company regulations stipulated that anyone bringing a guest onboard should have a visitor's pass, which one usually obtained from the officer-of-the-watch. The officer was supposed to enter the young lady's name on the chitty; but seeing as we often didn't know who we would be bringing onboard, we would simply name her as Miss Jones/Evans/Smith/Brown etc. Tonight it was the 3rd mate that issued the chit. Mine was in the name of Miss Take!

After Monty's closed up, we took the girls back to the ship. John didn't hang about and took Rhonda straight into his cabin and firmly closed the door. I spun Rachel around so that her back was towards me and I wrapped my arms around her. She swivelled her head around and I kissed her and ran my nose through her hair, breathing in her scent. "Can you stay the night," I whispered, and she nodded.

And that was the way in which we spent the next seven days. During the day the girls had their jobs working in a shop in Bourke Street, whilst John and I worked aboard the Port Pirie. In the evening, after a shower and a change of clothes, they would return and stay for another night of passion.

A Drive in the Countryside

I sat on a wooden bench and watched the construction underway for the new Sydney Opera House. Gangs of workmen were pouring semi-liquid concrete into wooden shuttering to create foundations for the huge new structure.

An elderly woman in her mid-sixties came and sat down, and somehow we got talking. As she spoke I could detect a fruity Birmingham accent. The lady told me that she originally came from Wolverhampton, but had come to live in Australia after her husband had retired when he was 65 years old. "Did you come out by ship or plane?" I asked.

"Neither," she said matter-of-factly. "We drove out here from England."

"You drove here?" I said incredulously. "You drove from England to Australia? You've got to be joking?" I was flabbergasted.

"Nope," she said proudly. "It took us just over six months."

"What sort of car did you drive?"

"We had a Ford Anglia," she said, smiling at their foolhardiness. "I know it's only a small car, but it's all we had."

"How on earth did you manage to do it?"

"We did our homework. Worked out a route; and off we went." She said it as if it was the most natural thing in the world to do.

"That's incredible," I said in amazement. "When was this?"

"It was two years ago. We set off across the English Channel and drove down through France, Switzerland, and Italy. Then we passed through Yugoslavia and Greece until we arrived in Istanbul." She made it sound an everyday occurrence, like going out for a spin in the countryside on a Sunday afternoon.

"Weren't you scared?" I asked.

"No, that was the easy bit. It got a bit scary when we were driving through Iran – Oh my God that took ages," she remembered. "We went across Afghanistan; through the Khyber Pass, and into Pakistan."

"Did the car break down?"

"Just a few punctures, that's all. We were very lucky", she recalled. "After that, we drove through India, Burma, Thailand, Malaya, and all the way down to Singapore."

"What made you want to drive instead of going out by ship?" I asked.

She smiled as she remembered their reasoning. "We had never done anything adventurous before in our lives. My husband worked in an engineering drawing office and I was a school secretary, so our experience was very limited. We wanted some excitement before we got too old."

"What's your name?" I enquired.

"Sheila Martin." We shook hands and I introduced myself. She had short greying hair with animated eyes and a ready smile. She looked extremely fit.

"We stayed in Singapore for a month and had a garage completely overhaul the car," she continued. "We put the car aboard a cargo ship to Darwin, and then we drove across Australia to Queensland where we now live."

I shook my head in wonderment. That would have been an amazing achievement for a young couple, never mind old-age pensioners. "Whereabouts in Queensland do you live?"

"We've got a house out in the countryside - near Cairns."

"What made you want to move from Wolverhampton to the other side of the world?" I asked.

"We wanted to get away from the factories and the smoke," she explained. "We needed to live in clean fresh air."

"You're a long way from Cairns. What are you doing all this way down in Sydney?"

"We have some friends in Sydney, so we've come down to visit. My husband's out playing golf with them."

"How did you get from Cairns down to Sydney?" I asked, but I had already guessed the answer.

"We drove down," she said matter-of-factly. "It's 1700 miles. It took us six days."

I remembered a book by Nevil Shute which I had recently read. It was called "A Town Like Alice." In the novel the English heroine called Jean Paget, who was a prisoner of the Japanese in Malaya, gets into conversation with an Australian POW. In peacetime the Aussie works as a stockman on a cattle station in Northern Queensland. "How big is your cattle station?" Jean Paget asks him.

"Aah struth, I should think it's about 2500 or 3000," he guessed.

"Gosh that's awfully big," she says, "3000 acres is an enormously huge area."

"It's not 3000 acres," he said casually. "It's 3000 square miles."

These vast distances in the novel made me recollect that Sheila had said she lived near Cairns. "When you say you live near Cairns – How near?" I asked.

"Oh my," she said offhandedly. "Oh - It's no more than about 150 miles away."

That's synonymous to saying that Birmingham is just near Dover! Sometimes, maybe once in a lifetime, one meets a person who is a one-off. Sheila Martin was just such a person.

⚓

We were in Monty's bar one evening. The music was playing and the beer was flowing. Over at the bar were a group of Swedish sailors having a quiet drink. Their ship was unloading on the opposite pier to ours. One of the Swedes was a tall blonde handsome looking fellow. He must have been 6ft 4" in stockinged feet.

Weaving drunkenly at the far end of the room was Shirley the Abbo. God, she was ugly. Apart from the typical Aboriginal features of a very wide nose and a squashed-up jet-black face, Shirley had a scar running down the side of her cheek that had the effect of making her look extremely scary. Shirley was short and dumpy, but as solid as an ox with thick muscle on her arms and chest. There were not many men who would take her on in a fight, because when Shirley was in the mood for fighting, it was best to buy her a drink and keep out of her way. Notwithstanding her physical features; she had other bad habits. On every occasion that I saw her in Monty's, she was either drunk, or attempting to get that way; usually by bumming drinks from sailors who were too scared not to buy her one.

On unsteady feet Shirley made her way towards the bar. She spotted the tall Swede and was instantly smitten. Within her drunken booze-laden world she had fallen in love. She drank her beer and looked up into his big blue eyes. "I like you Big Boy. You're ever so handsome," she said, slurring her words.

"Thanking you for saying so," he said in his fractured English.

"Have you got a girlfriend? Are you married?"

"No, I am not having a wife or having not the girlfriend," he said. His open and honest face was totally unaware of the unmitigated grief that was heading his way.

"In that case, do you wanna take me home tonight? You can f*ck me if you want to," invited Shirley with garbled speech.

His eyes bulged with horror at the very thought of it. "I am thinking not," he said - a bit too quickly for her liking.

"Why the f*ck not," she said indignantly. "Ain't I bloody good enough for ya?" Without further ado she grabbed the back of his shirt collar whilst her other hand dived between his legs and grasped his testicles. With her full weight she spun him around and ran him towards the glass doors. As the handsome Swede hit the doors, they splintered and smashed into a thousand pieces and he cart-wheeled out onto the pavement. The poor man lay in an untidy heap and with blood seeping from cuts across his whole body. Shirley, never a one to pass-up the offer of a free drink, went back to the bar and picked up his glass of beer.

Aotearoa – The Land of the Long White Cloud

At last we had unloaded the last of our cargo and said goodbye to Sydney. As Port Pirie cleared Sydney Heads, an easterly course was set and she headed across the Tasman Sea for a three and a half day voyage to Auckland, New Zealand. The ship was ballasted down with sea water, which made her more comfortable and easier to handle. En-route the deck crew cleaned out the cargo spaces to be ready to load our cargo of butter, milk powder, shellfish and lamb. The cargo holds had to be scrupulously clean so as to comply with the strict hygiene regulations of New Zealand. The same high standards of cleanliness also applied in Australia. The ship would undergo a hygiene inspection on arrival at Auckland. We deckies washed and scrubbed every square inch of the six massive cargo spaces to ensure she was ready to begin loading.

It was mid-afternoon as we sailed past Rangitoto Island and into Auckland harbour. The harbour was bustling with a multitude of yachts and motor boats. We passed by sandy beached coves lined with neat wooden clapboard houses along the shoreline. On the hills above were thick forests of coniferous trees. It all looked so idyllic and healthy. Within the hour we were berthed at the dock which was located near to the city centre.

On arrival, the chief officer gave the deck crew an early knock-off, and they piled ashore quickly. New Zealand's bars closed at 6pm – and with the 6-o'clock swill still very much in operation - time was beer. However, I had been on duty very early on the 4-8 watch, so I badly needed some sleep, and so I went to bed for a few hours. But firstly I had to read a blue air-mail letter from my mum, which had been delivered via our ship's agent. There was not a lot of news. She told me snippets about baby Toni and what my sisters were doing. My younger sister Glynis was now 16 years old and had a boyfriend. It was all quite mundane stuff.

Later that evening John returned onboard with a delicious Maori girl on his arm and immediately took her into his cabin. I regretted having a snooze instead joining the lads ashore, but with the pubs now closed, there was little I could do about it.

I wandered along the crews' alleyway. There was loud music coming from Phil Trevelyan's cabin and I could hear shrill female voices. He had a party going on. I put my head in the door and said hello. "Hiya Graham, come on in. Help yourself to a beer," he said. I grabbed a can and looked around. Apart from Phil there were four girls and two stewards squeezed into the cabin. Everyone was getting sloshed on cans of Heineken. I planted myself in the middle of the ladies and made myself comfortable. Mostly the girls were attractive, but one girl in particular was very nice indeed. The problem was that one of the pantry stewards was trying to lay claim to her by having his arm around her waist and his hand casually on her thigh. She had shoulder length jet-black hair and nice brown eyes that crinkled at the corners. While the steward was busy looking elsewhere, I made eye contact and gave her a secret smile. She briefly grinned back at me then looked away. A few moments later she asked where the bathroom was, and Phil waved his hand in the general direction of the toilets. A few minutes after that, I drained my beer and said goodnight. I went along to stand outside the toilets. I could hear her flushing the toilet and washing her hands. She came out and looked startled when she found me loitering outside. "Oh you surprised me there," she said, and began to giggle.

"I just came along to make sure you ended up back in the right cabin," I said as I took her by the hand. Within a few moments I had led her into my own cabin and had my arms around her waist. She didn't pull away so I kissed her. She had soft and yielding lips and her breath smelt of mint. I ran both my hands across her bottom and pulled her closer into me. I leaned across and threw the bolt on the door. Outside I heard the pantry steward searching for her at the toilets. I wasn't worried. "What's your name sweetie," I whispered.

"My name's Debbie," she murmured. "Will anyone find us here?" I shook my head and undid the button to her jeans and helped them to slide to the floor. I guided her into the narrow bunk and killed the cabin lights. Much later, after a luxuriant and languid sleep curled within each others' limbs, I turned her onto her side so that we were in the spoons position and we again made slow sensual love, and fell into a comfortable doze.

A few hours later I opened my eyes. Through the porthole the sun was attempting to push its way above the horizon. She was sleeping beside me and ever so slightly snoring. I smiled at the thought and silently watched her for some minutes. She slowly opened her eyes and was eventually awake. It was time for her to go home - and for me to start work. We quickly dressed and I took her ashore to the taxi rank. I gave her a long and deep kiss as the cab slid to a stop beside us. She gave me a wink and got into the back seat and waved as it pulled away. Sadly, I never saw her again.

Ma Gleason's

One of the most famous, or should I say infamous, seaman's bars in the world would probably be Ma Gleason's in Auckland. It's renowned across the seven seas for being a rough and ready bar where the beer flows non-stop, fights are common, and the women are easy.

Apart from the front entrance and the off-licence, the main bar of Ma Gleason's was one large room with a fairly small bar. Around the room ran a shoulder height shelf. It was a handy place to park your beer so that it didn't get spilt when a fight started. There were no seating arrangements, but sometimes you could find a beer crate to sit upon. Very often the place was full of girls. However, they were not the type of ugly women, like Shirley from Monty's Bar. These were mostly attractive regular girls who worked in shops and offices and hospitals. Until October 1967, the "6-o-clock swill" was in operation and between 5pm and 6pm the place was a madhouse. Speed-drinking was the name of the game. After 1967, when 10pm closing came into being, there wasn't the suspense and excitement and it didn't seem so much fun anymore.

But this was 1964, and my first visit to Ma Gleason's was on our second afternoon in Auckland. John, Dave Knight, Dave Moorcroft and I were drinking as fast as we could. The place was buzzing with seamen, pretty girls, and locals. There were also four very large Maori guys who were intent on causing trouble. They were huge. Tall, with plenty of bodyweight, they would very easily be able to overwhelm us in a fight. The problems began when one of them picked up John's beer. John politely said, "Hey, that's my beer you're drinking."
The Maori took a gulp - all the while staring John straight in the eye as if to say, "Come on tough guy, do something about it." The three others casually came to stand close to us. He picked up John's glass again, and as soon as John made a grab for it, the other three jumped us. Their huge fists were fast, 1-2-3-4 and we were out of the game. But without warning the rest of

our crew, including the nasty Kevin, piled in and threw them out of the bar. A big cheer went up as they were ejected out the door.

A little while later, we were drinking with Kevin and the Jocks, when an empty beer bottle hit me on the back of the head. I looked around to see who had thrown it, but Ma Gleason's was so packed out that it was impossible to see who the culprit was. Moments later, another bottle came flying through the air and hit one of the Jocks. We looked around. "Hey, who the hell threw that?" he shouted.

"Aah, don't worry", said a nearby sailor, "that's Queenie the Maori. She's always doing that." He indicated a drunken wild-haired Maori woman who was standing beside a stack of beer crates. As I watched, she selected another empty bottle from the crate, and lobbed it across to the far end of the room.

⚓

Even now I don't know what possessed me to do it, but I felt a sudden urge to take myself off to a tattooist. Perhaps I thought that any real sailor worth his salt would almost certainly have a tattoo. Anyway, an hour or so later I returned onboard sporting a Kiwi Tiki on my left arm. The Tiki, in Maori legend, is a fertility sign and is represented by a squat humanoid charm that supposedly brings good luck and plenty of healthy children - although I wasn't planning on having any children any time soon. Also on the tattoo were the Maori words Kia-Ora which mean – Be well or be healthy; but these days it's just another form of saying Hi or G'day.

To complement the tattoo I decided that, just like many sailors, I should also wear a single gold earring. However, firstly I needed to have my ear pierced and I opted on doing the job myself. I bought a 9 ct gold earring – or ringbolt in sailor's parlance – and got the necessary equipment ready-to-hand. I needed a thick darning needle with a cork rammed onto the blunt end, some cotton wool and a jar of Vaseline. I had a few cans of beer to give me some Dutch courage. Taking my earlobe between thumb and forefinger, I began to squeeze tightly. Harder and harder I exerted pressure on the fleshy lobe until, after a few minutes, it had become quite numb and I couldn't feel a thing. Picking up the disinfected needle, I bravely rammed it through my ear and looked aghast in the mirror as it came through the other side. I quickly slid the gold earring – or sleeper - into the vacant hole and that was it – job done.

⚓

On the following Sunday we were off-duty, and so Phil Trevelyan organised a self-drive minibus which could take 8 passengers. We planned to drive north to visit the Bay of Islands up near Opua and then return via Ninety Mile Beach on the west coast. We aimed on being back in Auckland

113

by evening. Dave Knight came along and so did Chris Morling. John Sheppard brought along a girl called Sandy whom we had met in the Great Northern Hotel, and I was accompanied by her friend Georgia, a slim blonde with nice blue eyes and cute dimples. They were both 18 years old. We had met them only yesterday, but they seemed rather nice and they had brought along a picnic.

We set off early and headed for the Auckland harbour bridge. The weather was sunny and the sky cloudless as we motored northwards. Phil was driving, and I sat with Georgia at the back of the minibus. Within a short time we were holding hands, and soon she was leaning against me as the coach trundled along the undulating road. The scenery was beautiful as we drove through the towns of Orewa, Ruakaka, Hikurangi, and then into our destination - Paihia.

At Paihia we went along to visit the Maori Meeting House where, in 1840, the Treaty of Waitangi, which gave sovereignty of New Zealand to Great Britain, was signed by the British and the Maori chieftains. Nearby in an open-sided shed, was a huge replica war canoe – the biggest in the world. We looked out over the waters of the bay, and as far as the eye could see there were countless islands and rocky inlets to explore. We went down to the quayside and joined a tour cruise that would take us around the numerous islands and coves and past sandy beaches. Our trip aboard the cruise boat was wonderful. The skipper and crew were very helpful and pointed out places of interest and the spot where, in 1769, Captain James Cook supposedly dropped the Endeavour's anchor whilst surveying the waters around New Zealand.

Meanwhile dolphins were swimming around the vessel's bow-wave and jumping high out of the water; and although as seamen we had seen dolphins many times before, Georgia and Sandy were city girls, and had never seen these wonderful mammals up close in their natural element. Phil and Chris meanwhile were taking lots of photographs and Dave had a cine camera. The cruise boat came back alongside and we disembarked.

We drove across to Hokianga Harbour on the west coast, and had a slow drive around this huge inland estuary. After some suitable liquid refreshment at a pub at Opononi, and devouring the contents of the picnic hamper, we drove onto 90-mile Beach and headed southwards. The wide beach was almost deserted and we saw only two other vehicles during the hour's drive on the hard compacted sand. It was great fun to drive through the surf and to scatter flocks of seagulls feeding at the water's edge as our minibus motored along with ease and reached a fair speed. The beach's name is a misnomer as its length is actually 55-miles long, but nevertheless, it was a pleasant and entertaining drive.

114

We were back at the ship by early evening and popped onboard for a quick wash and change while the girls waited in the messroom. We hopped into a cab and took them home, where they shared a sizeable apartment with two other girls out at Mount Eden. We made ourselves at home, and whilst Sandy and Georgia had their showers, we chatted to the two cute flatmates Annette and Sophia. When our girlfriends came out the shower we were all sitting around talking about travel. It was then that Annette came out with a very strange statement. She said that she was saving up her money because she wanted to travel "Back home to England." "Oh," I said. "I didn't know you were English. How old were you when you left England?"

She looked confused. "I've never been to England before. That's why I'm saving up to go."

"But you just said that you were going back home to England." It was my turn to be confused.

"Oh well – that's just the way us Kiwis say it. Everyone calls it 'Going Home.' It was a phrase I was to hear many times again, both in New Zealand and Australia. Even though the average New Zealander had never stepped outside of their own country, they had been brought up to look upon England as their Mother Country. Their grandfathers and great grandfathers had all made the long voyage out from England, and the British history and way of life was instilled in them and had been handed down from father to son. Wherever one went in New Zealand you would see English place names. Wellington was named after the great general. Auckland and Napier named after ancient lords of the British realm. Nelson in the South Island bears the name of Admiral Horatio Nelson There's Marlborough and Blenheim, New Plymouth, Palmeston, Hastings, Canterbury etc. The list was endless. Just as young rich Englishmen in the 19th century would embark upon The Grand Tour of Europe, so the young New Zealander would set out on a journey to the other side of the world because, by tradition, they were magnetically drawn there by a need to make this Rite of Passage back to the Old Country. They were 'Going Home.'

The day had gone very well indeed. Everyone had enjoyed the trip to the Bay of Islands, and the closeness between Georgia and myself, which had tentatively started with holding hands, had got better as the day progressed. John and Sandy were likewise getting on like a house on fire. We were laid out on the sofa and Georgia was in my arms and nuzzling my neck.

She whispered in my ear. "Do you want to stay tonight?" I nodded.

"Sandy and I share a bedroom. Will that be a problem?"

I playfully dug her in the ribs. "If you want to shag me, then you'll have to do it quietly." She laughed and dug me right back. "Ooh you naughty boy. I may have to do just that."

⚓

We left Auckland on a Tuesday and our next port-of-call was Gisborne, a small port on the east coast in Poverty Bay. John and I had been told by some seamen who we had met in Ma Gleason's that Gisborne was a great run-ashore. They said that there was no large quay in the port, so therefore ships had to anchor off the harbour to load and discharge from barges. However, they said that the male/female ratio was so high in favour of the female species, that there were ten females for every male. That's just the sort of ratio's we liked, so John and I decided that we would definitely like to give Gisborne a visit.

We dropped anchor in the afternoon and rigged the ship's derricks ready to work cargo. Tugs brought barges and wharfies alongside and they started work loading the cartons of butter for export to the UK. However, the chief officer informed us that the captain would not permit shore leave as there were no proper launches to transport us. John was devastated. He had been so looking forward to getting ashore, but only for the simple reason that he wanted to be the first British seamen to bonk a Gisborne woman in a very long time. I said that if the captain wasn't allowing shore-leave, then we were buggered. He suggested that if we could get a lift ashore aboard one of the small tugs, then we would be okay. I reluctantly agreed to it. The decision was made, and we prepared to go ashore. We asked a tug skipper, and he agreed to take us – for a price. As darkness fell, we climbed unsteadily down a rope ladder and onto the tug which took us ashore to a small pier.

As John and I walked along the main street, we could immediately see that the town was very small indeed, and the nightlife was non-existent. There were very few shops and hardly any street lights, and after a few hundred yards, the town simply petered out into countryside. Those nasty sailors back at Ma Gleason's had been spinning us a porkie-pie! We found a solitary ice-cream parlour. We were the only persons in there. The owner asked if we had come ashore from the cargo ship. He told us that he was about to shut-up for the night. He said, "I dunno why you've bothered to come ashore in Gisborne – there's sod-all here." We didn't even see any females!

The Port Pirie was due to stay anchored off Gisborne for five nights whilst we loaded more dairy produce. With what we had just experienced, it would seem more like a month. We returned to the ship aboard the tug and climbed precariously up the shaky Jacobs ladder to get back aboard. As my eyes became level with the deck, a pair of legs were standing there. Attached to the legs was the chief officer Jack Newbery, and as we climbed up onto the deck he was fuming. He said, "You knew full well that you were not allowed shore-leave, didn't you?" We both nodded miserably. He regarded us sternly. "You will both report to my cabin tomorrow morning."

At 09:00 John and I were stood before the Mate. He sat behind his desk and stared at us with annoyance. We were for the high-jump, that's for sure. For disobeying the master's orders we could each be fined a day's pay, plus forfeit another day's pay or whatever the chief mate thought it deserved. The whole procedure was known as a logging because the offence and the punishment would be recorded within the ship's official logbook. For any second or subsequent offence, the fines were doubled up. Being a naughty boy aboard ship could be a very costly exercise!

"Well," said the mate harshly. "What have you got to say for yourselves?" I couldn't think of any plausible story that he would even begin to believe, so I decided to tell the truth. I told him about the alleged ratio of ten women to every man and how we'd been stitched up with a pack of lies. I informed him how small the town actually was and about the ice-cream parlour and not having actually spotted any females and having to pay the tug skipper. There was silence in the cabin as he deliberated what our punishment should be. Suddenly he threw his head back and roared with laughter. He couldn't stop. Eventually he said, "I haven't had such a good laugh for a long time. What a hard luck story that was. Go on – get outta here."

⚓

The capital of New Zealand is known as Windy Wellington for good reason. As the Port Pirie entered the port, a brisk wind slanted in from the Cook Strait as some rain clouds scurried ahead of the warm front. We picked up our harbour pilot and steamed through the heads between the Miramar Peninsular and Barrett Reef. An hour later we were tied up in Lambton Harbour right in the city centre. By the time we raised the derricks, opened the cargo hatches, and got the vessel ready to load, it was time to go for a pint. We headed for the Duke of Edinburgh Hotel on the corner of Manners and Willis Streets. The bar upstairs was fabulous with a long polished bar with large mirrors along the wall and chrome fittings and leather sofas and club chairs. It looked like the sort of place to get seriously drunk in.

A short while later Christine came into the bar accompanied by a perfectly beautiful creature. She introduced me to Krystle, a leggy blonde dressed simply in black leggings and lemon woollen top. While I bought them a drink, Christine brought me up to date on the latest rumours and goings-on aboard the Port Pirie. The girl meanwhile was very quiet and didn't say an awful lot. When she did speak her voice had rather a deep but pleasant timbre. When Christine went to the toilet I made my move with the girl. I tried giving her some chat-up lines, but was not having much luck. I asked what she did for a living and she told me she was a waitress. I enquired how she knew Chris, and she said she'd simply known her for years. I tried other tactics, but she wasn't playing my game and I got the brush-off. With that, Chris came back from the loo and Krystle said she had to get back to work. We said goodbye, but I tried one more time for a date and asked if she would be around later. She said offhandedly, "No sorry, but you never know, I may bump into you at some time." I watched her rear-end as she walked out. It looked rather nice from where I was standing. I turned to Christine. "Where the hell do you know her from?" I said excitedly. "She's bloody gorgeous."

Chris laughed out loud. "Ooh Graham. You're a silly sod. Couldn't you tell? That was a bloke. He's a waiter aboard the big passenger liner that's in port!" To say I was embarrassed would be an understatement. Apart from that first visit to Danny's Bar, it was the only time I had ever not been able to tell the difference between a real female and a woofter.

Christine had gone back aboard and so I rejoined John Sheppard and Dave Knight at the bar. They were getting beer down their necks rather rapidly and I had some catching up to do. A little later two girls came in the pub and we got talking to them when they came to the bar for drinks. I rather fancied a tall blonde and I could see that she was keen on me, so I slid my hand around her waist and pulled her closer. John nonchalantly draped his arm across the shoulders of the second blonde and they were in deep conversation. The day was turning out very well indeed. Maybe I couldn't chat-up a ship's poofy waiter, but the blonde would do me nicely, thank you very much. Dave, who'd had too much to drink, went off back onboard to sleep it off, which left John and myself and the two blondes. My girl was called Caron and John's was Erica. It was getting close to 6pm and the bar was about to shut. We asked if they would like to come back aboard the ship with us, but they had to go to work shortly. I asked where they worked. "We're at the Pussy Cat Club," said Caron. "Hey, why don't you come by the club about 10 o' clock, then you can take us home later?"

You will dear reader, have noticed by now that my shyness when in the company of women, was abating rapidly, and my sexual libido was coming along by leaps and bounds, and I was speedily making up for lost time.

It was now late evening and we were walking through the rain soaked streets of Wellington on our way to the Pussy Cat Club. At the entrance to the club we spoke to the doorman, who had been told to expect us. We were let inside and made ourselves comfortable at a table with a glass of beer.

"Where are the girls, Gra," asked John. "What do they do here? Are they waitresses?"

"Dunno John. I'm sure they'll turn up soon. They may be busy." We asked a passing waitress where Caron and Erica were, but she just shrugged her shoulders. Another hour went by and the girls still didn't show. John was all for buggering off, but I pointed out that Caron had very definitely said that we would be taking them home after they finished work. We were on a promise!

However, I was getting tired. I laid my head down on the table, and somehow I fell asleep. Much later, John was shaking my arm roughly. "Graham, wake up – they're here. Look - up on the stage." My bleary eyes slowly focused and followed his pointing finger. There, up on the stage were the girls – taking their clothes off. They were the strip act!

Culture Vulture

The Port Pirie was gradually sinking lower in the water as she was loaded with thousands of tons of apples, lamb, shellfish and dairy produce and our departure day loomed ever closer. From Wellington the ship would make the long voyage across the Pacific Ocean and back to London.

After breakfast one Sunday morning, I decided to take a walk around the city. Thus far I had only been to the Duke of Edinburgh Hotel and the Pussy Cat Club. I remembered my promise that I would endeavour to see some sights and culture of countries I had visited, and I didn't think that Ma Gleasons somehow fell into this category. I set off at a brisk pace along Lambton Quay where there were interesting shops and buskers and street artists, and very soon came upon the city's main railway station. With its marble cladding and neo Georgian exterior, it was a magnificent building, and so I walked inside and was impressed by the classical architecture in the huge entrance hall with its vaulted ceilings. I wangled a free city information pamphlet and map from the tourist office and retraced my steps back along Lambton Quay. Shortly, I came upon some impressive and elegant buildings, the Edwardian Baroque Building and the Public Trust Building, both looking as if they had stood there for a thousand years. Other nearby heritage buildings, with their cared-for appearance, gave the impression that the city council put a lot of effort into preserving these fine old structures. With Wellington abounding with all these wonderful edifices, I was pleased not to find any garish billboards proclaiming the presence of the NZ branch of "Whelan the Wrecker!"

119

I found the entrance to the cable car and I paid my fare. On this beautifully sunny morning it whisked me up past the Victoria University and then onwards to the Botanical Gardens. The view from the top was magical, with the whole of Wellington laid out before me in a beautiful panoramic landscape. The botanical gardens were stunning and I took many photographs with my camera. Although I wasn't remotely interested in horticulture, the exhibits included many native exotic trees and plants and I was very impressed. I was having a good day.

⚓

Two days later the Port Pirie, loaded down to her Plimsoll marks, pushed her nose out into the Cook Strait and turned eastwards on her 6500 mile passage across the Pacific to the Panama Canal. The sea conditions were good as the vessel cut through the swells at a steady 16 knots and we were making good time on our 17-day long haul journey. The sun shone down remorselessly every day and the heat was kept in check only by the vessels forward speed. Port Pirie wasn't air-conditioned, so the only way to keep the hot and sultry temperature down inside one's cabin, especially at night, was to slide a metal scoop out of the porthole which would literally scoop the passing flow of air into the ship's accommodation. For those cabins which didn't possess a scoop, we would slide a sheet of thick cardboard out the porthole, which served the same purpose.

A day and a half's steaming from Wellington, the Port Pirie passed across the International Date Line. This is an imaginary line running in a north/south direction through the 180 degree meridian of longitude. The line is necessary in order to have a fixed boundary on the earth's surface where the calendar date resets. As we were travelling eastbound, we repeated the day in which we had previously been. We had crossed over on a Tuesday which meant that the next day was also Tuesday.

Day after day, work continued upon the open decks. Painting and chipping was a never ending process to keep the rust at bay, as was the routine maintenance for the upkeep of every moving part. There was always some task or other that needed doing. And if there wasn't? - There was always holystoning!

Very occasionally one may see another vessel hull down on the distant horizon or perhaps at night as a dim light many miles away. Rarely would one see another ship at close quarters and it brought home the message of how vast was the Pacific Ocean.

If the navigation lights of a distant ship were sighted, the officer-of-the-watch would occasionally call it up by using an Aldis lamp. This is a hand held signalling lamp with which they could exchange information using the Morse code. He would normally flash, "What ship? Where are you bound? And the answer would be flashed back by the receiving vessel.

Gradually our ship moved little by little across the small scale chart, never coming within sight of any island groups or landmass. Every day the captain would order the clocks put forward by a half hour, so as to correspond with the local time of the area.

The talk on the lower decks was of when we would reach London, and if any crew member intended signing-on again for the next voyage. I had already decided that, as this was my fourth trip aboard the Port Pirie, I would take some leave, and then look for a berth in another ship. I wasn't alone in this decision. Although she was a happy ship, many of the crew had been aboard for a considerable time and they wanted a change of scenery.

The Panama Canal

The eighteenth day out of Wellington was the 15th October 1964. As we steamed into the Gulf of Panama, we got news from home via the radio officer. There had been a general election in the United Kingdom, and after 13 years of Conservative Party government, Harold Wilson's Labour Party had won the election by a narrow margin.

We took aboard our American pilot for passage through the Panama Canal. The transit of the 50-mile canal would take 8–10 hours, but would save many weeks and thousands of miles, rather than going via the alternative route – around dangerous Cape Horn on the southern tip of South America.

The building of the canal was originally attempted by the French, under the command of Ferdinand de Lesseps, who had gained great fame and success in building the 105-mile long Suez Canal. However, de Lesseps was to find conditions far more difficult in the Isthmus of Panama. In the 10-year period of the 1880's when he attempted to carve his way through dense jungle and swamps, 22,000 men had died, mostly due to malaria and yellow fever. The real culprit of the disease was of course, the mosquito, but so little was known about this innocuous, but deadly, insect at that time. French doctors on site thought that these diseases were spread by the armies of ants in this tropical region. Field hospitals were set up, and bowls of water were placed under each leg of the beds so as to deter the ants from climbing up onto their patients. The bowls of water were, of course, a perfect environment for the mosquito to breed, and the workers consequently died in their thousands. Eventually, in 1903, the French gave up, and with the company on the brink of bankruptcy, they abandoned their equipment and departed. Slowly but surely the dense jungle began to reclaim the land.

In 1904 the American US Army Corps began work to forge a way through the isthmus. The army medical staff did tests upon the mosquito and pinpointed the cause of so much suffering and death. Therefore, their first task was to drain vast areas of swamps, ponds and streams so as to deny the mosquito anywhere to breed. Water sources were sprayed with tons of insecticide, so as to kill the mosquito eggs where they lay ready to hatch. At last, after 18-months of work, the disease was largely eradicated, and work could begin in earnest.

The largest earth dam in the world was built so as to control the wild Chagres River, and its waters would be used to fill the enormous lock chambers by gravity, thereby negating the need to install high-capacity pumps. Huge steam shovels were brought in from the US, and a heavy gauge railway system was built so as to remove the millions of tons of mud and spoil from the workings. Immense concrete locks systems were installed in three separate locations, each with innovative hollow lock gates that could, not only hold back the heavy weight of water, but were operated by a simple 25hp motor. In tandem with these works, housing, roads and general infrastructure all had to be built from scratch. At last, when the excavations were complete, and the canal was almost ready to begin operations, it only remained to dynamite the last narrow strip of land that held back the water. Then the sluice gates of the giant Chagres Dam were opened wide and countless millions of tons of water soon filled the canal, and created the huge Gatun Lake. It was a colossal feat of engineering, and when it opened for business in 1914 it changed forever the enormous distances that ships would otherwise have had to travel.

As we began our passage, we passed under the Bridge of the Americas, a towering suspension bridge that spanned the canal to form part of the Pan-American Highway that linked North and South America. At a sedate pace we came to our first set of locks. I had heard stories about what a wonderful sight the canal was; some even called it the eighth wonder of the world; but I wasn't prepared for my first sight of one of man's greatest engineering achievements. It was breathtaking.

Port Pirie nosed gently into the Miraflores Lock, and thick mooring wires were quickly passed across from four electric locomotives, known as mules. Once the mules were secured, two on each side, they would use their tensioning winches to keep our vessel in the centre of the lock. The water came into the lock at such a fast rate that it created fierce whirlpools and vortexes that could easily cause large ships to bump against the concrete sides and be damaged, so the mules were a real necessity. Even though we were a big 10,500 ton ship, we were dwarfed by the sheer size of the vast locks, each of them 1050 feet long, into which Panamax vessels of up 75,000 tons could be accommodated. At each of the lock system locations, two locks were sited side-by-side. One was for vessels ascending and the other, just 100 feet away, was for descending vessels. As the water rose up in our lock, a large grey painted American troop transport came into view, its decks filled with US troops and trucks and military equipment of every kind. Some of the troops gave us a desultory wave, but none of them looked particularly overjoyed. One of our crew shouted over to them. "Hey, where are you guys going to?" The answer came back, "We're going to Vietnam." Astern of our ship, the lock gates closed, and water was pumped in at such a prodigious volume that the ship rose up the sides of the lock at an alarming rate. However, the mules did their jobs and kept us dead centre. Once we had risen up to the top, the gates ahead of the ship now opened and the mules gently towed us into the next lock.

One impressive aspect of Panama was how clean and tidy the whole canal area was kept. The canal authority offices were smart two-storey wooden buildings with a veranda all around. Neat mown lawns ran alongside the locks, and everywhere one could see the Stars and Stripes fluttering from flagpoles. Port Pirie was secured in the next lock, and up she went in a faultlessly orchestrated procedure. At a stately pace we moved just one mile through the Miraflores Lake to the next lock system, the Pedro Miguel Lock, and once again, with the assistance of the mules, rose up until we were some 85 feet above sea level.

Once clear of Pedro Miguel, we entered the Gaillard Cut, a steep sided rock gorge that runs for 8-miles. When the canal was being built, the Gaillard (or Culebra Cut), had to be hand blasted and cleared by vast gangs of men. It's rumoured that one man died for each yard of progress in forging through that rock. Exiting from The Cut, we now sailed via a series of dogleg courses through the Gatun Lake before reaching the last lock system.

At last we entered Gatun Locks, a 3-stage system that brought the Port Pirie down 85 feet so as to be level with the Caribbean Sea. Ten hours after leaving the Pacific Ocean, we passed the Port of Colon and we were out into the Atlantic.

Sailing Across the Pond

Our voyage across the Atlantic would take 12-days. The ship briefly stopped off at Curacao in the Dutch Antilles for fuel bunkers, then continued on our passage across the Atlantic, commonly called "The Pond." Most of the voyage was uneventful except that, as we travelled further northwards, the temperature cooled considerably. Port Pirie took a position fix as she passed close by the volcanic islands of the Azores and altered course for the Ile de Ushant – the entrance to the English Channel.

It was as we neared the Bay of Biscay that the storm hit us. The storm had started as storms often do. The pressure reading of the barometer had dropped like a stone, and on the western horizon the darkening cumulonimbus rainclouds took on a threatening grey hue, which stretched right down to the horizon and the billowing cloud formations stood like pyramids toppling end-over-end. The long oceanic swells gradually shortened in length, becoming steeply sided with cresting wave-tops falling over into the trough. The whitecaps built up in size, slowly at first, but enough so as to feel the ride aboard Port Pirie become extremely uncomfortable. The depression had started a thousand miles to the south-west as a small dip in the atmospheric pressure as it fed off the rising warm air currents of the eastern Caribbean. This was the hurricane season. The isobars of the barometric pressure packed tightly together as the storm went active and careered north-easterly across the Atlantic Ocean and the wind-speed was now in the region of 45 mph and rising.

I awoke in my bunk and felt the ship's see-sawing movement and the vibrations as the propellers came out of the water and raced at high speed until the engine governor cut in. Immense waves were now smashing into the ship's side, and a torrent of water was coming onboard and washing across the decks. The ship lifted her blunt bow and crashed down into the sea as a solid phalanx of green seas and spray came over the bow and ran down the foredeck in a river of white water. Even though Captain Conby had drastically reduced our speed, each colossal wave that smashed into us would cause the ship's hull to shudder throughout its length and the noise would reverberate through the crew's quarters. Conditions inside the ship were pretty bad, as anything not lashed down came adrift and was thrown noisily about the accommodation. The situation in the galley was dreadful as plates, pots, pans, and cooking equipment rolled around the galley cupboards. The captain wisely sent down word not to attempt cooking hot meals until the storm had abated.

The size of the breakers became very large and some rogue waves towered over the ship before crashing onboard in a frightening cacophony of noise. When Port Pirie had reached the furthest arc of her roll, she hung there for a long periods, seemingly wanting to topple over even further onto her beam ends. The captain altered the ship's course so as to bring the wind more onto her stern and perhaps reduce the violent rolling and make the passage more comfortable. The view when one looked out of the porthole was of massive crested waves, each one looking very solid and heading interminably at our ship. The whole scene was one of white foam swept along the wave-tops. The occasional monster wave sent solid crested rollers crashing over the decks and resulted in the forward well-deck filling with hundreds of tons of white water. The extra weight caused her to lean over at an acute angle. Eventually – like a terrier shaking water off its fur – she would shake the water free from her decks and come back upright.

The nightmare voyage continued all through the morning watch, during which one could only hang on for dear life as Port Pirie rolled incessantly back and forth and dug her nose into the solid rollers. After midday, as the low pressure system passed to the south and careered away on its north-easterly track, the winds gradually veered to a more north-westerly direction and reduced in speed. By tea-time the engine revolutions were increased and we were once again making full speed towards the French coast and the Ile de Ushant. Through the night watches the seas abated and the wind-speed reduced to a light north-westerly wind. The ship came abeam of Ushant lighthouse at dawn, and with just over 400 miles to run, we would soon be back home.

The next morning, we entered King George V Dock, where tugs towed us along to our regular berth. The crew, with great excitement and a good dose of "The Channels", had already packed their suitcases and were eager to get off home. Within the hour we were in the saloon and being signed-off articles and getting our pay. I didn't pay-off with an awful lot of money, just £68 1s 11d for nearly five months work – but I'd had a bloody brilliant time!

We said fond farewells to our shipmates, Dave Knight, Dave Moorcroft, Phil Trevelyan, the Jocks, Finn, nasty Kevin, Sammy the bosun, Christine and Lily and many more. I very much doubted if I would ever see them again. A half hour later, John and I were in a taxi and back home in Silvertown. Mum made us a large fried breakfast with a mug of tea. We were in heaven! Soon afterwards, John caught the train to go spend some time with his dad who lived in Hampshire.

5: The Port Melbourne

Falling Out in Farnborough

John Sheppard's parents were divorced. His mother ran a cafe in Portsmouth and his father was a mechanical engineer who lived in Farnborough, Hampshire. The plan was that I would spend a week at home, and was then invited to stay at his father's house. John knew of plenty of places to pick up girls in the area, so it seemed we would be having a great time.

I arrived at the house in Farnborough on a Friday afternoon. I was introduced to his father, a man of about 55 years old. Tom Sheppard appeared to live in an olden day era. He smoked a pipe and wore a wartime leather jerkin, and his slow drawling voice reminded me of a country farmer, although behind that rustic facade, I detected a man who was used to his orders being obeyed. His wife Phyllis was a quiet mousy woman who looked as if she did as she was told. However, she was a pleasant enough lady and made me welcome. They made me comfortable in the spare guest room and she served me a meal of sausage and mash.

John had arranged that we meet up with some girls and go dancing at the Mecca Ballroom in Aldershot, and so we ordered a cab. At the Mecca we met up with a girl he knew called Irene and her friend Brenda who, it was arranged, would be my date for the night. Irene was a fabulous girl, full of fun and vitality. However, she was one of life's rebels and didn't give a toss about anything or anyone - especially the police! She had several serious motoring convictions and fines for crimes outstanding. Whenever the police caught her, she never bothered turning up at court or paying her fines, so they were always chasing her. It seems that Irene was married to a truck-driver who was presently delivering a load somewhere in Europe, but she straight away made it plain to John that he would be sharing her bed tonight.

We didn't do much dancing that night. We stayed by the bar in the Mecca and got drunk. Brenda was passably attractive in a prissy kind of way, and for want of anything better to do, I made a move on her. However, I found her rather standoffish and her body language told me that she wanted to be courted and wooed, but I couldn't be bothered. Thank the Lord for beer!

Irene had consumed far too much drink. However, she insisted on driving Brenda home in her red mini. I sat in the back seat as drunk as a skunk, and John rode shotgun in the passenger seat. After dropping Brenda, we continued towards Irene's house in the village of Hartley Whitney, with

Irene weaving all over the road and taking sharp bends almost on two wheels!

As we pulled up outside her house, her vehicle was suddenly surrounded by several police cars with blue flashing lights and sirens wailing. She was dragged out, arrested for multiple motoring offences and unpaid fines, and put into the back of a police car. Torches were shone into the mini, and I was apparently asked for my name, but I was far too drunk to understand what the police were saying. John was just about sober enough to give his name. The police took notes, and satisfied that we were simply a pair of drunkards, drove off with their target – the incorrigible Irene!

On the Sunday morning John had a starring role in the 'News of the World' newspaper. The front page headline said that Irene had been arrested for numerous motoring crimes and had been carted off to the women's prison at Holloway. Important news must have been thin on the ground on that Sunday, because this was hardly groundbreaking headlines. But the newspaper did reveal that Irene was pregnant with a child not thought to be her husband's. She must have got herself a very good lawyer, because he made capital of the fact that she was banged-up whilst expecting, even though dozens of women in prison were similarly pregnant. The press made a meal of it, and the local MP even got involved. She was later released due to being pregnant.

When the article got to the arrest, the newspaper stated that the other occupants of the red mini were a Mr John Sheppard and "an unknown drunken man." Hey - fame at last!

⚓

Our big problem was lack of transport, which meant that we couldn't get ourselves to where the damsels hung out. So, as we sat around the kitchen table, John suggested that we share the cost of buying a motor car. John had a driving licence. I on the other hand couldn't even drive. I suggested that we should both pay for fuel and running costs, but if we parted company, then he should reimburse my share of the initial cost of the vehicle, to which he agreed. Tom Sheppard sat at the kitchen table puffing on his pipe and stayed silent.

The next day we went to a car showroom and bought a second hand Austin Mini; and our love lives improved drastically. For the next two weeks we had ourselves a wonderful time chasing and bedding girls. But alas, all good things come to an end. After paying for half the cost of the car I was almost broke and needed to go back to sea, whereas John was an only child on whom his father doted. As we ate supper I broached the subject of repaying back my half.

Tom Sheppard bristled with anger and asked how dare I expect to get back what I had paid? Didn't I understand that cars depreciate in value? He put forward a figure that was about one tenth of what I had forked out. Yes I agreed, cars do depreciate; but not by as much within the two weeks that we had owned it. Unaccountably, John appeared completely dominated by his father, and although he seemed unhappy with what was being proposed, he kept silent. Old Tom trotted out the fact that he had accommodated his guest completely free-of-charge; as if his guest should have paid him some rent, and likewise for the sausage and mash. Within the hour I slid my suitcase into the back of a waiting taxi and departed for Silvertown. John Sheppard was being strangled by the wishes of his father, and I wasn't to see him again for almost a year.

⚓

My niece Toni was now 13 months old and almost walking. During the following week I spent my days taking her out in her buggy, and my evenings taking my sisters out to the pub. Albert was still as busy as ever, and I helped out cleaning the bar in the Tate Institute. Throughout my week at home I told my family all about my travels, being careful to edit the raunchy tales of my love life. I couldn't spend too much time on leave because, as I had blown most of my wages on beer and women, and that damn car, so cash was tight. I hadn't paid-off with much money, so I had to find another sea-going job.

The Port Line crew offices were located in King George V Dock adjacent to the ship's regular berth. A seafarer could gain employment either by attending The Pool, and possibly be stitched up by the likes of Reggie the Rat, or go direct to the superintendant of whatever shipping line he wished to be considered for. The marine superintendant of Port Line Ltd was Mr John Aitchison, a jovial Scot who always seemed happy to get crews assigned onto their preferred ships. He found me a berth in the Port Melbourne which was departing soon on a coastal voyage, known colloquially to seamen as 'going around the land' or 'rock-dodging.'

I took my gear onboard, made myself at home in the ordinary seaman's cabin, and went to find the bosun. He was an elderly Irishman who told me that we would depart in two days time bound for a quick dry-docking in Cardiff, then back to London.

⚓

Cardiff can be a dismal place at the best of times. Cardiff in November, with gloomy fog and grey overcast skies made it a cheerless place to be. We arrived on a Wednesday, and tugs very gently guided us into the dock. Once we were inside the dry-dock, the foreman ganger took charge. Armed with a copy of the vessel's hull plan, he gave his orders to carefully position the ship over the wooden keel blocks that lined the bottom of the dock, and which would take the full weight of the ship. Once in position, long lengths of timber, much like telephone poles, were hung between the ship and the sides of the dry dock. These would take the weight when the dock was pumped out and would prevent the ship from falling over onto her side and causing great damage.

This was my first visit to Wales, and it was strange to hear the lilting accents of the Welshmen. Cardiff also had a high population of Welsh-born coloured immigrants, and it was weird to hear these black people talking just like their white cousins.

As the dry-dock was pumped out, the ship sank lower into the dock and settled onto the keel blocks. As the water receded, so men in small punts with high-pressure water lances were washing off the slime and algae from the ship's plating.

It is a known fact that a thick growth of algae and barnacles can slow a ship down drastically and add 15% -20% to her fuel consumption, so it is well worth while keeping the hull free of growth. By the time all the water was pumped out of the dock, the hull had been washed off. Tomorrow they would begin the huge task of repainting the whole of the ship's bottom and topsides. Running in tandem with the hull painting, a ship's surveyor would inspect the propeller, rudder, overside valves, cathodic protection and shell plating for any damage. If there were any problems, then we were in the right place to get them fixed. However, this was 1964 and I was only 18 years old and these were not my problems. I had no responsibilities whatsoever – so myself and a couple of the lads headed for the pub.

The Ship & Pilot pub in James Street may have improved by now. For its own sake, I sincerely hope it has. On a bleak November evening, Charlie Osborne the Peggy, myself, and my cabinmate, who had the unlikely name of Norton Caulfield, walked into the bar and ordered beers. The carpets smelt of spilt beer; the walls and curtains smelt of stale cigarette smoke; and if I wasn't mistaken - I could smell a fight brewing at the other end of the bar.

The two combatants were squaring up to each other with looks of evil aforethought. Almost on cue a bottle was smashed and the jagged end jabbed into the stomach of the larger bloke. He clutched his stomach tightly as bright red blood seeped through his fingers, and his face showed a look of utter surprise that he had been bottled. His assailant stood nearby staring at the said raggedy bottle, and equally surprised that his quick jab had caused so much blood. Bottle jousting must have been a common pastime in the pub, because the landlord came bustling along carrying a handful of spare bar-towels. "You boys want to be more careful when you're playing around," he said, quite unconcerned with the casualty's pallid appearance. He threw the bundle of towels onto the bar. "Here Boyo, go off to the toilet and clean yourself up; and watch you don't go dripping your blood all over my carpets."

An hour or so later, we had consumed several beers and were feeling quite squiffy. Two girls entered the bar and ordered rum and cokes and settled in at the next table. One could tell instantly that they were prostitutes 'on the game.' Perhaps the clue was in the revealing low-cut blouses, or maybe the very short miniskirts, or perhaps the bright crimson lipstick, or the fishnet stockings; but I suspect the answer was in the discount she offered me for "a quick fuck behind the back wall of the pub." Over the following days we had a few more visits to the Ship and Pilot. The decor wasn't up to much, but one could get seriously drunk without feeling as if you were out your league.

Back at the dry-dock, work continued with coating the ship's bottom with special paints called antifouling and boot topping. As soon as this was completed, the dock was flooded and Port Melbourne made a quick escape back to the King George V Dock in London.

The ship began loading for Australia immediately on arrival in London. We were due to stay for eleven days, then sail to Hamburg and Rotterdam to pick up more cargo, after which we would return to London to finalise loading. Norton, my new cabinmate was a nice bloke and we got on very well indeed. He was a tall blonde haired and blue-eyed guy with a ready smile who I suspected might be an instant hit with the ladies. I wondered if perhaps we would be as good a team as John Sheppard and I had been at picking up the damsels. Only time would tell.

It felt good to be back in Silvertown, and although it was often a smoky dirty place, I had missed it. It was a great time to meet up with old contacts and spend time with my family. I bumped into an old friend, Len Ficken, who had a souped-up Mini Cooper. Now, with some hot wheels to get us around, we spent many happy hours pulling girls and watching blues bands in the smoky London pubs. His parents had a seaside chalet at Leysdown-on-Sea, on the Isle of Sheppey in Kent, so Len and I drove down there. We had the place to ourselves for a long weekend and promptly pulled a couple of likely looking girls. There was just one problem. The chalet didn't offer enough privacy for all four of us to partake in any sexual shenanigans; therefore my date and I had to use the Mini Cooper. If you dear reader, have ever attempted to have sex in the back of a Mini on a freezing cold December evening, you will know that the word difficult would surely be an understatement!

On 9th December Port Melbourne left the Royal Docks and was bound up the North Sea to Hamburg, where we arrived the next evening. Unlike the stevedores in the London docks, the German's began work upon arrival, loading tons of diesel engines and generators packed in heavy wooden crates. I had been to Hamburg once before aboard the Port Pirie, but hadn't had too much cash available with which to go shoreside. Norton and I went ashore and found a bar with tables outside on the pavement; and as we sipped our lager, the sun went down to the west of the River Elbe. As I became aware of our surroundings, I noticed that all the buildings both in the neighbourhood and across the river were of modern design. It was then that I remembered that the city of Hamburg had been largely flattened by allied bombers during the war, and hardly any of the original buildings had been left standing; and so the city had been rebuilt almost from scratch.

We had a few more beers then took a water taxi to the St Pauli district. We had heard about Hamburg's thriving red-light area, and we were keen to see the place at first hand. The Reeperbahn is the main street where all the action takes place, and it was certainly an eye-opener. The streets around the Reeperbahn were crammed with bars, strip joints, night clubs, discotheques, sex-shops and prostitutes.

The Beatles, who had played in the clubs when they were an unknown band in the early 1960s, now rejuvenated the area with their fame, even though they were no longer here. We had a drink in the Star Club, which boasted that the Fab Four had found stardom within its walls. The same message was put out also at the Kaiserkeller, and the Top Ten Club, all of which festooned their walls with photos of the Boys from Liverpool. Most of the strip clubs had a beefy doorman in a smart uniform whose job, it appeared, was to literally drag potential customers off the street and into the club's front door. They were quite forceful. "Vee haff vays of making you vatch zee girls take zee clothing off, Englander."

After a few more beers Norton and I went to see the prostitutes in the Herbertstrasse, an offshoot of the Reeperbahn. The street is screened off from the prying eyes of children and respectable ladies, and a policeman was stationed at each end. This was legal prostitution. The houses would in daytime look much like any law-abiding street with their neat painted doors and polished brass doorknockers. But at night, the curtains were pulled back to reveal girls laid upon a chaise longue in erotic poses and illuminated by a red light. To me they looked quite sad characters; as if they would much rather be reading a good book than sitting here, awaiting perhaps a fat middle-aged man who would degrade them. I found it all rather dispiriting.

131

As we walked slowly up and down the street, the girls would open their window to whisper to a prospective customer what the rate for a wide variety of sex would be. Not one of the women looked to be German, but were mostly dark skinned eastern Europeans. The going rate for a quickie appeared to be the equivalent of my month's wages. I had no intention of spending good money on the services of a prostitute. Why should I do that, I reasoned, when I was getting all the girls I could handle?

Two days later we had finished loading and, after being piloted back down the winding River Elbe, we were on our way southwards to the Port of Rotterdam.

$$\downarrow$$

Rotterdam is one of the busiest ports in the world, and manoeuvring room is very restricted for big ships. Port Melbourne picked up two pilots at Maas Centre pilot station near the harbour entrance and proceeded sedately along the Nieuwe Waterweg Canal. We passed the ferry-port at Hoek van Holland where British Rail ferryboats were loading or disgorging shiploads of cars and passengers. The Nieuwe Waterweg is 25 miles in length with numerous offshoot canals and dock systems going in all directions. Scores of ships of all nations were coming and going. Large oil tankers discharged their Saudi Arabian crude oil into massive storage facilities, whilst small harbour tugs bustled with long strings of barges. The waterway links up with the Rhine and Meuse rivers, so traffic comes from all over the European canal system. Large motorised commercial barges are the lifeblood of the canal system, and dozens of them passed us on our way along the waterway. It was interesting to observe that these huge barges were, in many cases, family owned and crewed. As they motored by, the husband could be seen working out on the deck with perhaps, a small boy and the family dog for company, whilst his wife may be holding a baby, and at the same time be manoeuvring this 1000 ton monster. I was impressed by how well the barges were maintained and painted with bright glossy colours and varnished woodwork. On the deck behind the funnel, they usually parked the family car, which was lifted on and off the barge by a small hydraulic crane. In the large windows of the family accommodation I spotted softly furnished rooms with lacy gingerbread curtains and pots of flowers. It truly was a floating home-from-home. It seemed the perfect family lifestyle.

Luckily, Port Melbourne's berth was well upriver near the city centre, and as we tied up I looked about me to see the modern city streets. Much like Hamburg, there appeared to be very few old buildings, until I recalled that in 1940 the German Stuka and Heinkel bombers had flattened a greater part of the city of Rotterdam. It was a great shame, because

132

negotiations between the Dutch and German governments had already been successful to save the city from being ravaged by the marauding Luftwaffe, but due to a lack of communications, the city was blitzed unnecessarily. Rotterdam had been a beautiful city with many medieval buildings and wonderful museums, but after the bombing there was very little left standing.

Several of our deck crew had previously visited Rotterdam and I had been warned that the dances held at The Mission to Seamen could be a comical riot. I am not by nature a deeply religious person and tend to stay away from any institution that tries to ram their beliefs down one's throat. However, the Mission to Seamen is different. Although they do hold holy worship services, they also provide a huge array of assistance for seafarers in their various missions that are located worldwide. In the past I had used the missions to post letters, make phone calls, watch TV, use their library, and even have a game of ping-pong. I admired the unpaid volunteers who worked in the missions, and generally found that their chaplains and staff worked very hard to make seafarers feel right at home.

The Port of Rotterdam Mission to Seamen was understandably much larger than its counterparts in the smaller ports. It had a bar to purchase beer, a games room, a snack bar, library, and many other facilities. On this particular night the central meeting room was being used as the dance hall. Respectable young ladies were brought to the mission by coach as dancing partners for the sailors, and the elderly chaplain took his responsibilities very seriously in ensuring that the randy sailors didn't get their grubby little hands on his virginal charges.

Almost every girl was gorgeous. I don't know what it is about Dutch women, but they are mostly tall and slim with a healthy scrubbed clean look and sparkling eyes and big smiles. The fact that they are slim, I put down to nearly every Dutch person owning a bicycle. Someone once told me, "You'll never see a fat Dutchman," and I've found that to be very true. They are so fit and active because they pedal everywhere and are inordinately healthy. I personally think that Dutch girls are the sexiest looking females on earth, and this, together with their accomplished use of English, which they speak in a sensual sultry tone, I find extremely attractive.

However, I was totally unprepared for the modus operandi used by the chaplain during the weekly dances. He was stationed at one end of the dance hall, and sat up high in a tennis umpires chair. Beside him was a table on which he had a record player and a stack of the latest records. The chaplain was basically the DJ – but a DJ with a difference! As he played the music and couples danced, he would from his lofty perch, keep an eagle eye on them to ensure that they were not getting too friendly, and this was especially so during the slow smoochy numbers. If the chaplain even suspected that there was any untoward hanky-panky going on, then he would stop the music and bellow out to the whole room, "Everyone must change partners. All change your partner immediately." One had to give up the dishy girl that you were dancing with, and move onto another one who was perhaps not so pretty. The average time allotted with any dance partner was two minutes – then it was, "All change again."

It was every English sailors dream to pull one of the mission girls, but try as they might I never heard of one single sailor who had managed to have some nooky with one of the Mission Maidens. In any event they never stood a chance because at the end of the evening the chaplain rounded up the girls and counted them back onto the coach.

"Mustn't Grumble"

Three days later we returned to London, and I was back home in Silvertown. I had been away for just nine days, but I had plenty of stories to tell my family. My mum, who had never stepped foot outside of England in her life, could hardly believe the tales of my voyages around Europe. She was shocked at the stories of the clubs and the bars and the whores in the Reeperbahn, and she laughed about the two-minute dances at the mission in Rotterdam. As my mum and I sat in our living room one evening, we laughed at some of the tricks I had been getting up to on my travels. Just lately, she said, she could see a distinct change in me. She now seemed to look at me in a different light, as she realised that her little boy was growing into an adult.

I chatted to a couple of ex school-friends in a pub one day, and after telling them snippets of my exploits around the world, I asked how their lives were progressing. Their voices seemed to take on a flat monotone as they related how their mundane lives hardly changed from one week till the next. "Mustn't grumble" was a phrase repeated more than once. Compared with my fast-paced activities, their lives seemed so humdrum and boring. They both worked Monday to Friday in one of the Silvertown factories, and although they earned more than I did, they never had enough money to enjoy themselves. Both had steady girlfriends and each was engaged and saving up for a big white wedding; so having fun was not on the menu. To make matters worse, they weren't even getting much nooky, as many 'decent' English girls were brought up to practice chastity before marriage. I knew in my heart that I had made the right decision in not working in a factory, but in choosing a sea-going career that took me to some of the world's most exotic locations.

⚓

It was unusual for ships to have to go far afield to pick up a cargo as we had done in Europe. Normally, the whole cargo was loaded in the Royal Docks, but on this voyage we would also be loading in the Mediterranean on our way to the Suez Canal. As departure day approached new crew stepped onboard with their suitcases.

Our new bosun arrived aboard. Jack Franks was a tall muscular man in his late thirties who was forever singing tunes to which he would put his own dirty lyrics. There was something about him that I didn't quite trust. He seemed a bit too over-friendly with the younger boys in the deck crew, and he wasn't someone I would want to be alone with. Having said that, he was a superb seaman, and he could splice any rope or wire and rig any tackle with his eyes closed.

The deck crew were a great bunch of lads. Charlie Osborne and Norton Caulfield were returning for the deep-sea voyage and several new able seamen had just joined. Robbie Adams was from Epsom and Steve Goddard from East Anglia whilst Mick Haywood came from Leicester. They all had a great sense of humour and intent on having a good time. An old reprobate among us was George Meredith who must have been almost 70 years old, and should probably have retired years ago; but George was very fit and a damn fine seaman. He was one of those people whom you could never dislike. He was very tanned from years of being at sea, and his sparkling eyes and lop-sided grin gave him the air of a buccaneering pirate. He was full of banter and had a wonderful sense of quirky humour. He would also show the younger deckhands little nuggets of seamanship.

This was in direct contrast to our bosun who seemed to look at the young boys with lustful eyes. Whenever Jack Franks spoke to one of the younger lads, his demeanour changed as he blatantly and shamelessly ogled them. I was convinced that he thought his rank and his muscular size gave him *carte blanche* to do as he pleased. He gave me the creeps and the rest of the deck crew, a mixture of soft-spoken Hebrideans and lowland Jocks, looked upon him with distaste. A new steam queen called Blossom joined the catering department. She was a slim blonde haired waif-like figure from Essex. She straight away set about turning her nondescript cabin into a very comfy retreat with soft lighting and plenty of bright cushions and flowery curtains.

Just before Christmas most of the ship's company, except for a skeleton crew, were sent home and ordered to return after Boxing Day. I volunteered to be onboard so that the crew from further afield could get away home. The chief officer said that I need only pop aboard every day to see if I was required for anything in particular. The dock workers would also be stopping work over the Christmas period which would leave just a few days available to finish loading before departure day.

Prior to Christmas a huge floating crane, the 'Mammoth,' was manoeuvred alongside. Upon its decks were two diesel locomotives, each 50 feet long and weighing almost 70 tons apiece. Space on the foredeck had been reinforced and railway sleepers had been laid to spread the weight. Dock riggers were in attendance as the Mammoth lifted these huge behemoths onboard; and as they were placed upon the deck, the ship listed over at an alarming angle. However, the second loco was placed on the opposite side and that evened things up. The riggers then strapped them down securely and covered them with green tarpaulins and we were almost ready to go.

I went home for the festivities and enjoyed a terrific time with my family. Apart from the usual roast turkey dinner and exchange of presents, we had a superb dinner/dance held in the Tate Institute which was packed to the rafters with revellers. All my family were there of course, including aunts, uncles, and cousins, and we occupied two tables pushed together. My sister Glynis had invited along her friend Pat, a pretty girl with curly brown hair and a nice figure. Seventeen year old Pat and I were soon getting along famously and dancing to smoochy music as the lights were dimmed on the dance floor. I was never quite sure if it was the effect of the alcohol that caused her to nibble my ears, but, as we danced, Pat was getting quite turned on, and I didn't need a printed invitation to partake in some delicious extracurricular activities. My Christmas leave was turning out perfectly.

Bound for Australia

We signed articles on 30th December and sailed from King George V Dock on New Year's Eve. Once again I was signed-on as a JOS, a junior ordinary seaman. Some of the crew, especially the Jocks, grumbled that they had missed out on celebrating Hogmanay, but I figured that, as soon as we arrived in Australia, then every night would be party night.

As was usual, the Port Melbourne carried her maximum twelve passengers in luxuriously appointed staterooms located on the promenade deck, from where they had a good forward view through their cabin windows. As we sailed down channel past Folkestone, the captain sounded the alarm bells that signalled emergency boat drill, and we quickly swung the lifeboats out as if it were a real emergency and our lives depended upon it. The elderly passengers, who stood about wearing bright orange lifejackets and thick overcoats against the December chill, seemed the usual mix of well-bred upper class travellers. Gratefully there wasn't a blue rinse in sight.

As midnight came, the officer-of-the-watch sounded the ship's horn for some minutes to welcome in the New Year. It was now 1965. Being a Silvertown lad, I missed the traditional cockney way of bringing in the New Year. As midnight approached, everyone would gather out in the streets and make as much noise as humanly possible. We would bang dustbin lids together or use pots and pans or any implement that could make a cacophony of noise. The pubs and clubs would empty out and everyone would be smiling and cheering and hugging their neighbour and wishing everyone a Happy New Year. Often, someone would start dancing and a conga line would begin. Everyone would rush to join in, and one would see a long snake of happy faces as the conga wound its way around the streets. Soon after midnight, all the ships within the Royal Docks and berthed at quays in the River Thames, began sounding their fog horns. Imagine the noise as dozens of ocean-going ships all sounding their horns, each trying to outdo their neighbour. It was a wonderful way to welcome in a new year which would hopefully herald an improvement in their impoverished and underprivileged lives.

We were lucky with the weather and made good time going down channel and crossing the Bay of Biscay. Once in the Mediterranean Sea, we would be loading even more cargo at Genoa and Livorno, before heading off to the Suez Canal. Port Melbourne, with her 17 knot cruising speed, was a whole knot faster and more modern than the older Port Pirie. In place of the canvas covered cargo hatches with their time-consuming hatch-boards and tarpaulins, she was fitted with Macgregor hatches that opened and closed simply by heaving on a wire. The steel hatch lids then trundled along their track-ways into their open or closed position. Easy-peasy!

We steamed southwards, parallel to the coast of Spain and Portugal, and as we did so, the deck crew got busy overhauling the cargo handling gear. Three days later we were abeam of Cape St. Vincent lighthouse, and made our port hand turn towards the Straits of Gibraltar.

Sometime after midnight on 5th January, during the pitch dark 'graveyard watch,' the ship was passing Gibraltar and entered the Mediterranean. I was carrying out a look-out duty above the bridge deck when I noticed the navigation lights of another vessel coming towards us from the port side. I reported it to the 2nd mate who, after taking compass bearings, found that we were on a collision course and that the other vessel, whose responsibility it was to take avoiding action, hadn't altered course at all. The 2nd mate flashed an Aldis lamp at the other ship, but got no response, and she came steadily onwards on a bearing that would hit us squarely amidships and probably sink us. The captain was called to the bridge, and he ordered that our powerful searchlight be trained to shine

137

directly into the other ship's wheelhouse. We switched it on and lit up the other ship like a Christmas tree, but still got no reaction. We could however see that she was a large black painted cargo ship and thought to belong to the French Compagnie des Messageries Maritimes.

Aboard the other vessel there appeared to be no one on duty in their wheelhouse! Meanwhile it had closed the distance to a worryingly close quarter's position. Finally we could wait no longer. The captain gave a double ring on the ship's engine telegraph which meant "Full power. Give me everything you've got."

Down below in the engine room, the duty engineer quickly worked the massive twin engines up to their maximum power, and the Port Melbourne began to shudder as the stresses and strains made the ship's hull quiver. The huge phosphor bronze propellers spun faster and faster, giving the ship an extra 4 knots of speed and we began to pull away clear of the mystery vessel, but even so it passed across our stern at a mere quarter mile distance. That was much too close for comfort.

Midday on the 6th January found us south of the Balearic Island. The weather forecast was not good. Severe gale to storm force winds were due along our track within the next six hours. One doesn't usually associate storms with the Mediterranean. Normally the shore is thronged with holidaymakers lounging upon sun-kissed beaches and the sea is full of bikini clad girls and muscular men enjoying the balmy climate. But this was January, and even the Mediterranean is susceptible to inclement weather. The crew rigged lifelines along the decks and generally ensured that everything was lashed down tight. Everything was double checked. Slowly the winds picked up speed and the seas began to gain in height By late afternoon a full gale was running, with waves that smashed into our bow and threw white spray across the decks.

However, this was just a foretaste as the weather was predicted to become much worse. It was now pitch-dark and the seas had become even higher. The wind-speed had gone way beyond storm force and, at 80 knots was now classed as a hurricane. The seas piled up into massive white topped rollers that battered the ship from every angle. The captain slowed the ship down to a speed that would allow her to be steered, but hopefully prevent any damage to the vessel. The screaming of the wind as it wailed through the rigging was a wild cacophony of noise.

Inside, the accommodation was pandemonium as small objects were thrown about and crockery from a cabinet which had been ripped loose smashed into a thousand pieces. We could only hope to hold on for dear life to prevent ourselves being tossed clear across the messroom. All attempts by the galley staff at cooking any meals were forgotten, as any pots and pans on the stove were slung across the decks. Later in the evening the chef managed to make mounds of sandwiches which were much appreciated, but for now the galley was out of action. I wondered how the elderly passengers, most of whom had never been to sea before, were coping; but I was certain that their stewards would be there to look after them. We were now meeting the waves head-on. They were so enormous that the bow reared clear of the water – hung there for an eternity – and slammed back down into the trough with a resounding crash. Back at the stern, the propellers came clear out of the water, making the whole ship vibrate. The bow was being hit by such huge waves that it would rear skywards and slam down with such force that I was sure that damage was being done to the ship's structure. I certainly heard the sound of tearing metal at one stage, and thought that perhaps one of the locomotives had become loose. If that was the case then it would have caused very serious damage and would have posed a real danger with a 70 ton monster loose upon the decks. I peered through the spray lashed foredeck porthole and was gratified to see that both loco's were still in place, and gave thanks to the London riggers who had loaded them so securely.

The storm went on throughout the night, during which the whole forward part of the ship was awash as hundreds of tons of white water cascaded about the decks. Eventually, as dawn broke, the seas began to calm down as the low pressure passed over us and scudded away to the east. The wind-speed dropped and by breakfast time the engines could be put back to full speed. One of the Jocks who had been on bridge look-out duty, told us that there was damage up in the forward part of the ship. The jackstaff, a ten foot long steel pole upon which the company's house-flag is flown, had been completely bent over by the force of the waves, and the steel guardrails had been ripped away. It was thought that there was also damage to the big electric winches located on the No. 1 cargo hatch; but sea conditions still weren't ideal to send someone up forward to assess any damage.

Port Melbourne docked at the Italian port of Genoa the next afternoon, and as we steamed into the busy harbour, the sun was shining amid clear blue skies. Local welders came aboard and the damaged guardrails were cut away and new ones welded into place. The welders renewed the bent jackstaff, and by the following day the deck crew had repainted it all in gloss white, and it looked brand new once more.

What little I saw of Genoa in a short stroll ashore was a dirty city strewn with rubbish whose car drivers drove on their horns and the filthy streets were a cacophony of honking cars. Meanwhile work continued loading cargo into the holds. There wasn't much to load, just two hundred tons, which was quickly stowed away and we sailed that night.

Port Melbourne (Port Line Ltd) 10,470 gross tons

The next morning we entered the Tuscan port of Livorno, and began loading more cargo bound for Melbourne. In the afternoon we got an early job-and- knock, and so Norton, Charlie Osborne and I caught the bus into the historic city of Pisa, just 12 miles away. Of course no visit to Pisa would be complete without going to see the Leaning Tower.

We made ourselves comfortable in a cafe just across the road from the famous tower. I found it most disconcerting to look up and see the 183 foot tower leaning towards us at such an acute angle, that it seemed about to come crashing through the window at any moment. I picked up a free information brochure and found that the tower was actually the bell tower (or campanile) for the nearby cathedral and had started to be built in 1173.

It was a pleasant afternoon, so we had a stroll around the cathedral in the *Piazza del Duomo,* after which we made our way along *Via Roma* to the River Arno. We had a beer at a decent pavement cafe and watched the pretty dark haired office girls go walking by, then caught the bus back to the ship.

Port Melbourne departed Livorno two days later bound for the Suez Canal, but first we had to proceed southwards down the coast of Italy and through the Straits of Messina on the toe of Italy's boot. The January mornings were chilly as we steamed down the Tyrrhenian Sea past Rome and Naples, and as we drew near the volcanic Lipari Islands, located to the north of Sicily, the 3000 foot high Stromboli reared out of the sea belching smoke from its almost constant volcanic eruptions. Three hours later, we entered the narrow Straits of Messina between the Sicilian city of Messina and Reggio on the Italian mainland. As the ship passed through the confined waters of the straits and set a direct course for Suez, a much larger volcano could be seen forty miles away on the starboard bow. It was the 11,000 foot Mount Etna, the largest active volcano in Europe, and generally in a constant state of activity, as it was at this moment. It spewed grey volcanic ash up into the atmosphere which was then whisked away on the winds.

The Heavy Gang

Work on the cargo-handling gear carried on. I often worked with Mick Haywood, Robbie Adams and Steve Goddard. We were getting so slick at being hauled aloft in a bosun's chair, unbolting the cargo blocks, lowering them to the deck for maintenance, then re-bolting them back up on the mast, that the rest of the crew called us 'The Heavy Gang.' The cargo gear had to be stringently overhauled so as to satisfy the Australian Stevedores Union, who ensured that every piece of cargo equipment that their members would use was certificated and up-to-date as regards maintenance.

The weather vastly improved as we neared the Suez Canal, and it was warm enough to wear just shorts and T-shirt. I found myself working with the elderly George Meredith, who was such an accomplished seaman, that he taught me more in a week than I had learnt in my entire three months at the Vindicatrix. George was a happy character who always had a cheeky grin and was such an easy-going individual. However, on one particular afternoon, when the deck crew were having smoko together on the foredeck, George had a scowl upon his face.

"What's up, George?" I asked. "You look a bit down in the mouth." He indicated the bosun sitting upon the hatch-lid just thirty feet across the deck. He was seated next to Charlie Osborne the young peggy, and whispering in his ear. Charlie didn't look at all happy with whatever Jack Franks was saying to him, and he seemed even unhappier when the bosun laid his hand on his thigh.

"Graham, I'm bloody sure that bastard Franks is a bum-bandit," said George. "Look at him. Poor Charlie doesn't know what to do with himself."

I agreed. "The trouble is, George, that unless Charlie makes a complaint, then there's not much you can do about it, is there?"

"Suppose not," said George unhappily.

"I'll have a quiet word with Charlie later," I promised.

After our evening meal I had a chat with Charlie. The poor lad's mind was in turmoil. "The bosun said he wants to teach me the Morse code. He said he'll teach me in his cabin. I don't wanna be alone with him, Gra. I'm supposed to be there right now. What the hell am I gonna do?" he said desperately.

I thought for a second. "Charlie, go sit in my cabin and stay there, okay? Franks won't come looking for you there. If he says anything later, just say that you've changed your mind about learning the Morse code." Charlie went off like a man saved from the hangman's noose. He had no more problems from Franks for the next week or so, but I noticed that our bosun was paying an inordinate amount of attention to Miles, one of the young catering boys. Although I was fairly certain that Jack Franks was a predatory bum-bandit, it was a hard fact to prove. If anyone cared to report the powerfully built bosun to a senior officer, then Franks could simply say that he was trying to help the lad become a better seaman with some private coaching. The nub of the problem was that, unless he attempted to sexually force himself upon someone, then he was in the clear. But by then it would be too late.

Meanwhile the Port Melbourne reached the Suez Canal and we prepared to steam through on that afternoon's southbound convoy. At Port Said our pilot came aboard, together with his entourage of boatmen, who would run mooring lines ashore when we entered the Bitter Lakes, and a gang of 'electricians' who rigged the heavy searchlight hung high up on the bow. Once the ship was underway, the pilot's helpers usually set up shop on deck to sell cheap souvenirs, fake papyrus, pen knives, brass pyramids, and stuffed camels.

Pilotage was compulsory to transit the canal, and a ship's passage was made rather easier if the pilot received a gift of a carton of Marlboro cigarettes. To ensure that there were no hold-ups whatsoever, it was always best to additionally give him a bottle of Scotch whisky. I'm quite sure that these bribes were simply a fact of life, and a cheap means with which to overcome any potential problems caused by over-zealous officials. It was most probably written off in the company's accounts as "for services rendered."

Many of our passengers, who apart from quick forays ashore when in Genoa and Livorno, now came out on deck to view the sights. No doubt there were plenty of odd and strange things for them to see. Among the passengers were a young doctor and his wife, on their way to make a new life in Victoria, a Scottish civil engineer and his wife, and a priest who was travelling to serve in a diocese in New South Wales. The doctor, who as usual was signed-on as ship's surgeon, was an official crew member and kept a regular surgery for an hour each morning, when he could be found in the ship's tiny one-bed sick bay. The rest of the day was his own to do as he pleased.

As Port Melbourne entered the canal, we passed the statue of Ferdinand de Lesseps, the French diplomat who had planned and accomplished the building of the canal which opened in 1869. On the waterfront of Port Said was the world famous department store of Simon Artz with its art deco and ornate exterior. As we glided past the city, one could smell spices and incense and other odours of the Middle East, and from the towering minarets, the loudspeakers stridently summoned the believers of Islam to attend prayers. The transit of the canal took all day and a part of the night, but by late evening, we had disembarked the pilot and his gang, and were steaming at full speed down the Red Sea and bound for Aden.

⚓

Our voyage southwards along the Red Sea was full to the brim with spectacular sights and scenery. On the starboard side were the high mountain ranges of the Nubian Desert, and a day later, we were sailing past the mountainous coastal regions of Sudan and Ethiopia. Far over the horizon on the port side were the deserts of Saudi Arabia. The dolphins, as if on cue, leapt out of the water and played in our bow-wave, and flying fish furiously flapped their wing-like fins to propel them 100 yards or more across the water. Every day brought sights of exotic sea creatures such as turtles, manta rays, sharks, and sea-snakes, and all the while the sun shone down mercilessly. I was in seventh heaven.

At Aden we tied up to an offshore buoy, and a bunker barge came alongside to replenish our fuel tanks. The Port Melbourne had an enormous diesel fuel capacity of 2800 tons which was stowed low down in the ship's double-bottom storage tanks. Further wing tanks and ready-use tanks were located in the engine room. The ship guzzled some 52 tons of diesel every day at full speed, which meant she used over two tons every hour! On the two week voyage from London; our engines had therefore gulped down over 700 tons of fuel.

We cast off and set an easterly course for Cape Gaurdafui on the Horn of Africa. With a 6445 nautical mile passage ahead of us, it would take 16 days to sail to Melbourne. This would be the longest leg of the voyage. One day later we passed the cape and set a south easterly course for Cape Leeuwin in Western Australia.

The days passed by, each much like the day before. Decks got painted, masts were painted, bulkheads were painted, and there was always the never-ending holystoning. The Equator came and went with the usual mix of first-timers entering King Neptune's domain. Charlie Osborne, Miles Bentley the catering boy, and two young cadets were among the noviciates who received the obligatory dousing with foam, flour, and galley slops, followed by an official looking certificate from the captain.

A week after we had departed from Aden, the Port Melbourne was sailing through smooth and balmy seas. We had just passed across the equator in the Indian Ocean when news came, on Sunday 24th January, of the death of Sir Winston Churchill. He had suffered a stroke nine days previously, and hadn't regained consciousness before he died at home in London. He was 90 years old, and would always be remembered as an historic Englishman. He was first elected to parliament as the MP for Oldham back in 1900, and went on to serve as Britain's wartime prime minister 1940 – 1945 and again 1951 – 1955. Only ill health forced him to retire from politics in 1964. Port Melbourne flew her Red Duster at half-mast until the day of his funeral at St. Pauls Cathedral. Sir Winston was given a state funeral in which his casket was borne along a stretch of the Thames aboard a launch. As his mortal remains were piped onboard, the crane-drivers at nearby Hays Wharf dipped their cranes jibs in salute to this most English of Englishmen. Sir Winston was laid to rest in the family plot at Bladon in Oxfordshire, near Blenheim Palace where he was born in 1874.

One evening I went to have a look around the engine room. The Port Melbourne was fitted with two 6-cylinder Doxford diesel engines which drove twin phosphor-bronze screws. They gave the ship a service speed of 17 knots, which could be increased to 20 knots in an emergency. From the upper catwalk I looked down on the huge engines, each as big as a bungalow. I had never been in a ship's engine room before and I was surprised at the level of noise down there. It was very loud indeed. The decibel level was off the scale!

I descended the ladder so that I was right next to the big diesels. My ears were ringing with the cacophony of noise and I began to wonder how the engineering staff could work in such conditions.

The duty engineer and a stoker were standing at the engine control position and appeared to be having a normal conversation. I was just three feet away and couldn't hear one word of what they were saying. It was only when I noticed that they were wearing ear defenders that I realised they were probably lip-reading!

They handed me a spare pair of ear defenders and I had a cursory look around the rest of the machinery spaces. At the rear of the Doxford engines I watched the propeller shafts as they spun around at two revolutions per second. The thick steel shafts, each as wide as a man's torso, ran from the engine room and along the shaft tunnel to the very stern of the ship – a distance of some 150 feet – until it connects up to the propellers.

The typical engine room of a ship is crammed full with all manner of engines, electricity generators, fuel pumps, water pumps, oil pumps, compressed air motors, compressors, fuel separators and much much more. And everywhere there is pipework - miles of it that reached into every nook and cranny.

I decided that working in a ship's engine room definitely wasn't for me. I wouldn't be able to endure the noise. Much better to be a deckie. In any case, you don't get suntanned working in an engine room!

Medical Emergency

With four days to go before we were due to sight the coast at Cape Leeuwin, Mick Haywood was taken sick. The duty watchman found him looking pasty and with stomach pains when he had gone to awaken him for duty. Doctor Ian Forsythe was called, and he carried out an examination. Mick was by this time feeling nauseous and vomiting. In an ideal world the doctor would have given Mick a blood test, a urine test, and an x-ray to determine the cause of his illness, but the Port Melbourne carried none of these testing facilities. However, with the clear symptoms that Mick was exhibiting, the doctor was fairly certain what the problem was. With a rapidly worsening fever, and a lower right abdomen that was tender and sensitive to the touch, the prognosis was that Mick had acute appendicitis. The ship's medical kit and facilities was fairly basic, and certainly not geared to the doctor carrying out an appendectomy operation upon the messroom table. Mick would require the services of a surgeon and a trained theatre staff which would be available only in a hospital. Doctor Forsythe had Mick transferred to the sick-bay and gave him medications to alleviate his pain and fever. He then went off to see Captain Forster.

145

The captain was advised of the symptoms, prognosis, treatment, and possible outcomes. The appendix, he was told, is a pouch-like structure located at the junction of the small and large intestine in the lower right abdomen, and normally measures approximately 4 inches long. It doesn't have any proper function in the human body, but is thought to have had a purpose for its existence in ancient or prehistoric humans, such as digesting leaves or vegetable matter. If the appendix suffers an inflammation and becomes enlarged, then that's where the problems begin. The correct treatment normally consists of a surgical operation to remove the appendix, called an appendectomy, after which, if acute appendicitis is treated quickly, the recovery rate is usually good. The keyword is rapid treatment. If it is not treated quickly, then the enlarged appendix may rupture and the patient may suffer peritonitis, with which he could then suffer shock, renal failure, and death. It's a potentially life-threatening situation, and if untreated, the mortality rate is high.

The captain thanked the doctor and called the radio officer to the bridge. Meanwhile he measured distances off the chart to the nearest port to disembark their patient. The radio officer, usually referred to as 'Sparks,' came onto the bridge with notepad in hand, ready to copy a signal. News on a ship travels fast, and everyone by now knew of Mick Haywood's plight and his fight for life.

"I'm declaring a medical emergency," said the captain. "Contact Western Australia Department of Health in Perth, and a copy to WA Coastguard," he went on. "Signal reads – From Port Melbourne. Have 20 year old male patient suffering acute appendicitis. Doctor onboard concurs diagnosis. Require emergency medical evacuation (MedEvac) soonest. Suggest disembark Albany. ETA (Estimated time of arrival) 14:00 hours 30th January 1965. Message ends."

Sparky hurried off to his radio room where he began tapping out the long signal in Morse Code. He got a response via Perth coast radio station, logged it in his record book, and returned to the bridge to report to the captain.

Meanwhile Captain Forster called up the chief engineer who came to the bridge wearing his pristine white overalls. "Good morning, Chief. You've obviously heard of the problem we've got with young Haywood?" The chief nodded. "I need all the speed you can give me. It doesn't matter what it costs in extra fuel. Give me the extra speed, but without shaking the old girl to pieces, okay chief?" Derek Parnell, our chief engineer went off to the engine room, and within a few minutes the whole ship began to vibrate as the massive 12,200 hp 6-cylinder Doxford diesels spun the twin

146

propellers faster and faster until Port Melbourne was cutting through the Indian Ocean swells at over 20 knots.

Meanwhile, in the sick-bay, Mick's condition was fairly stable. Doctor Forsythe was treating him with antibiotics and tablets to relieve the pain, but if his condition worsened, then we could only pray that we could get him to a hospital in time. Several times a day Mick could receive visitors, most of whom good-naturedly accused Mick of being a malingerer and a slacker. Mick knew just how serious his situation actually was, so simply gave a weak grin and a two-fingered salute in return.

Three hours before dawn on the 30th the ship rounded Cape Leeuwin, and by midday the Port Melbourne anchored in Albany Harbour. The harbour masters launch came alongside with a doctor and two paramedics onboard. Mick was loaded onto a stretcher and taken down the gangway and onto the launch, followed by his suitcase into which someone had packed fresh clothes. He was expected to go into the operating theatre that very afternoon, and would be a minimum of ten days recuperating on the ward. The whole crew lined the rails to give him a good send-off, and there were many ribald remarks to wish him 'God Speed.' Most were along the lines of, "Don't shag too many nurses." Shortly afterwards, Port Melbourne had weighed anchor and was heading eastbound through the Great Australian Bight - bound for Melbourne.

Jumbo Rigging

On arrival at Melbourne the deck crew's first task after topping up the cargo derricks and opening the hatches, was to rig the jumbo derrick. The jumbo is an extra large derrick which is clamped to the foremast in a vertical position and has a heavy lift capacity; in our case 77 tons. There was no heavy lift shore-side crane available in the port, so we would be using the ship's equipment to offload the two 70 ton diesel locomotives secured on the foredeck.

It took us two days to rig the giant jumbo derrick. Heavy-duty blocks and tackles and thick lifting wires all had to be rigged by seamen going aloft in bosun's chairs so as to bolt the unwieldy gear in place; and it was no easy task. This is where Jack Franks showed his mettle as a knowledgeable seaman. He knew exactly what to do and how to organize his crew. Franks was in a jovial and ebullient mood as he coordinated his crew with the various rigging tasks. He was in his element. His songs with dirty lyrics just got filthier.

During the afternoon Charlie Osborne brought a tray of tea and tab-nabs out on deck for the crew's smoko, and work stopped while we relaxed for a break. The deck crew were sat atop No. 2 cargo hatch drinking and

147

smoking when Franks came over and joined us. He sat next to young Charlie, and quite openly and blatantly began rubbing his hand up and down the lad's bare thigh. "You're a beautiful boy. I'm gonna have you tonight," he chuckled. Poor Charlie went red-faced and was clearly embarrassed. Franks thought it was hilarious and grabbed a chunk of the boy's buttocks and squeezed him tightly. "Ooh you've got such a lovely arse, Charlie," chortled Franks. "I'm gonna have myself a piece of that soon enough." The bosun obviously thought his overtly homosexual antics were funny and acceptable, but I could see from the looks on the faces of the crew that they didn't share Franks' attempt at camp banter. No one laughed. Franks body rippled with muscle and he exuded a silent undercurrent of violence. Even though he hadn't actually threatened anyone, it was always there. I looked across at George Meredith. He was staring pure venom at Franks, and if looks could kill then he would be a dead man.

I'm not sure what made me go along to Charlie's cabin that evening; but as I got to the door, I could hear a subdued voice coming from inside. I knocked, and without waiting for an answer, stepped inside. Charlie was sat on the bench seat - and looked petrified. Sat next to him, with his hand upon Charlie's thigh, was Jack Franks. Our bosun didn't look at all pleased to see me, as I was clearly upsetting his plans to have his wicked way with the innocent fresh-faced teenager. Franks had a book of Morse code and a torch beside him as evidence that he was here to tutor the 16-year old in the finer points of ship signalling.
"Hi - what are you doing?" I asked Charlie pointlessly.
"I'm trying to teach Charlie the Morse code," interjected Franks, "and we need some peace and quiet because we need to concentrate." He was clearly sending me a message - Fuck off!
I couldn't care less what he thought. I parked myself firmly onto the spare bunk and brazenly stared at him. "In that case I'll just keep you company. You can teach me as well, can't you?"
Franks silently harrumphed to himself but he knew he was beaten. He gathered up his things. "We'll continue your studies at some other time Charlie," he said as he went out the door. Charlie's face was a picture as he grinned from ear-to-ear. "Thank Christ you arrived on the scene," he said gratefully. "The bosun was just suggesting that we switch the cabin lights off. He said it was so that we could see the signals from the torch."

The next morning George Meredith told me that, late last night, he had seen Franks doggedly ferreting about the accommodation as if on a quest. He had become suspicious when the bosun had gone off in the direction of the stewards' cabins on the opposite side of the ship. A short while later, George had almost collided with Miles, the effeminate looking catering boy, as he came out of the shower room. The young lad appeared to have tears welling up in his eyes, but before George could ask any questions, Miles dived into his cabin and slammed the door.

During the course of the morning we unloaded the two locomotives in what was a potentially dicey procedure. Because of the complexity of the operation, which involved the possible negative stability of the vessel, the captain and chief officer were on hand to oversee the discharge of this important cargo. However, Jack Franks took charge of the actual mechanics of the task, and to give him his due, it all went off faultlessly. As each loco was lifted, and the weight transferred to the head of the jumbo derrick, the ship's centre of gravity lessened dramatically, and she listed over at an alarming angle towards the quayside, where two heavy duty transporters were awaiting.

The chief officer was extremely pleased with the offloading and gave us the rest of the day off. Tomorrow we would have the task of de-rigging the jumbo and stowing away the equipment in the forward bosun's store. But tomorrow was another day.

All the deck crew descended en-masse to Chloe's Bar that hot afternoon. It was the first time the entire deck crew had been ashore together, and it was a terrific feeling of camaraderie. The only person missing was Mick Haywood, who wasn't due to be rejoining Port Melbourne for another few days. We had heard via the ship's agent that Mick's appendectomy had gone well, and that he was presently recuperating. We all threw some money into a kitty, known as a tarpaulin muster, and the barman filled our jugs with beer. The Heavy Gang were on the booze!

Fortunately our beloved bosun got the message, and didn't attempt to tag along. If he had foisted himself upon us, then our booze up would have been a much different affair, with an atmosphere one could cut with a knife. As sunset approached, the 6-o-clock swill got underway and we intensified the drinking and were halfway to getting legless. George was worse for wear and had to be helped back aboard by Robbie and Steve and Angus, one of the Jocks. Norton and I purchased some beer and we began walking back to the ship. On the way, we spotted two pretty girls sitting on a bench, and because we were quite merry, we asked them if they would like to come to a party on the ship.

Back onboard, we took the girls around to Blossom's, who could usually be found with a party going on. Sure enough, there was the sound of blues music and the smell of joss sticks as we came to her cabin. She was similar to Christine aboard the Port Pirie, in that her cabin was an open house, and anyone could usually just drop in. There were already a couple

149

of pantry stewards and their girls there, so Blossom's cabin quickly filled up. My girl was called Natalie, and we made ourselves at home on the top bunk and drank cans of beer. The other girl, with whom Norton was paired up, was called Suzanne. Blossom was dressed outrageously in a bright yellow top and sequined ski-pants with a pair of gold lame mules on her feet. Natalie and I chatted about this and that, and generally flirted with each other. I impetuously asked her if she would like to see my cabin and she nodded eagerly.

As soon as Natalie and I were alone, I put some music on the record player and took her into my arms and kissed her. She was slim and above average height, with long black hair and dark eyes, which added to her attractiveness. "Will Suzanne know where I am?" she asked. I told her that Norton would tell her, and it put her mind at rest. I kissed her neck and her ears and our tongue's searched out for each other before intermingling in a lovely deep kiss.

I manoeuvred her into the bed and silently removed her clothes. I slid in alongside and held this beautiful woman into the contours of my body. The music seemed to go on forever as we made long slow love within the confines of the narrow bunk. Later, we lay spent on our sides in the spoons position and dozed with my arm thrown over her hip, and feeling the warmth of her slim body next to mine. The next morning Norton and I took the girls ashore to the cab rank and kissed them goodbye before returning aboard to grab breakfast and start work.

The remainder of our stay in port was taken up with de-rigging the jumbo gear and painting around the promenade deck. Three days later Mick Haywood was flown in from Albany and was glad to be back onboard, but the chief officer instructed the bosun to keep him on light duties for the next week.

During the two weeks that the ship was in Melbourne, Natalie and Suzanne would come aboard most evenings, and after a few drinks, we would cram ourselves into the narrow bunk bed and try to make love noiselessly, but could only manage to start giggling. Up above in the top bunk, Norton and Susanne were attempting to do the same thing. Life was one long laugh. On some nights Norton and I would sleep ashore at their two bedroom apartment. They rented the top half of a two-storey clapboard house with a veranda in a leafy street in the suburb of Fitzroy.

On one particular night towards the end of our stay, I went alone to their house because Norton was secretly getting bored with the relationship, and had arranged with Suzanne not to meet tonight, but to have a night off. When I got there, Suzanne met me at the door. She was dressed in loose ski pants and a red knitted sweater. She had just come out the shower, because her face was shiny clean and her hair was still damp. "Natalie's not here," she said. "She's had to go to see her father, whose been taken ill. She said to tell you she's sorry." She poured us both a glass of wine and I sat in one of the leather sofas. She brought the bottle over and joined me. "I don't think she'll be back at all tonight because her folks live out in Geelong and the bus service is terrible." I must have looked disappointed, because she said, "Just because she's not here doesn't mean you've got to leave, does it? You can stay for a while, can't you?" She smirked. "You can stay the night if you want to, couldn't you?" The implication seemed crystal clear, but I still didn't make any move on her. She shrugged and got up and went to the kitchen to open a second bottle. My mind was in turmoil, and I wasn't sure s how to react. Suzanne was a very pretty and sexy looking girl, and I would be untruthful if I said that I didn't fancy her. Anyway, this was only ever going to be a transient fling that would last just as long as the ship remained in Melbourne. This was never going to be a long-term affair. Furthermore, we were due to sail in two days and would probably never see the girls again, so no harm done.

I made up my mind and went to the kitchen, where Suzanne was standing at the sink struggling to open the wine bottle. I came up behind her and slipped my arms around her midriff. She tilted her face around and we kissed with a forbidden passion. I slipped my hands under her loose sweater and happily found that she wasn't wearing a bra. I took her hand. "Come on, I'm taking you to bed," I said, and she followed me submissively to her bedroom. I peeled back the bedcover, but she had other ideas and yanked my arm in another direction. "Let's go out on the veranda," she suggested. "It can be much more exciting, don't you think?" It was still warm even though the sun had set three hours ago. I wrapped my arms around her and gave her a long passionate kiss. She responded as if she were a wild animal. She moaned and squirmed and rubbed herself against me in the manner of a lioness in oestrus that is trying to sexually attract her mate. "Do it to me out here," she whispered urgently, and we made love outside in the warm open-air. Again during the night, as the urge of desire overtook us, she insisted that we leave the warm bed and have sex alfresco. This was a new experience for me, and I must admit that I found it strangely exciting.

The Mind of a Pervert

Port Melbourne sailed at midday on Wednesday bound for Sydney. The voyage would take a day and a half. As we cleared Port Phillip Bay and disembarked the pilot, the course was set for Wilson's Promontory 115 miles away to the eastwards. The ship reached the rocky promontory just after sunset at 18:00 hours, and then altered onto a north-easterly course

151

towards Cape Howe. The wind was blowing from the south, with sea conditions of moderate swells. It was not enough to cause any real problems, but sufficient that the ship could roll and pitch.

During the evening, the bosun had sat in the petty officers' mess with the ship's carpenter, the lamp-trimmer and engine-room storekeeper. As was his usual habit, he drank a half bottle of rum and coke. Sometime after 22:00 he went out on deck to get a breath of fresh air and to clear his head to prepare for the day ahead. The ship would arrive in Sydney in the early hours of Friday, and he wanted to be one jump ahead of the chief officer, who was certain to ask how the crew were to be employed. The ship's side required a fresh coat of paint, which entailed seamen going over the side on painting stages to apply gallons of grey paint. It was a big undertaking; one that would take the best part of three days. There would be a lot of work to do, and he mentally ticked off the equipment that would be required, and who would carry out what task.

Jack Franks promised himself a night ashore next week. He was looking forward to it with barely suppressed anticipation. He knew a club in the red-light district of Kings Cross in Sydney that he had visited on a previous voyage and his mind mentally visualised the layout of the gay bar where rent boys hung out. He had used rent boys on other occasions, and he liked the way in which he could do as he pleased with them; bugger them senseless if he wanted to. But what he really preferred was to tie them up and smack them about a bit. He recalled the last rent boy he had used. It had accidentally got messy when he slapped him too hard and he'd screamed blue murder. He had disappeared from the cheap hotel room a bit sharpish, because the boy was screaming his lungs out. The problem with rent boys was that they cost too much money. That last one had demanded payment up front, and it had cost him more than two weeks wages. What he really wanted, he mused, was a virgin, a genuine unused cherry boy, and not one of those soiled sluts from the gay bar. If he could just get his hands on one of the boys onboard the ship. He pondered on how it would feel to have young Charlie Osborne, or perhaps the girlie looking Miles, captive in his bunk whilst he buggered him forcefully. He remembered how, just a few evenings ago, he had almost got Charlie into his clutches, but his pal had come blundering into the cabin and queered his pitch. He had cornered the catering boy in the shower room that same night, and he'd almost forced the boy to fellate him, but the silly bugger had started to cry, and ran away. He leant on the starboard side guardrail and watched the waves slip by. A grim smirk played on his lips as he remembered when he had last lured a young boy into his cabin. It had been on a voyage last year aboard another ship. The kid had actually thought he was there for Morse code tuition. Franks smiled as he clearly recalled the tears in the boy's frightened eyes as he had pinned his wrists down and slid his large penis between the boy's buttocks.

John (Jack) Alfred Franks, 38 years old, born Chelmsford, Essex, heard nothing as the man moved silently up behind him out of the darkness. His mind was busy fantasizing about sodomising Charlie Osborne, and perhaps smacking him about for awhile, when the unknown man reached down, grabbed Franks' ankles, and heaved upwards. In the space of two seconds, Franks' body tipped over the guardrail as he lost his equilibrium, and apart from briefly making a grab for a handrail, his arms flailed as he went over the ship's side. A half second later his body hit the water and he was taken rapidly astern as the Port Melbourne steamed onwards at 17 knots. He hadn't even had time to scream!

It wasn't until after 08:00 the next morning that Jack Franks was reported missing. A very thorough top-to-bottom search of the ship was ordered, which of course discovered nothing. His colleague's in the petty officers' mess reported to Captain Forster that the bosun had left the messroom sometime about 22:00, after consuming a half bottle of rum. The captain decided that due to the long period of time that Franks would have been in the water, the ship would not be turned around to search for his body. The sea conditions were such that, anybody who fell into the sea would have quickly been overwhelmed by the sizeable waves. In addition, this part of the Tasman Sea was infested with sharks, including the savage Bull Shark, and that had been a further consideration as to the bosun's chances of survival. Captain Forster ordered Sparks to send a signal to the NSW Coastguard and to Port Line head offices in London and Sydney. Another signal to all ships in the vicinity to keep a sharp lookout was made via VHF radio. Finally the captain made a full entry in the ship's official logbook.

On arrival at Sydney, the Police, Coastguard, Ship's Agent, and Port Line Operations Manager came aboard to receive further information. All went up into the captain's suite where he gave a statement and made another entry into the official logbook.

The deck crew went en-masse to Monty's Bar, where we consumed oodles of beer and talked about the key topic of conversation on everyone's lips; the death of Jack Franks. Not one of the crew believed that he had accidentally fallen overboard, and no one was saddened by his death. The sea conditions last night were not all that bad, and the ship had hardly rolled or pitched much at all. Franks had only consumed the same amount that he drank every night, so it's not as if he was staggering drunk.

"So, hands up, who pushed him over the side then?" I asked.

153

"Someone pushed him, that's for sure," said Steve Goddard seriously. "Tell me who it was and I'll buy him a drink," said Robbie Adams. "He was an arsehole, and every one of us hated his guts, didn't we?" We all nodded.

"He was an arse bandit. It was as plain as day. He deserved whatever he got," said Mick Haywood.

I noticed that the three people whom I would have thought hated him the most, Charlie Osborne, Miles Bentley, and George Meredith, all stayed silent. Whoever it was that pushed Jack Franks over the side, I couldn't condemn him. Although I had no proof, I was quite sure that Franks was a predatory homosexual of the worst kind. Earlier I had spoken to Blossom about Franks' variety of homosexuality. A few years ago, Franks had been bosun aboard a ship upon which Blossom had been a steward, and she knew for a fact that he had routinely sodomised a young catering boy, whom he had then intimidated into keeping silent. She had said that anyone who practises rape and violence upon young boys was hated by everyone, especially in the camp community.

As the days went by, Jack Franks was quickly forgotten as a bad memory. The captain had called the lamp-trimmer, Eric Roberts, to his cabin and immediately promoted him to the post of bosun. The lamp-trimmer is a petty officer who, in the days before electric lamps aboard ship, maintained all the oil lamps and trimmed the wicks, especially the navigation lamps. Nowadays, he is the bosun's right hand man and is basically the deck storekeeper who is responsible for the paint, rope, tools, general deck stores, and the rope and wire splicing. Eric was well liked by the crew because he always had a smile and a cheery word, and in addition, he was an excellent seaman. He was a good choice.

Death of the Aborigines

The cargo discharge went on day-after-day, and as thousands of tons of goods were unloaded, the ship rose further out of the water. We would soon be ready to sail to New Zealand to begin loading our cargo of dairy produce and wool.

One Saturday afternoon there was no cargo work going on, and so I set out to have a leisurely stroll around the city. The sun was hot and muggy and there were dense clouds on the horizon. As I wandered through Sydney's Hyde Park the clouds drew overhead and the sky darkened. Rain began to come down, lightly at first, but quickly turned into a heavy downpour. This was quite normal in the Antipodes when high levels of rainfall would bucket down; especially further north in Queensland where it was known as 'The Wet', but it was also quite common further south.

I crossed into Macquarie Street and dived into the State Library of New South Wales to take shelter. By now the rain was slanting down like the proverbial stair-rods, and so I strolled through the marbled hallways and reading rooms to find something interesting to while away the time of my enforced visit. Dotted here and there was display cabinets of polished wood and glass, within which were various exhibits. I peered into one cabinet and came upon a very old newspaper, dated September 1838, and I began to read the stories on the front page. The news dealt mainly with the coronation of Queen Victoria on 28th June 1838, and showed an image of the state coach escorted by mounted soldiers and lancers. Another image showed the young 18 year old Victoria with the crown upon her head and an orb in her hand. It was all very interesting, but not enough to grab my attention for more than a few minutes.

I was about to stroll on to some other exhibits when something caught my eye in the bottom right hand corner of the newspaper. The story was barely three column inches. "Aborigines becoming a nuisance," it said, and I began to read the story written 127 years ago.

"From our correspondent: Police in NSW have recently been kept busy keeping the aborigines in check. On 28 January 1838 a detachment of Sydney mounted police was despatched by Acting Governor-General Colonel Kenneth Snodgrass. They attacked an encampment of Kamilaroi people at Waterloo Creek NSW and official reports indicated between 80 and 120 killed. Major James Nunn, officer in charge of the detachment stated that he thought the figure was somewhat higher at 200 – 300 natives, but that most of the Kamilaroi were successfully destroyed."

Underneath was a further story by the same correspondent. "Gwydir River July 1838: In a statement by the local magistrate, he stated that aboriginals in the district have been repeatedly pursued by parties of mounted stockmen, assembled for the purpose, and that a great number of them have been killed at various spots as war has been waged along the Gwydir River." And in the last of the stories from 'Our correspondent,' "Men from the Bowman, Ebden, and Yaldwyn sheep stations in search of stolen sheep, killed 14 aboriginals at the confluence of the Murrumbidgee and Murray Rivers in NSW".

One of the subjects which I thoroughly enjoyed reading at school was modern history, and I reckoned that this came under that heading. Therefore, I decided that, as I was stuck in here due to heavy rain, I should delve a little deeper.

Several months ago, I had got talking to an Aussie guy called Glen in Monty's bar. This was right after the ruckus with Shirley the Abbo and the Swedish sailor, and he had told me some interesting facts that seemed to

155

have a ring of truth to them. Glen said that most Australians don't like to discuss the aborigines because they are a problem that they don't quite know how to resolve. They just wish it would go away. Glen put forward the theory that most Australians knew deep in their hearts that their forefathers - the early settlers - had run the aborigines off the land that, for a thousand years previously, had been aboriginal hunting grounds, and they felt a sense of guilt. Much like the white settler in America had dispossessed the Native American Indians, so the aborigines had been similarly dispossessed.

The typical aboriginal, he said, will work hard when employed in a cattle or sheep station environment, because they are happy living off the land and working with animals, but bizarrely, without any warning they will just up and leave, or go walkabout. Aboriginals also seem to have further problems with alcohol. They cannot take their grog, said Glen, which gets them into all kinds of trouble, and they have problems holding down a job. Many aboriginals migrate to the cities and you can often see them loitering on street corners, which usually gets them into conflict with the police. And here's the strangest thing, added Glen; very often they cannot take being locked up for the night in police cells, and they attempt to commit suicide. Since 1960 the suicide rate for aborigines has without explanation trebled, even amongst those that are not in police custody. Never mind young Queen Victoria getting a crown bunged upon her head - this was interesting stuff!

These few stories, tucked away at the bottom of an ancient newspaper, had grabbed my interest and I wanted to know more. Looking at the newspaper story again, I quickly totalled up that perhaps 300 natives had been put to death, mainly because they were trying to prevent being over-run by the white man. Consider this. Those figures represented only those three reported incidents in NSW alone in the month of July 1838. How many more, before and after, were put to death in the name of progress across the whole of Australia? I decided to enquire into the circumstances of these ancient people who had inhabited Australia for the past 40,000 years, but who were looked upon, by certain newspaper correspondents, as "a nuisance."

At the reception desk I asked a uniformed attendant how one could get further information on a particular subject. "And what subject would that be?" enquired the surly looking man.

"I want any articles you have regarding the killing of aborigines in the last century up to the present day," I said. He gave me a haughty look as if I'd just let off a loud fart.

"Can't think why the hell you'd wanna look into summat like that for, but that young lady over there will help you out." He pointed at one of the lady curators dressed in a simple uniform of light brown shirt and trousers.

As I walked over, she gave me the benefit of a stunning smile. "Hello, can I help you?" She had a plastic nameplate pinned onto the pocket of her shirt. It said Paula Curtis. She was quite attractive.

I smiled back. "Actually, I've just read an article in the newspaper in the cabinet over there, and I'd like some further information please. It's in regard to the killing of aboriginals by white settlers." She didn't seem at all put out by my request, and in fact showed me her pearly white teeth again. "Oh yes, I know the one you're talking about. We're sure to have plenty of information on the subject." She considered something for a moment. "Have you ever used a microfiche before?" she asked. My blank look must have told its own story. "Never mind, it's ever so easy. It's a fairly new invention, where a whole newspaper is reduced to the size of a tiny dot, and at the press of a button it's displayed onto a screen. If you'd care to follow me, the microfiche are in the reading room next door."

I followed her rather delectable bottom into the next room where, at a long polished table were three microfiche displays. The room was otherwise empty and I was the sole user of this new-fangled equipment. "Please sit down there and I'll show you how to display the information." She dragged a nearby chair over and sat close next to me to begin the tutoring session. She looked older than me, but in excellent shape. She wasn't what one could term beautiful, but she looked as sexy as hell. Perhaps it was the uniform? She was slim and above average height with light brown hair. The outline of her perfectly shaped small breasts jutted impertinently out from under her shirt. As she began showing me the simple buttons to press, and how to display the data onto the reader, I caught a whiff of her perfume. She smelt fantastic. She smiled again and wandered off and left me to get on with it. I quickly mastered the simple reader and, using the index, soon had the ancient newspaper articles on the monitor as I required them.

The first newspaper article came up on the screen. Dated 1833, it told the story of a beached whale that had come ashore at a place called The Convincing Ground near to the whaling station at Portland, Victoria. A dispute ensued between the local Gunditjmara tribe who tried to assert their right to the carcass, and the whalers who saw it as part of their catch. In the ensuing battle, some reports mention figures of between 50 to 200 aborigines slain, including women and children. The incident became known as The Convincing Ground Massacre.

Another article reported the story in which white settlers put to death 28 aborigines on 10th June 1838 at Myall Creek, NSW. It was to become known as the Myall Creek Massacre, and was famously the first incident where the settlers were convicted of the murders. At the first hearing, eleven of the white men were acquitted by the jury, but the State Governor ordered a retrial, in which seven of the defendants were found guilty of the murder of an aboriginal child, and hanged.

Wading through pages of newspapers of the era, I came across reports of a new and effective way in which the white settlers kept the aborigines off their land. They poisoned them! The settlers would often leave flour or other foodstuffs laced with poison at different locations, and the unsuspecting aborigines would eat it. After the Myall Creek incident and the hanging of white men convicted of killing natives, even innocent settlers clammed-up. They were wary of reporting any information to the authorities, lest the European perpetrators be prosecuted for the murders of people whom they viewed as being little more than sub-humans. No evidence or statements could be gathered, and nothing could be proven as to whom had left the poisoned food. And so the settlers literally got away with murder!

On the Brisbane River in 1842 settlers poisoned 50 aborigines, and at Kilcoy station between 30 – 60 people of the Kabi Kabi tribe were poisoned using strychnine. I was deep into my inquiries when Paula Curtis came back. She gave me that smile again. "I'm afraid the library will close in a half hour. Will you be finished here?" I looked at my wristwatch, and found to my astonishment that I had been searching for over two hours. I put a pained expression on my face. "Well, if you're going to chuck me out onto the street, then you must." She went off giggling.

There were many more killings of the indigenous tribesmen and their families. Sometimes hundreds at a time were massacred simply to keep them from hunting on the land which they and their forefathers had hunted for centuries, but which the newly arrived white men claimed was their own. Over a ten year span I counted over a thousand put to death. I skipped forward to more recent times and found an incident called the Coniston Massacre. In 1928 a WW1 veteran had shot 32 aborigines in the Northern Territories after a white dingo trapper and a station owner were attacked by aborigines. It was not proven that the aborigines who were shot were the same aborigines who had carried out the attack, but a court of inquiry stated that the action of the white European was justified. I was astonished. How can the killing of 32 people be justified? Just to think; this incident had happened a mere 37 years beforehand. I didn't have enough time to scour through all the articles, but they seemed to point to the fact that the indiscriminate killing of aborigines was a nationwide problem, not simply endemic to NSW.

With these grim accounts running around my brain, I got ready to leave. However, Paula Curtis beat me to it and appeared at the door. She looked at her wristwatch. "It's 4-o-clock. I'm afraid that it's time to close the library," she said apologetically.

"That's alright. Where are you going now?" I asked innocently. She looked bewildered. "Erm, well I'm going home I suppose." I decided to be bold. "Can I possibly take you out for a drink, Paula? Is it alright to call you Paula?" I gave her my name. She went red in the cheeks and looked genuinely flustered. "Oh my, I've never had this situation before at work. I don't think it's allowed for staff to fraternise with customers."

I wasn't to be put off. I whispered, "Well, if you don't tell anyone, then I promise not too either." I held my hands up in simulated surrender. "I assure you that my intentions are strictly honourable," I lied.

"Well, I don't suppose it would do any harm, would it?" she said..

"Of course not," I agreed, "Shall we go?" She was unsure of the fraternisation issue and didn't want tittle-tattle among her work colleagues, so she insisted on meeting me further along Macquarie Street.

The rain had long gone and the pavements were dry. I offered my arm, and she linked hers into mine as we went in search of a suitable hostelry in which to take a lady. By the time we found a hotel bar in a nearby street, we were laughing loudly at some inspired banter on my part. She had the most wonderful hazel eyes that crinkled into crow's-feet when she laughed. We went inside and sat in a secluded booth with red leather seats. She told me that she was 28 years old and threw her hands up in mock horror when I revealed that I was a mere 18 years old. She laughed and mimicked my earlier statement. "Well, if you don't tell anyone," she said, "then I promise not to either." We both roared with laughter, but while she was still laughing, I took her by surprise and kissed her rather passionately. This flustered her even more than earlier and she went bright red. I ordered more drinks and we continued talking.

She had, she said, worked as a curator at the state library since she was 19 years old and enjoyed it enormously. Paula lived with a tabby cat in a rented house in the suburb of Balmain, near Darling Harbour, and she was unmarried. I asked when she had last been in a relationship, and was surprised to hear that it was over 18 months ago, and even that had sounded quite platonic. However, although she was a real stunner, she was quite shy and came over as reserved, so perhaps it put anyone off trying to date her. She certainly wasn't putting me off. I was in seventh heaven with her in my arms and sipping a beer. What more could a man want?

She asked me questions about my travels around the world and wanted to know the details of the places I had visited. I found myself relaxed in her company and she was comfortable to be with and knowledgeable in the subjects that we covered. After two hours, the time had simply flown by as we had chatted. I had drank a few pints of beer and she had drank three gin & tonics and her face was quite flushed. She said she thought that perhaps she ought to be getting home. However, it was only just past 6pm and I wanted to see more of her. I felt so at ease with her snuggled close beside me, and I felt the warm glow of euphoria every time I even brushed against her. I didn't want to let her go. "Look Paula," I said. "I don't want to outstay my welcome, but could I take you out again tonight? Why don't I take you home, then I could wait while you get changed, and we could perhaps go out for a bite to eat?" She gave me that stunning smile again. "Yes, that would be lovely. Are you sure you don't mind taking me home?" she asked in her wide-eyed innocence.

We caught a cab out to Balmain. Her house was an old wooden affair with the obligatory veranda that I had seen so many times in Australia and New Zealand. We went inside, and a tabby tom-cat purred loudly and brushed himself against her legs until she fed him from a bowl on the floor. "Would you like another beer? I think I've got one in the fridge?"

I relaxed on the veranda with a can of beer and she went off to shower and change. A little later, I heard her come out of the shower and go into her bedroom. I went and stood by the bedroom door. The door was slightly ajar and I could hear her towelling herself down. I pushed the door with my toe, and as she saw it open, she grabbed the towel and pressed it to her body to hide her nudity, but in that brief second I caught sight of her small breasts standing proud. She was stood by the dressing table holding the towel tightly to her body and her eyes were uncertain and were tinged with fear. I smiled to put her at her ease, but I nonetheless continued walking into the bedroom. "I'm sorry if I frightened you. It's just that I was getting lonely out there."

"I wasn't expecting you to just walk in," she whispered. "You surprised me." I put my arms around her and kissed her neck, then lifted her chin and kissed her softly on the lips. I kissed her harder with more urgency and she responded. As she did so, a part of her bath-towel fell away at the back. In the mirror I could see the reflection of her bottom with small perfectly formed cheeks, each one a milky white orb covered in goosebumps. I took her hand and led her to the bed and pulled the covers back. She kept the towel tightly clutched across her body as she climbed into the bed and pulled the sheets up to her chin. I drew the curtains closed, even though it was dark outside, and silently got undressed and slid in beside her. I took her into my arms, and kissed her again. My hand began wandering across her body and down her legs and back again countless times. We lay like that for ages, both of us finding and exploring the others erogenous zones. There was no rush whatsoever. We had all the time in the world to probe and investigate each other's bodies. This shy and self-conscious girl began to come out of her shell, and gradually she transformed into a passionate and sensual woman.

I never took her aboard the ship, because she wasn't the type of girl, like some of the Monty's Bar females, who permanently hung out aboard the cargo boats. Every evening I would get a bus out to Balmain and we would lounge out on the veranda or cuddle on the sofa as she and I would perhaps read a book. For some unknown reason her cat, Snooks, never left my side, but would cuddle up beside me on the sofa. I had, it seems, made another friend. Every night we would sleep in her comfortable double bed, but as the ship's departure day drew nearer, our relationship was overshadowed by the realisation that we wouldn't see each other for many months to come. Eventually, sailing day arrived and she came to the ship to wave me off. She never came aboard, but stood on the quayside waving a white handkerchief as the ship slid out of Sydney harbour.

Return to Auckland

Three days later, in the early dawn, the ship berthed almost in the city centre of Auckland and we were given a job-and-finish to sugi down the ship's funnel. By midday we were finished, so Mick, Norton, Charlie and I made a beeline for Ma Gleason's, where the boozing was in full swing. As we entered, the noise from the jam-packed bar was the usual cacophony of raucous pandemonium as the sailors put beer down their throats as fast as humanly possible. Alongside the wharves were three other British cargo ships, one Port Line, a Shaw Savill, and a Blue Star cargo ship. As I looked around, I could see many of the crew from those ships all busily getting legless. Queenie the Maori monster was getting ready to launch her latest barrage of missiles into the packed clientele, and Port Line Sue was creating havoc at the other end of the bar by giving a Blue Star sailor a slap. We decided not to stay too long and bought a carry-out of beer and departed. Ma Gleason's was getting to be such a rough pub, that even I could only take it in short measures.

On the way back to the ship we stopped at the Pandora coffee bar in Fanshawe Street. I'd heard reports that it was a good place to pick up the ladies, and sure enough it was full of girls and sailors. We sat in a booth with green leather seats and ordered coffee. While the bar-girl brewed the coffee, I looked around at the young ladies on offer. I spotted a group of three girls at the far end and in particular a slim blonde with a lovely fresh complexion. She had her back to me, but I caught a quick glimpse as she turned to speak to her friend and she looked gorgeous. Her friend must have told her that I was taking an interest, because she turned to look at who it was that was interested. In that fraction of a second I smiled and gave her a wink. I wondered how I could engineer an introduction with her, and realised that I would have to take the bull by the horns and make it happen.

You may, dear reader, have noticed the difference in my character which had changed from that naive and shy 17 year old boy of just a year ago, into a bolder and more decisive character. Most of this new-found confidence stemmed from being in competition with the cocksure John Sheppard, which perhaps compelled me to be more self-assured. Since leaving Farnborough I had often wondered how he was and where he was. I suppose it wasn't his fault that he couldn't stand by his word with regard to returning the money for the car. After all, his father was a forthright and assertive person, and I'm sure that John had been obliged to carry out his father's wishes, whether they were right or wrong.

Mick, Norton, and I made our way through the packed coffee bar to where the group of girls stood. One of the girls, a brunette, saw us coming and whispered to the blonde, who turned as we reached them. Close up, she was even prettier than I had first supposed, except for a small scar on the side of her cheek, which simply enhanced her attractiveness. Without any waffling I launched into a well tried chat-up line. "Hello, my name's Graham. If you're not busy I wondered if you'd like to come to a party." I indicated her two pals. "Your friends are quite welcome to come as well." As you can tell, I favoured the direct approach. She deliberated this for all of ten seconds. "Where's the party being held?" she asked coolly.
"It's onboard the Port Melbourne," I told her. "We've just arrived this morning. I really would like you to come. I hope you'll say yes."
While she put on an expression of considering my proposal, I smiled at the other two girls and introduced Mick and Norton who were standing on the sidelines. Apart from the short brunette, the third girl was a quite pretty blonde who was dressed all in black. I decided that I'd stir things up a bit by giving them the option to come along as well. They were nodding as I asked if they would like to come onboard, which left my blonde with no way out. "Yes alright then," she said cautiously.

On the walk back to the wharf, she told me that her name was Karen and that she worked as a receptionist in a car showroom. By the time we had walked halfway I was holding her hand, and as we arrived at the ship's gangway, I gave her a kiss. We made our way to Blossom's cabin, and as always, there was a party already under way.

Later, when I took Karen ashore, we arranged to meet tomorrow night at her house in Mount Eden, where she shared with four other girls. She would be taking me to a friend's party near where she lived, and I jokingly asked her if I'd need to bring my pyjamas. She threw her arms around my shoulders and whispered huskily into my ear. "I reckon you'd look a lot better without any pyjamas, sailor!" As the taxi pulled into the rank, I gave her a long deep kiss and squeezed her bum!

The deck crew had thoroughly cleaned out the refrigerated cargo spaces during the passage from Sydney and the ship was now ready to begin loading. The cargo holds had been inspected for cleanliness by the New Zealand Department of Health and the wharfies began to load lamb and all manner of dairy produce.

The voyage was barely halfway completed. After departure from Auckland, the Port Melbourne would be loading in Wellington, Lyttelton, Bluff, Timaru, and then back to Wellington. Once loaded she would sail across the Pacific Ocean, through the Panama Canal, and call at several ports on the eastern seaboard of the United States and Canada. After that, we would voyage across the Atlantic Ocean and back to Silvertown.

Thoughts of Silvertown reminded me of the airmail letter I had received from home yesterday. Everyone back home was well, and mum was keen to know how I was and all about my travels. Baby Toni was now 18 months old and running around the house causing mayhem, and both my sisters were fine. Apart from a funny story about my stepfather Albert, who spent half his life smiling as if he had not a care in the world, things back home were quite normal and tickety-boo. I made a promise to myself that I would write back within the week. After months away from home I really should have been feeling homesick, but I was having far too much fun. Oh what an insensitive youth I really was!

⚓

Since the demise of Jack Franks over two weeks ago, there had been no clue as to the guilty perpetrator. As far as the authorities were concerned, his disappearance had been an accident and no one else had been implicated in his death. Not one of the crew had given the slightest indication that they knew anything, even amongst ourselves. There was a wall of silence. Even though most were agreed that he was pushed, it seemed to be the general consensus of opinion that Jack Franks deserved what he got, and no one was sorry to see the back of him. Whoever had given him a helping hand over the side had done everyone a favour. The new atmosphere onboard was laid back and relaxed, and the Port Melbourne had become a happy ship to serve upon. Eric Roberts, our new bosun, was always in a cheerful mood and this rubbed off on the deck crew. We would go about our tasks with a smile and a new found enthusiasm to please Eric. He was one of life's real gentleman and we would do anything for him.

The Pillion Passenger

Karen answered my knock at the door of her rented house in the suburb of Mount Eden. She gave me the benefit of a welcoming smile. "Come on in and meet the untidy mob I live with." We went inside and met her house-mates. Carol was a big-boned girl with a zany sense of humour who worked as a nurse, and Trish was a petite platinum blonde with enormous breasts. The other two girls were Lydia and Denise, who could almost have been twins, with their dark brown hair cut in the same short style. It was arranged that we were all going off to a party at Carol's friend's house; but there was a hitch. "We've got a problem," said Carol. "We can't all go to the party in one taxi. We'd never squeeze into it. So, how about four of us go in the taxi and Trish gives Graham a lift on the back of her scooter?" And with that, our travel arrangements were concluded.

As the taxi drove away, Trish started the scooter. "Have you ridden on one of these before?" I admitted that I hadn't. "No problem, just hold on tight. It's only a ten minute ride." I hopped aboard onto the pillion seat and we zoomed off up the road so fast, I almost fell off. I had nothing to hold onto, so I lightly held onto her hips. She slowed down and swivelled her neck around. "You'd better hang on tight. I don't want you falling off." I took this as an invitation and reaching around, cupped her sizeable breasts in my hands. It must have surprised her, because the scooter's engine gave a cough and momentarily slowed down, but we were soon poodling along again with no complaints from Trish. I decided, "In for a penny – In for a pound," and became bolder. I slid my hands under her blouse and worked my way under her bra. Still she rode on at a steady 30 mph without saying a word. I whispered hoarsely in her ear. "Can you slow down?" She slowed to 10mph and we took an extra five minutes to get to our destination. She moved her bottom backwards and we could feel the warmth of each other as she snuggled into my crotch. As we got within a few hundred yards of the house-party she pulled over and adjusted her clothes. "Well, that was a most interesting ride," she said primly. "We must do that again one day." I simply nodded, because we were both aware that when we arrived at the party, I would be with Karen.

⚓

It was a warm and sunny Saturday afternoon as the ship sailed through the heads into Wellington, although a stiff breeze followed us in from the Cook Strait. Within the hour the ship was moored onto one of the finger wharves in Lambton Harbour and the deck crew set about getting the vessel ready to load a cargo of butter and lamb first thing Monday morning. With cargo derricks topped-up and steel hatch-lids in readiness to load cargo, we went ashore for a few beers. Mick Haywood, Norton, Charlie and I rushed to the bar at the Duke of Edinburgh Hotel, and with just two hours still to go before last orders, we quickly set about getting tanked-up. As usual, the bar was packed with sailors, girls and locals all attempting to get legless before the bar closed at 6pm.

I was in conversation with Norton when there was a tap upon my shoulder. I turned to find a girl standing there. "Are you here with anyone?" she enquired seriously. "What I mean to say is, have you got a girlfriend at the moment?" It's not very often that a chap is on the receiving end of such a direct question as that. She saw the look of puzzlement on my face and quickly added, "I'm not asking for myself, but for my friend who's hiding around the corner. She's very shy," she explained. I was in a spot and didn't quite know how to react. For all I knew, her unseen friend may have a face like the back of a bus. The girl must have read my mind.

She said, "You don't need to worry. Marianne's very pretty. She's somehow taken a shine to you, and wondered if you'd like to have a drink together. She's just a bit shy," she repeated.

"Well," I said, a little perplexed, "I'm at a loss at what to say, but I suppose you'd better ask her to come on over." The girl went off to find my mystery admirer, and the lads gathered in a huddle. "Bloody hell, Gra, that's a turn up for the book, ain't it?" said Norton. "What ya gonna do if she's as ugly as sin?" I shook my head as I hadn't a clue.

A few moments later the girl came back accompanied by a perfectly beautiful creature with dark shoulder length hair and lovely hazel eyes. She had a slim body, which was accentuated by her figure-hugging black jeans. She hung back anxiously looking frightened and vulnerable, like an abandoned waif. She looked ever so young, and it crossed my mind that she may be an underage minor. She smiled nervously and waited for me to say something. Inexplicably I shook her hand and said, "Hello, my name's Graham. What's yours?"

"My name's Marianne," she said in barely a whisper.

"That's a lovely name. It suits you. How old are you, Marianne?" I asked.

"I'm seventeen. I'll be eighteen next month," she murmured. Well, at least she didn't appear to be a juvenile, and after all, I myself was a mere eighteen years old.

"Why don't we go sit over there by the window? It's a bit quieter and we can have a chat."

Marianne's friend was stood between Norton and Mick and seemed quite happy at all the attention she was getting, so I left them to it. I took Marianne's arm and led her to a quiet corner of the room. I decided to tease her a little. "Do you usually send your friend over to ask a bloke if he's got a girlfriend?"

She smiled at the absurdity of the thought. "Good God no, it's the first time I've ever done anything like that." She had a nice smile which lit up the room, and suddenly she didn't look like the underage girl that I had originally suspected. She somehow looked more confident and worldly-wise, but I may have been mistaken.

"Well, your friend said that you wanted to have a drink with me. Why's that?"

Her face went red with embarrassment. "When I saw you, I thought that you had a kind face and nice eyes," she murmured. "I thought it would be nice to talk to you."

"I take it that you haven't got a boyfriend at present?" She shook her head, and for a fleeting second I thought I saw a look of regret briefly appear on her face; but I let the moment pass.

"Where do you live? Do you share an apartment?" I asked.

"I've only recently moved up from the South Island, so I don't know too many people here to share with." She indicated her friend, who I could see was soaking up the attention from my three shipmates and loving every minute of it. "Katherine's a good friend, but she's already sharing with some flatmates. So, at the moment I've got just a small flat over the top of a greengrocer's shop." I nodded and tucked this snippet of information away in the back recess of my brain. I asked Marianne did she have a job, and for a second I detected that same look of regret pass across her eyes. "I haven't managed to get a full time job just yet. I've got a temporary job which just about pays the rent."

"What job do you do? Is it very interesting?" I asked.

"No, it's not a very good job at all," she said, then quickly changed the subject and asked me about life aboard ship. I told her about the Port Melbourne, and my visits to exotic ports of the world and the sights which I had seen. She was ever so easy to talk to, and we felt relaxed in each other's company. She didn't appear to mind when I slid my arm around her waist and gave her a kiss. As closing time approached, there was an explicit but unsaid understanding that I would be taking her home.

Marianne's apartment was exactly as she had described it. We trudged up the stairs above a city greengrocers to a small bedroom with a kitchenette and bathroom. The furniture was mismatched and Spartan, but I could see she kept the place clean and tidy. The sun had barely set behind

166

the horizon, but Marianne closed the curtains, switched on a bedside lamp, and came into my arms. We kissed for many minutes, neither of us wanting to break the magic of the moment. We silently undressed and I was able to admire her body. She had a lovely slender figure with a tiny waist and small but full breasts. She was exquisite.

We slid into bed, and as traffic and the everyday noises of the city of Wellington passed by under the window, we made slow delicious love. When we had finally consummated our lovemaking, we lay spent in each other's arms until at last; we snuggled up and drifted into sleep.

The next morning was a Sunday and the sunshine blazed through the opened curtains as I sleepily opened my eyes. I looked at my wristwatch. It said 8-o-clock. The bed beside me was empty, and then I heard the shower running. I lay back in the warm bed and luxuriated with thoughts of our lovemaking last night. Just after midnight, Marianne had awoken me by running her hands across my back. No sooner was I half awake than she whispered, "Are you awake? Do you want to make love again?" She had managed to arouse me for a second time and it had been a perfectly wonderful night. As I lay in bed, I had more erotic thoughts which involved making love yet again when she came out of the shower.

A few moments later she stepped into the room with a bath towel wrapped tightly around her body, and another on her wet hair. "Come on sleepy eyes, time for you to get out of bed and back onboard," she said, a little unsympathetically. I had other ideas and reached out to grab her arm and drag her back into bed, but she pulled her arm away quite forcefully and surprised me with the suddenness of it. "Come on," she said harshly. "It's about time you were heading back to your ship. I've got things to do." There was no hiding the urgency in her voice. The message was loud and clear. Get the hell out of here! I was astounded by the complete change in her attitude. Last night, both in the bar and in this bedroom, we had been a romantic couple who couldn't keep their hands off each other. And now it seemed, she couldn't wait to get shot of me. It was all very strange, and I must admit to being confused by her change in personality.

"Why are you talking like that, Marianne?" I asked in annoyance. "All of a sudden you can't wait to get rid of me. Have I done something to upset you?"

Her eyes wouldn't meet mine as she looked down and mumbled, "No, it's time that you went back to your ship, that's all."

"Marianne, I think you owe me an explanation, don't you? I don't deserve to be treated this way," I was livid. "Yesterday in the bar, you sent Katherine across to ask me if I had a girlfriend, and now you're throwing me out. Something's not right. You're not telling me the truth, are you?"

167

As I looked, her eyes began brimming with tears and it triggered a bout of uncontrollable sobbing as wet teardrops ran down her cheeks. "I'm so sorry, Graham," she cried. "I never intended it to be like this. I just wanted you to leave so that you didn't discover the truth."

"I think you'd better tell me exactly what's going on, don't you?"

She nodded. "You're right; I should have told you the truth." She collected her thoughts, and went on to explain. "When I said I had a part time job, that was true enough, but I should have been honest with you." She took a deep breath and launched into what she viewed as extenuating circumstances as to why she had lied to me.

"I arrived in Wellington two weeks ago with very little money. My father had thrown me out because we've never got on, and we had another fight," she explained. "I had only enough money to pay the first weeks rent. If I didn't get more money, I'd be living on the street. I've been to dozens of places looking for a job, but no one's hiring at the moment." Her eyes became remorseful as she remembered the next part of her story. "Then I met a woman in a cafe who offered me a way to make some easy money."

The grim look on my face told its own story. I could think of only one way she'd make easy cash. "Are you on the game?" I asked. She nodded her head and her eyes spilled over with tears.

"I've only done it once. That was last week. It was a client that the woman sent along."

"Well, I hope you took some precautions," I said bitterly. "You could have given me a disease."

"No," she said. "I made sure he wore a condom."

"Well thanks a bunch," I said cynically. "Why is it you need me out of here in such a big hurry?"

Her voice was almost a whisper. "Because there's another client due here in two hours time." She started to cry again.

"Well, I won't get in your way then," I said, and began to get dressed.

"I'm so sorry, Graham. I didn't mean to hurt you. I just didn't know what to do."

I finished dressing and took some money from my wallet. I laid it on the bedside cabinet. "Here, I'll pay my money just like everyone else." I saw her face crumple as if I had slapped her and already I regretted saying it.

As I made my way down the stairs, I could hear her crying uncontrollably.

Back onboard the ship, I refrained from mentioning anything to my cabinmate or any of the crew. I was in a quiet and reflective mood as I lay on my bunk and ran the events through my mind for the umpteenth time. To be perfectly fair, Marianne hadn't actually lied to me about her "part-time job." She had simply omitted to tell me what that job was; which, of course, was quite understandable, as one is hardly likely to start off a conversation with such immortal words as, "Oh by the way, I've just started work as a prostitute." I tried to put myself into her position. She was a 17 year old girl in a strange city, and after paying a week's rent for the flat, had no more money and no friends who could give her a bed and some food. She had tried looking for a job, but without any success. What would I have done had I been in her shoes?

For a heterosexual man, becoming a prostitute wasn't an option, but try as I might, I couldn't think of any viable alternative as to how I would have handled the circumstances. Perhaps if someone such as the stranger in the cafe offers you an easy way out, then who knows what anyone may have done?

I couldn't understand why I'd become upset when she told me of the imminent arrival of another client. I decided that I was probably as jealous as hell that another man, albeit a man who would be paying for the pleasure, was going to be taking my place in her bed.

I just couldn't fathom why I was insanely jealous; it's not as if I expected Marianne to be a virgin. It's never bothered me before that a girlfriend hadn't been as pure as the driven snow, so why worry about it now? I concluded that I shouldn't make any negative judgement against her. She was quite simply a frightened young girl in a difficult situation.

After dinner on the Monday evening, the gangway watchman knocked at my cabin door. "Hey Graham, there's a young lady on the quayside who says she wants to speak to you." I went down to the quayside and found Marianne stood by the cargo warehouse. Her face appeared sad, and I could see that she had been crying. Perhaps she viewed our short-lived relationship as a lost possibility. "I came here to tell you again that I'm sorry, and to let you know that I've now got a job and a proper house to live in." This was great news and I couldn't have been more pleased. "That's fantastic, Marianne. I'm so pleased." I took her hand in mine. "Come onboard and tell me all about it." She followed me up the gangway and I settled her into my cabin.

She opened her purse and took out some banknotes and laid them on the seat. I guessed it was the money I'd put on her bedside table yesterday. Her voice was solemn, but tinged with pride as she said, "Graham, I cannot accept this money. I'm no longer a prostitute." She snorted a laugh. "Anyway, I was never a very good one, was I?" With a smile I agreed.

"So, what happened? How come you've got a job and another place to live?"

169

"I'm not sure you'll want to hear the story. It's linked to the client I had yesterday morning."

"Well, you've come this far," I said pensively. "You may as well tell me the rest."

"Well alright then." She took a deep breath. "Believe it or not, yesterday's client was actually booked by his mother."

I was amazed. "His mother hired you? You've gotta be joking?"

"No, it's the Gods honest truth. Her son – his name's Luke – is a bit erm', well backward. He's 23 years old. He isn't really mentally disabled, he's not a nutter or anything like that; it's just that he's not very social and quite introverted. He's quite bright really, but he won't talk to anyone." She hesitated momentarily then continued. "His mother saw my advert in the newsagents shop window, and it was her who got in touch and made the booking. She told me that her son is quite capable of speaking, but very rarely does, and even then he will only speak to her and to no one else," she went on. "She said he had been like it for the past 18 months. She's sent him to three different psychiatrists, but none have been able to help him. They said he had suffered some sort of mental trauma. She didn't know what else to do. She was kind of hoping that if he ...." Her voice tailed off and she blushed and looked embarrassed. "....if he went to bed with a girl, then it might bring him out of his shell."

"Go on, Marianne. Finish the story. Did it help at all?"

"Yes it did, but not in the way that you think."

She continued with the story. "His mother, Mrs Hamlyn, brought him along to my flat, and explained the mental problems with Luke. She warned me that he wouldn't talk, and that he would probably just sit there expressionless and totally uncommunicative. Then she left him with me."

"That must have seemed weird," I said.

"It was truly bizarre," she agreed. "The poor bloke just sat on the end of the bed and I didn't know what to do. I could hardly ravish the poor bugger, could I?" she said with a giggle. "So I took my blouse off to see if that could get him.....interested. But he just sat there staring into space with no expression on his face at all. His eyes didn't move. It was weird."

"What did you do?" I asked.

"I didn't know what to do, so I talked to him about this and that, but he just sat there silently. Then I asked him if he liked reading books, and it was as if I'd switched a light on in his head. He was grinning and nodding as I asked him what books he liked. His face sort of came alive and animated. Do you know what I mean?"

"Yes, I think I do," I said uncertainly, although I had no inkling what it must be like for someone to be in a permanent state of speechlessness.

"I told him what books I'd read and I could tell that he was taking an interest. Then I said that I used to like reading comics when I was a kid, and it was then that he spoke to me."

"He actually talked to you? You got him to speak?"

Her smiling face was filled with pride. "Yes, I got him to talk. He said – 'My mum used to read comics to me.' – "That's all he said, he never spoke anymore."

"But that was a good result just getting him to say those few words, wasn't it?"

There was that look of pride again. "Yes, for the first time in ages, I felt good about myself." As I looked at Marianne I could see a new person. She was someone reborn. She had changed. She looked and acted far beyond her seventeen years. She had pride in herself.

"So where does the job and a new place to live come into the picture?"

"Well, when Mrs Hamlyn returned, I told her about Luke saying those few words, and she was astonished to say the least. She got very excited by it all. She said it's the first time Luke had spoken in over 18 months. She was ecstatic. Right there and then she offered me a live-in job looking after Luke and reading to him and so on."

I took her hands in mine. "I'm very happy for you, Marianne. You seem to have turned your life around, don't you?"

She was nodding and smiling. "Oh Graham, I feel so happy."

I took her in my arms and kissed her. "I'm sorry about how I behaved yesterday. I shouldn't have said the things I did, especially leaving that money by the bedside."

"Well, you did get a bit of a shock, didn't you." She laughed self-consciously. "No one would expect their girlfriend to be on the game, would they?"

"No I don't suppose so," I agreed. "So - what's your new room like at Mrs Hamlyn's house?"

"It's lovely. It looks out over the garden. But it's still being decorated, so I can't move in for another two weeks, so I'm keeping my old flat for the time being."

"Oh really," I said, keeping a straight face. "You'll be requiring someone to keep you warm at night then, won't you?"

"Perhaps," she said smirking. "Are you volunteering for the job?"

"Well someone's got to do it, haven't they?" I joked, as I wrapped her in my arms and I gave her a passionate kiss.

For the remaining days while the ship loaded her cargo, Marianne and I were always together. Most evenings we would meet up at her flat and either go for a walk or to the cinema, or we would stay indoors and

171

make love in the noisy room above the greengrocers shop. Each day Marianne would travel to Mrs Hamlyn's large house in the suburbs and be a companion to Luke. She would take him for walks; and as they ambled along, she would chat about things around them. At first progress was slow, although she could tell that he was listening, but gradually she got some response, a grunt here and there, and she knew that she was winning the battle to bring him back into the real world.

Our departure day came, and Marianne stood on the quayside to wave me off. Beside her was a young chap who mostly stared into space and whom I took to be Luke. The ship would be loading cargo at several ports in the South Island and then return to Wellington, so we knew that we would be seeing each other again within a couple of weeks.

Ginger Macaulay

The next morning the Port Melbourne docked at Lyttelton, the port for Christchurch, which is the largest city in the South Island. Straight away the wharfies were busy loading more butter, lamb, shellfish and wool into the cargo holds. The deck crew worked on the quay painting the ship's side using paint rollers attached to long bamboo poles. Others were over the ship's side on painting stages. These were long wooden planks attached to the ship with gantlines from which they painted the parts not accessible by the men on the quayside. In the bright sunshine, gallons of Port Line grey paint were rollered onto the steel sides of the ship in an effort to delay the ravages of rust. On the neighbouring wharf was berthed another Port Line vessel, the Port Lincoln, which was almost fully loaded and would soon be departing for the UK.

After we had finished work for the day, some of us rushed off to have a few beers at The British Pub, the favourite seaman's hostelry in town. We met up with a few crew members from the Port Lincoln and one of them, an ordinary seaman called Bob Russell, I already knew after meeting him in the Round House pub in London the year previously. I promised Bob that I would pop onboard his ship tomorrow for a few beers.

The next evening I went aboard the Port Lincoln, and Bob took me into the crew's bar for a drink. The bar had been converted from the old crew's recreation room, which hitherto had contained just a ping-pong table and a darts board. With some new lighting and comfortable seating, the crew had made it into a snug and friendly place to relax after a hard day's work. Also in the bar on this evening were a couple of stewards, an engine room stoker who was acting as the barman, and a first trip deck boy who was with his girlfriend. Bob and I got chatting and I asked if he had a good crew to work with. "Yeah," said Bob. "We've got a really good crowd, a

172

great bunch of guys." The deck crew, on whatever British vessel were always known as The Crowd.

"Just one problem though," said Bob. "Our bosun is Ginger Macaulay. He's an absolute animal. Everyone's scared shitless of him. Anyone steps outta line and Macaulay beats him up." I had heard of Macaulay. He was one of three brothers from the Outer Hebrides, all of them ship's bosuns, and all serving with different shipping lines. I had heard from another source that Ginger Macaulay ruled his deck crews with his fists. One of his brothers was known as Mad Macaulay due to his habit of playing his bagpipes whilst strutting around the decks at all hours of the night.

A matter of minutes went by when, with great drama, the door was banged open and framed in the doorway stood a huge brute of a man with red hair and a lopsided mouth. As he stared around the room one could feel the menace emanating from him and I knew that this scary looking character must be Ginger Macaulay. The pleasant ambience of the room changed instantly to one where you could cut the atmosphere with a knife and there was stark fear in the room. He walked around the bar, staring threateningly at each face he saw through his booze laden eyes. He looked at me and gave a grunt when he couldn't put a name to my face. As he looked down at me I could smell the whisky on his breath. He ordered a pint of bitter from the barman and the room remained silent whilst it was poured. All the while Macaulay stared around the room with a menacing demeanour. He grabbed his pint and strutted over to the young deck boy, who sat hunched together with his girlfriend. Both had a look of abject terror on their faces as Macaulay stood towering over the peggy in an intimidating manner. "So peggy, is this your wee lady friend, is it?" he asked in his sibilant Hebridean accent. The petrified lad simply nodded his head.

"You'll be taking a drink with me won't you, peggy, eh? You'll have a drink on me." It was a demand, not a request. The poor lad was so frightened that he stayed silent. Macaulay, in his drunken stupor, took the silence as an insult and changed his tune. "Oh you don't want to have a wee drink with me, eh? In that case we'll have a wee drink on you." With that he poured his whole pint of bitter over the poor boy's head and stomped out of the room. The unfortunate lad was drenched from head to toe in beer, and his girlfriend was likewise spattered with it. The silence was deafening as Macaulay went out the door.

"You can see what we have to put up with, can't you?" said Bob as he helped the peggy to mop-up the beer. "Nearly every day he's on the booze. He's a bloody alcoholic and he often gets the DT's. Having him around is a nightmare."

The DTs, or to give it its Latin name, Delirium Tremens, is caused by withdrawal from an episode of heavy and sustained drinking of alcohol. The symptoms can include confusion, disorientation, impaired visual perception, anxiety, paranoia, and hallucinations.

The Port Lincoln sailed the next day bound for the Panama Canal, and onwards to the UK. The story which I heard many months later was as follows. As the ship sailed across the Pacific Ocean, the crew were having their afternoon smoko outside on the after deck. Ginger Macaulay staggered out onto the deck in a drunken stupor, and with a serious case of the DTs. He stared out over the ship's port side handrails, and in his hallucinatory state, spotted a non-existent fishing vessel to which he began shouting his orders. "Come alongside me shipmates. I'm coming aboard. That's right, come and tie-up alongside." He then began shouting more orders to his crew. "Stand-by to take the ropes from that there fishing boat. Come on, look lively, she's coming alongside."

The deck crew had seen these drunken episodes before and knew that he was suffering from DTs, but dared not refuse to obey his orders as they knew that Macaulay was still capable of inflicting a severe beating. They therefore went along with his confused requirements. He was still calling to the fishing boat that he would be coming aboard, and as Macaulay judged that the fishing vessel was close enough alongside – he jumped over the rail. The crowd looked aghast as he disappeared over the side and was swept swiftly astern as the Port Lincoln steamed onwards at her cruising speed of 16 knots.

Even though they had been trained to rapidly respond to their regular man-overboard drills, there was confusion. They didn't quite know how to react to this situation. One of the young seamen said, "Shall I run up to the bridge and tell the captain?" The eldest of the deck crew, an able seaman who had previously received a beating from Macaulay said, "No, let's finish our tea and smoke first, shall we?" Twenty minutes later, when Ginger Macaulay was five miles astern, the AB ambled up to the bridge and calmly told the officer-of-the-watch what had happened. His body was never found.

⚓

Bluff was noted as a meat-packing town located at the southern tip of the South Island. Eighteen miles away to the north-west is the city of Invercargill, and a thousand miles to the south lay Antarctica. There was not an awful lot to see or do there, and I mostly stayed onboard. Meanwhile the wharfies proceeded to load tons of lamb and butter into our refrigerated cargo holds. Our next stop was the pretty town of Timaru where we stayed for just two days as we loaded more lamb carcasses and butter.

Early the next Friday morning we sailed back into Wellington harbour to complete our loading. This was to be our final port of call before sailing for Panama. From the canal we would sail through the Caribbean Sea before discharging our cargo in the USA and Canada. I had sent a letter to Marianne telling her when the ship was due to return and I was eager to see her again. After work I grabbed a cab to her flat above the greengrocer's shop. She looked positively delicious. I brought her up-to-date on my travels and she in turn told me of her progress with Luke, small though it was.

For a further week the ship loaded the last of our lamb and butter cargo for the American markets. The Port Melbourne was weighed down with thousands of tons of cargo and her Plimsoll marks were almost submerged down to their limits. The final tonnage of cargo to load was heavy bales of wool, which were stowed as deck cargo atop of the cargo hatch. The wool was protected from any salt spray by being covered over with two layers of tarpaulins.

Meanwhile, I saw Marianne every evening. Early the next morning I would return to work aboard the ship, and she to be Luke's companion. All too soon it was time for the ship to depart. We had discussed the possibilities of seeing each other again, and how we would keep in touch. I had warned her that a long distance relationship would be difficult, and if in the meantime she met a decent guy, then she shouldn't feel she's tied to me, because I had no idea when I would return to Wellington.

As the Port Melbourne backed out of the berth, the beautiful Marianne, looking extra delectable on this sunny afternoon, waved and waved until she was just a dot in the distance. I felt a pang of guilt because I knew full well that whenever I met the next pretty girl, all my good intentions to remain faithful would be whipped away on the wind.

I wasn't the only crew-member being waved off. As the ship departed, Jimmy, our young peggy, was waving frantically to his girlfriend as we let go the ropes. Poor Jimmy had fallen hopelessly in love with his Kiwi maiden and he had tears in his eyes.

As we steamed slowly down harbour the deckies were closing up the cargo hatches and tidying up the decks. Number six hatch needed to be closed by attaching a wire and winching the two halves of the steel hatch lids together, thereby making it watertight. As the winch took the weight, the two heavy hatch lids slowly and inexorably trundled along their track-way to marry up. Suddenly, just at the last moment, Jimmy stepped forward, inserted his middle finger between the gap, and it was instantly severed off. There was lots of blood and Jim had turned a strange pallid colour. He was, it seems, desperate to remain in New Zealand with his girlfriend and he planned on getting a medical discharge. His plan certainly worked, because his bag was packed and he was taken ashore by the pilot boat, then onwards to the hospital. I often wonder what happened to young Jim. Did he make a success of his new life in Kiwi? Did he spend the rest of his life with his girl? Let's hope so.

⚓

The voyage across the Pacific was fairly uneventful. Eight days out from New Zealand we passed close by Pitcairn Island, and as we did so, the captain sounded our ship's horn as a salute to the islanders. Pitcairn is of course, famous as the island to which, in 1790, the Bounty mutineers, led by the mate, Fletcher Christian, and their Tahitian companions, fled after setting Captain Bligh and his loyal crew adrift in a longboat and taking over the ship. There are actually four islands in the group which are spread out over several hundred square miles of ocean, but Pitcairn is the only one which is inhabited.

After settling on Pitcairn, the mutineers set fire to the Bounty as it lay at anchor so that it would sink, and no passing ship would sight it and report back to the Admiralty in London, who would have undoubtedly sent a frigate to arrest the mutinous crew. The island's history is evident from the surnames of the inhabitants. Generally they are all descended from four families and are named Christian, Warren, Young and Brown.

No attempt was made to land ashore as there is no harbour, but just a narrow pier to which a small boat could get alongside. In any event the islands are remarkably productive and produce a wide variety of fruit, vegetables and fish. They are also served by cargo ships that regularly stop to offload imported goods. Within the hour Pitcairn had receded well astern and the Port Melbourne continued on her voyage to Panama.

Each night as we proceeded on our way to Panama, I was required for lookout duty. Usually the lookout was carried out from atop the bridge on a raised deck called the monkey island. The lookout would normally last for one hour, after which your watch-mate would relieve you.

The officer-of-the-watch or OOW usually remained below in the bridge wheelhouse from where he would perhaps take a navigational star-sight, check compasses, correct charts, or read a book. If you were to spot the navigation lights of another ship, then the lookout would report to the OOW by shouting down a tube, "Masthead lights bearing two points to port" or from whatever bearing it happened to be. When a ship steams across the vast Pacific Ocean then you may go days before spotting the dim lights of another vessel, so there isn't too much nautical traffic to see out there.

On just such a night I was gazing in awe at the millions of bright stars in the cloudless sky. Very often one may see a satellite or one of the thousands of items of space junk that constantly orbit the Earth's atmosphere. These were quite easy to distinguish, because these space vehicles always travel in a straight line orbit around the Earth. Shooting stars or asteroids are likewise easy to spot, as they travel extremely fast and burn up as they enter the Earth's atmosphere. If the bright light has flashing white lights – then it's an aircraft!

I know the following story may seem hard to believe, but it's perfectly true. After craning my neck upwards for some minutes, I spotted a white light travelling in a south westerly direction and thought that it was simply a satellite. However, as I watched, I was amazed to see that it changed course to head on a completely new heading that took it towards a distant star. It didn't show any flashing lights! This I knew was unbelievable because we know that satellites travel in straight line orbits – so what could this be? This, (for want of a better word I shall call it a space vehicle) then reached the next distant star, went around it and headed off to yet another star. As I watched intently - never taking my eyes off the light in case I lost sight of it – the light veered from one star to the next in maybe twenty seconds. This was incredible because we are told by leading astrophysicists that, not only are some of the stars many light years away from planet Earth, but they are also light years away from each other. I watched this space vehicle or UFO for another half an hour, during which the UFO travelled through space at an extraordinary rate as it passed by or appeared to inspect dozens of stars. When my lookout relief arrived, I pointed it out to him, and he was just as baffled as I was

To put the distances travelled into perspective, it is important to understand what a light year is. The speed of light in vacuum is 186,282 miles per second. Therefore this equates to a speed of 671 million miles per hour. There are 8760 hours in one year, so for a space vehicle to travel just one light year, the speed would be astronomical. The closest star to planet Earth is Proximi Centauri at a mere 4.2 light years away. The UFO that I saw easily motored from one star to the next in a matter of seconds. I shall leave you dear reader, to come to your own conclusions.

⚓

The transit of the Panama Canal was again a wonder to behold as our ship was efficiently taken through the several lock systems and out into the Atlantic Ocean. The only unfortunate incident that occurred involved the first-trip galley boy. When the ship had departed from New Zealand he had been tricked into saving up the stale bread for arrival at Panama. His so-called shipmates had strung him a tale that it is customary for the galley boy to save up all the stale bread so as to feed the mules that would pull the ship through the canal. The mules were of course not the four-legged variety, but the powerful electric mules that would guide us faultlessly through the locks.

As the ship entered the first lock, the lad came out on deck dragging a heavy sack of bread and expecting to see a mule train all harnessed up and towing the Port Melbourne through the canal. "Where are these bloody mules that I'm supposed to feed?" he shouted. When the electric mules were pointed out to him with comments of "You've been had, mate," he didn't see the funny side, and in a fit of pique threw the sack of bread onto the quayside, where it split wide open and the stale bread was strewn all over the mowed lawns of the pristine canal.

Up on the bridge the American pilot had been chatting to Captain Forster. The crew-cut pilot resembled the prototype American tourist with a Hawaiian shirt, shorts, sunglasses and chomping a large cigar. When he saw the galley boy throw the sack onto the dock and the mess it made of the meticulously mown lawns he went apoplectic. "Aaww, Jeez Christ Captain, what the hell is going on here?" He said in a loud and angry voice that could be heard up on the fo'castle head. "I'm not puttin' up with this kinda shit. I'm gonna have this ship pulled into the side of the lock so that goddam idiot can climb ashore and clear up that mess." The ship was winched into the side and the poor galley boy, his head hung in embarrassment, was instructed by a very furious Captain Forster to leap ashore and clean up every last crumb. Without any further incidents our passage of the canal went smoothly and we sailed out into the sparkling blue waters of the Caribbean Sea and headed northwards towards the United States.

⚓

Four days later, in the early morning, we berthed at Charleston, South Carolina, but stayed discharging cargo for just a matter of 12 hours. This was my first visit to the USA and I found it strange listening to the deep southern drawls of the stevedores. On arrival we were boarded by stone-faced officers of the US Immigration Service who checked our documents and asked pertinent questions regarding our political affiliations. The war in Vietnam, the purpose of which was to halt the spread of the communist North Vietnamese, was at its height and the yanks viewed any visitor to their shores with mistrust in case they were there to spread the word of communism.

The era of McCarthyism and the witch hunts against anyone viewed as red – or even pink for that matter – had ended just six years previously. Therefore the immigration officers would ask stock questions which were supposedly designed to wheedle out any red-under-the-bed. The questioning would begin along the lines of, "Have you ever been a member of a communist organisation?" or "Do you intend to overthrow the government of the United States of America?" These questions were delivered in deadly serious tones by the deadpan granite faced immigration officials, and woe betide any crew member who tried to be a Smart Alec or to even inject the slightest comedy into this inane questioning. I mean, who in their right mind would own up to such an allegation?

We of course encountered no problems and our shore passes were duly stamped by the boys in blue. But I heard a story of one crew member aboard another ship who thought he was a comedian. When asked, "Have you ever been a member of a communist organisation?" he joked, "No I haven't, but my grandma wears red socks on May Day."
The US Immigration officer said, "Oh a wise guy, huh? Mister you won't be stepping ashore in the USA." He was deadly serious and armed guards were posted on the gangway – at the shipping company's expense - to ensure that the seaman didn't set foot on American soil.

The next day we arrived at Norfolk, Virginia at the entrance to Chesapeake Bay. The city of Norfolk is home to the largest naval base in the world, and across the bay I could see whole fleets of aircraft carriers, cruisers, and destroyers. From horizon to horizon was a sea of grey painted ships. This was to be another short visit as we stayed for only 48 hours. In any event, I had spent too much of my wages in New Zealand, so didn't have the inclination to take a long cab ride, just to share a bar with hordes of fresh-faced American sailors who seemed to display an inordinate amount of medals on their chests.

Onwards we sailed to Philadelphia for another short stay before sailing that same evening for New York. The next morning we sailed past the Statue of Liberty and the skyscrapers of Manhattan as we proceeded to our berth. We sailed again that same evening and sadly, I wasn't seeing anything of America as I had hardly stepped ashore. The same thing applied at Boston, our next port-of-call, where we discharged cargo for less than 24 hours. During our entire time in America I had done no more than have a couple of beers in a dockside bar.

⚓

We sailed again for Montreal in Canada. The voyage up past Nova Scotia and westwards along the St Lawrence River took three and a half days, but at least the ship would be in port for much longer. Montreal in Quebec province was a lovely city, and in 1965 was the largest city in Canada, only surpassed by Toronto in 1976. It is in fact the second largest French speaking city in the western world, apart from Paris.

We were given a job-and-finish by the chief officer, and so on a gloriously sunny afternoon I strode out to explore the city. First stop was Place d'Armes square where stands the Notre-Dame Basilica, a solid-looking gothic cathedral which looked cool and inviting on this hot afternoon. As they were free, I helped myself to a pamphlet at the tourist information kiosk and stepped inside through the enormous arched main entrance. The interior of the church was very grand and fabulous, with the high ceilings coloured deep blue and decorated with golden stars. In the Sanctuary the stained glass windows showed scenes from the history of the city, and everywhere there were hundreds of intricate wooden carvings. At the far end of the nave sat a huge pipe organ with uncountable numbers of pipes that reached almost to the domed ceiling.

As I sat in a pew to study my pamphlet, the basilica's organist began playing Handel's Messiah, and the whole effect was wonderful. I could only sit there mesmerised by the rich notes that echoed around the vast church. I was later to learn that the enormous pipe organ had 9000 individual pipes, and that Notre Dame was at one time the largest church in all of North America. After the organist had finished his piece, I opened the pamphlet and studied the history of Montreal.

The city is in fact (I read) an island connected to the mainland by dozens of bridges, and sits at the confluence of the St Lawrence and Ottawa rivers. Montreal is named after the triple peaks of Mont Royale which are located in the heart of the city centre. When the explorer Jacques Cartier arrived there back in 1535, it was inhabited by the Iroquois Indians; however seventy five years later, when Samuel de Champlain set up a fur trading post on the site, the Iroquois had unaccountably disappeared.

It was now late afternoon, and with sore feet I reluctantly returned to the Port Melbourne. I stood on the upper deck and gazed out into the St Lawrence River. Nearby, on the mid-river island of Ile Sainte Helene and the artificial island of Ile Notre-Dame, frantic construction was taking place to build pavilions, and exhibition centres which would showcase the culture of scores of the world's countries in the forthcoming EXPO 67 world's fair. When it was held two years later, this cultural festival was a resounding success which attracted 50 million visitors to Montreal.

After four days and a few visits to the local bars for liquid refreshments, it was time to leave this lovely city and head back home to London on the last leg of our round-the-world voyage. I had enjoyed my time in Montreal. The city was interesting and vibrant and I couldn't have been more pleased.

⚓

The voyage across the Atlantic took eight days, and like our passage through the Pacific, was also uneventful. It was uneventful except for one comical incident. George Meredith, who had an almost school-boyish sense of humour, liked to play practical jokes and he had been fairly active during the whole voyage, but particularly just lately. Even though he was past 70 years of age, he still got a kick out of causing mayhem. His latest trick had been that age-old prank of balancing a bucket of water across the top of a door, and whoever opened it got soaked. In this case it had been Robbie Adams on the receiving end. So, Robbie and his best buddy, Steve Goddard, decided it was time for some friendly retribution.

It was well known that George was a deep sleeper and that he slept like the proverbial log – complete with some serious snoring! Therefore a plan was hatched to inflict payback whilst he was in the Land of Nod. George's single berth cabin porthole looked out over the ship's side, and he usually liked to get some fresh air circulating by keeping his porthole wide open.

One morning whilst George was off-watch and catching up with some sleep, Robbie and Steve manoeuvred an empty 45 gallon drum into his cabin and set it up in the centre of the floor, firstly ensuring that it was perfectly clean. Then they fed a fresh water hose through the cabin porthole – into the drum – and turned on the tap. Fill her up!

Next they set-to with needle and thread, and whilst George snored loudly, they sewed his bed-sheets tightly together so that he couldn't escape. George was cocooned. Lastly a few thick dollops of strawberry jam were ladled into the toes of George's carpet slippers which always lay ready-to-use at the foot of his bunk. And so the stage was set.

We will never know what went through George's brain as he awoke and found that he was trapped in his bedding, or as his bleary eyes focused, and wondered what a 45-gallon oil drum was doing in the middle of his cabin. What we do know, is that George screamed blue-murder as he struggled to break free of his bed-sheets, and once free, screamed even louder at whomever was responsible for planting an immoveable oil drum in his cabin. However, this was nothing compared with George's outburst as he tried on his carpet slippers and was rewarded with an audible squelch as the strawberry jam oozed out between his toes. It would have taken him hours to pump the water out of the drum and remove it, so we took pity and lent a hand, but he grumbled for days afterwards. But as Robbie rightly pointed out, "If you can't take the flak - then don't dish it out."

We berthed at the King George V dock in Silvertown on Friday 28 May 1965 and within the hour the crew were paid-off and were ordering taxi's to take them to the railway station. I had already made the decision that I wouldn't be returning for the next trip. I had completed three voyages aboard Port Melbourne, this latest being an around-the-world voyage, and although I had enjoyed every minute, it was time for a change. I said fond farewells to all my shipmates, once again promising after five happy months with them, to keep in touch and send the occasional postcard. Like the Board of Trade acquaintances we would always be – we never did.

⚓

Within the hour I had signed-off, packed my suitcase, and was tucking in to mum's home cooking. Mum brought me up to speed on what was going on in the family, and even Soupy took an hour from his busy work schedule to listen to some of my stories. His youngest children Teddy and Betty had moved out as and when they had got a flat or become married, and so the only occupants were Soupy, Mum, Linda, baby Toni, Glynis, and myself. As Toni was now 20 months old, my sister Linda was able to get a job in the office at a local company, so it kept mum busy and brought in some much needed extra cash. Throughout the week I kept my mum in stitches with tales of my travels and people I had met. It was now 18 months since, as a shy and self-conscious character, I had first gone to sea in the Port Pirie, and my mum was amazed at the changes in my personality and independence. Whereas I was once an introverted and quiet boy; now I was a man and could openly share some of the more risqué encounters with her. We laughed all day long.

During that first week, I wanted to upgrade my certification. I was presently an ordinary seaman, but needed to take an examination to upgrade to efficient deckhand or EDH. This was basically the same as an able seaman, except that it lacked the lifeboat certificate. As I hadn't much leave I travelled up to Great Yarmouth in Norfolk to complete the exam in one day. The examination I found fairly easy and the examiner didn't try to throw me any trick questions. I was back home by late that same night. The new certificate entitled me to far more pay per month.

To Belfast and back

I stayed at home on leave for a week or so, during which I resurrected old friendships and generally went clubbing and pubbing. It was good to have my family around me after being away from home for five months, but alas the magnetic quality of the sea-going life drew me back, and so I went to see John Aitchison, Port Line's Marine Superintendent. He gave me a rail warrant and instructions to join the Port St Lawrence in Liverpool which would soon be departing on a 19-day coastal voyage.

Port St Lawrence 10,486 gross tons

I caught the train the next morning, and after a long and tiresome rail journey, found the smart looking ship berthed in the Canada Dock. I went aboard, and as I entered the crew's messroom my face dropped. Sitting there was Nasty Kevin, who had been a trouble-maker aboard the Port Pirie when I had sailed with John Sheppard. He looked up, and with a sneer of his lips said, "Well, look who we have here. Where's your pal Sheppard...Or maybe ya think you can take me on by yourself?" I remained non-committal and introduced myself to the other deck crew. They appeared to be a decent bunch of guys, and I busied myself getting settled in. Nasty Kevin was at least consistent, and it wasn't long before he was causing mayhem and got into a fight with another deckhand, in which I'm glad to report, he came out of it second best and sustained damage to his shoulder. I simply kept out of his way.

We signed articles of agreement and the Port St Lawrence sailed that same day on an unspectacular voyage unloading her cargo of lamb and apples and butter that she'd brought from Australasia. We called at Dunkirk and Hull, then back to the London Docks, where we stayed for just two days whilst we discharged the last of the butter. The cargo holds were now empty and our ship was scheduled to sail to a Belfast shipyard where she would go into dry-dock for a bottom scrape and be coated with red antifouling paint. Captain Coombs departed on leave and a new master took over. It was none other than Captain Harry Conby, who had been our skipper aboard Port Pirie.

We sailed out of King George V dock and headed towards Lands End, then north up the Irish Sea to Belfast. On arrival at the shipyard we were signed-off and given ferry and train tickets to return home. The ferryboat, which would take us across the Irish Sea to Liverpool, was old and decrepit, and the overnight voyage was a nightmare. Our ship's officers were accommodated in warm and cosy cabins, whilst the crew had only bench seats to sit on. Most people stretched out full length on the seats, whilst the rest just lay about on the wooden decks. Upon departure the ferry's crew immediately set up shop and began selling cans of beer at exorbitant prices so as to supplement their wages. As the ferry cleared Belfast harbour we ran into a severe gale that caused dozens of passengers to be seasick where they lay, and the ship stank of puke and piss. By the time I got back home to Silvertown I had never wanted a bath so desperately in my whole life.

6: Bumming Around

The Crown Prince

Whilst I had been away on the Port St Lawrence, John Sheppard had called to enquire when my ship was due back to London, and a few days after I had returned home, I had a phone call from him. He asked about my trip and where I had been, and what my plans were, and how much leave was due to me. He also had been away on a voyage aboard a Blue Star Line refrigerated meat vessel to Buenos Aires in South America. Not one word was said about the reason I had left his father's house in Farnborough, nor for that matter had he apologised for the way in which I had felt it necessary to leave. However, I don't hold a grudge; life's too short for that. In any case I had genuinely missed having him around. So when he asked me if I would like to join him in Portsmouth to get a summer season job on the British Rail Isle of Wight ferries, I jumped at the chance. I instinctively knew we would have a wonderful time. He suggested that I get the train down on the Saturday afternoon, and there would be accommodation for me in a room above his mum's cafe; but I was instructed to bring a sleeping-bag. My family were quite used to my need to always be on the move, and so after just one week back at home, I repacked my suitcase and made my way to Portsmouth.

My train arrived at Portsmouth Central in the evening, and John picked me up from the station in a tired looking Triumph Herald motor car. I hadn't seen him in almost a year, but he hadn't changed one bit. Although at 19 years old he was just seven months older than me, he had deep clefts under his eyes which somehow enhanced his face, and together with his ready smile, gave him the look of a cheeky but confident conman.

We drove to the White Swan pub and sank a few pints while we caught up on each other's news. To be perfectly honest, we had much more than just a few pints. We swapped stories of our travels to the other side of the world, and talked about the pubs and clubs of Portsmouth and Southsea where we would be hanging out. We also discussed our chances of getting a job aboard the ferries. By the time we left the pub dragging my suitcase, it was chucking out time, and John was almost too drunk to drive anywhere. As we got in the car he said, "Oh yeah, did I mention that your room at my mum's cafe ain't ready to occupy until Monday. Never mind, I've booked you into a nice cheap place to stay." He drove down Queen Street and parked outside the Salvation Army Hostel. No sooner had I picked my suitcase from the boot than he said, "Sleep tight, mate. See you tomorrow," and he drove away.

My cheap accommodation at the Sally Army couldn't rightfully be called a room. It was simply a wooden cubicle with a single bed. The mattress was covered with a plastic sheet designed to prevent the drunken inhabitants from urinating onto it. In the corner was a narrow locker with space to hang almost nothing, and the top three feet of the bare plywood cubicle was made of steel wire mesh that allowed the noise of the inmates to permeate throughout the dormitory and be heard by everyone. There must have been three dozen men of varying states of homelessness and cleanliness staying in that dormitory, and throughout the night I could hear wheezing, coughing, retching, farting and heavy snoring, and I slept not a wink. Despite the expense I moved out the next morning into a bed and breakfast guest house.

On the Monday morning we presented ourselves at the office of the shipping superintendent of British Rail Ferries at Portsmouth Harbour railway station. He was a snotty looking man with a moustache, but he was only too glad to employ two proper deep-sea sailors, rather than the usual grunts whose sea-going experience consisted of a one-way trip on the Gosport ferry. We would start work as able-seamen in two days time for a busy summer season that would last until September.

John's mum, Molly Haynes, ran a cafe in New Road, in Portsmouth's North End, and it was here that both John and I would be occupying the attic room. "There's not much furniture, but we'll soon make it comfy," said John as we climbed the stairs to show me my new home. It was a complete understatement - there was no furniture at all! The floorboards were bare except for two small cheap rugs, upon which sat two single blow-up Lilo beds. The fly-blown windows had no curtains and were covered in cobwebs. I must have looked crestfallen as I inspected this dump which was to be my new lodgings. He tried to inject some optimism. "Yeah, we'll soon have this place looking like a home-from-home, won't we, Gra?" said John. He certainly had lots of confidence.

Molly and her taciturn husband Sunny Jim lived a few streets away in Laburnum Grove, so I was grateful that she wouldn't be around to get in our way. Molly was a flame-haired Irishwoman and was a complete chatterbox. She talked so fast and without pause that she hardly drew breath.

⚓

That night we went out to scour the pubs of Southsea and see if we could pull some girls. John was driving the Triumph Herald, so we didn't have to worry about getting a taxi. This was prior to the drink-drive laws and the use of the breathalyser. We were having a few pints in the Apsley House pub when he struck upon a stupid brainwave. John had always reckoned we were a couple of debonair and suave fellows, so why not tell any girls which we chatted up, that we were from the tiny Eastern European kingdom of Sauvolia? We'd drank a gutful of beer, so it had seemed like a good idea at the time.

Plan A went into operation as I marched up to two pretty blonde girls standing by the bar. John stood back a few paces.

"Excuse me. ladies, but I've been instructed by my friend over there," I said as I indicated John, "to ask if you would like to join us for a drink? He would ask you himself, but he doesn't speak any English."

"Where's he from then?" the shorter one asked warily.

"Well," I explained. "I'm his official guide and interpreter whilst he's here on a state visit. The crown prince is from the Kingdom of Sauvolia in Eastern Europe. Perhaps you've heard of it?" They shook their heads, but seemed delighted that they had been singled out to join a prince for a drink. This good looking bloke standing just six feet away was from a royal family. They couldn't believe their luck. I introduced myself and asked their names. They were called Lorna and Fiona. I told them that the crown prince wished to visit a typical English pub, and wanted to meet some pretty English girls. "He thinks that you're the prettiest girls in here, and so he hoped you wouldn't mind having a drink with us."

The tall one called Lorna asked what the prince's name was. "His name is crown prince Johann, but he is usually addressed as Your Highness, okay?" They both nodded solemnly. When I think about it all these years later, it sounds so far-fetched that anyone would be so stupid or gullible and fall for such an outlandish chat-up line.

Now came the difficult part. I waved John over and began speaking to him in a language that I thought may fit somewhere between a guttural German tongue and the romantic sounding dialect of Bohemia. It was all utter gibberish of course, and it was as much as I could do to keep a straight face, but John stood looking distant and aloof, as I suppose a crown prince from Sauvolia would do. I introduced the two fawning ladies, and as he stood ramrod straight, he clicked his heels together and inclined his royal head. John delivered some unintelligible gibberish in my direction and I explained to the girls what he had just said. "His Royal Highness has asked me to tell you that you are the most beautiful girls he has met while he's been in England." This agreeable snippet of royal commendation brought about a visible preening of their feathers with a coquettish, "Ooh my...whatever next," from Lorna.

"Could you tell His Highness, that it's very nice of him to say so," said Fiona gratefully.

We now became bolder, and after an exchange of more double-dutch the girls were keen to know what had transpired. "What did His Highness say just then?" asked Lorna.

"Um...Well, it's a bit embarrassing really," I said, attempting to sound a little reticent. "It's rather personal. I do hope you won't take offence?"

"Oh go on, tell us. We won't mind. What did he just say?"

"Well, he said that he thought that you both have perfect breasts and beautiful bottoms."

"Oh my...," said the lovely Fiona fanning her face with a beer-mat. Her cheeks had visibly reddened, but I could see she was very pleased indeed for her tits and her bum to be given the royal seal of approval. I ordered drinks; pints of foaming bitter for the crown prince and I, and Babychams for the girls. When I enquired where they lived, Lorna told me that they shared a two-bedroom apartment nearby in Southsea. I noticed the prince's ears pricking up as he heard this item of very important information. I slipped my arm around Lorna's waist and guided them to a vacant table in the far corner of the bar. Prince Johann, not to be left behind, took Fiona's hand and was soon ensconced on the seat opposite and was blatantly stroking her bottom which she seemed to be rather enjoying. He suddenly launched into some more meaningless mumbo-jumbo and the girls again wanted to know what he had said. This was the cruncher. "Ahem....well, two things actually," I said, dragging out the anticipation. "Firstly, His Royal Highness wondered if it would be alright if he gave Lady Fiona a kiss." Fiona began to giggle, but John simply took her into his arms and gave her the benefit of a long and passionate kiss. She came up for air breathing heavily and looking flummoxed, but nonetheless with a smile upon her face. I think that the sudden promotion to "Lady Fiona" hadn't done any harm either. Meanwhile, I tightened my grip on Lorna's slim waist and without further ado gave her a kiss as well. Other people in the bar briefly stared, but it was a young persons' hang-out and kissing and the odd quick grope were commonplace. In the quiet aftermath Lorna said, "You said there were two things. What was the other thing?"

"His Royal Highness," I said loftily, "wondered if you would both consent to us taking you back to your apartment." With a little experience I thought that I was getting rather good at the lingo, and my role playing as the laid-back royal personal secretary and interpreter. Fiona and Lorna meanwhile went into a huddle to discuss taking us back to their place. John surreptitiously slipped me some money and I got up to go to the bar for more drinks. It would after all not be in keeping for the crown prince to have to fetch his own drinks, would it? Anyhow, he didn't speak any English.

Lorna came to the bar with me to help carry the drinks, and whilst I stood there with my arm around this beautiful woman's waist, I basked in the euphoria of guessing that I would be sharing her bed tonight. Suddenly the bare floorboards and the Lilo bed of the attic room were forgotten, and I was starting to warm to the idea of living in the City of Portsmouth. As we waited for our drinks Lorna looked me in the eye. She said, "Graham, tell me the truth. Is he really a prince?"

I began to laugh. "Nah, don't be silly. Of course he isn't. His name's John and we're sailors who are starting work on the Isle of Wight ferryboats on Wednesday."

"Ha – I thought as much," she said and began to giggle.

"Are you going to tell Fiona," I asked, silently begging her not to.

"I don't think she needs to know just yet, do you?" she whispered secretively.

Much later, after we had consumed inordinate amounts of alcohol, we escorted them back to their apartment above a shoe shop in Fawcett Road.

We left the Triumph Herald where we'd parked it, because Fiona may have smelt a rat if the crown prince had slid into the driving seat of a rusty jalopy.

Lorna and I were laid upon her bed semi-naked and having a passionate kiss. Suddenly we heard Fiona's raised voice cry out from her bedroom, where she and Prince Johann were laying in bed. "I thought you couldn't speak English?" she shouted at John. Then, after some low-level mumbling explanation she cried out, "You're not really a prince at all, are you?" More mumbling was followed by, "I thought so." Lorna and I began to giggle at the absurdity of the scene. However, the next morning when I peeped into their bedroom, I found the two of them wrapped in each other's arms. They were both in a deep sleep, but I could see that Fiona had the trace of a satisfied smile upon her lips.

⚓

Portsmouth Harbour railway station was built on a pier that juts out into the grey waters of the harbour. It was upon the end of the pier where the passenger ferryboats berthed. Passengers would disembark from the trains and walk the few dozen yards along the platform to board the ferry, which would take them across the Solent to the Isle of Wight. The three ferries ran throughout the day taking hundreds of residents, holidaymakers and day-trippers on the 45-minute trip to Ryde IOW. However, as we deckhands loitered around the platform awaiting the arrival of the next train, we had ways to make the passengers part with their hard-earned cash. As they descended from the train we would grab their luggage. "Carry your bags Madam?" we would cry, and carry it to the ferry, dump it on the deck then hold out our hands expectantly for a tip. We'd rush back to the railway platform to grab the bags of yet another unsuspecting tourist.

This was easy money. We were required only to tie-up the ship; take turns at steering, and perhaps a short lookout duty. The rest of the time was spent in the crew's messroom drinking tea and reading the newspaper. If one of the diesel powered ferryboats was at refit or out of commission, a spare ferry was brought into service. This was the ancient steam powered coal-burning paddle steamer 'Ryde,' and every Monday morning it was our task to replenish the coal bunkers from a coal-barge that would be brought alongside. It's not often one can say that they've served aboard an old coal-burner, but I'm rather glad I did just for the experience.

British Rail/Sealink passenger ferry "Southsea"

That warm summer was idyllic as we went to and fro across the Solent countless times, and in the evenings we would cruise the busy streets and bars of Southsea to pick up suntanned girls in their short miniskirts and crop-tops. This was heaven. Even the attic room got a revamp when, after unsuccessfully attempting to seduce some girls upon the plastic Lilo beds, we went to a second hand furniture store and invested in two old beds, a pair of wardrobes, and a set of curtains.

Occasionally we deckhands would be required to serve upon the car ferries that berthed and departed just a few hundred yards along the harbour at The Camber Docks. Although they were also owned by British Rail, the car ferries were run as a separate operation, in that they carried only cars and their passengers. They didn't cater for foot passengers coming from the trains. However, where we now lost the opportunity to make money carrying their luggage, we could now make extra cash washing cars. As they drove up the car ramp and we took their tickets, we would ask, "Would you like your car washed, sir?" On a 40-minute trip we could wash and leather half a dozen cars. It was a great way to supplement our wages. Running six trips per shift worked out pretty good, and we deckhands would have a share-out at the end of the day. Easy-peasy

Car ferry 'Camber Queen'

Our downfall came one day in September when we were running trips aboard the car ferry. We were inbound to Portsmouth, and due to berth at 7:30pm on our last scheduled trip of the day. Our captain then sent down the unexpected news that the crew would be required to work overtime by doing an extra round trip. This, it was explained, was because, due to a very busy period, dozens of cars were still at the ferry terminal at Fishbourne on the Isle of Wight, and unless a car ferry was sent to collect them, they would be stranded there throughout the night. "Can't be helped," said the captain. "We should be finished by about 10-o-clock tonight. You'll just be in time to get a last pint before the pubs shut."

"Bugger that," said John. "We've got a hot date tonight." What he said was perfectly true. We had chatted up two heavenly girls just the night before in a pub near Southsea Common, and we had got along like a house on fire.

At the end of the evening, on a park bench, some heavy petting had ensued. Unfortunately, they explained, they couldn't invite us back to their apartment due to a visiting relative staying the night. However, if we cared to meet them in the same pub tonight, then we could stay the night and we were left in no doubt that hot sex was definitely on the menu and we would be sharing their respective beds.

Looking back, I was uncomfortable with the stance that John had taken, but which I had agreed to go along with it. After all, if I had been stranded on the Isle of Wight, I would be very grateful indeed that a ship had come to my rescue. But John was quite adamant. He marched up to the bridge and informed the captain that overtime was not compulsory, and that therefore we would not be sailing on the extra trip. The captain could only take note and try to find some replacement crew at very short notice. "Fuck 'em," said John as we made our way off home for a quick shower before our red-hot date.

The next morning as we joined the ship for our scheduled shift, the captain met us at the gangway. "The shipping superintendent wants to see both of you in his office right now," he barked. As we waited in the superintendent's outer office I looked out of the window. Things didn't look good as our ship let go and sailed without us. We had been replaced!
The superintendent came out of his office and simply handed us our outstanding pay and documentation. He said, "Your services are no longer required. Now please get out of my office and don't ever come onto British Rail property again."

As we made our way home, John said, "I'm sorry, mate. I'm to blame. It's my fault entirely." And so our summer season came to an abrupt end, and we now had to find alternative employment. It would mean going back to the pool and find ourselves another ship.

 As for the red-hot dates - the heavenly girls hadn't even bothered to turn up at the pub!

⚓

Before leaving Portsmouth, we briefly got a job at a local factory called MacMurdo's; for the simple reason that it employed 900 people – 700 of whom were female. On our first day in the factory, John was assigned to work in the battery shop where he did things that involved working with copious amounts of battery acid and having to wear heavy rubber gloves, long steel toe-capped boots, and a thick rubber smock. It all looked very dangerous.

I was assigned to work in a large workshop where, I was pleased to find myself surrounded by lots of young girls. The foreman sat me at a strange looking machine and gave me my instructions. On one end of the machine lay a 3 inch wide reel of thin shiny stainless steel, and this was fed, by a series of rollers, onto the die moulding tool that would then punch out the steel into a round shape. I was then required to place the shape onto another mould, and a heavy hammer-like column would descend and press the shape into a thimble-like mould. This would all take just a second and the finished product - the purpose of which escapes me - would be ejected by a noisy blast of compressed air and the thingamabob would fall down a chute and into a sack.

Picture if you will, yours truly sitting at this monstrous contraption for hour after hour where, in strict sequence, I must open the gate – place shape on the mould – close the gate – stamp the pedal – whoosh! It was farcical.

However, there were fringe benefits in the shape of the lovely Rosie, who introduced herself to me on my first day at MacMurdo's. After a night out together at a local pub, she shared my bed in the attic room for the rest of the week. She was not only a lovely girl, but was, beyond a doubt, definitely adventurous in the bedroom department, and we had lots of fun. Our brief sojourn at MacMurdo's was brought to a conclusion when, at the end of our first week, John Sheppard came along to the workshop to see what my job entailed. He took one look and fell about laughing. I'd had enough. "Come on, John; let's bugger off back to sea."

⚓

Back in Silvertown we went to the offices of the Federal Steamship Navigation Company who, together with the New Zealand Shipping Company, ran a sizeable fleet of refrigerated cargo liners trading mostly to Australasia. There we saw their marine superintendent, Ginger Moxley, who assigned us to do a 16-day 'around the land' voyage aboard the mv Somerset. It was a pleasant trip with a great crew. We joined her in London's Royal Albert Dock and were given a variety of maintenance tasks until we were due to sail.

One morning John, myself and other deckies were loitering near the gangway when I happened to look along the quayside and spotted a wonderful sight approaching. Striding purposefully towards us in full Vindicatrix uniform was a fresh-faced Vindi Boy. Over his shoulder he carried a canvas kitbag and he swaggered from side to side like Popeye the Sailor Man. He was about to join his first ship, yet he acted as if he had been at sea all his life. Upon his upper arms he wore the crossed anchors that signified that he had been a bosun at Sharpness. Back at the Vindi, with his bosun's rank, he maybe thought he was the 'Big Cheese,' but here in the real world he was about to become a lowly peggy – the lowest form of nautical life. I decided that I would have some fun. I winked at the lads. "Watch this," I said and ran down to the quayside to intercept him as he came to the gangway. "Good morning, sir," I said in my most obsequious manner. "Welcome to the Somerset. Are you just joining the ship, sir?" This spotty youth looked at me doubtfully, as he wasn't expecting such a rich welcome. "Er...well, yes I am actually."

"I see by your crossed anchors that you're a bosun. Let me take care of your kitbag, sir." I scooped up his kitbag and we set off up the gangway. The rest of the crowd took my cue and respectfully said, "Good morning, Bosun." Our Vindi Boy thought this was so wonderful that he was being treated with such deference. "I'll get you settled into your cabin sir," I said. Like a smarmy hotel porter, I escorted him into the crews' accommodation and sat him in the bosun's well appointed single berth cabin. Our muscular Scottish bosun, Willy Campbell, was at this very moment in the forward storeroom with the lamp-trimmer, so he was suitably well out of the way. "What's your name, sir?" I asked the Vindi Boy. "It's Ian Partridge," he said innocently, not guessing what misfortune was about to befall him.

"I'm afraid that the last occupant of the cabin hasn't cleared his gear out yet, so it's not quite ready for you to move into. Meanwhile, I'll make you a nice cup of tea, shall I?"

"That's ever so nice of you," he said. "I never expected to have such a nice cabin and be looked after like this." I delivered his tea. "There you are, sir. You put your feet up for a while and I'll call you when it's time to have your lunch, okay?" I left him to relax, and together with my crewmates loitered just along the alleyway to await events. It wasn't long in coming. John had spotted Willy Campbell ambling towards his cabin and we listened for the uproar.

"WHAT THE FOOK ARE YAE DOIN' ON ME FOOKIN BUNK, WEE MAN. GET THE FOOK OUTTA HERE." We could hear the Vindi boy mumble apologies as the bosun threw him out into the alleyway, quickly followed by his overcoat and kitbag. I must own up to feeling a trifle guilty in the way in which we had mistreated the lad; but after things had calmed down, and the real bosun had given us a right royal rollicking for winding him up, we showed the Vindi Boy to the deckboy's cabin and made him comfortable. I must say, he took it well, and later he saw the funny side and we all got on famously afterwards.

194

Somerset 10,256 gross tons. Federal Steamship Co.

We sailed from London two days later and discharged cargo at Liverpool, Avonmouth and then back to Liverpool where we paid-off and once again found ourselves unemployed.

My Dad's Dead – Again!

John went back to Farnborough to stay with the redoubtable Tom Sheppard, whilst I kicked my heels in Silvertown. After just a week and with dwindling resources, I somehow found my way to the P & O/Orient Line crew offices in Aldgate, London, where they offered me an able seaman's job aboard the cruise liner Oriana. Although the Oriana was presently away on a cruise, and wouldn't dock in Southampton for a further three weeks, the superintendent put me on pay for the whole time I would be standing-by at home.

I didn't hear anything from John until a few days before I was due to join Oriana for a six-month series of world cruises. The phone rang. "Hello, mate," said John. "Hey, I'm aboard the Middlesex in the Royal Albert Dock. She's signing articles on Tuesday for an 18-month round-the-world trip. She's a brilliant ship and got a great crew. All nice blokes. How'd you fancy joining me, eh? It'll be just like old times."

The Middlesex was a refrigerated cargo ship of the Federal Steamship Company. I was sorely tempted as I knew that, although an 18-month trip was a very long voyage, we would indeed have a great time together. However, he should have given me more notice, instead of a last minute phone call. I explained about my unwritten contract to join the Oriana and how I had been paid for doing nothing. "Well, see if you can wriggle out of it, can you? If you can - then go see Ginger Moxley, because they're still looking for more crew." I promised to do what I could, but didn't hold out much hope.

The more I thought about it, the more I wanted to sail with John. I was certain we'd have a fabulous time on a voyage around the world. Over the course of that weekend I tried to find a decent excuse that I could give to P & O as to why - after keeping me on full pay for three weeks - this ungrateful bugger could not possibly join their cruise ship. In spite of this, my sense of fairplay was frustrating the creation of a believable lie that the superintendent might swallow. The Oriana was due to dock in Southampton on Wednesday and I was expecting a call at any minute with instructions to join her there. I was at my wit's end.

Finally, on the Monday morning, I somehow found the courage to call the P & O offices and mumbled down the phone that I wouldn't be able to join the Oriana as I was unwell. A junior office gopher took the call and informed me that the superintendent, Mister McCall, wanted to see me, and could I be in his office at midday? My heart sank.

As I waited in his outer office my mind was in turmoil. My legs turned to jelly as he came out of his office to greet me with a smile and a warm handshake. He was a tall rotund man with a pleasant florid face. "Hello, nice to see you again. I'm told that you're not well, and you've said that you cannot join the Oriana. Why's that?"

I stared like a rabbit caught in the headlights of a motor car and I began to mumble some lame excuse, but suddenly my mind cleared and I rapidly formulated the lie to end all lies.

"Sir, it's not me that was sick. The truth is that my father died over the weekend." My face took on a forlorn and sad look. Mister McCall looked genuinely saddened and put a fatherly hand on my shoulder. "I'm very sorry to hear that. Of course I quite understand why you can't join Oriana, and we wouldn't expect you to in the circumstances." I nodded my head gratefully in the knowledge that I was getting away with it. Hey, this was easy, I thought.

"I know its early days," he went on, "but do you have any idea when you'd be ready to return to work? We could perhaps offer you another cruise ship." Oh dear, I'd spoken too soon. He seemed to be offering another

196

extended fully paid period of standing-by to join one of his ships. But as kind as it was, I simply wanted to be free to sail with John.

"Er...Well, Mister McCall, you've been awfully kind, and I appreciate your offer, but perhaps it would be better if you simply released me from my obligations, because I shall have to remain at home for some time to care for my mother," I lied.

"Of course, yes of course," said Mr McCall with concern. "Whatever suits your best interests." We shook hands, and I felt a real bastard as I thanked him for his kindness and compassion. If anyone from senior management at P & O is reading this, then may I give you my heartfelt apologies for any problems caused all those years ago, but I would like to remind you that the statute of limitations most probably applies – I sincerely hope so.

As I waited at the bus stop to take me back to Silvertown, the citizens in the streets of Aldgate must have wondered what kind of lunatic I was as I repeatedly punched the air in triumph at wriggling out of my commitment to P & O/Orient Line. My grin was as wide as the Nile.

It was only when I was riding along on the bus that I wondered what my father, who had been dead these past six years, would have thought about me declaring him dead for a second time. I imagine that my very healthy and robust step-father, Soupy Edwards, wouldn't have been too happy either. Oh the ruthlessness of a callow youth!

The Wonderful Ginger Moxley

I went straightaway to the Royal Albert Dock where the Middlesex lay in readiness for her forthcoming voyage. The quayside was busy as freight, bound for Australasia, was being loaded into the ship's massive cargo holds. Trucks, forklifts and trolleys bustled about and one had to be quick on one's feet to dodge the myriad number of vehicles that whizzed around the dockside.

I easily spotted John Sheppard and the rest of crew. They were working seventy feet above me whilst slung into bosun's chairs and washing the soot and grime off the ship's funnel. I shouted up at him and he waved back at me. I heard fragments of his words as he shouted back, but it was a windy day, and together with the noise and bustle on the quayside, it whipped his words away on the wind. I cupped my hands together and bellowed up at him. "Not sailing on Oriana. Gonna go see Ginger Moxley and sail on the Middlesex with you, okay?" He appeared to understand and waved back at me, and then shouted something else, but a gust of wind made his words unintelligible.

I walked off to the nearby Federal offices and saw the crew superintendent, Mr Moxley. Ginger was a tall kindly character with a mop

197

of red hair and bushy eyebrows. I was already well acquainted with him from when I had sought jobs in the past. I asked if I might be allowed to join the Middlesex. "Are you sure?" he asked. "You do realise that the Middlesex is sailing on an 18-month voyage, don't you?" From his desk he brought out an important looking document and laid it onto his blotter. He looked at me rather quizzically. "Are you quite sure you want me to put your name down for the Middlesex?" he again asked me curiously. Once again I nodded and the deal was done. He shook my hand. "We sign-on ship's articles tomorrow morning. I hope you enjoy the trip." I walked out of his office with a feeling of euphoria. I had not only wriggled out of sailing on the Oriana, but had now lined up what should be a fantastic voyage.

When I returned to the Middlesex the crew had finished the funnel job and were having lunch as I walked into the messroom. John greeted me with a wide grin. "Did Ginger Moxley get you all sorted?" he asked.
"Yes mate," I said cheerily, "I've spoken to him, and I've got my name down for signing-on the Middlesex tomorrow morning."
His face took on a disbelieving look. "You've done what?"
I was confused.
"You soppy bugger," he said. "I was trying to shout to you that I'm not sailing on the Middlesex now. Everything's changed. Didn't Moxley tell you? I'm getting the train up to Liverpool this afternoon and joining the Sussex instead."

What the hell had I let myself in for? I realised that, because I had given my word to Mr. Moxley, I would feel obligated to sail aboard the Middlesex, as agreed. It also became clear why he had repeatedly asked if I was quite certain I wanted to join the Middlesex. Perhaps he thought that John and I had fallen out?

Within the hour John had packed his suitcase and taken a taxi to the railway station for his journey to Liverpool, and I traipsed off home. I had to accept that I would be sailing on an 18-month voyage without my good friend John. I told my mum what I had done. Of course there was nothing she could do about it except to say, "Oh dear. Never mind, Graham, I'm sure you'll have a good time,"

The next day I brought my gear aboard the Middlesex in readiness to sign-on and to depart on the high tide tomorrow. I reported to the bosun. He was a stern looking elderly man who showed me to a vacant cabin. "You can have this cabin," he barked. "The deckhand who had it last has gone off to join the Sussex." I hadn't felt so down in the dumps in ages as I sat in that bare cabin that John had previously occupied. I opened a drawer, and found a pair of old socks which he had somehow left behind. I put them into the pocket of my windcheater for safekeeping, not knowing if we would ever meet again.

Later that morning the crew made their way up to the officers' saloon to sign the ship's Articles of Agreement, which was the formal contract between the crew and the shipping company. On hand to witness our signatures were the Superintendent of Shipping from the Board of Trade and the ship's captain. Ginger Moxley sat in a far corner of the saloon having coffee with the chief engineer. He was here to represent the Middlesex's owners, the Federal Steamship Co. The crew formed an orderly line to sign the legal agreement. When my turn came, I picked up the pen to sign where indicated, but just as I was about to do so, the voice of Ginger Moxley came from over my shoulder. "Don't sign the articles, Mr Mcglone. I've got another job lined up for you." I was somewhat mystified, but he took me to one side and explained. "I don't think you'll be happy without your mate Sheppard to keep you company, will you? So here's a rail warrant to go up to Liverpool to join the Sussex." He lowered his deep voice conspiratorially and grinned. "It's always better if you can sail with a good friend, isn't it?" He shook my hand and I was just so gratified that I was almost speechless and could only mumble my thanks. Ginger Moxley went to number one in my personal hall of fame.

7: The Sussex

The Navigation Lamp

The 11,272 gross ton Sussex lay in the Gladstone Dock at Liverpool as I joined her on the bitterly cold evening of Tuesday 14th December 1965. No crew were around as I lugged my suitcase up the gangway and inside the warm accommodation. I found the messroom where the crew had just eaten dinner, and sitting at a table with his back to me was John Sheppard. As a nasty surprise I cuffed him around the head and stood back. He jumped like he'd been electrified, and had a look of complete bewilderment on his face when he saw me standing there laughing. The rest of the crew wondered what the hell was going on.

"What the hell are you doing here?" he demanded happily.

"Ginger Moxley thought you could do with a decent mate to have a run ashore with. Anyway John, someone's gotta get the ugly women, so it may as well be you." I delved into my jacket and pulled out a navy blue ball of material and tossed it onto the table. "Here, you can have your smelly socks back." To the other crew it must have seemed implausible that the superintendent would go out of his way to ensure that two friends could ship-out together.

We signed-on articles the next day, and sailed on the high tide on the 18th December. Very shortly the Sussex was steaming down through the turbulent waters of the Irish Sea and she was bound for New Zealand. But firstly we had to sail through the rough waters of the Bay of Biscay and via the Azores out across the Atlantic Ocean to Jamaica. After discharging cargo in Kingston, we would sail through the blue waters of the Caribbean, and transit the Panama Canal and across the wide Pacific Ocean. There was a very long way to go.

The next morning found the Sussex rolling from side to side as we steamed south-south-westerly through the Bay of Biscay. During the night the navigation lamp, which is situated at the very top of the mainmast, had blown its filament, and the ship was now without an electric lamp; which at night was intended to show other ships the aspect of our vessel. There was still the possibility of hauling up an emergency oil lamp instead, but our bosun, a short wiry Liverpudlian called Jeff Lee, wanted the electric lamp replaced quickly. The entire deck crew were gathered around the mast, but he singled me out carry out this risky task. I looked up with apprehension. The ship rolled 15 degrees either way and the top of the mast swung way out over the sea.

"That looks ever so unsafe, Jeff. Can't we wait until after the weather improves and the ship stops rolling so much? Perhaps we could use the emergency oil lamp?" Some of the crew chipped in and made it plain that they also found it bloody dangerous and not a top priority as the ship was rolling so much. But Jeff would have none of it. "Don't be such a wimp, lad. Go on, get up there." He slung a canvas satchel containing the replacement lamp across my shoulder.

Orders were orders, and so I began to climb up the steel rungs of the ladder. I now readily admit that I was shit-scared. Before I had climbed even halfway up, a violent roll caused my feet to slip off the ladder and my body was taken out almost at right angles to the mast. My fingers were wrapped around the rungs as I hung on for grim death. The ship rolled back the opposite way and I went crashing into the steelwork. This was far too dangerous. I began to creep down the ladder again. "What the hell are you doing?" shouted Jeff from far below. "Get back up there. The jobs gotta be done." But there was no way I was going to put my life at risk. I wasn't ready to die!

Jeff Lee was about 50 years old, and after whinging about me having no courage, he decided that he would climb the mast himself, and show us youngsters how it's done. He set off up the crazily swaying mast and reached the same height where I had lost my footing. Suddenly the ship rolled violently to starboard and his feet were likewise swept off the ladder. Only his tight grip on the rungs prevented him from being thrown to the deck. As the ship rolled back again, his body was smashed into the steel ladder and we were all sure that Jeff would lose his grip and be killed. He hung on for some minutes as he got his breath back, and we all thought that he would make his way down and call it a day. There would have been no shame in that. But Jeff began to slowly climb again, and the higher he went, the more precarious it became. The mast reduced in circumference and there were much smaller ladder rungs to hold onto. But little by little he crept gingerly upwards, until at last he was sat astride of the navigation light housing at the very top of the wildly swaying mainmast. At times the top-mast hung way out over the sea, and would then sway wildly in the opposite direction. I could see him open up the access flap in the watertight box and replace the blown lamp. Then came the perilous task of getting down again. Ever so cautiously he descended, and twice almost lost his footing. As he got to the lower mast, I went back up and perched just below him to give some encouragement, and we slowly came down to the deck together.

Jeff was visibly trembling as he sat on a bollard and drank a mug of hot tea. We lit a cigarette for him, as he was shaking too much to light his own. Jeff looked at me and said graciously, "I can see what you mean about

201

it being risky. I wouldn't want to do that again in a hurry." It was the nearest he could ever come to an apology, but I was grateful for the thought.

By the next day the swells had abated, and the Sussex cut through the waves with hardly a roll. As the weather improved, the deck crew set about the usual task of overhauling the cargo gear. It was a major task and would take many days to complete. As the Sussex steamed further towards the Caribbean, the sun became warmer and we could work out on deck in shorts and t-shirt.

The Sussex was a typical general cargo ship that was designed for the Australasian trade. She had six cargo hatches, all 523,000 cubic feet of which could be refrigerated, so as to carry meat and dairy produce. On this outward voyage we would, as usual, carry heavy machinery and general cargo that had been manufactured in the industrial heartlands of Great Britain. The Sussex had been built at John Brown's Clydebank Shipyard in 1949 for the Federal Steamship Navigation Company. She was fitted with twin Doxford 5-cylinder diesel engines producing 12,800 bhp. This gave her a service speed of 16 knots.

Naturally I shared a cabin with John, but we were quickly getting to know our shipmates. Simon Holroyd was a lanky Yorkshireman from Scarborough, and Gwyn "Taffy" Evans was from Swansea, and Robin Hedges was a Croydon lad. There was also Dave Bowyer from Brighton and Trevor Russell, one of the two ordinary seamen, hailed from Essex, The peggy was Ronnie Packard. There was also a middle-aged South African from Durban who had the most boring voice imaginable and would almost send me to sleep. Some of the other crew were still getting to know each other, but I got the feeling that we would soon be a close-knit crew.

Just before midnight, a week after sailing from Liverpool, I went up to the bridge to do a look-out duty. As I relieved Kenny Roberts, the able seaman on the 8 -12 watch, he pointed out the dim navigation lights of two other vessels on the far horizon, and began to make his way below for some well earned sleep. As he descended the bridge ladder he looked back as if he had forgotten something. "Oh by the way, Graham, a happy Christmas mate." Of course, I hadn't realised - It was Christmas Day! This would be my second Christmas Day spent at sea, and I sincerely hoped that it would be better than the first one aboard the Port Pirie, when the Scotsman Willy had gone overboard. Although I didn't have my family around me, the day turned out quite pleasant with just the minimum of work required, except for duty watches. The chef and his galley staff pulled out all the stops to ensure that we were served a superb four course dinner. Captain Richard Baker and his entourage, including the chief engineer, chief officer and the chief steward, made a visit to the crew's messroom to wish us a Merry

Christmas, and more importantly, made a bottle of rum and two cases of beer available for the lower deck crew.

Five days later, we berthed at the port of Kingston in Jamaica to load a small amount of general cargo which was due to take just 24 hours. When we had left Liverpool, less than two weeks ago, the December weather had been bitterly cold, and now here in Jamaica, it was so warm and sunny, that we strode around the decks bare-chested.

I had heard some disturbing stories about the high crime rate and violence of Jamaica, and decided that I wouldn't be venturing very far afield. Apparently criminal gangs ruled whole areas of the cities where it was unsafe to go, and Jamaica had one of the highest murder rates in the world. One section of people who were particularly at risk were homosexuals. Jamaica has the highest incidence of homophobic attacks in the western world, and Stella, one of our queer stewards, was warned not to even attempt to go ashore.

However, that night we arranged for a dozen of us to go ashore *en masse*, and we descended upon Doris's Bar; renowned as the place where sailors went to get drunk. The music was Caribbean reggae, and all the girls at the bar and on the dance floor were unmistakably prostitutes. The whores didn't interest me at all, so I got steadily drunk on the local rum called Appleton Estate.

Sitting just a few seats away at the bar was what I presumed to be another prostitute, who I noticed was very heavily pregnant. In her expectant state she obviously couldn't be carrying on her trade, so she was getting drunk on neat cheap rum. As the night wore on, she was getting more tanked-up by the minute, and by 9pm she gave out an awful moan as she held her lower abdomen in pain. Two girls helped her off the stool and they left the bar. It occurred to me that she was possibly very close to her baby's delivery. I thought nothing more of it until almost midnight when she and her two cohorts returned. They helped her back onto her bar stool and she ordered more rum. I immediately noticed a vast difference in her silhouette. The sizeable bulge of her pregnant abdomen had disappeared, and her tummy was almost flat again. In the three hours during which she had been away from the bar, her baby had been born, and she'd returned to Doris's to continue drinking where she had left off. God knows what happened to the baby. Suffice to say, that in places like Kingston, Jamaica – life was cheap!

We sailed from Kingston early morning on the last day of the year, and set course for Curacao in the Netherlands Antilles to top up the ship's fuel bunkers. From Curacao we would head for the Panama Canal. As midnight came and we travelled into 1966, there appeared to be no difference to any other day of the year, except that the captain came onto the bridge and wished everyone a Happy New Year.

Happy Valley

In the late afternoon of New Years Day the Sussex arrived at Willemstad, the capital of Curacao. The ship glided through the narrow harbour entrance and into St Anna Bay, which straddles the heart of the city. With its tall narrow Dutch style houses it looked to be a charming city and I would love to have explored it further; but alas we would be here for only a matter of hours whilst the ship had her fuel tanks topped up for the long voyage across the Pacific. Our pilot navigated the Sussex into the inland lake called the Schottegat and we tied-up at the fuel facility wharf. The ship's engineers quickly coupled a thick rubber hose onto the inlet valve, and tons of diesel fuel was soon pulsing through the fuel line to supply our engine's lifeblood.

Curacao is the largest of the Netherlands Antilles, the other two islands being Aruba and Bonaire; and because of their alphabetic lettering, they are sometimes called the ABC Islands. They have had a fairly chequered history. The islands were firstly occupied by the Spaniards in 1499. They forcibly exported the original indigenous inhabitants, the Arawaks, to a life of slavery onto other islands, where the Spanish needed manual workers. The Dutch took over the islands in 1634, and quickly recognised that the natural harbour at Willemstad was an ideal location for commerce, trade - and piracy! For some considerable time, piracy was the most important trade within the region. In the mid-1600s the Dutch West India Company made Curacao a major centre for the Atlantic slave trade. Greedy Dutch merchants would bring slaves from Africa; and under an agreement with Spain, would ship and sell large numbers of slaves to be worked throughout the Caribbean or South America. Even when slavery was officially abolished in 1863, the former slaves had nowhere to go, and so under a system called Paga Tera, they remained working for the plantation owners. The Negroes leased a piece of land, and in exchange had to give up most of their harvest to their former slave-masters. This form of neo-slavery lasted until the beginning of the 20th century. Fortunes changed dramatically in 1915 when oil was discovered in the Maracaibo Lakes of nearby Venezuela. The Royal Dutch Shell Company built an extensive oil refinery at Willemstad and the islands prospered as Curacao became a major oil refiner and fuel facility for shipping.

As the deck crew sat having our morning smoko, the South African called Louis, revealed that he had been to Curacao before, and he told us about a brothel located at a place called Happy Valley. My ears pricked up because, even though I have never paid for the services of a prostitute, girls were girls.

Happy Valley, or to give it its proper name, Campo Alegre, said Louis, is a extensive club within a walled compound set up by the Curacao government in 1949 for the purposes of legal prostitution. Prior to that, whores and their pimps infested the city centre of Willemstad, and so the government looked at ways to make the streets safe and pleasant to walk in again. Campo Alegre was build out by the airport on the far side of the island, and overnight the prostitution problem was solved. Only the most beautiful girls were employed and were brought in from faraway Caribbean islands and from South America. Louis thought that there were over 100 girls out at Campo Alegre when he had visited a few years previously. A qualified resident doctor is on hand to ensure that the girls are regularly tested for nasty diseases, and all the girls charge a set rate for their services – give or take an extra amount for 'personal services.' Louis said that most sailors thought the club was built and maintained by the Shell Oil Company, and most referred to it as Shell Oil's Happy Valley. But that is not the case, as the brothel was wholly instigated by the Curacao government. However, with the majority of customers being workers from the huge refinery, he thought it was unthinkable that Shell Oil had no hand in the setting up of the facility. None of our crew would have the time to savour the delights of Happy Valley because after just four hours pumping diesel fuel aboard, the ship departed and we headed for the Panama Canal. I never did get to visit Campo Alegre.

All these years later I searched for details of the brothel that I had missed visiting. It's still there, and doing a roaring trade, and in fact has been modernised with rows of quaint looking bungalows. The ladies rent a room at a reasonable rate, and whatever they earn – they keep. It now employs roughly 130 girls and also has its own website and calls itself an adult resort. Campo Alegre has a credit card facility and one can even take a virtual tour around the brothel. That seems much too clinical and kinda takes the fun out of it, doesn't it?

⚓

At the port of Colon on the Atlantic side of the canal we stayed for almost two days whilst more cargo was offloaded. Although I had been through the canal twice, the ship had never stopped off in port, and so it was a new experience for me, and another country to tick off on my list of places I had visited.

In January1880 the French, under the command of Ferdinand de Lesseps, attempted to build a sea level canal i.e. one without locks, through the Isthmus of Panama. The attempt was an unmitigated disaster, and after

13 years toil and the loss of 22,000 lives – mostly due to malaria and yellow fever, the French gave up in 1893. Ten years later the United States decided that they themselves could successfully build a canal.

Panama was, at the turn of the 20th century, a province of Columbia, and so in order to build the canal, the United States needed to sign a treaty with Columbia that would give the US control of what would be a very expensive undertaking. A treaty was signed that stipulated a renewable lease in perpetuity. However, the Columbian Senate did not ratify the treaty, which left the US somewhat in limbo. President Theodore Roosevelt then changed tactics by supporting Panamanian separatists to revolt against Columbia, and in November 1903, with American help, they achieved independence. The United States immediately recognised the Republic of Panama and a new country was born. The United States paid-off France for the digging equipment which had been abandoned and later paid-off Columbia for the loss of her province.

Work could now begin in earnest. In May 1904 the US Army Corps began the huge engineering task of draining vast areas of swamp, bringing in massive steam shovels, building dams, laying heavy duty railway tracks, installing huge locks systems, and building the associated housing and infrastructure. The Panama Canal opened for business in August 1914 and saved every nation's shipping from travelling the vast distance around the dangerous Cape Horn on the southern tip of South America.

When a ship transited through the canal, it travelled through what was known as the Panama Canal Zone, a part of the US territory which extended roughly five miles on each side of the canal's centreline. It was almost a mini state of the USA, in that it was run by the American controlled Panama Canal Company, which had its own shops and housing and even postage stamps. A large US military presence, an infantry brigade, was in place and the Canal Zone Company provided its own police force as well as courts and judges. All this changed when on 31 December 1999 the US and Panama signed a treaty handing full control of the canal back to Panama so long as Panama guaranteed permanent neutrality to the canal zone.

However, back in 1966 when I was trotting down the gangway to go ashore, the port of Colon was not within the Canal Zone, so we were in the actual Republic of Panama. I went ashore to the local pharmacy and purchased, quite legally it would appear, a dozen Benzedrine tablets so as to keep me awake and dancing throughout the night. Cheap marijuana was openly on sale in one kilo bags.

Later that evening, John and I went to Tony's Bar. It was heaving with beautiful creamy skinned girls wearing skimpy short skirts and tassel-tops. I suspect that most of the women were prostitutes, because they did appear to go upstairs to the private rooms with a variety of different men at frequent intervals. In the bar the music was thumpin' out salsa, and it was so sensual that one of the girls began dancing with me on the small dance floor. She must have drawn the conclusion that I was a potential customer, because she manoeuvred me out onto the palm fringed patio at the rear and began kissing me. When I kissed her back, she took that as her cue to tell me what her tariff was for the receiving of sexual favours. As I had no interest whatsoever in paying a prostitute, when there was so much free totty in New Zealand, I made it plain that sex wasn't on the menu, and that was the end of another beautiful relationship.

⚓

Two days after leaving the Panama Canal, the Sussex was steaming west-south-westwards on her 6533 nautical mile voyage to New Zealand. During the morning watch she was sailing close to the Galapagos Islands that straddle the equator.

The Galapagos are a volcanic archipelago located some 530 miles to the west of Ecuador, to whom they belong. They are made up of 18 main islands and numerous rocks that are spread out over 17,000 sq mi of the Pacific Ocean. In 1684 a buccaneer called Ambrose Cowley began a mapmaking survey and named the individual islands after fellow pirates or after noblemen who were financial patrons of his voyage. Since that time they have been given Spanish names, but they are still referred to by their ancient piratical names. In the 1820s American whalers from Nantucket came to kill the profusion of sperm whales and the giant tortoises that abounded around the archipelago, and in doing so, almost wiped them out.

In 1835 the survey ship Beagle, under the command of Captain Robert Fitzroy, came to survey the approaches to the harbours. Onboard was a young geologist, naturalist and biologist called Charles Darwin. He studied the different species of flora and fauna, and in particular the giant tortoise; but he especially studied the mockingbirds that were markedly dissimilar between the separate islands. It was these birds, now called Darwin's Finches, which were unique and crucial in the development of his theory of evolution in his written work - The Origin of Species.

Across the Pacific Again

That same afternoon we passed across zero latitude – the equator - as we steamed into the southern hemisphere. The 'crossing the line' initiation ceremony included those crew members who had never crossed the equator. Like thousands before them, they were welcomed into Neptune's kingdom by being trussed up and splattered with galley slops and coloured foam. After being hosed down they were thrown into the swimming pool which had been erected upon the after deck.

Sussex 11,272 grt Federal Steam Navigation Company

The weather sailing across the Pacific was warm and balmy with just a long low swell on which the Sussex motored easily. The deck crew were kept busy chipping rust off the steel decks with the aid of an electric chipping machine on which tungsten tipped cutters mounted onto a rapidly rotating flexible shaft would scale the paint and rust off the decks and back to bare steelwork. The noise made by the chipping machine was deafening, and the very rapid vibrations as it flailed the rusty deck caused our hands and arms to become numb. So as not to be covered in dust and rust, we would cover our faces with a muslin material which had two eye holes cut into a mask, somewhat like a balaclava. We also had to wear eye and ear protection, so it wasn't a very comfortable task in the heat of the tropics, and the sweat would run down our faces. During the course of a day's work we could normally scale off tens of square yards of rusty decks and coat it with a rust protecting paint called red lead. So as not to suffer dehydration, lime juice cordial and salt tablets were made available.

New Zealand is made up of two main landmasses – North Island and South Island. It also has about 600 smaller offshore islands, many of which are volcanic. Although New Zealand's size (103,483 sq mi) is 10% bigger than the United Kingdom (93,627 sq mi), the population is far less. In 1966 the population of the UK was 54.2 million, whereas the number of people living in Kiwi was a mere 2.6 million. To put the population into perspective; in 1966 there were 54 million sheep being reared on NZ farms – that's 20 sheep for every man, woman and child. They're gonna need an awful lot of mint sauce!

After our 17-day Pacific voyage, our first stop was the pretty town of Picton, nestled at the top of the South Island. Picton is at the southern extremity of the Marlborough Sound, and to reach it, the Sussex sailed for almost two hours through the most wonderful scenery imaginable. The Sound looks much like a Norwegian fjord and is surrounded by high hills on which houses are perched and sheep graze in the fields.

The town was named after Sir Thomas Picton, a Welshman from Pembrokeshire who was a Lieutenant General in the Duke of Wellington's army who fought and died at the Battle of Waterloo

Picton was (and is) the terminus for the inter-island ferry, which today has a roll-on-roll-off facility. However, in 1966 things were much more basic, and the town had just one pier and a pub or maybe two. All the same it was a beautiful place to step ashore and to recharge our batteries before proceeding onwards to Auckland. We stayed for just two days and then headed northwards.

⚓

Soon after the Sussex sailed into Auckland harbour, we lifted the derricks and opened the hatches ready to discharge cargo. By late afternoon we were heading for Ma Gleason's. The place hadn't changed one bit. It was still packed to the rafters and the atmosphere was manic as the serious drinkers were getting tanked-up.

After 6pm when the bars closed, there was normally a house party going on somewhere that one could wangle an invite to. Mind you, you'd have to take a decent supply of beer along with you. It was very bad form to try to scrounge other people's booze.

The other type of party going on after the pubs closed was a cabin party onboard ship. The wharfs at which the ships berthed were located close to the city centre and it was just a short walk from the bars. The girls who drank in bars like Ma Gleason's, The Great Northern or the Snake Pit were extraordinarily eager to get themselves invited to a party aboard a ship. However, the ship had to be British because the girls were almost exclusively drawn towards British sailors. As long as the ship was flying the Red Duster (New Zealand flagged ships didn't count), then the women would flock onboard. There would normally be half a dozen girls to be found enjoying themselves down on the crew decks.

However, as stated in a previous chapter, one was first required to obtain a guest chitty from the OOW (officer-of-the-watch) prior to entertaining a young lady onboard. Therefore it was advisable to obtain one's guest permit before venturing ashore; but seeing as we often had no idea which girl we would be bringing onboard, the chits were often made out in a variety of comical names. Most of the permits used the common names of, Smith, Jones or Brown etc; but others that spring to mind were in the names of, Miss Tress, Miss Chief, Miss Fitt or Miss Take.

A typical scenario might be that a sailor has chatted up a girl in one of the bars and invites her back onboard for a few drinks. Her eyes light up. The Auckland girls liked to have a good time. As the pubs chucked out at 6pm, the sailors would head back to their ship with a girl on his arm. Once onboard, he would get her alone in his cabin and ply her with more alcohol. She would insist that she couldn't possibly get her kit off – she's not that type of girl! After plying her with more alcohol and telling her that she was a most beautiful creature on earth, all this play-acting would be forgotten and the virginal princess would slip out of her jeans and eagerly hop into bed.

Meanwhile, up in the officers' accommodation, they would be entertaining a whole bevy of nurses from the local hospital who, at the first sniff of a party, would pile aboard in droves. Those nurses sure knew how to let their hair down!

If a sailor and his girlfriend become closely attached, then it caused difficulties when it was time for the ship to depart. However, some seamen overcome this problem with a simple solution. He takes the girl with him! It was known as ring-bolting.

If say the ship was sailing from Auckland to Wellington, he would hide her in his cabin for the day and a half's voyage and hope that no officers caught sight of her. If she was discovered, then she would more than likely find the police waiting for her on the quayside at their destination. Of course, for the sailor, there were fringe benefits with ring-bolting your girlfriend. Firstly you had her nice warm and curvy body beside you in your bunk, and could if you wish; bonk your brains out en-route to the next port. Secondly, one may be able to sweet-talk her into doing your cabin cleaning and dhobying whilst you're working out on deck. It's a win/win situation.

Our two week stay progressed along typical lines. Apart from working aboard ship, we drank in the bars, occasionally picked up girls, and added them to our tally of conquests. However, I was rather glad when we sailed out of the harbour bound for Napier. I needed a change of scenery – and a rest!

The heavy swells that rolled into Napier harbour caused the ship to range up and down the quayside. Therefore we had to haul very thick coir ropes onboard which were designed to stretch, and not snap as regular mooring ropes would tend to do. It should have been an easy task, but as we were making them fast, yours truly managed to get into a perilous position between the ship's rail and the mooring bollards. When the rope somehow slipped, I was trapped with nowhere to go, and the coir rope scraped down my thigh, taking a sizeable area of skin with it. I looked a dreadful mess and had to wear a bandage soaked in cold cream for a week before it healed.

Being in Napier was akin to being in a convalescent home – not too much to do - but quite relaxing. I do hope the town has improved over the years. Back in 1966, Napier seemed soulless and needed a heavy shot of vitality pumped into the place. Even the sailors' hangout, the Criterion Hotel, wasn't too exciting. We stayed only for two days as we loaded more meat and dairy cargo, and sailed for New Plymouth.

⚓

The town of New Plymouth lay on the west coast of the North Island and is overlooked by the 8284 foot high volcano, Mount Taranaki. It was just after midday on a lovely sunny day in early February as we berthed at the port; and after getting the ship ready to work cargo, the chief officer gave the deck crew a job and finish. I went for a walk around the town to stretch my legs. John Sheppard didn't come with me. He wasn't the type of guy to go sightseeing or to sample the culture and scenery of a country. He would sooner get himself comfortable in a pub with a rum and coke and attempt to chat-up a girl and add her to his list of promiscuous maidens who have fallen for his charms.

The Sussex was due to be in New Plymouth for twelve days whilst we unloaded the last of our general cargo from England and reload with lamb, butter, cheese and other dairy products. On the adjacent berth another ship, a Shaw Savill cargo liner, was loading lamb carcasses and heavy bales of wool.

I walked through the pleasant streets of the town and aimlessly window-shopped along the busy streets. I popped into the museum and picked up a pamphlet which gave me some basic information about the town. It was settled in 1841 by colonists who came from the west country of England, and of course, it was named after the city of Plymouth in Devon.

Walking south and almost in the heart of the town, I came across Pukekura Park, a thickly forested parkland that was bisected by a lake with quaint bridges spanning across the water. I walked around its leafy trails and found formal gardens, specimen trees, and an exotic plant collection within heated greenhouses. It was interesting, but not riveting enough to hold my attention for more than a few minutes. It was time to go for a beer.

Near the docks I came across the Breakwater Hotel, and unsurprisingly found John installed in the bar drinking a Bacardi and coke. The bar was noisy and busy with sailors, wharfies and locals getting beer down their throats. Over in the far corner, some sailors from the Shaw Savill ship were boozing with two girls who I suspect would have easily won an ugly contest had their names been entered. As John didn't get off his arse to buy me a drink, I ordered a glass of beer for myself and settled down in a comfortable leather chair for some leisurely afternoon's drinking. I began telling John about my walk around the park and nature trails, but his eyes clouded over and I could tell he wasn't remotely interested in tales of flora or fauna.

Into the bar came two perfectly lovely girls. The dark haired girl was very pretty with shoulder length hair, a nice figure, and hazel eyes, but it was her taller blonde companion who I just couldn't take my eyes away from. The blonde was very slim, almost waif-like, and with short cropped hair and clear blue eyes. John, who had been half asleep after I had insisted on telling him about the park's exotic plants and specimen trees, suddenly sat up and took notice as his 'fanny scanner radar' detected the girl's presence and went into automatic mode. He grinned and winked back at me. I knew it was our signal for us to go into chat-up mode.

The Shaw Savill sailors were looking over this way, and I presumed they were wondering how they could dump the ugly sisters and snare these two stunning girls. I decided to get in first and marched over. I didn't try any clever chat-up lines, but simply stated the obvious. "Good afternoon ladies. My friend and I were wondering if you would care to join us for a drink." They looked at each other, and in that mystifying way in which females signal between the species, silently decided that they were attracted to us. It's always baffled me how they do it.

We sat at a table and introduced ourselves. The dark haired beauty was called Michelle and Miss Wonderful the blonde was Beverley, but she said she preferred Bev. They shared a house together in town, and whilst Michelle worked at an estate agents office, Bev was a civil servant at the district council offices. They pretty much guessed that we were off the cargo ship, and so we talked about our travels, and of course they both had plans to 'Go home' to England when they had saved up enough money. With all these Kiwi lads and lasses planning on 'going home' to England, it was a wonder to me that there would be anyone left in the country!

Bev somehow knew with a woman's intuition that I fancied her, and likewise with John and Michelle. Very soon we were sitting close together and laughing and joking; and after a while when I held her hand, she seemed relaxed and squeezed it. I couldn't stop looking at her. Although she couldn't be called beautiful in the truest sense, her lovely eyes and wonderful smile simply added to her attractiveness.

They took us back to their house, where we sat around the kitchen table drinking beer, smoking, and playing a noisy game of cards. John was getting along famously with Michelle and they were quite intimate as they held hands and occasionally kissed. However, I was unsure if I would be invited to stay the night, and I didn't want to upset the applecart by suggesting it and offending her, so without any preamble I leaned over and kissed her. "Mmmm, that was nice," she said. A few minutes later Bev gave a huge yawn and said, "I'm tired, it's time for bed – Goodnight all." She took hold of my hand and led me into her bedroom. I was a happy man indeed.

⚓

The Sussex sailed on a balmy Saturday evening bound for Port Chalmers down on the east coast of the South Island where we would be loading more of the same type of cargo; lamb and dairy products. The voyage of almost 500 nautical miles would get us there for late on Sunday.

John and I were sad to be leaving New Plymouth as we'd had a wonderful time with the girls. Every night after work we would show up at their comfortable rented house with some food that we'd liberated from the ship's storerooms, and they would cook a delicious meal. Afterwards we would play cards or games and drink beer, and of course, go to bed and make love. It had been an idyllic time, but all good things come to an end, and the good ship Sussex eventually slid out of the harbour, heading south.

Port Chalmers was a nice little town which is tucked away on the north side of Otago Harbour. It is the main port, and almost a suburb of the city of Dunedin, the second biggest city of the South Island. We arrived at almost midnight on the Sunday and got the derricks topped up in readiness for the wharfies to work cargo as soon as they came aboard on the Monday morning.

The port is overlooked by steep granite cliffs, perhaps two hundred feet high. They were dotted with numerous gorse bushes and interspersed

213

with flat grassy areas which I imagined was a perfect spot to have a panoramic view across the whole of Otago Harbour. On some parts of the rock face, the granite escarpment was almost sheer sided. Over the years, sailors had climbed up onto the cliffs with ropes and pots of paint, and had hung over the abyss while attached to bosun's chairs. As they were suspended over the sheer drop, they would paint the name of their ship upon the flat face of the precipice. I could see names of ships from many nations daubed onto the rock, together with the date of its visit. Some dates went back many years, and several of the paintings, with decorative funnel markings and company house-flags, were pure works of art.

The next afternoon some of our crew went to the pub for a few pints, and Dave Bowyer pulled a dark haired girl who took him home to stay the night. Back on board the next morning, Dave shared the innermost secrets about his night of debauchery and carnal lust with anyone who would care to listen. He also told us that the girl had organised a picnic up on the granite cliffs that very evening, with just her and Dave as the participants.

"Hey, how would you like to see me shagging her when I get her up there?" Dave asked the deck crew. Dave was known as something of a pervert.

"How are you gonna arrange that, Dave?" said Gwyn. "We wouldn't be able to see a thing from this far away, would we?"

"Borrow some binoculars from the 3rd mate," suggested Dave, "and I'll make sure I'm shagging her at 6-o-clock on-the-dot. It'll be a great laugh."

"Where will you picnicking?" enquired Kenny Roberts. Dave scanned the area, and then pointed at a grassy knoll at the very top of the hill. "That's where we'll be. Right there."

After work that evening, the bridge binoculars had been loaned, and several of the crew were stationed on the boat-deck, including the 3rd mate, who wasn't going to miss out on any alfresco sex. He had his own pair of binoculars. Dave and the girl were spotted climbing up the footpath carrying a wicker hamper and a tartan blanket. As the girl led the way, Dave managed to give us a wave without the girl noticing. They spread the blanket and made themselves comfortable way up on the designated knoll, and we could see Dave munching on a sandwich. We looked at our wristwatches. The minute hand was nearing the magic hour.

"He's getting her jeans off," reported Kenny. Even without the benefit of binoculars, we could see the two figures high on the hill get into the doggy position, and Dave was careful to position her facing away from the watchers below. They began humping and were going at it hammer and tongs, and we could see Dave was putting a lot of effort into it. Just about then he must have remembered his perverted voyeuristic shipmates, because

214

without missing a beat, he turned around and gave the crew a triumphant wave.

Beautiful Dunedin

The chief officer gave the deck crew another job n' knock to sugi down the ship's funnel, and so after a quick lunch we shared a cab into the City of Dunedin. Whilst my shipmates made themselves comfortable in the bar of the Gresham Hotel, I decided to have a walk around and discover the town.

By way of Princes Street I found my way to The Octagon in the very heart of the city. The Octagon is a circular orbital road that houses many of the city's important public and municipal buildings. Despite the lack of any proper plan of action, I was drawn to a massive granite structure on the far side of the eight-sided plaza, and found that it was the town hall. Dunedin Town Hall was a solid looking Victorian building made of local hewn granite that, according to a brass plate at the front entrance, had been built back in 1880. A fine four-tiered clock tower rose up dramatically from the centre of the building and the whole edifice gave the impression of permanency and the belief that it had been standing for a thousand years, and would remain standing for yet another thousand. Inside the foyer was a rack of free literature, and so I grabbed a city map and a guide to Dunedin which helpfully included the main attractions and a history of the city. On what was a warm and sunny afternoon, I sat on a bench across the road and skimmed through the brochures.

Captain James Cook, in his ship Endeavour, had anchored off what is now Dunedin in February 1770 and surveyed the surrounding waters of Otago Harbour. In doing so, he inconsiderately reported penguins and seals in the area, which later brought an influx of commercial whalers and the setting up of several whaling stations in the outlying vicinity.

The Free Church of Scotland founded the town in 1848 as its principal settlement, and after the discovery of gold just inland in 1861, and much later the export of frozen meat, it provided extra impetus for the town's rapid growth and importance. The name of Dunedin, I found, comes from Dun Eideann, the Scottish Gaelic name for Edinburgh, and all around the city one can still see many examples of Scottish influence and many place names are of Scottish origin.

Walking around The Octagon I couldn't fail to see the massive Anglican St. Paul's Cathedral, which towered over much of the city. A broad stone staircase leads up to its enormous imposing doors, and inside was a stunning vaulted ceiling that rose from the ground and formed the nave. All around the outside of this huge Gothic building are large piers that reach upwards to support the roof, and to my weird and quirky mind, were reminiscent of the legs of a gigantic praying mantis. Behind the cathedral, in Moray Place, I found more beautifully preserved buildings. The regal Dunedin public library was opened in 1908 and was funded by a grant from the American philanthropist Andrew Carnegie, and just along the road was the gothic monstrosity of the Fortune Theatre, whose claim to fame is that it is the world's most southerly theatre. There were numerous other grand Victorian buildings, and the multitude of shops looked quaint with their cast iron balustrades and verandas that brought shade to the shoppers on hot days. I thought that Dunedin was a wonderful city. Not only were its buildings looked after and sympathetically preserved, but the streets were clean and there was plenty of parkland and open spaces. If ever I felt like jumping ship and moving to the Antipodes – then this would be the place.

I would like to have spent longer mooching around the city, but I had promised the lads that I would meet up with them later in the Gresham Hotel. I wanted to see the art gallery in Logan Park and to walk around the University of Otago, but there wasn't the time. However, there was still one more place to visit, and so I strode briskly down past the Victorian Law Courts in Stuart Street, and over to the main railway station in Anzac Square.

The railway station was constructed in the early part of the 20th century to serve the busy main line traffic to Christchurch and Invercargill and beyond. The station is possibly one of the best known buildings in New Zealand, and is the jewel in the country's architectural crown with its easily identifiable Flemish renaissance style. The building is constructed of dark basalt with lighter Oamaru stone for the facings. Pink granite was used for a series of supporting pillars for the colonnade at the front of the building, and the roof is tiled in terracotta shingles and is surmounted by copper domed cupolas. At the south end is a 120 foot high clock tower that is visible from many parts of the city. With its distinctive architecture, the building resembles a gingerbread design, and consequently the building's designer, George Troup, was thereafter know as Gingerbread George.

I stepped inside the main booking hall and was bowled over by the beautiful mosaic floor that my brochure said, was made up of 750,000 Minton tiles. Around the balcony above, runs a Royal Doulton porcelain frieze, and as I climbed the stairs up onto the balcony, the mosaic on the floor below, with its central design of a locomotive, stood out clearly.

However, I had promised to meet up with the chaps later, so I set off for the pub. As I sauntered along Castle Street towards the Gresham, I reflected on my day's travels, and decided that I'd had a superb day out. I would have liked to have seen even more of the city. However, that was something to save for another day. Now for some beer.

As I entered the bar at the Gresham, a loud cheer went up from my lunatic shipmates, as if I was the Prodigal Son returning after years of travel in the wilderness. That was the trouble with being a typical British seaman. When ashore in a foreign port, one was rarely inclined to discover the cultural beauty of a city or to explore the diverse attractions that any country had to offer. Instead, we simply went on the piss. John Sheppard, Kenny Roberts, Simon Holroyd and Gwyn Evans had a four hour start on getting themselves tanked up, and as I rejoined my idiot mates, I recognised that I had no chance whatsoever of catching them up. They had somehow managed to attach themselves to three girls, and the whole troupe of them sat around in a circle talking gibberish. I got myself a jug of beer and did my best to catch up. Ten minutes later a girl entered the bar and sat at our table, where she appeared to be friends with the other three. She was modestly attractive, and so I slid my arm around her slim waist. She didn't seem to mind at all.

I don't want you to think that I'm being blasé, or taking for granted the plethora of women it's possible to drag into one's bed, but unless the young lady in question is someone really special, I want you, dear reader, to know that I'm getting rather bored with describing the many sexual encounters that occurred, especially whilst on the New Zealand coast. You may also be finding it rather tedious and repetitive. Therefore I have a plan. I shall not bother you with intimate details, but I'll simply use a codeword to infer that some action of a sexual nature took place. That word will be "wonderful." Needless to say that all these young ladies came back onboard the ship with us for a cabin party and I had a wonderful time with whatever her name was!

We loaded many more thousands of carcasses of lamb within our refrigerated cargo spaces and stayed in Port Chalmers for another five days. Late on a Friday afternoon the Sussex departed the port bound for Wellington. The 330 mile voyage up the coast took only 20 hours and so we were alongside in Wellington just after midday on Saturday.

By coincidence my cousin Norman, who was a dining room steward on the Shaw Savill liner Corinthic, was berthed on the dock just ahead of the Sussex. Norman, whose brother Steve donated his old Vindicatrix uniform to me, was older than me by about seven years. Our two families had spent several years hop-picking together when we were kids, and so I knew Norman very well indeed. I popped aboard Corinthic, and we repaired to the crew's Pig & Whistle where he plied me with copious amounts of alcohol. We had a pleasant couple of hours catching up with family news and the latest gossip about people in the shipping world, and then it was time for him to get back to work, and for me to meet up with John and a few other lunatic cronies in the saloon bar of the Duke of Edinburgh.

The next day on a whim, I took a cab out to the house in the suburbs where Marianne worked as a companion, helping the young Luke to come back into the real world. The door was answered by her employer, Mrs Hamlyn. I introduced myself, and in answer to my enquiry she said, "I'm terribly sorry, but Marianne doesn't work for me anymore. She moved back to her parent's house on the South Island. Somewhere near Christchurch. Her father was taken ill, and she went home to help care for him." I wanted to know more. "Do you have her address? I really would like to write to her," I asked.
"I'm terribly sorry, but she left in rather a hurry. I'm afraid I can't help you." It looked like it was a dead-end and so I thanked her and hailed a cab back into town.

We stayed in Wellington for another week whilst we loaded thousands more tons of lamb, butter, cheese, shellfish, and lastly bales of wool. Without spending too much time recounting every detail, I had a marvellous time during that period. John and I went to many parties and dallied with quite a few ladies affections. In short, we had a wonderful time (if you see what I mean?)

In early March the Sussex was almost ready to depart from New Zealand. Her cargo holds were crammed to capacity with lamb and dairy products, and she was eager to slide her bow out into the blue waters of the Pacific, and head out across the ocean to Panama. She was almost ready except for one thing - the deck crew didn't want to leave!

We'd had a brilliant time in Wellington. Our last day in port was a Saturday, and we all went on the lash and got drunk. The ship was due to depart at 5pm, but we wouldn't come out of the pub until 6pm when it closed-up. Even then, John Sheppard and I, Dave Bowyer, Kenny Roberts, Simon Holroyd and some stewards had sat cross-legged on the quayside and sang our lungs out and were generally being silly and refusing to come onboard. The ship's engines were ticking over and the harbour pilot was aboard, but still we didn't want to leave. Eventually, Jeff Lee came onto the quay and talked us into coming aboard to let go the ropes, and a little while later we slipped the moorings and departed for Panama.

The next morning we were all summoned to the chief officer's cabin and he logged us all and made an entry of the incident in the ship's official log book. My fine for going AWOL was one day's wages, £1 15s

3d. I wish I could tell you that it was my very last logging, but it wasn't to be. There were a few more occasions when I fell by the wayside.

Mama – Where's the Donkey?

I cannot recall why we spent two days in Balboa, Panama. It may have been to offload cargo, or it may have been an engine repair problem, but we did indeed spend two glorious days there, and it was one of the best ports I've ever been to for a run ashore. Once again I took myself to a pharmacy and bought some Benzedrine tablets so as to keep me awake for the coming pub crawl; I would never have been able to stand the pace otherwise. A whole section of the deck crew went ashore together including, Simon, Kenny, Dave Bowyer, Taffy Evans, Ronnie Packard, John Sheppard and me. We would work aboard the ship all day long, carrying out general maintenance or painting, and then go ashore after 10pm when the town started to come alive. The bars were heaving with creamy skinned girls, and the music was loud and thumpin' as we drank Cuba Libre's and danced the night away. We would drag ourselves back onboard at maybe 4-o-clock as the dawn was breaking, and after a few hours shut-eye, we would be working on deck for the rest of the day. Only the Benzedrine kept me going.

On our last night in Panama we went ashore early to Charlie's Bar, and after a few drinks and some nifty haggling on my part, I hired a spaced-out cab driver called Sylvester for the whole night. Sylvester drove a highly polished classic example of a Lincoln Continental limousine – the one with a long bonnet that went on forever – it was huge.
"Sylvester, I want you to take us to the best whore houses in town, okay?" He took a deep drag on his marijuana spliff. "You've come to the right place, man – I know all the best joints hereabouts." We shook hands to seal the deal and piled into the limo, which easily swallowed the seven of us. Sylvester lit up another spliff and we set off.

We were soon out of the city and onto bumpy back-roads out into the countryside. Even with the large crowd of us onboard, it was a little worrying in case he drove us to some God-forsaken place where a gang of armed men were waiting to rob us.

However, we needn't have worried, because we shortly drove through some ornate double gates into a brightly lit complex that comprised several cabanas, a circular palm roofed bar, a dance floor and dozens of comfortable chairs and tables dotted around the lawned garden area. Exotic flowers of red bougainvillea hung from trellis, and from the multitude of palm trees hung gaily coloured lights. And everywhere were beautiful girls. They were gorgeous. As we disgorged from the limo a large roly-poly lady, who I correctly guessed to be the madam, bustled over to greet us. She had a treble chin and the skin on the underside of her upper arms hung slackly down in dewlaps. "Welcome my friends. Senors, you are most welcome. Please make yourself at home." She pulled tables and chairs together for our large group to sit, and clicked her fingers for an aged uniformed waiter to come serve drinks.

Although I had never visited a real brothel before, I was somewhat surprised at the pleasant atmosphere, because it didn't correspond with the mental picture I had of such places. I had always thought of brothels as dark sleazy dirty establishments where they couldn't wait to relieve you of your hard-earned cash before some big muscled gorilla threw you back out onto the street.

After drinks were served, several girls came over and began to get friendly without being pushy. But as pleasant as it was, I had no intention of paying good money to a prostitute when, just a few weeks ago, I was getting all the totty I could handle – for free! However, Simon, Taff, and young Ronnie Packard were eager to sample the attractive ladies, and almost like magic the madam reappeared and sorted out the financial side of the transaction, and strangely, even gave the lads some sort of receipt. Perhaps she thought they could claim for the girl's services on an expense account? The girl who had been chatting to me asked if I wished to take her to bed, but as I didn't want to hurt her feelings, I told her, "Thanks very much, but I'm happily married with a wife and two bambinos." She didn't seem to mind.

The beady-eyed madam, who went by the name of Big Mama, hustled over and asked John and myself if we would like to partake in some jiggy-jig with any one of her beautiful girls. John said "No thanks, Mama, but how about putting on a sex exhibition with a girl and a donkey?" Big Mama's face took on a sad look as she said, "I'm very sorry senor, but the donkey – he die."
"Awww, that's a shame," said John, not believing one word of it.
"Never mind," said Big Mama, "I arrange another exhibition for you. Two lesbians, okay?" John looked at me for agreement, and I shrugged my shoulders to signal that we may as well. The guys who had been having some jiggy-jig had now returned with satisfied smiles upon their faces, and were eager to sample more of the brothel's services.

Big Mama directed us to one of the brightly painted cabañas and some money exchanged hands. The room consisted of simply a bed, a bedside chair, and a crucifix hanging on the wall. Big Mama hustled in carrying some more chairs and departed again to make arrangements. We made ourselves comfortable at the foot of the bed whilst we waited for the two girls who would engage in the lesbian exhibition. We had no illusions that the show would not be for real, but just a sham show for us punters. A short while later a mousy-haired woman entered the room, and without the slightest trace of embarrassment, proceeded to get undressed. She was in her late thirties and from her careworn demeanour; she looked as if she had been around the track a few times. We were all ready and needed only the second participant. Some of us glanced at our wrist-watches - we were raring to go.

The door opened and in walked Big Mama holding an enormous leather dildo and looking as if she meant business. "Hey Mama, what's going on? C'mon where's the other girl for this lesbian exhibition?" demanded John.

"No other girl available, senor" she apologised. "So I'm gonna be doing the show myself, comprende?" The lads gave a loud groan "Oh God, you've gotta be joking," John complained.

"Sorry Senor, it's either me or nothing," said Big Mama.

"Alright then, let's get on with it," I said, resigned to the fact that we were stuffed for choice. Big Mama, with her rolls of fat and cellulited legs, wasn't the prettiest creature on the planet, and as she proceeded to get undressed and strapped on the huge dildo, her unattractiveness became a source of hilarity and things started to get comical. These two women, in complete seriousness, began making movements and noises that they thought emulated two women in the throes of passion, whereas I could only find it hilarious, and thought it looked more like two dogs on heat. Sprinkled in amongst the heavy breathing were lots of Ooohs, Aahhs and Mmmms. We all knew that it was put on for our benefit, and I couldn't help it and started to laugh uproariously. The laughter was infectious, which started off the other lads who began to see the funny side. The two women, who meanwhile had got into the 69 position, and were trying to give their play-acting some theatrical dignity, glanced at each other with alarm and wondered what the hell was going on. But eventually, when we were all braying like lunatic donkeys, even they saw the comical side and began to laugh.

Later Sylvester took us to another brothel where we danced and drank - but, apart from Dave Bowyer and Kenny Roberts, we didn't partake of the beautiful girls. We got back to the ship just an hour before we were due to sail. Without a doubt, we'd had a fantastic night and the port of Balboa went on my list of fabulous places in which to go ashore.

By this time the effects of the Benzedrine had worn off, and my poor tired body just wanted to sleep. Only God knows how I kept going for the next 24 hours until my body was back to normal. That day we transited through the canal and out into the Atlantic Ocean.

Twelve days later, on 12 April 1966, after completing a 25,000 nautical mile voyage, the Sussex tied up in the Royal Albert Dock. The crew were signed-off articles and went on leave. Once again I said cheerio to many good friends and shipmates, knowing full well that I probably wouldn't ever see them again. After eating one of my mum's fried breakfasts, John caught the train to Portsmouth and went to spend some precious leave with his mum.

Some days later I was walking along Albert Road, the main thoroughfare of Silvertown, when I bumped into Roy Kane, who you may remember was the boy I had a fight with when attending Lizzo almost five years ago.

"Hello Graham, how's it going?" he asked. "Where have you been to on your latest trip?" I told him a shortened version of my recent travels across the Pacific Ocean to New Zealand.

"How long does it take you to cross the oceans to get to New Zealand?" he asked.

"About a month," I told him.

"A whole month?" he exclaimed. "Jeezus, that's an awful long time to be at sea. It must be so bloody boring. Don't you think that you're wasting your life?"

Wasting my life? This pretentious prick was getting up my nose. I pointed up at the nearby animal feed factory. "Do you still work in that factory, Roy?" I asked him. He nodded. "Do you have a steady girlfriend?" Again he nodded. "Yes, we're saving up to get married."

From my pocket I brought out a thick roll of banknotes secured with an elastic band. His eyes bulged at all that cash. My pay-off wages for the voyage aboard the Sussex was £163 1s 9d and it was probably more money than he had ever seen in his miserable life.

"Listen to me, Roy. As you can see, I earn good money. In the past four months I've been to some of the most exotic places on earth. I've been to parties almost every night, and made love to a dozen beautiful women," I reminded him. "Yet you, who spend every weekday in that miserable bloody factory and get a bit of nooky every now and then, are telling me that I'm wasting my life? What an idiot!" He went on his way looking embarrassed. I don't mind admitting, it made me smile, because it was people like Roy, with their insular lives and narrow-minded outlook that brought it home to me just how lucky I was to be a sailor.

I had been to the other side of the world and back. I had drank from the cup of cornucopia - and that cup had overflowed. I had stood on palm-fringed beaches: had watched as beautiful sunsets had sunk below far horizons and had witnessed every kind of marine and bird life that the oceans had to offer. I had been in the arms, and in the beds, of beautiful women; and Roy Kane wanted to tell me that I was wasting my life? What a bloody fool!

⚓

John and I had enjoyed a great time aboard the Sussex, but after just ten days of being at home on leave, we sailed off aboard another ship. However, this would be only a short trip of one week's duration. We sailed on 22nd April aboard the Blue Star Line cargo ship Argentina Star, bound for Rotterdam. Once again we went to the Mission dance and tried to pull one of the delicious mission girls (fat chance!), and we also went to a few bars, so I don't suppose we saved too much cash

On the passage back to London, the deck crew were cleaning out the refrigerated tween deck cargo holds, when a heavy metal bull-bar - used for the hanging stowage of beef carcasses - fell onto my foot and injured my toe. Within half an hour it had turned black. This was in the days before one could claim for injuries sustained in the course of one's work or to sue in the courts for damages. The very next day we again tied-up in the Victoria Docks.

Argentina Star (Blue Star Line) 10,716 gross tons

223

It was aboard the Argentina Star that I encountered a guy who was renowned throughout the Merchant Navy as being a totally loopy individual. His name was John Grimes, but he was known far and wide as The Vicar. He could be so funny that he'd make one's ribs ache with laughter. However, he could also be accurately described as somewhere between demented and unhinged. There was never a dull moment when The Vicar was around. I had met him when he'd joined the ship in London and we'd had a few beers together in the Round House pub. Right there and then I had known that, here is someone who is such a strange oddball – that you'll never forget him. I liked him straight away. John's claim to fame, other than being as mad as a box of frogs, was that when ashore, he always dressed entirely in black; and mostly with a dog-collar attached. As he walked along the city streets, he would take it upon himself to bless all and sundry that passed by. "Bless you my child," would intone The Vicar to little old ladies. He would make the sign of the cross and give blessings to one and all - even to other clergymen.

Another renowned character was Nelson from Folkestone. I never got to sail with him, but he was a character whose eccentric behaviour was legendary throughout the Merchant Navy. The story goes that Nelson was serving as an able seaman aboard the Dover to Calais ferries when he got into a heated argument with the captain. As the vessel left its berth at Dover, the argument became more intense. By the time the ferry was ready to proceed out the harbour entrance, Nelson decided he'd had enough. "F**k you and your frikken ship," he announced, and dived over the ship's side. He swam ashore and went up the pub!

My cousin, who was a deckie aboard a Blue Star ship, told me of a humorous incident which occurred when he walked into a bar in Rio Grande, Brazil. Inside, he found the crew of a neighbouring British vessel were dancing the conga with a crowd of laughing bar girls. The long line of dancers snaked right around the bar. Nothing strange in that you may think – except that every one of them – girls and sailors - were stark naked!

That's what I liked about being in the Merchant Navy. On almost every ship I ever served upon, one met weird and crazy individuals, too numerous to mention, who made life interesting. With shore-side jobs where workers largely carry out mundane and mind-numbingly repetitive jobs, there tends not to be the individualistic characters one meets aboard ship.

8: The Icenic

Strike? What Strike?

It was in early May of 1966 that John Sheppard and I stood in the King George V Federation office and perused the blackboard for a suitable berth aboard a ship. The Federation or 'pool' office was where one went to obtain a sea-going job, and the blackboard listed the many ships requiring crew. There were several suitable vessels sailing to far-flung places. However, I spotted just what we wanted halfway down the board.

"Icenic – Shaw Savill Line – requires 2 x able-seamen – deep sea voyage to New Zealand," I read out aloud.

"That'll do nicely," said John and we went across to the counter - behind which sat Reggie the Rat.

Reggie was the allocation officer whose sole purpose in life was to see that ships which required crew - got crew. Sometimes Reggie was a little over-zealous, and could be ever so economical with the truth. Occasionally he would send a sailor to a real pig of a ship which he'd previously described as a luxury floating gin palace which was sailing on just a three month voyage. Sometimes, half-starved after many months away on this rust-bucket, the aggrieved sailor returned wanting revenge from the official who had stitched him up, and his first port-of-call was to go see Reggie and duff him up. Therefore, Reggie's counter was protected by steel bars from any victimized sailor who wanted to cause him physical harm.

Reggie's name wasn't a misnomer. With his thick pebbledash spectacles and buck teeth, he really did look like Ratty in Kenneth Grahame's story The Wind in the Willows. John and I were in the Pool so often these days that Reggie actually knew who we were.

"Mornin," he said with a strange whiney voice. "I suppose you two prima donnas' want a nice ship with female stewardesses, great food, plenty of overtime and sailing to Tahiti?"

"That'd be very nice," I said. "But in the meantime we'd like to take the two AB's jobs on the Icenic, please."

"You two wanna sail together again?" he asked.

"Of course we do," I said. "Why – is there a problem?"

He lifted his eyes towards heaven. "From what I've heard about you two, I need to say a prayer for the girls of New Zealand."

"Thanks Reggie," I laughed. "I'll bear that in mind."

He quickly peered at our seamens' discharge books to ensure they were in order. "The ships berthed in Avonmouth Docks," he informed us. "You can get the train tomorrow. She's signing articles later in the week and the trips due to be five months duration, okay?"

He began making out two rail travel warrants to Avonmouth, together with joining notes which we should give to the chief officer on arrival at the ship. "That'll do nicely," I said.

"There you go," he said with a lopsided grin. "That ought to keep you away from the strike, shouldn't it?"

What he said was quite correct. The real reason we were in such a hurry to get away to sea, was that there was a National Union of Seaman strike looming. It was due to commence on 16th May and it would go on indefinitely, or until the ship-owners bent to the will of the union – which could take an awfully long time. However, if a seaman was already signed-on ship's articles, then it would, within the terms of the Merchant Shipping Act of 1894, be unlawful for him to go on strike. If he did so, it amounted to mutiny. To have a sea-going career, one had to be a paid-up member of the National Union of Seamen. It was compulsory – a closed-shop agreement. We were between a rock and a hard place.

The supposed reason that we were coming out on strike was for higher wages and a shorter working week. There had been unofficial disputes in 1960 and again in 1961 pushing for a shorter working week. By 1964 the rank-and-file militancy had achieved an agreement with the ship-owners for a 42-hour week by 1965, followed by a 40-hour week in 1966. However, the NUS senior officials, led by General Secretary Bill Hogarth, signed a backdoor agreement with the ship-owner's association contracting seamen to work a 56-hour week, working eight hours per day, and seven days per week. This put the clock back to the way in which seamen were worked in the Victorian era. It was an unholy alliance, which most ordinary rank-and-file members thought was a cosy state-of-affairs with the senior NUS officials 'in bed' with the ship-owners.

Most of us had previously had dealings with our union convenors and officials, and we didn't trust them one little bit. A lot of us thought that they were conniving bastards who would sell their own mothers down the river for the hell of it. However, like most rank-and-file members of any union, we were not politically driven and just wanted a quiet life. Like millions of Britain's workers, we suffered from a generalised apathy. This was how any union's membership can be undermined; simply by the militants turning up at committee meetings and taking a lead in policy-making and getting voted into positions of power. Our union's membership was in a strange situation, whereby 90% of its members were away at sea at any given time, and so didn't vote or take any active part in the way the union's affairs were conducted. Consequently our union became a hotbed of dissent and leaned very much to the left. Most seamen were disgruntled and wanted no part of the strike, and that's why many seamen were signing-on and sailing away from the coming strike – John and I included.

The Icenic had been built in 1960 for the Shaw Savill Line by Harland & Woolf, Belfast. She was a 6-hatch refrigerated cargo ship of 11,239 tons designed for the European/Australasian trade. We joined her at Avonmouth Docks in early May and my first impression was that she was a well maintained and tidy ship. The deck crew were accommodated in single berth cabins on the port side, and the crew's messroom was forward on the main deck. The owners, Shaw Savill, had us signed-on articles soon after joining the ship on 5th May 1966, so that we couldn't take part in the seamen's strike. The last thing they wanted was a mutinous crew on their hands.

However, thoughts of going on strike and mutinies were furthest from our minds as we went ashore to sample the delights of Bristol. We got a cab to the city centre and made ourselves comfortable in a bar that had music and dancing. We sat at a table with our foaming pints and watched the local talent walk by as we tapped our feet to the music.

We spotted two pretty girls and invited ourselves to sit at their table. John opted for Tanya, and I paired up with a dark haired beauty called Verity. She was very pretty and had an infectious grin which indicated she had a good sense of humour. The music wasn't too loud, and so we were able to chat. I found that she worked in a solicitor's office and lived in a suburb of Bristol. I found her easy company and we laughed a lot as the night wore on. John and Tanya were similarly getting along just fine. It was during a quiet moment, when Verity had gone off to spend a penny that Tanya leaned over and said, "Do you really like my friend Verity?"

"Well of course I do," I replied. "I think she's lovely. Why do you ask?"

She looked at me seriously. "I just wondered if you would like her as much if you were aware that she wears a calliper on her leg?" I must admit that it came as a surprise because, even though we'd had a slow smoochy dance, I hadn't noticed a thing.

What could I say? "Of course, it doesn't make any difference," I answered. "She's a very pretty girl."

"That's okay then. She's my best friend and I wouldn't like to see her get hurt if you dumped her because of a slight incapacity." When Verity returned to the table it was difficult not to stare at the calliper. I decided to ask her about it. I leant over and whispered. "Tell me why you wear a calliper. Did you have polio as a child?"

"Yes," she said candidly. "I contracted polio when I was 7 years old. It took years of hard physiotherapy to be able to walk properly again. Even now, I've got to wear this damn thing because my leg's not quite strong enough." As she spoke, she pulled up the hem of her midi dress to reveal the steel calliper that ran from her ankle to her knee.

"Mind you," she went on, "I'm luckier than some polio sufferers. At least I'm only affected in one leg. It could have been a lot worse." I nodded as I remembered Chris Morling, my cabinmate aboard Port Pirie, with his withered arm.

I held her hand. "That's the spirit. You've got a very strong character, haven't you?"

"Yes I have," she answered, and her eyes crinkled in the corners as she laughed. "But I'll get over it." At that moment I thought she looked so pretty that I couldn't resist leaning across and giving her a soft kiss on the lips. I shall never forget her reaction. She almost purred. "Mmmm, that was nice. I could get used to that." It was a nice thing for her to say, but of course it was completely wrong, as I would be sailing shortly and heading for the other side of the world.

Later that night as the pub was about to close, John asked Tanya if they would like to come back onboard the ship for a few drinks, and they accepted. It was only when we were climbing the gangway that Verity's disability was apparent, and I saw that she couldn't lift her leg very high to clear each step, and her leg travelled out in a sideways crablike movement. We settled ourselves in John's cabin, but very soon he and Tanya were getting amorous and he gave me the wink and a movement of the eyes to indicate that I should take Verity into my own cabin. He was planning something very sexual for Tanya and I think she was looking forward to it.

I laid Verity on my bunk and killed the main cabin lights, just leaving a low watt bunk light on. She didn't resist as I slowly undressed her and laid her clothes neatly to one side. There was an embarrassing moment when she was dressed only in her panties, and I wondered how I could get them over the top of the calliper without them getting snagged up. She came to my rescue by switching out the light and slipping them off. She came into my arms and that brief awkward moment was forgotten as I crushed her tightly into my body. In that instant I felt very protective to this lady who had lots of guts to battle against her disability.

A few hours later, as the dawn was breaking, we took the girls ashore and put them into a cab with promises to meet them again later that same night. One last kiss and she was gone. We went back onboard and I got my head down, and was asleep as my head hit the pillow. I would have just a few hours before I was called to turn-to on deck.

I was awoken by a banging every few seconds on the wooden deck above my cabin, and it was so loud that I couldn't sleep through it. I looked at my wristwatch and it was almost time to start work. I struggled into my work-clothes and went to investigate the source of the noise. On the deck above I found two so-called shipmates, Terry and Gordon, guiltily holding a broom-handle with which they had been pounding the deck with the blunt end.

"Wassup?" I asked moodily. "What's your game?"

"Sorry Gra," said Gordon, "but John told us about your girlfriend. He said she had a wooden leg, so we were making you feel right at home. Sorry mate."

"Yeah sorry, Gra," repeated Terry. "No offence meant."

Things didn't improve. At breakfast time some jokes were bandied around regarding how Graham's girlfriend would need some creosote so as to stop her wooden leg from getting woodworm. Someone else said I should buy her 3-in-1 oil to prevent her calliper from squeaking. There were many more jokes in the same vein. Although the jokes were in bad taste, there was not a lot I could do about it, so I just smiled benignly. After all, I was about to sail with these guys for the next five months. No use in getting upset. I couldn't fight them all, could I? However, I later gave John a piece of my mind for telling the crowd about Verity's disability, and he was very apologetic.

⚓

That night we went ashore early with the intention of meeting the girls later. We found a snug bar in Bristol city centre and proceeded to have a few pints. Above the bar was a selection of sherry barrels that were labelled with the name of each sherry. There was Oloroso, Amontillado, Pedro Ximenez, Moscatel, Manzanilla, Pale Cream, and Fino. I ordered another beer, and unwisely decided that we would have a different sherry accompaniment with each pint of ale. Of course we had to start with Bristol Cream. As we worked our way steadily along the barrels – each with an accompanying foaming pint, our preoccupied minds forgot about our date with the ladies. We needed all our concentration just to stand upright!

Needless to say, that by chucking out time we were pretty legless and got a taxi back to Avonmouth Docks. The taxi driver stopped just outside the dock gate. "This is as far as I can take you. I'm not licensed to drive inside the docks. Sorry fellas."

"Bloody hell," said John testily. "Our ship's miles away down the other end of the docks. Can't you just drive down there this once?"

"Sorry matey," said the cabby. "I'd lose my job if I tried that stunt." He obviously didn't get a tip. We started to trudge to wherever we thought the ship was parked. We were weaving all over the road as we went along our drunken way, and mostly our progress was one step forward – two steps back!

I spotted a gent's bicycle leaning against a warehouse. I was dog-tired and my legs were like jelly. The little demon inside my befuddled brain said, "Go on Graham. Hop aboard and cycle back to the ship. No one will ever know. It's not stealing. You're only gonna borrow it, aren't you?" We climbed aboard. John managed to sit on the crossbar and we set off towards the good ship Icenic. The bike was weaving all over the road, and by the time we reached the gangway I was worn out. I leant the bike against a bollard and went off to my bunk for some well-earned rest.

I was roused just an hour later by the 3rd mate who was the duty officer. He didn't look at all pleased. "There's a dock policeman on the gangway who wants a word with you and your pal Sheppard regarding a stolen bicycle." I got dressed and warily followed him to the gangway. A uniformed police constable was waiting for us, and I began to sober up rapidly. John was leaning against the guardrail looking pensive. The policeman had brought the aforesaid bicycle aboard, and it was parked by the gangway watchman's cubby-hole. The night-watchman - who I'd never clapped eyes on before - had presumably informed the copper which of the crew had stepped aboard in the past hour or so, hence we had been roused. The 3rd mate said he was going back to bed.

The constable stared at me. "Is this your bike?" he asked. "No," I answered quickly. "I've never seen it before in my life, officer."

"Well that's strange," he said suspiciously. "It was stolen just over an hour ago from number three warehouse where the duty dispatcher had parked it; and now it's turned up here at the bottom of your gangway. Your gangway watchman's log records you pair as coming aboard at about that time. What have you got to say about that?"

I glanced over at John for some helpful input, but he only managed to shrug his shoulders. A fat lot of good he was! My mind was in turmoil because I had never in my life stolen anything before, albeit in a drunken state.

The constable began to reason with me. "Come on, son, if you admit to it, then they'll be no official action. We'll say no more. But you've got to own up, okay?"

I put my hands up in surrender. "Okay officer, I borrowed it. I'm sorry."

The policeman turned to John. "I don't think I need to detain you any further, sir, you can go back to bed. Goodnight." John was gone before the copper could change his mind!

"As for you, young man," said PC Plod. "You had better return the bicycle to where you found it, hadn't you?"

"But that's miles away and I'll have to walk all the way back," I protested. "Aren't you gonna ride it back for me?"

"You've got to be joking," he said. "Think yourself lucky that I'm letting you off so lightly."

Minutes later I set off to return that damn bike. It had just started to rain. I could only think of John Sheppard cosily tucked up in his warm bed.

⚓

We didn't have an awful lot of cargo in the holds, and I suspect that the company's plan was to just get the Icenic the hell out of UK waters so that we weren't caught up in the planned seaman's strike. We would be calling in at several European ports to pick up small amounts of cargo wherever we could.

The ship sailed on Sunday 8th May and headed for Hamburg. Once berthed in the German port, the stevedores began loading cargo almost before we had finished tying-up. John and I and a few of the crowd, rushed ashore to once again taste the pleasures of the Reeperbahn, where we drank copious amounts of pilsner in the bars, and chatted to the prostitutes in the Herbertstrasse. We stayed only for one night in Hamburg and then headed off for Bremen for another one night stay. The next port-of-call was Antwerp in Belgium, where we would stay for two days. Of course, no call at Antwerp would be complete without a visit to Danny's Bar, where there was no closing time, and every one of the gorgeous waitresses was a fella! We departed Antwerp in the late evening of 16th May, and it was the day that the NUS strike was due to start. When we slipped our moorings, it was found that two engine-room greasers had deserted and had taken their personal effects off with them. Perhaps they were ardent union men and had decided to join the strike? Who knows?

Our next port was a four day stopover in Rotterdam where we sampled the delights of the Mission to Seamen dance and drank in the bars. Just before departure, a Blue Star cargo vessel glided slowly past us to tie-up in the berth ahead of the Icenic. We called to the crew as she passed by. "Where are you bound for?"

"We've just arrived from Australia, and we're going back to London," they shouted. "Have you heard any news about the strike?" they asked. We told them the latest NUS strike news; which was that they would be lucky to be able to berth anywhere, because the docks were crammed full with strikebound ships. They thanked us by dropping their trousers and showing us their arses – a quaint sailor's ritual called 'spreaders' or otherwise known as 'mooning.' Our crew, not to be outdone, obviously returned the compliment.

On the BBC radio news, we were getting reports from home with regard to the seaman's strike. Any ship that made it into a British port was immediately strikebound because, under the terms of the crew's agreement or articles, as soon as a ship returned to a British port, then the crew should be signed-off. The crew then had to join the strike and the ship sat unmanned. As more ships arrived, then the ports became clogged with tonnage, and were being berthed double-banked. The Royal Docks couldn't accept any more ships, as they were so chock-a-block. Any further arrivals bound for the London docks had to anchor at the anchorage off Southend-on-Sea in the Thames estuary. It was rumoured that more than 100 ships were anchored there.

The Prime Minister, Harold Wilson, was strongly critical of the seamen, as the strike had not only caused an adverse effect on Britain's precarious balance of payments, but had also triggered a run on the pound. On 23rd May, Mr Wilson declared a State of Emergency, although he never invoked its powers. He claimed that the NUS had been taken over by communists whose sole aim was to bring down his administration. The strike lasted for just over six weeks, and eventually came to an end on 1st July. Even so, it took many months to clear the backlog. However, the strike did irreparable damage to the way in which shippers did business. If they couldn't trust British ships to carry their goods, then what else could they do except to use foreign tonnage? British ship-owners lost trade and that had an adverse effect on the UK's merchant fleets.

And what did the strike achieve for the seamen? – Nothing! The NUS senior officials put out a statement that they were bringing the strike to an end because, "We're putting the country's interests before our own; otherwise the strike could seriously damage the future welfare of Britain's economy." But they had already done the damage, and once again the seamen were sold down the river by their own union.

Our next port was Le Havre in France, where we stayed for only 19 hours, before setting off across the Bay of Biscay, and into the Mediterranean Sea. We headed for Genoa. We spent five days in the Italian city, and the weather was gorgeous and the temperature was such that we spent our time working on deck in just shorts and t-shirt. This was my third visit to Genoa, and I didn't enjoy it any better than I did on the first two occasions. It was still just a dirty and noisy industrial city, where motorists drove on their horns with much strident honking and tooting. Genoa must have had some attraction though, because just prior to sailing it was discovered that one of our engine-room greasers packed his bags and deserted.

Genoa was to be our last port-of-call before heading eastwards towards New Zealand. The voyage to the Suez Canal took just four days, and our transit through the canal and down the Red Sea to Aden was uneventful.

The voyage began to take on the usual day-to-day routines, whereby the deckies would overhaul the cargo equipment and begin chipping and painting the ship's steelwork. We began this huge task by being hoisted aloft in a bosun's chair and washing the salt spray from the masts and Sampson posts. Next we would coat every part of the steel masts with gallons of primer and buff coloured paint. This was one of my favourite jobs. It felt wonderful to be suspended high above the deck with the ship gently swaying on the ocean swells and with the sun beating down. The forward speed of the ship generated a gentle breeze that made our work even more enjoyable. On the boat deck and bridge deck, the more experienced hands would sand down and re-varnish the weatherdeck doors and teak handrails.

Amongst the deckies, some strange words could be found in general usage, many of which don't appear to make any sense. For instance, the deck crew on whatever British ship were always known as, 'The Crowd.' ("The deck crowd were a great bunch of fellas.") Another was the term used for the ship's side. It was always called 'The Wall.' ("He fell over the wall and was drowned.") There are dozens more bizarre words which are in common use. A holiday is an area that has somehow been missed when painting and a dog's leg is an angled paint brush. Another strange description is that which is used to describe the deck above the wheelhouse. It's called, The Monkey Island!

Meanwhile, whilst the deckies were busy fighting the ever present ravages of rust, the officers were equally as busy with their own responsibilities. The captain (otherwise known as 'The Old Man) would read through mountains of documents to ensure that the vessel complied with the laws and maritime regulations. He was, of course, in overall command of the entire ship and the buck stopped with him.

The chief officer, who was also simply known as 'The Mate,' was responsible for the cargo stowage plans and ship's stability. Another of his tasks was to ensure that all lifting gear – especially the derricks (aka sticks) and their associated lifting tackle, underwent periodic maintenance. Each block and shackle and hook and wire had to have its own certificate and was assigned a SWL – a safe working load.. This was especially important when the ship was loading or discharging on the Australian coast. The Australian

Stevedores Union's had very stringent rules regarding any ship's cargo equipment or lifting gear which their members would use. Via the bosun, the mate would also oversee how the deck crew were being employed.

Meanwhile the 2nd mate was responsible for keeping navigational charts updated. If the vessel traded worldwide, as the Icenic was on this particular voyage, then she was required to carry dozens of navigation charts so as undertake voyages to anywhere that her owners required. Every week the Admiralty issued a list of 'chart corrections', each of which may require the 2nd mate to update dozens of charts, pilot books, almanacs and other nautical publications. Keeping this hydrographical data up-to-date was an exacting and time consuming task. Nowadays, ships are routinely fitted with electronic charts which are corrected via a computer input.

The 3rd mate may generally be charged with the upkeep of all safety equipment carried onboard. His responsibilities ranged from ensuring that the lifeboats were fully equipped, and that all liferafts, pyrotechnics and fire-fighting gear were in-date. A minor role often given to the 3rd mate was to procure reels of Hollywood movies which would be regularly shown to the crew when crossing the oceans. These movies were acquired from a commercial company based in London whose speciality was to provide films to shipping companies. A movie would normally be shown outside on the after-deck, where he would set up the 8mm film projector and screen. When the ship arrived in port, he would also oversee an exchange of movies with other ships in harbour. These days life is much easier with vessels carrying dozens of DVDs.

In some respects the cadets sometimes had the hardest of tasks. It seemed to be the rule throughout the Merchant Navy that cadets were to be given the dirtiest or most difficult of jobs. These ranged from cleaning out the bilges, to swabbing out the toilets. Normally cadets were well-educated lads who were offered an apprenticeship by a shipping company for a period of four years. Part of this time was spent onboard so as to gain practical experience and sea-time; and later they would attend nautical college so as to enable them to sit examinations and gain their 2nd mates certificate. In the evenings, when off duty, they were expected to study for their upcoming certificates of competency. It was a long hard slog to climb the promotion ladder from lowly cadet to ship's master.

Of course it's not just the deck department that makes a ship run smoothly. Down below in the engine room, the engineers and greasers work hard to ensure that the propeller keeps turning and the electricity generators, oil pumps, water pumps, compressors, motors and air-conditioning units continue to work perfectly. A major aspect of the engineer's task is to ensure that the refrigerated cargo spaces maintain the ideal temperature to keep the meat and dairy produce in tip-top condition.

We shouldn't forget the catering department. Under the direction of the Chief Steward, all manner of things seemed to occur faultlessly. The Chief Cook and his galley staff somehow manage to cook three meals per day, sometimes in the most appalling weather conditions. Things that we take for granted, such as loading fresh food stores, obtaining clean laundry, taking care of passengers, fresh bread, fresh milk, tab-nabs, supplying beer for the crew's bar, and most importantly, obtaining a sub of wages which will be squandered ashore, are a list of essentials which are all taken care of by the catering department.

The only crew-member about whose duties I was never quite clear was the radio officer. Aboard a typical cargo ship, there didn't seem to be enough radio traffic so as to keep the 'sparkie' very busy throughout the day; and in harbour I would have though his duties would have been minimal. But what the hell did I know? I was just a 19-year old jumped up deckie! The strange thing about radio officers back in the 1960s is that they were not directly employed by the shipping company itself, but were employees of The Marconi Company. With the modern trends in digital equipment, the radio officer's job, except on cruise liners, is mostly obsolete and his role has been overtaken by the advent of satellite communications.

⚓

At the end of June, after a 10,785 nautical mile voyage, we arrived in Auckland. Our long 29 day passage had taken us across the Mediterranean, the Red Sea, Indian Ocean, the Great Australian Bight and the Tasman Sea. The voyage had been almost non-stop, in that we had simply transited through the Suez Canal and briefly called in at Aden for fuel bunkers – neither of which place could we step ashore Two days before our arrival in Auckland, I celebrated my 20th birthday.

After getting the derricks topped up and the hatch-lids opened and ready to discharge cargo, the chief officer gave the deck crew the rest of the day off. We made straight for the Great Northern Hotel to sink some beer. John and I re-ignited old friendships with a few girls we had known from previous trips, and got to know many new friends as well. Of course after the pub chucked out at 6pm, there was always someone who knew where a party was going on. One simply grabbed a carry-out of beer from the off-licence, and followed the throng of party-goers; and if the party wasn't much cop – then there was always another one somewhere else. There were usually pretty girls to be romanced and seduced, and if there wasn't – there was always plenty of beer. We stayed eleven days in Auckland, and almost every night was party night. I'm not sure if this debauched lifestyle came under the heading of experiencing other country's cultures – but it came pretty damn close.

The Icenic's next port-of-call was the small port of Whangarei, located 100 miles north of Auckland, where we spent three days unloading our industrial cargo. It was a tidy little town, and as long as you didn't expect too much night life and excitement, it was quite a relaxing place to be.

The harbour had been discovered by Captain James Cook in November 1769. As his ship Endeavour anchored in the harbour entrance, some of his sailors began fishing with rod and line and caught over 100 fish, which Cook believed were bream. Captain Cook therefore named the harbour Bream Bay.

We sailed onwards to Wellington which lay some 650 miles to the south, and there we remained pissing-up and partying for a delicious eleven days. Life was manic. After the quiet time we'd had in Whangarei, we made up for lost opportunities. No girls were safe as John and I assailed them like marauding Vikings, pillaging and looting their chastity.

Moving southwards, we headed for Bluff, a town in the far south of New Zealand. It is so far south that the next stop is Antarctica! With its chilled warehouses and cold stores, it's a chief exporter of lamb carcasses and dairy products. The forbidding aspect of the 872 foot Bluff Hill looks down on the town; and as we tied up alongside the pier in the early morning, a deluge of heavy rain gave us a Southland welcome. The hill came alive with dozens of mini waterfalls and rivulets as the cloudburst literally dumped thousands of tons of water upon its slopes. But the sun came out later that day, and for want of anything better to do in this dreary town, the deck crew repaired to the Bay View Hotel, a rough joint on Gore Street, where we did our best to get as drunk as skunks!

The Senhouse Slip Two-Step!

It was towards the end of July and the Icenic's next stop was Lyttelton where we loaded more lamb, butter and cheese, and in between times drank in the British Bar.

Captain Falkiner went on leave, and our new ship's master, Captain James Richmond, took command of the vessel. Our new captain brought with him his wife Jean and son Alick and daughter Helen. I thought that it must be rather nice to be able to sail around the world and have one's family with you at the same time. Captain Richmond was a tall patrician figure who was known to be strict, but fair in his dealings with his crew.

Icenic (Shaw Savill Line) 11,239 gross tons

On Saturday 30th July there was a very special event taking place. Surprisingly, the English football squad had made it to the FIFA World Cup Final and would be playing against West Germany at Wembley Stadium in London. There was great interest in the football match throughout New Zealand because, as previously stated, the Kiwi's regarded England as their mother country. New Zealand is 12-hours ahead of the UK and so the afternoon match took place in the early hours of the morning, Lyttelton time. We were told that there would be a lock-in at the British Hotel, the local seaman's watering hole, and that the police would not be bothering to raid the place. The hotel landlord had placed a television in the bar, and crews from all the ships in harbour gathered to watch the match. Of course the television was of the old black & white variety, but it didn't matter because the beer was being consumed in copious amounts and everyone was getting quite legless. I have never been a great aficionado of football, but I was there in the pub to witness this once-in-a-lifetime event.

The match kicked off, and after just 12-minutes of play, the German, Helmut Haller, put the ball into the back of England's net and there was a loud groan from the dozens of British seamen assembled in the bar. In the 19th minute, Geoff Hurst smacked the ball into the German's net to equalise. In the second half, both teams scored to make it 2-2 and the match went into extra time. The atmosphere in the British Hotel was electric as we watched the events taking place 12,000 miles away. Eleven minutes into extra time, Alan Ball put in a cross and Geoff Hurst shot from close range. The ball hit the underside of the crossbar and bounced down, and no one was quite sure if the ball had actually gone over the line. We all waited with baited breath whilst the Swiss referee consulted with the Russian linesman. He awarded the goal, and with the score at 3-2 to England, the room went wild and the British crews were dancing jigs and hugging each other.

However, the excitement wasn't yet over. There were still a few minutes of play remaining, and the West Germans had sent all their defenders forward in a desperate attempt to score an equaliser. Bobby Moore got possession, and sent a long pass down to an unmarked Geoff Hurst; and the rest is history. The words of the BBC commentator Kenneth Wolstenholme gave rise to one of the most famous football commentaries of all time. He said, "And here comes Hurst. He's got....Ooh...Some people are on the pitch.....They think it's all over ... (Hurst scores). It is now. It's four!"

⚓

Eventually, after ten days in the port, it was time to sail to Auckland, where we would finish off our loading – but there was a complication. Via the chief officer, we learnt that our shipment of butter and wool cargo that awaited us in Auckland was not guaranteed. The cargo would be assigned on a first come, first served basis. The first ship to arrive in Auckland received the cargo. It reminded me of the ancient tea clippers who would race each other across the oceans from China to be the first to arrive in London.

The captain was in touch with our shipping agent in Auckland, who informed him that there were two other ships vying for the same cargo, but if we left on time tonight, then we should arrive with time to spare. However, the problem was that this was the antipodean winter, and there was presently a raging storm centred just to the south of us, and the wind speeds were exceptionally high – over 50 knots. This would make letting go and manoeuvring out of Lyttelton Harbour almost impossible.

The problem with sailing from the port was that the harbour entrance is fairly narrow, and a ship wouldn't have enough forward speed after letting go her lines to enable her to steer very well. We were tied up to a wooden wharf with our bow pointing outwards towards the open sea, but even so, the violent wind could easily take hold of the Icenic and dash her into an adjacent wharf or another ship, or even smash her into the harbour wall. What our ship required, was to come out of our berth very quickly and point her bow directly through the harbour entrance. It would be a tricky manoeuvre, but our captain had a plan.

The deck crew rigged thick wires from the stern of the Icenic that were then led ashore, around strong shoreside bollards that were set into concrete, and thence back onboard ship in what is known as a bight of wire. The eye of the wire was then put into a 'Senhouse Slip,' a solid steel heavy duty quick release hook. These rigs were positioned one on each side of the stern. Everything was ready to roll. It would be a dangerous situation, and so just the bosun and the 2nd mate would be allowed on the stern when they were to be let go. They were issued with hammers, so that on the order from the captain, they could knock-away the clips. Captain Richmond set the engines at 'dead slow ahead' and the wires took the strain. The crew let go every mooring line and brought them inboard. Only the thick wires back aft were holding us now. The engines were powered up to 'slow ahead,' and the water boiled under her stern. Meanwhile the wind was howling in the rigging and was now gusting to 60 knots plus. "Clear the after deck," shouted the chief officer, and our deck crew stood clear of any danger. If one of the wires had snapped, then it could whip through the air, and slice through a human body like a hot knife through butter – and so we kept well out of the way. With just these two wires holding her to the shore, the Icenic vibrated and hummed as if impatient to be away. The engines power was increased even more to 'half ahead.' and the bar tight wires began to sing. Strange noises came from the pier, and it made one wonder if the ship was doing damage with the huge strain. I thought that perhaps the Icenic's 12,200 horse power diesel engines would tear the wharf apart.

I heard the order shouted from the bridge, "Let go aft," and the bosun and 2nd mate knocked away the clips on the Senhouse Slips. There was a loud bang as the wires simultaneously shot out of the stern rails, and with nothing to hold her to the shore, the Icenic leapt out of her berth like a racing greyhound coming out of its trap. We were away. The ship rapidly gathered speed and headed for the harbour entrance. Up on the bridge, the captain lined up the bow and gave his helm orders to the quartermaster, and she slid out of Lyttelton with not a scratch. It remained only for the deck crew to winch aboard the lengths of wire that were now being towed astern of us and tidy up the deck gear. It would be a rough trip, but we were on our way to Auckland.

⚓

It was the third week of August when we were about to depart Auckland, homeward bound via South Africa. The ship's engines were ticking over; the harbour pilot was aboard and a mooring gang were stood by ready to throw our ropes from the bollards.

Down on the quayside beside the warehouse were five girls. They were obviously here to wave someone off, but I couldn't for the life of me think who it might be. Who has that many girlfriends who would come to wave goodbye?

Just then a police van drove onto the quay and parked at the foot of the gangway. Two officers unlocked the back doors and a young guy emerged. As they unlocked his handcuffs, he indicated towards the girls and was pleading with the officers for a favour. They walked him over to the warehouse, and one-by-one the girls took turns to embrace him. He was a good looking bloke of average height and build. I guessed it was his cheeky grin which the women probably found so attractive. Some of them were openly crying, and they had to be physically pulled apart as they hung on with their arms around him. "Bloody hell, Gra, he looks like he's got quite a fan club there, hasn't he?" said John.

Eventually he was brought up the gangway where he was handed over to the chief officer. John and I could only look on in bemusement. We stood nearby to secure the gangway for sea, just as soon as the police officers returned to the quayside. Meanwhile, as the chief officer signed a receipt for their prisoner, our new arrival looked over and smiled. "Hello lads. I've just been released from Mount Eden prison, and I'm coming home with you as a DBS," he said. "Flash Green's my name."

We introduced ourselves. "That's quite some sending-off party you've got there, Flash," I said indicating the girls. "Who the hell are they?"

"Oh they were all girlfriends at one time or another," he explained. "They didn't know each other then; but once I got picked up and went into prison, they all somehow met up at visiting times, and now they're all the best of friends. Great eh?" I was somewhat jealous. I'd never before had my own fan club.

Minutes after the police had departed, the mooring lines were let go and the Icenic moved astern out into the harbour. We were bound for Durban in the Republic of South Africa, some 6850 nautical miles away. It would take us almost 19 days, by way of the Tasman Sea, the Great Australian Bight, and the Indian Ocean to get there.

Our voyage around the Kiwi coast had been fabulous. We had been to some interesting and lively ports. Our ship had called at half a dozen European cities, and then come halfway around the world with cargo for Auckland, Whangarei, Wellington, Bluff and Lyttelton. Coming north, we had lastly spent a second idyllic time in Auckland. The crew had been close-knit and great to work with, and the parties had been almost constant.

The term DBS stands for Distressed British Seaman, and is usually associated with the forced repatriation (i.e. being deported), from a foreign country back to the UK. Potentially, a DBS could also be a seaman whose vessel has sank or foundered, or it could be a seaman who had been in hospital, and now needed to return to the UK. In any event they were getting a lift back home, usually with the assistance of the British Consul, who would find them a suitable ship. The deserters like Flash Green were put onboard via a Conveyance Order, which is an official document that requires the master of a vessel to comply with the Merchant Shipping (Repatriation) Regulations and deliver that seaman back to Blighty. There was a plentiful supply of wayward sailors who had decided to jump ship and stay in New Zealand; especially after falling head-over-heels in love with one of the Kiwi maidens. Mount Eden prison was full of them. Usually, when a sailor jumped ship, he would walk off the vessel with his suitcase packed with his personal effects, because apart from the clothes he stood up in, that is all he would possess. Unless the sailor had saved up some cash, then he wouldn't normally have any money either – he was potless.

In addition, any deserting sailor must leave behind a very important document – their seaman's discharge book, without which they would find it difficult to get another seagoing job. Their discharge book would usually be securely locked away in the captain's safe; and when the wandering sailor didn't return, it would be marked with the entry VNC which means "Voyage Not Completed." If the seaman had also been of bad behaviour or unsuitable ability, then the captain could put a stamp in his discharge book marked "Decline to Report" – known as a DR. It was possible that if the seaman left much to be desired, then the captain could give him a DR for both behaviour and ability. A double DR usually ensured that your chances of getting another seagoing job was made even more difficult. Even though Decline to Report was non-committal, and divulged nothing about the seaman, it was the worst possible discharge one could receive from a captain. Our two captains had both been strict disciplinarians and had already handed out five DR's to seamen who had deserted ship.

Sometimes the jumpers would get some casual work ashore and maybe set up home with the girlfriend, but the lure of their former shipmates would be too great, and they would frequent the seamen's bars and haunts. That's when they would be picked up by the police. In Auckland, the person who normally carried out the arrest was Detective Sergeant Richard Bird, who was in charge of a small unit that kept a weather eye open for deserting seamen. He would arrest them at the appropriate moment, and they would be banged up in Mount Eden Prison awaiting deportation aboard a ship that would return them to the UK. We shall hear more about Dickie Bird a little later on.

⚓

Durban was a lovely city. It had numerous public parks with colourful plants and flowers on display and its white sandy beaches were beautiful. Of course it was hot, and after our long oceanic voyage we were given an afternoon off. Some of us chose to relax on the beach. Up on the promenade, muscular Zulu rickshaw runners, wearing leopard or lion skin capes, waited in line hoping for customers, just like any taxi on a cab-rank back in England. It was rumoured the Zulu's had so much stamina; they could run all day long if need be.

John, Flash Green and I hired surf boards, and due to my inexperience it almost killed me. The incoming waves were quite high as I paddled my board further out with the intention of catching a roller and scudding along on the crest of a wave. However, my total knowledge with regard to surfing is whatever I picked up from listening to the Beach Boys records!

As I reached a point about 25 yards offshore, a sizeable incoming wave bowled me over and I was sucked under by a strong undertow. It must have been very strong indeed, because my surfboard was likewise dragged under. Suddenly I popped to the surface and in my panic looked around for the board. I had visions of either being swept out to sea, or having to pay a hefty penalty to the hirer. Without warning the surfboard shot to the surface and caught me square under the chin. It smacked into my jaw with such force that I momentarily though it had broken some bones. I was so dazed that I began to lose consciousness, and I think I lay lifeless in the rough water. I began to splutter as my mouth and nose filled with sea-water and I thought I was a goner.

Suddenly a strong black arm was around my waist and was carrying me ashore as if I was a mere featherweight. He laid me down on the beach to recover, and I was breathing heavily and spluttering. I looked up to find that my rescuer was one of the big Zulu rickshaw-runners. "You wanna watch dem big waves out der, boss," he said. This big black man had almost certainly saved my life. Without his quick action, I may never have made it. I thanked him gratefully, and he nodded just once to acknowledge my appreciation. He looked nervously around him and ran back up the beach to rejoin the other rickshaw runners on the promenade. It was only then that I understood why he had been in such a hurry to get off the beach. A nearby sign said in Afrikaans and English, ***"WHITES ONLY – NO COLOUREDS."***

Whilst we're busy sailing around the African coast, here's an amusing tale about being buried at sea. My cousin Norman was an assistant steward aboard a Union Castle liner when an elderly passenger had a heart attack and died after the ship had departed Mombasa. The poor widow was told that her late husband would have to be buried at sea, as there were no facilities onboard to refrigerate and store his body. The corpse, encased in the traditional weighted canvas overcoat, had to be carried through the passenger accommodation, with hundreds of them rubber-necking as the funeral cortege passed by. Everyone then followed the funeral party outside onto the after-deck where the committal was to take place.

As the captain finished reading the scripture, he gave the nod to tip the dearly departed into the Indian Ocean and send him on his way. Suddenly, the hundreds of passengers who were gathered to witness the ceremony, rushed to the ship's side to see the splash! I am reliably informed that the sudden movement of hundreds of well-fed and overweight passengers caused the ship to momentarily lurch over to starboard. Dunno if I believe the last bit. The jury's out on that!

District 6

The 800 nautical mile voyage from Durban to Cape Town took us two days. As the Icenic slid her bow into Cape Town harbour and headed for the docks, I was bowled over to see the wonderful sight of Table Mountain that overlooks the whole of the city. On top of the mountain she displayed her crowning glory. An air mass coming up from the south-east, and travelling up the slopes of the 3500 foot mountain, had condensed to cover the top with thick white clouds. She had her tablecloth on!

We arrived at noon and work began immediately to offload the small amount of cargo. We were due to discharge in Cape Town only for two days before heading northwards towards England. In the evening we had a swift drink or two in a favourite seaman's haunt - Delmonico's Bar. The bar was well used by the crews from the Union Castle liners who were regular visitors to South Africa.

Later that evening we went to a disco, where I began to understand why Mister Green was known as Flash. Boy, that guy could really dance. Put him on a disco dance floor and he was poetry in motion. He simply grabbed a gorgeous girl and boogied so expertly, that he made the other couples look like rank amateurs. He was so brilliant, that the rest of the dancers cleared the floor and formed a circle just to watch him.

Flash, who hailed from North London, also shared with me the secret of his success with the ladies. It was a simple, though very basic tactic. He would, he said, often target the most beautiful woman in a club or bar, on the assumption that every other guy thought that she was out of their league. Flash would simply walk up and say something along the lines of, "I hope you won't be offended, but I find you extremely attractive, and without beating around the bush, can I take you to bed?" On the odd occasion he got his face slapped, but his success rate he claimed, was very good, because by the law of averages, if he asked ten women that question, and just one of them accepted, he had a different woman every night.

"Why do you want a different girl every night, Flash? You don't have time to get to know her."

"Wadya wanna do that for, Gra?" he laughed. "Variety's the spice of life, mate."

On our final night in Cape Town, John and I and other crewmates were in a bar, when a local South African (who us British sailors referred to as Yarpie's) latched onto us and joined our group. No one knew him from Adam. He simply stood grinning gormlessly on the periphery of our merry band. Later, John and I said that we were getting a cab back to the ship and the Yarpie offered to give us a lift. We hopped into his car, a Ford Anglia if I remember correctly; and so began a sedate drive through the streets towards the docks. However, as we approached a rundown part of the city centre, he steadily increased speed until we were almost flying! "Why are we going so fast," I asked anxiously. "We're not in any hurry."

"Have you ever heard of District 6?" he asked in his broad Afrikaans voice. My cousin Steve had told me tales about the lawlessness in this part of Cape Town. He had served on Union Castle liners that regularly ran down to The Cape. District 6, Steve had told me, was almost exclusively a black district located right within the city centre, and it could be dangerous if one was caught inside it by a gang of blacks.

"If this is District 6," I said angrily, "then why the hell have you brought us through here?"

"I thought it would be a bit adventurous," he said lamely.

"You've gotta be a twat for bringing us through here. What an idiot." He kept his foot on the gas and the car raced through some of the most run-down areas I thought possible. As we sped through the streets, people sat outside on their front stoep and glared at us with hateful eyes. Gangs of black youths congregated on street corners; and when they saw us white men in their territory, they screamed at us as we drove by. They were mostly made up of Cape Malays and Xhosa. The place was truly a ghetto, and I don't mind admitting – I was scared. If the car were to have broken down, I had no doubts that we wouldn't have survived.

I wasn't aware at the time, but earlier that year in February 1966, the apartheid government of Hendrik Verwoerd's National Party had, without even consulting the district's black residents, arbitrarily declared that, under the Group Areas Act (a law which specified where black people may live) District 6 was to become a white's only residential area. The 60,000 residents weren't going to be given any say in the matter, and would be forcibly expelled if necessary. Many black people thought that, because district 6 was located smack bang in the city centre, close to the docks, and to Table Mountain, the white man's government wanted to redevelop the area. From 1968 to 1982 the government forcibly relocated over 60,000 residents 25 kilometres away out to the bleak Cape Flats Township. Then the bulldozers moved in!

But to return back to 1966 - On 30 March of that year, Verwoerd's government was re-elected with a huge landslide victory at the general elections. It didn't surprise many black people, because the available seats in parliament consisted of 166 seats reserved exclusively for whites, and just four seats for blacks – but the four seats were represented by white men! Not one black man was allowed to sit in parliament. With what the blacks saw as a rigged election, and being removed from their homes, then there's no doubt in my mind that we couldn't have driven through district 6 at a worse time. The neighbourhood was a hotbed of dissent.

But that wasn't the worst of the matter. On 6th September; five days before the Icenic reached Durban; Hendrik Verwoerd, who some called the architect of apartheid, had entered the House of Assembly building and was about to take his seat. A parliamentary page named Dimitri Tsafendas approached the Prime Minister as if to deliver a message. As he did so, he drew out a large sheath knife and stabbed Verwoerd four times in the chest. The Prime Minister died almost instantly.

However, the events in District 6 and the assassination of the hated Prime Minister had no effect whatsoever on the black population of South Africa, and the white man's apartheid regime continued unabated for many years to come. Verwoerd's death certainly brought no change for the most famous resident of the state prison on Robben Island. Nelson Mandela, who at 48 years old, had served just four years of his life sentence. He still had to serve a further 24 years of incarceration until his release in February 1990

The Icenic departed Cape Town on 19th September, and ten days later, after crossing the Equator back into the northern hemisphere, and passing close to the West African states of Guinea, Senegal, Mauritania, and Morocco, tied up in Las Palmas in the Canary Islands. Icenic would be here for only a matter of hours; just long enough to top up her fuel tanks and continue her voyage to London. Four days later, after completing a 5-month voyage, in which we had steamed 27,000 miles, the Icenic tied up in the Royal Albert Dock, Silvertown. I was back home.

⚓

I stayed hardly any length of time at home because John had asked me to come to stay at his father's house in Farnborough again. I was a bit reticent after falling out the last time, but he changed my mind after telling me that, "The old man doesn't hold any grudges" – and so I agreed. I arrived there on the Friday afternoon and John picked me up from the station in an Austin Mini which his dad had paid for. I was surprised at the welcome I received when we arrived at the house. Bearing in mind that the last time I had seen Tom, we had argued about the repayment of my half of a motor car, Tom Sheppard appeared full of bonhomie and treated me like a long lost son. However, I didn't want to be seen as a bum, and so I insisted that I should pay some rent for my room and meals, which we agreed upon. The bonhomie wasn't to last too long.

We applied for a job as painters and decorators at an old folk's residential home that was being built in Farnborough. The foreman painter asked us what jobs we had previously worked upon. We said we had painted at locations worldwide (it wasn't actually a lie!). The contractor supplied the paint, but we had to supply our own rollers and paint brushes. We didn't have much cash, so we bought just two rollers and one paint brush each. The apartments consisted of a lounge, one bedroom, kitchen, bath/shower room and hallway. Other painters in the block usually worked alone and took on several apartments at one time. We of course worked together, and found ourselves so slow in comparison to the other guys, that we were still painting the lounge when they were moving on to their next apartment. Eventually the foreman painter came along to inspect our work and sussed out that we had previously slapped paint onto ship's hulls for a living and advised us to leave. He paid us up to date and said, "You two will never make any money at painting. You've gotta be fast. You're far too slow and it's just too painful to watch."

In early December John, his dad and I were drinking coffee in Tom's kitchen when we heard the squeaky front gate opening. John looked out through the net curtains and saw a middle aged man and a girl approaching up the driveway.

"Oh shit," said John in panic. "It's an ex-girlfriend, and she looks as if she's brought her dad along with her. Dunno what this is about." Tom rose languidly to his feet and gazed at the approaching duo.

"She looks as if she's rather pregnant to me," he said in his slow lazy drawl. He made a quick decision. "You two go into the living room and keep very quiet. Don't say a word." There was a knock at the door, and from the

246

safety of the living room we could hear the exchange of words between Tom Sheppard and the girl's father.

"Hello, are you John Sheppard's father?"

"Yes I am. Can I help you?" Tom said cordially, but deliberately not inviting the pair inside.

"Well, your son's gone and got my daughter here pregnant, and I want to know what he's going to do about it," said the father.

"Oh dear," said Tom putting some concern into his voice. "I'm so sorry to hear that."

"Is he at home? I want a word with him because this ain't right," he said, pointing at his daughter's swollen belly.

"I'm afraid he's not here," said Tom, puffing on his pipe. "He's in Canada."

"Oh, when will he return?" said the father.

"He's not coming back at all, I'm afraid," lied Tom. "He's emigrated. He's gone for good."

We heard the girl's voice chip-in. "Come on Dad, let's go home. We're not going to get anywhere here, are we?" We heard them move off up the gravel drive, and the front door closed. We came out from our hiding place, and John beamed at his father. "Thanks Dad."

In Aldershot we got a job on a building site painting wooden window frames with thick pink primer. We worked out in the open air. It was late November and it was not only bitterly cold, but by 3:30pm it was almost dark and you couldn't see what you were doing.

At this time John rekindled a romance with an old flame called Jenny, and for a few nights, whilst he went out on a date with her, I was left to spend evenings watching something boring on the TV with Tom Sheppard and Phyllis for company. It was either that, or to stay alone in my room. Mostly I preferred my own company rather than have to endure the atmosphere with the gruesome twosome.

Eventually I'd had enough. My money was running out rapidly and there was nothing coming in. To make matters worse, John and I weren't going out pulling damsels and having a great time. I was spending my evenings with Tom and Phil, and I definitely wasn't having fun. I told John that either we go see Reggie the Rat, and get a ship departing on a deep-sea trip, or I'm going home and ship-out by myself. I couldn't spend my days on a cold building site, and my evenings in a cold atmosphere. It was time to leave.

John asked me to stay for a while. "Give it another chance," he said. "Perhaps if you got a steady job and a girlfriend of your own, then things will be better," he said hoping to talk me into staying. That sounded very much like settling down to married life. He had to be joking!

One of the problems with being John Sheppard's friend was that he took you for granted and wanted to be in control. Although I enjoyed his company tremendously and loved him like a twin brother, he would always let you down – it was instinctive. It was difficult to defend his somewhat strange ways. He was inclined to be tight fisted, and he found it hilarious to say, leap out of a cab when you'd reached the destination, and leave others to pay the fare. He would routinely stand at the back of a crowd in a pub and not get his round of drinks in. He found it funny; but I found it embarrassing to keep having to remind him to pay his way. At other times he could be extremely generous.

I hopped on a train and returned home, but after spending a week or so back at Silvertown I was stony broke. I couldn't be bumming food and keep from my mum. I wanted to pay my own way in life. Being an only child, John had his father who would dote upon him and he would want for nothing,

After some weeks of working on dreary building sites, I needed some sunshine; and so in mid-December I went to see John Aitchison, the deck department superintendent at Port Line Ltd. He offered me an able-seaman's job aboard a cargo ship that was shortly departing for Australia. That seemed perfect, except that it was sailing just before Christmas – still, beggars couldn't be choosers, could they?

9: The Port Victor

A Nightmare Voyage

The Port Victor had been built in 1943 at John Brown Shipbuilders on the River Clyde. She was to have been a 6-hatch general cargo ship; but halfway through construction she was taken over by the Admiralty, had a flight deck welded on, and became the fleet escort carrier HMS Nairana. She spent the war years escorting convoys in the Atlantic Ocean and on Arctic convoys to Russia. At the end of hostilities she spent some months on loan to the Dutch Navy, after which she was returned to her builders, and rebuilt as originally intended as the Port Victor.

I joined her just before Christmas 1966 at Glasgow, for what was planned to be a short voyage to Australia and back - a mere five month trip.

The three deck crew who I winged up with were Roger Blake, an EDH from Warwick, Neil Hudson, a JOS from London, and Tom Cooper, a deck boy from Hackney. I shared a two-berth cabin with Roger. The bosun was a supercilious bastard called John Huntingdon, and the remainder of the deck crew were mostly Jocks who all banded together.

Last, but by no means least, was Kevin Callaghan. Callaghan was a tall, well-built Irishman, who at 18 years old was just two years younger than me. However, he made up for his lack of years by being a natural fighter and a bully. He was scared of nothing and he would be constantly brawling with anyone who upset him. He was persistently getting logged for a variety of offences including drunkenness and absenteeism, and I found out much later that he had paid off with a double-DR in his discharge book.

We thought Callaghan was a psycho, as he would seek to cause chaos at any time of the day. This, together with the constant fights and threats, made our lives a misery. He appeared to take great delight in being the source of instigating mayhem and went through life with a permanent sneer on his lip. The Jocks had no problems with him because they had safety in numbers, whereas we four were slightly built, and I don't mind admitting, we were all scared shitless whenever Kevin was around and spoiling for a fight.

The ship sailed three days before Christmas and headed for Bremerhaven in Germany, where we arrived late afternoon on Christmas Day. This wasn't to be a memorable Christmas. The Port Victor was not what one could call a "good feeder", as the food was not of a decent quality and there was never enough of it. On some ships, this could be because the chief steward and the chief cook were operating a scam whereby the crew were kept on short measures, and they made money from back-handers. I couldn't say if this was the case with our senior catering staff, but it was not a very happy Christmas.

The Port Victor left Bremerhaven on the 28th December, then leap-frogged to Hamburg (Happy New Year!), Rotterdam, and Antwerp (Danny's Bar again!). But after just two days in port, the ship set out for the long 2000 mile trip down to Marseilles in Southern France.

For six whole days there was no respite from the cold and turbulent weather as the ship rolled and dived virtually all the way through the dreaded Bay of Biscay and down the Spanish and Portuguese coasts, and into the Mediterranean. After three day stopovers to load cargo in both Marseilles and Livorno, we headed for the Italian port of Genoa. By this time I was wishing that I had never clapped eyes on the Port Victor. However, at least it became warmer as we loaded more cargo bound for Australia.

Roger, Neil, Tom and I decided to take the afternoon off and have a leisurely drinking session at a pavement bar. Neither the bosun nor the captain was very pleased with our nonchalant behaviour, because the following morning, he fined us each a day's pay as our penance.

We found a novelty shop in the city centre, and each of us purchased lifelike replica revolvers, complete with leather holsters and boxes of brass capped cartridges. The guns felt heavy and looked quite authentic and hard to tell from the real thing. We found a bar with bat-winged doors, and entered with wild whoops as if we were drunken cowboys. Just for a laugh we shot the place up with our newly purchased firearms. They made an awfully loud noise and sounded very business-like. The brave barman, who was unaware if the guns were real or not, promptly threw us out.

After leaving Genoa, the ship was bound for Port Said at the northern entrance to the Suez Canal. The passage would take four days. One evening, my friends and I were having a few beers in my cabin when Kevin attempted to bulldoze his way in uninvited. Although we bolted the wooden door, he wouldn't be put off, and tried to barge the door down, but luckily the sturdy door held fast.

The deck crew's accommodation was on the ship's port side, and the porthole was open to let a breeze into the non air-conditioned cabin. Unbeknown to us, the fearless Kevin went to the deck above - threw over a thick gantline rope - and with the ship steaming along in the dark at full speed, he clambered over the ship's side and slid down the shell plating and came feet first in through the porthole. We were petrified as his body slithered through the narrow opening and he landed with a heavy crash onto the wooden desk and broke it into a dozen pieces. A demonic grin creased his face as he obviously though that it was hilariously funny, but we were out of there and made a run for it. We hid out on deck for hours.

The rest of the voyage out to Australia took the familiar route via Suez, Aden and across the Indian Ocean. It was largely uneventful except that, as we went further southwards towards Australia and the antipodean summer, the weather improved dramatically. I enjoyed nothing more than to be working out on the open decks in shorts and t-shirt and get pleasure from the sight of marine creatures and birdlife as we steamed along at our cruising speed of 16 knots.

As we departed Aden to commence our long oceanic voyage, an albatross with a ten foot wingspan, continuously flew around the ship in the hope of picking up food scraps that were thrown overboard. With a crew of 65 plus 12 passengers, I don't suppose that huge bird went very hungry; but it looked so comical and ungainly after it had landed on the water to feed, and then had difficulty taking off again with a full stomach. Every morning when I came out onto the deck I would search for my friend Albert (Albert-Ross!), and very soon he – or maybe it was a she? – would go flying down the side of the ship like an incoming missile as its wingtips almost touched the waves.

251

The Port Victor reached Adelaide in late February of 1967 On arrival we were boarded by a squad of Customs & Excise (aka The Black Gang), who proceeded to rummage around the ship from top to bottom in search of contraband cigarettes or any other illicit or exotic goods. Down in the depths of the engine room, they discovered several tins of St. Bruno pipe tobacco secreted beneath the floor plates. It was easy enough for them to ascertain the owner of the aforementioned tobacco – they simply went to see the ship's purser and asked to inspect his sales sheets. Throughout the voyage, only two crew-members had purchased St. Bruno. One was the captain and the other was an engineer cadet. Obviously they suspected the cadet, as no one in their right mind would suspect the captain of tip-toeing down to the engine room to hide his stash of baccy. The young cadet was interviewed and told that, if he owned up to the attempted smuggling, there would be no further action, save for having his goods confiscated. It was made plain that the only other consumer of St. Bruno pipe tobacco was the ship's master – so come clean! The lad must have been rather dense or had a few marbles missing, because even when presented with such cast iron evidence, he refused to own up, The Customs & Excise boys threw the book at him and he received a hefty fine.

Smuggling was a common pastime among ship's crews. Mostly they would hide cigarettes or booze or marijuana for their own personal use, but some ships were well known for smuggling goods on a grand scale so as to supplement their meagre wages.

One such ship was the mv Turakina, a refrigerated cargo vessel owned by the New Zealand Shipping Company. The 7707grt Turakina was a tidy and well cared for ship which was otherwise known as 'the company yacht.' She was on the Crusader run, which meant she traded between New Zealand, West coast of the USA and Japan.

A good friend of mine was an able seaman aboard her back in the 1960s and the tales he told regarding smuggling were legendary. The crew would purchase large quantities of Japanese watches, transistor radios and tape recorders. These items were the latest cutting-edge technology which were either unavailable or would cost a fortune in New Zealand. They weren't just hidden away in the bottom of one's wardrobe or under engine room floor plates; this contraband was professionally hidden from the custom's prying eyes using false bulkheads or creating secret compartments which were welded shut. Whenever the Turakina arrived back in New Zealand, the Black Gang would make a beeline for the ship and it almost became a battle of wills as to who could overcome their adversary.

As the cargo hatches were made ready to discharge, the stevedores (otherwise known as wharfies) began unloading our industrial cargo. The weather was hot and we worked all day in the blistering sun. The bosun was a hard taskmaster and a downright miserable git, which made every day a hard day to be overcome; and apart from my already mentioned crewmates, the Scottish able-seamen were taciturn and kept to themselves.

Whilst we were in Adelaide some young girls came aboard for a cabin party. After plenty of beer had been consumed, we decided to play a game of Russian roulette. We brought out one of the fake guns and made a great show of loading a chamber with a single brass cartridge. The girls looked on apprehensively, and as Roger pointed the barrel at his head and pulled the trigger, the cabin was filled with panic as the girls screamed hysterically. However, the chamber was empty and only a loud click was heard. The girls really did believe the guns to be the real thing. We all took turns at pulling the trigger, during the course of which the girls pleaded and begged us to stop. Some had tears in their eyes as they implored us to pack it in. Eventually, it was on Tom Cooper's turn that he pulled the trigger and the cabin was filled with a loud explosion and acrid blue smoke and the smell of gunpowder. The girls were screaming and crying, and one girl I think wet herself. They very quickly departed.

Imelda

By early March, when the ship arrived in Melbourne, I wasn't a happy camper. Although I got on well with Roger, Tom and Neil, the Jocks were still a separate entity, and Kevin was becoming dangerous. I was wishing I had never stepped aboard the Port Victor.

On arrival in harbour, I received an air-mail parcel from home which contained a 3-piece navy blue pinstripe suit that I'd had made-to-measure at John Collier the Tailors. I had promised to meet up with the lads at a hotel in St Kilda later that evening. The 6-o-clock swill had ended the year previously, and the bars and hotels were now open until 10pm. Until the new licensing laws had come into force, most bars were jam-packed with men throwing beer down their throats as fast as humanly possible; but now, with the later opening hours, the wives would join their husbands and the event would become a social occasion. I put on my new suit and it fitted a treat. I looked and felt like a million dollars. I got a cab to the St Kilda Hotel and found my crewmates sitting at a table with several nice looking girls

I immediately noticed among them a dark haired girl with laughing eyes. She was about my age and was the most beautiful creature I had ever seen. I couldn't take my eyes off her. I cannot begin to tell you how lovely

253

she was. Our eyes met and she smiled back at me. I sat beside her, and over the course of the next hour, I found that her name was Imelda, and she came from Geraldton in Western Australia. She and some of her friends at the table worked as waitresses at the Victoria Hotel on Little Collins Street in Melbourne city centre.

Imelda and I saw each other every day. Some days she would work at the Victoria and spend the night onboard the ship, and on others she would sneak me into her staff quarters where we would spend a passionate night together. On some occasions I needed to get back to the ship early, and so as not to be spotted by the hotel's management, she would provide bed sheets with which to lower myself down from her bedroom window.

By mid-March the Port Victor was ready to head for Sydney to discharge more of the heavy machinery and industrial goods which we had brought out from Europe. In the short time we had been together, Imelda and I had fallen in love, and so after much debate, we had agreed that she would hitch-hike the 560 miles to Sydney, and there I would somehow get off the ship and we would live together in wonderful bliss.

Soon after departure from Melbourne, Captain Wright came down upon the after deck where the deck crew were having smoko. "I've got some bad news for you I'm afraid," said the captain. "We've just received a signal from head office in London. This voyage, which was supposed to be just five months long, has now been extended to 11-months duration." The crew groaned with displeasure. This new voyage plan was known as a MANZ run. It's an acronym for Montreal, Australia, New Zealand and indicates which loading/discharging ports the vessel will call at. This bad news made me even more determined to get off this ship as quickly as possible.

Imelda was waiting on the quayside as the ship glided into her berth at Pyrmont. The Port Victor was due to be in Sydney for two weeks before sailing south to Hobart to continue unloading. My mind fleetingly thought of Valentina and I wondered if she was married or in a relationship, or even if she was still living in Hobart.

Imelda luckily got a job waitressing at the Great Southern Hotel, and in the meantime we tried to make a plan of action for me to get off the ship. However, if I simply jumped ship I would have no money, no job and I would be in Australia illegally. There was also the strong possibility of my being deported! There seemed to be no way out of our predicament. "Couldn't you just ask the captain if he could let you come and live with me?" she asked naively. I laughed at her innocence. "He'd probably have me tossed in jail and throw away the key." I promised to keep thinking about it and come up with a viable strategy.

254

By the end of March the ship was almost ready for departure and I was frantically wracking my brains for a feasible plan to get off the ship. Suddenly I had a brainwave. I was taking a bucket of grit up to the boat-deck, where it was to be used for holystoning. As I began to climb the steel ladder, I looked around and noticed that the wharfies were all busy loading cargo, and that no other crew were around. No one was looking in my direction and so, on the spur of the moment, I made my move. In one swirling movement I let my feet slip from under me and let go the bucket of grit as I fell dramatically backwards. As my head and my spine was about to come into contact with the bottom rungs, my hand grabbed the handrail and gripped it very hard, which considerably broke my fall. I let my body easily slide the rest of the way down onto the deck, and even had the good fortune to end up in a position with one leg draped over the side of the ladder, whilst the other slid through the rungs and hung limply in mid air. An untidy heap of grit was scattered all over the deck and I lay there as if unable to move and awaited events. It all looked very realistic. Wharfies quickly came over and laid me onto the deck. One of them, presumably a first-aider, ordered his colleagues not to move me more than necessary in case I had injured my spine. The chief officer came along and attempted to ascertain if I had any feeling in my lower legs by jabbing the soles of my feet with a sharp pin. I groaned at him to stop.

An ambulance was soon on the scene and I was evacuated from the ship by being laid onto a pallet and lifted ashore on the ship's cargo derricks. My ambulance had blue flashing lights and wailed its siren all the way to Sydney General Hospital.

In the accident and emergency room I was examined, prodded, x-rayed and tested every which way. I was then put into a nice warm bed out on a wide open-air veranda, where it was cool during the heat of the Australian autumn. A nurse came by and took my details and made out forms and asked about next-of-kin and suchlike. I had a neck-brace fitted and I was instructed not to attempt to sit up or move in any way. The doctor and the ward sister came by. As the doctor flourished the x-ray photographs, he gave me the surprise of my life. "I'm afraid that you do indeed have a bent spine," he said. I was very taken aback, because I knew for certain that I had suffered no injury whatsoever when I fell. "Look at this x-ray," said the doctor holding it up to the light. "Your spine is shaped like a dog's hind leg." Sure enough, the spine was misshapen and most definitely looked bent. "However," continued the Doc. "I don't think you've damaged your spine by falling down the ship's ladder. I suspect that you were born with a wonky backbone." I nodded but was nevertheless surprised. "But, just to be on the safe side we'll keep you in hospital under

255

observation." I gave a silent smile of gratitude. I needed only to stay here until the Port Victor had sailed, then I would be home-free.

That evening Imelda swept onto the ward looking very anxious. "Darling, I've just come straight from the ship. The crew told me about your accident. Oh darling, how are you feeling? I do hope you're going to be alright." A nurse was hovering nearby, taking the temperature of the patient in the next bed. I grinned and gave Imelda a wink and she instantly understood the situation.

She whispered conspiritually. "When do you think you'll be able to leave hospital?"

I shook my head. "Not until the ship has sailed, otherwise I may have to rejoin her if I'm discharged." The nurse moved away, and we chatted about getting an apartment together, and how we would pay rent, buying bedding, cups and plates, and the million and one other things to take care of. Imelda was still living in the YWCA at the moment, but she went off to look for an available apartment and organise other stuff. Meanwhile I ensured that I didn't show any movement of my body that would draw suspicious looks from the nursing staff. I simply laid there in bed and didn't move.

The next day, in the late afternoon, two nurses came by. "Graham, has your ship got a grey hull and a red funnel with a black top?" I thought it was a strange question, but nevertheless nodded.

"Yes it has. Why do you ask," I said. They wheeled my bed over to the edge of the veranda, where there was a panoramic view.

"Can you see that ship sailing down the harbour? Is that your vessel?" In the distance the Port Victor had just sailed under Sydney Harbour Bridge and was heading for the open sea. I couldn't help myself; I sprang upright from my bed and craned my neck to watch as the ship gathered speed. "Yippee" I cried out jubilantly and punched the air in triumph.

"No you mustn't sit up," cried out the nurses. "You could injure yourself again," they said. "You should stay absolutely still." I promised to lay immobile, and they went on their way. My mind was now in a quandaras to what to do next.

Later that night I decided that I would meet up with Imelda, so taking my clothes out of the bedside locker, I got dressed - combed my hair - and left the hospital and went off to meet her. We had a drink at a hotel, and then went to see a movie at the cinema. Afterwards, towards midnight, we made love on the grass in a city centre park, and then I took her back to the YWCA and kissed her goodnight. I trudged back to the hospital and made my way up to my bed on the veranda. The ward was quiet and no one was around, so I got undressed and hopped into bed.

In the early hours of the morning I heard one of the nurses walking along the stone tiled flooring of the veranda. I pretended to be asleep and played possum. She saw me laying there and hurried away. She returned minutes later with a whole bevy of medical staff. The bedclothes were ripped off me, and I instantly became awake. The matron, the doctor, the ward sister and the nurse were standing there, and they didn't look pleased. "Where the bloody hell have you been all night?" sneered the ward sister furiously.

"I got really bored lying in bed, so I went off to the cinema to see a movie," I said innocently.

"What the hell do you think this is - a hotel?" She was red-faced and very angry.

"There's nothing whatsoever wrong with you," said the doctor. "You're malingering."

I didn't know what to say. The game was up and I had been found out. I hung my head in defeat.

"Get the hell outta here," said the livid matron pointing at the door. "Go on - get dressed and get out of my hospital right this minute, or I'll have you thrown out on your bloody ear."

I threw my few possessions into a bag and trudged out of the hospital under the ever watchful eye of the Dragon Lady – the ward sister. I found myself a park bench to sleep on. Strangely enough, it was the same park where we'd earlier made love!

10: Living in Australia and New Zealand

I think I might be an Australian!

Soon after the Port Line office opened for business, I walked in and introduced myself to the office manager, a man in his late thirties with sparse blonde hair and thin lips. He knew all about the circumstances surrounding my onboard accident and my stay in hospital.

"I was discharged from the hospital last night," I said, refraining from telling him that I had been thrown out in the middle of the night.

"That's a shame. The ship sailed only yesterday evening. You could almost have rejoined her before she sailed," he said, as if it was entirely my fault. "Now we're going to have to fly you down to Hobart at extra expense." I was non-committal on the subject of flying to Hobart to rejoin the Port Victor.

"Have I been signed-off the ship's articles?" I asked.

"Yes you have. The captain will sign you back onto the agreement when you rejoin the ship."

"Do you have my seaman's' discharge book and my personal effects?" I asked. He opened his desk drawer and took out my light blue seaman's discharge book and handed it over.

"You'll need this as identification at the airport so as to fly down to Hobart," he informed me. I was more interested as to whether I had been given a good report by the captain. My discharge had a stamp for both ability and conduct. They both read "very good" and were signed by the captain and an official from the mercantile marine office. My discharge was dated 31 March 1967. This was good news. I slipped the book into my jacket pocket. He picked up the phone and appeared to speak to someone at the Qantas Airlines office at Sydney airport.

"That's all arranged," he said as he recradled the phone. "There's a seat reserved for you on the midday Hobart flight tomorrow. If you come here at 9am, there'll be a car to take you out to the airport, okay?" I nodded my head in agreement, but knew full well that I never intended ever seeing the Port Victor again.

"Your clothes and personal effects have all been packed away by your crewmates," he said, pointing to my suitcase sat at the rear of the office beside a filing cabinet. "You can leave that here overnight, and then collect it when you come here tomorrow morning," he suggested.

I shook my head. "I'll need some fresh clothes, so I'll take my suitcase with me."

Now came the difficult part. "How much money have I accumulated in my wages account?" I asked.

He took out a document and placed it onto his desk blotter. "You have £123 15s 6d," he said. "That amount will be added to your next account of wages when you rejoin the Port Victor."

"Can you pay me my wages now - in full?" I asked.

He looked at me with astonishment. "But that's ridiculous. That's an awful lot of money. It's three months wages. You don't need all that cash. After all, you'll be back aboard the ship by tomorrow."

I looked him steadily in the eye. "It is my money, isn't it? I am legally entitled to it, am I not?"

He threw his hands up in defeat. "Well, of course you are, young man," he said, knowing he'd lost the argument, "but you might mislay it and lose everything. It would be far better locked up in my safe over-night."

"I'll take the chance," I said firmly. He wasn't happy regarding me demanding the entire amount, but nevertheless he did some calculations and opened the office safe. He counted out cash into different denominations. The total sum of wages included all the overtime I had worked since leaving Glasgow, and I would need every last penny if I was to survive until I could get a job.

He put the banknotes into a brown envelope. "That's all your wages in equivalent Australian currency, okay?" I thanked him and picked up my suitcase from the far corner of the office.

"There's one other thing," he said. "Because of import regulations, the Department of Customs & Revenue have put your valuable items into a bonded warehouse, which you can collect yourself." He consulted a list. "There was a camera, a portable record player, 400 cigarettes, and a tape recorder." He gave me the address of the warehouse where they could be picked up. He shook my hand. "See you tomorrow at 9-o-clock."

Outside the offices of Port Line Ltd, I hailed a cab and threw my suitcase in the back and disappeared. I never went aboard the Port Victor again.

⚓

Imelda and I rented a small furnished apartment above a men's clothes shop in George Street, one of the main thoroughfares of Sydney. However, we still needed to buy household items, and it was a wonderful time as we shopped together and discovered markets and shops where we could purchase the things we required. I imagined that it was just like being a married couple as we walked around the city hand in hand.

A week after I was discharged from hospital, I decided to retrieve my 'valuable items' from the Department of Customs and Revenue. I didn't think there should be any problem. After all, they were my personal

259

possessions. I made my way to the city centre customs warehouse and made myself known to the duty customs officer behind the reception desk. "Yeah, no worries, mate," he said casually. "You'll just need to pay a small storage charge, and then go see the judge."

Alarm bells went off inside my head. "What do I need to see a judge for?"

"It's just a formality, mate. Nuthin' to worry about." I paid the few dollars storage fee and followed him up to a small office on the 2nd floor where the sign on the door said, "Rt Hon Judge Ronald Bright."

Judge Bright was a bored looking elderly man who sat in an untidy room with stacks of books littering the floor space. He consulted some papers on his desk. "It says here that you were admitted into hospital last week from the mv Port Victor after having an onboard accident and your goods were transferred into the bonded store to await your collection. Is that correct?" I nodded in agreement, but quite unsure where this conversation was leading.

"I need to ascertain if you are required to pay import tax on your goods," he explained. "There are different rules for Australian citizens and for tourists and visitors. Do you understand?"

"Yes your honour," I said, although still very much in the dark.

"So, is it your intention to become an Australian citizen and remain here, Mister Mcglone, or to rejoin the Port Victor and return to the United Kingdom?" asked the judge seriously. I almost panicked, but decided to stay nearest to the truth. "I'm going to become an Australian citizen, your honour."

He shoved a holy bible across the desk. "Alright then, in that case put your left hand on the bible, raise your right arm, and repeat after me." He read from a prompt card on his desk. "From this time forward under God, I, Graham Mcglone, do hereby pledge my loyalty to Australia and its people, whose democratic beliefs I share, whose rights and liberties I respect, and whose laws I will uphold and obey."

"I will," I invoked with all seriousness. The judge shook my hand. "Welcome to Australia young man. I hope that you have a successful life here." He looked across at the duty customs officer. "Right, Bob, you can hand over his stuff now."

Ten minutes later, as I loaded my 'stuff' into the back of a cab, it occurred to me that Australian troops were currently helping fight the war in Vietnam, and I could easily get drafted into the military, given a rifle and shipped out to South East Asia. As I made my way back to George Street, it also crossed my mind that, without meaning to, I had just become an Australian!

Imelda had her job at the Great Southern Hotel which brought in some money. Meanwhile I searched the length and breadth of the city for a job, but could find nothing at all. However, my pay-off wages kept us afloat and we even had enough to go on a coach tour to the Blue Mountains at Katoomba. One evening we went to the city's red-light district of Kings Cross and saw a brilliant stage show at a nightclub called Les Girls. The girls in question were beautiful with stunning figures and danced exotically with sequined costumes, fans, and feather boas and for the most part were very nearly stark naked. It was a fabulous show and we enjoyed it enormously. However, every single one of "Les Girls" was a man in drag!

But as the days and weeks went by, life for me became so very boring. Apart from searching unsuccessfully for work, there was nothing for me to do, but to look forward to Imelda walk in the door when her shift at the Great Southern had finished. My days began to centre around her arrival back at the flat when I could take her into my arms and just look at her. She was so beautiful.

Life aboard the ships had been easy. My wages were guaranteed, and my accommodation was assured, as was my food and utility bills. But, even though Imelda was a lovely girl in both character and beauty; with nothing whatsoever to occupy me as the Australian winter approached, I'm afraid that I soon began to lose interest in playing at happy families. She also detected my unhappiness and so, after a short discussion, we agreed to part and go our separate ways. We gave up the George Street apartment, and she was lucky to get some staff quarters at the Great Southern. I cannot recall where I lived in the interim, but I made plans to try my luck in New Zealand. Almost as soon as we parted I began to regret not being with her. Imelda had tried so hard to make our relationship work, and I knew in my heart that I had put very little effort into it. I missed her so much.

In late May I booked a flight to New Zealand. The night before my departure, I was walking across the city to see Imelda, and to say goodbye. As I approached a liquor store near Tumbalong Park, three young lads unexpectedly jumped me. They pushed me into an alley and wrestled me to the ground. As the largest of them sat on my chest and began to pummel my face, the other two returned to the street to keep a lookout. The large fellow began screaming, "Gimme your money - gimme ya money, right now" I was being mugged!

Every penny I possessed was in my wallet in my jeans back pocket, and I had no intention of letting anyone get their hands on it. "Alright - don't hit me anymore," I cried. "I'll give you all the money I've got. It's in my jacket pocket." I slid my hand into my windcheater as if to retrieve my wallet, but when my hand reappeared it was holding the life-like revolver that I had purchased in Genoa. Without a seconds thought I shoved the barrel between his teeth and cocked the hammer back with a loud click. As his eyes opened wide in fear, I was on my feet. I shouted at his two mates. "Get over here against the wall or I'm gonna blow his frikken head off." Like lambs they put their hands up in surrender. "Right, all of you - undo your belts and drop your trousers." They quickly did as they were told. I think one of them peed himself. As soon as their strides were at half-mast, I ran as fast as my legs would take me. I didn't stop to look over my shoulder, as I defy anyone to catch you up if they've got their trousers around their ankles. That same night, after saying goodbye to the lovely Imelda, I wiped the weapon clean and threw the gun and holster underneath a parked car and walked away. I couldn't take any chances of trying to smuggle it aboard an airplane.

⚓

My first ever flight was aboard a Qantas Boeing 707 for the three hour flight to Auckland. Merchant seamen weren't required to possess a passport in those days, as their seaman's discharge book was a recognised form of identification which would enable them to fly worldwide so as to join a ship.

As the aircraft lost altitude on its final approach to the airport, we glided in over the blue waters of Auckland harbour. I looked down from the window and got the surprise if my life. I couldn't believe my eyes! Berthed alongside at a cargo wharf was the bloody Port Victor!

On arrival at the airport I was rather worried when I was required to submit an immigration card for the New Zealand authorities, but I needn't have fretted because I sailed through both immigration and customs formalities.

I got a cab into town and within an hour was having drinks with Roger, Neil and Tom in the Great Northern Hotel on Queen Street. As we quaffed copious amounts of beer, we exchanged tales of our respective lives since I had done my disappearing act. They told me that life aboard the Port Victor had become even more unbearable. Kevin Callaghan had become a nightmare with his fists, whilst the Jocks simply stayed out of his way and remained neutral. The bosun cared nothing that they were frequently beaten by the big Irishman, but continued to ride them hard by dishing out every difficult and filthy job on deck. Within the hour all three had stated that they could no longer carry on, but would jump ship. We then agreed that we would rent a house together.

Later that night I turned up slightly drunk on Karen's doorstep, and lugged my suitcase inside when she agreed that I could stay for a few days until us lads could rent a house. I hadn't seen Karen since my days aboard the Port Melbourne, but her former housemates Carol and Denise were still in residence, and so also, I was pleased to see, was the big-breasted Trish, with whom I had ridden on that most interesting scooter ride, and who had invited me to "Hang on tight."

A few days later I rented a very nice 3-bedroom bungalow on a quiet residential street in the suburb of Mount Eden. However, we would all need to get work very soon, as the deposit and rent had been paid from my fast diminishing pay-off wages from the Port Victor. That evening the Port Victor sailed from Auckland - minus three deckhands who had simply packed their suitcases and walked off the ship. They moved in that same night.

I found a job selling encyclopaedias, but would firstly need to attend a few days training at the company's office in town. Tom Cooper quickly found a job with an elderly watchmaker who planned to train him in every facet of horology and make Tom his apprentice. But our house-share didn't start well. I sadly discovered that Neil and Roger could hardly be bothered to get out of bed so as to find a job, and when I returned home in the evening, they would often still be in their pyjamas. This meant that there would be only the two of us contributing to any rent. I threatened to throw them out if they didn't make an effort to find employment.

Flogging Books

The Caxton Publishing Company occupied a second floor office just off Queen Street. The job entailed going from door-to-door to sell our wares. To enable us to get our foot in the door, we were trained to tell householders that we were carrying out a children's educational survey. After ascertaining if Mr & Mrs Bloggs possessed any young offspring ("You have? - Oh good!"), and any formal educational credentials (the answer to which was usually - no), we would ask if they wanted their children to attend university (to which the answer would obviously be - yes). "Do you want your kids to be a success, or to end up in a dead-end job?" This then gave us the argument to sell them a 25-book set of leather bound encyclopaedias (complete with a teak bookcase). I would then show them, with the aid of large posters and the sample book, how easy it was to locate any information and any subject simply by flicking through the index. I would challenge customers to ask for any fact, and have it at my fingertips in just a few seconds. This was called the production. After more high-pressure salesmanship, which could include switching off their TV set so as to get their complete attention, or maybe opening a bottle of strong wine, they were invited to sign an18-month hire purchase contract - "You can purchase your children's future for just the daily price of a pack of cigarettes. They'll not only be brainy - but their mum and dad will be so much healthier." It was a good sales pitch. After signing their lives away, yours truly would then be paid a whacking great sales commission. We needed every penny, because the job attracted no guaranteed pay - but was commission only. After some intensive training sessions, which included reading text upside down from the sample encyclopaedia, we new book salesmen were sent out on the road to try our hand at real live salesmanship.

Craig, the good-looking sales manager and his girlfriend Tracy, would drive us in his estate car to what would hopefully be virgin territory, and a location that had not been visited by book salesmen in a very long while. Craig would allocate each salesman several streets in the town, and would arrange a time and place when we would be picked up for the ride home. If any lucky salesman was in the process of making a sale, then we would all have to wait for him or her, no matter how long it took.

My first day selling encyclopaedias was in a quiet village 25 miles outside Auckland. Armed with my company's leather briefcase and sporting a suit and tie, I knocked on my first door with a positive attitude.

An unshaven man wearing a dirty string vest and boxer shorts opened the door. "Wassup? Wadya want?" he demanded.

"G'day, sir," I said, flashing a big smile. "I'm carrying out an educational survey to......"

"Fuck off!" he said, and firmly slammed the door in my face. Not a brilliant start. Things didn't improve. With each house I visited, I was given the bum's rush and asked to leave. At the ninth door, the householder at least had the decency to inform me that only just yesterday, our competitors, Collier Publishing Company, had blitzed the village with salesmen, and the villagers were bloody fed up with it. However, as the week progressed, I found that when it came to selling snow to Eskimo's - I was a natural. In my first week I made three sales, which was not only decent money, but put me right at the top of the company's sales league table. I was a success and I felt on top of the world.

⚓

Whilst I was busy selling useless books to those who should have known better, far away in the Middle East there were much larger forces at play between opposing nations who should also have known better. Israel on the one side was being opposed by the armed forces of Egypt, Jordan and Syria. The latter three countries should definitely have known better than to mess with the Israeli's, because Israel began a pre-emptive strike against its three Arab neighbours, and within the first few hours of the war, decimated their aircraft and air bases and quickly had supremacy over the skies.

264

What was to become known as the Six-Day War started on 5th June 1967 and by the 10th June it was all over for the Arab nations as Israel ran roughshod across their territory.

This had a knock-on effect for the worlds shipping when the Suez Canal was blockaded and forced to close. Fifteen ships were trapped in the Great Bitter Lakes, and the canal was closed to all shipping until 1975, forcing all vessels bound east of Suez to take the long passage around Africa via the Cape of Good Hope.

⚓

One afternoon we book salesmen were taken to a town to the north of Auckland. Apart from the paper mill which was the town's major employer, it consisted of just a small convenience store and a bakery. I knocked on a door with some optimism and got the surprise of my life when it was opened by none other than Lydia, who you may recall at one time shared Karen's house in Auckland.

"Oh my God. Hello Graham." Her face lit up. "What the hell are you doing here? Come on inside." Her house was a plain semi-detached property with two bedrooms and not very much furniture. I told her how and why I came to be in New Zealand and she did the same.

"I got married six months ago to a bloke who was an able-seaman on a Blue Star Line boat," she said. "He jumped ship and managed to get a job at the paper mill. We've been living here ever since," she said unhappily.

"How long did you know him before you decided to get married?" I enquired.

"Not very long." Her brow creased up in deep thought. "Hey. I think you met him once when we had a party at Karen's apartment. His name's Stanley and he's from Yorkshire. He's tall and he's got long black hair with a tattoo on his arm. Do you remember him?"

"I don't think I know him," I said, as I attempted to recall any Blue Star sailors I may once have met.

We chatted about life in general and she wanted to know all about my time in Australia, and my job selling encyclopaedias. We spoke for ages, and it became abundantly clear that life with Stanley, and living in this small town, was not all that it was cracked up to be.

"What's it like living way out here in the sticks?" I asked. She rolled her eyes. "It's so bloody boring. There's nothing to do. There's nothing but the paper mill."

"And how is life with your new hubby?" I enquired. "Are you still on honeymoon?"

"You've gotta be joking," snorted Lydia. "He's even more boring than this bloody town, and he's so jealous. He hates me talking to any men at all."

The words were hardly out of her mouth when we heard a key being inserted into the front door. "Oh my God, it's Stanley," she said with a hint of fear in her eyes. "Oh bloody hell's bells. He's come home from work. I didn't realise the time. I hope he's in a good mood."

A tall unshaven dark haired man in working overalls came into the room. He looked at his wife, together with this total stranger, and was perhaps about to come to the conclusion that there may have been some hanky-panky going on, when I jumped in to diffuse the situation. I rushed over and thrust my hand out and greeted him warmly. "Hey, Stanley, how the hell are you?" I said with as much friendliness and bonhomie as I could muster. "Blimey Stan, the last time we met must surely have been at Karen's party in Mount Eden, wasn't it, mate? D'you remember me from the Federal line ship? I'm Graham."

I could tell by the cogs turning slowly inside his head that he was trying hard to recognise me, but he didn't want to seem as if he didn't know me from Adam. "Err...yeah...of course I remember you, Gra. What ship were you on?" he asked, as if this would identify his mystery guest. He had a broad Yorkshire accent and his manner seemed uncultured and childlike. He was definitely not the brightest star in the sky.

"I was a deckhand aboard the Sussex, Stanley. I remember you getting pretty wrecked at that party." I said, lying through my teeth.

"Oh yeah, I remember now," lied Stanley. "That was a reet good night. So - wadya doin' all the way out here?"

I told him about living in Sydney, and my recent arrival in Auckland and my new job with Caxton's. He appeared very interested in my job, and asked me how I go about selling an expensive set of encyclopaedias. With a friendly wink I reminded him that I didn't sell books, but simply carried out educational surveys to ascertain if the encyclopaedias would be of benefit to people who had no formal schooling, and perhaps hoped to gain education for themselves or their kids. It was told in a very tongue-in-cheek manner, and I hoped that he wasn't taking it too seriously.

"D'you think yon books would teach me anythin'?" he asked. "A've bin thinkin'aboot educatin' meself agin, an if we 'ave some bairns in't future, then they'll need some educatin' an schoolin', won't they, Gra?" he said in all seriousness.

"I suppose you're right," I said uncertainly. I could see where this conversation was leading.

"Why don't yea shew us 'ow yea do the sellin," he asked like some rustic simpleton. Was he kidding? Did he really want me to go through the whole production? Oh well, here goes.

An hour later, after going through the entire show and dazzling him with facts and figures, he couldn't wait to sign the sales document. I tried hard to discourage him, by reminding him that it was all a show to bamboozle the punters, but he was quite adamant and wouldn't be put off. To make matters worse, Lydia did nothing to dissuade him as Stanley signed the purchase order. I felt as guilty as hell when I walked out of their front door, and Craig's words of congratulations did nothing to dispel that feeling.

⚓

Monday 26th June 1967 was my 21st birthday and my mum had sent me a card, together with a £5 note; a princely sum in those days. Roger and Neil had still not got any employment, and didn't seem particularly bothered about it, or with regard to paying their part of the rent. I had therefore only to make the decision whether to pay our overdue rent with mum's fiver, or to go out and celebrate.

We repaired to the Great Northern Hotel, and within the meagre sum we possessed for serious drinking, managed to have a few beers and to bring home a flagon of very inexpensive red plonk. None of us had girlfriends at that stage, and so after the six-o-clock swill had brought our celebrations to an early conclusion, we sat around our bungalow in a morose mood whilst Neil strummed his guitar in a lacklustre fashion and we drank the cheap red wine. I was having a lousy time and this was no way to celebrate one's 21st birthday.

A short while later the doorbell rang and I opened the front door. Standing there was a good-looking Kiwi chap with a case of Dominion Bitter resting on his shoulder. "Is this where the party's being held? Is this the right address?" he asked. I'd never clapped eyes on him before.

Quick as a flash I said, "Yeah, you've got the right place. Come on in."

He said, "Hang on, mate. Leave the door open. There's a whole bunch of people coming along the street." Within ten minutes there were dozens of New Zealanders, including several pretty girls in our lounge, together with plenty of booze and some musical instruments. We had an accordion, a guitar, a clarinet, and some drums. The girls began dancing. Within a short space of time, my miserable and depressing 21st birthday party had been transformed. I even managed to pull a pretty redhead, and she was quickly whisked off to my bed where she gave me the finest birthday present any man could desire. At last, my life was beginning to improve again.

Dickie Bird

On the following Sunday evening there was yet another ring on the doorbell. I answered the door and found a middle aged man wearing a dark suit. He had a face like carved granite and ice-cold blue eyes. His lips were like razor blades. He held up an identification card. "My name's Detective Sergeant Dickie Bird. Perhaps you've heard of me before? Don't go running out the back door because one of my constables is out there - and he'll get quite upset." He casually invited himself inside and began to identify everyone.

"You're all under arrest," he informed us. "I believe that you're illegal aliens and have no right of abode in New Zealand. You're all British seamen who have jumped ship off the Port Victor" He brought out a notebook and pen. He pointed at Roger Blake. "What's your name, son?" Roger answered the question. This was followed by identification of Neil Hudson and Tom Cooper. The constable came through from the back-door and began putting handcuffs on the boys. All of us looked crestfallen at being nicked by the police and Roger sat with his head in his hands.

Dickie Bird looked at me with a puzzled countenance. "Who are you? What's your name?" I told him my name, and in answer to how I came to be in New Zealand, I told him that I had submitted a proper immigration slip when I had flown into Auckland from Sydney, and therefore I was here quite legally.

"Hhmm, we'll see about that, young man. If I can't get you as an illegal, and have you deported like you're mates here, then I can have you charged with harbouring illegal aliens. How's that grab you?"

My three friends were taken off to the police station, whilst I spent a lonely and sleepless night in the bungalow worrying about my future. With the boys in jail, I would have to give up the rental and find some cheaper accommodation.

After being processed, the lads were imprisoned in Mount Eden jail, just a few hundred yards from our bungalow. They spent a month or so in jail, and when a suitable ship could be found with which to return them to the UK, they were deported and sent home as a DBS - a Distressed British Seaman.

I appeared in court a month later and gave the magistrate a good account of how I came to be in New Zealand, and why I should not be convicted of harbouring illegal aliens. I told him that I had flown into Auckland from Australia and had signed an immigration form on arrival and was in New Zealand quite legally. I declared that I was completely unaware that my ex-shipmates had jumped ship, or that they were living in New Zealand unlawfully. The magistrate believed my story and the charge was thrown out.

Meanwhile I gave up the bungalow and moved in with an English chap called Neil Truscott from London, who had advertised for someone to share his apartment in the suburb of Ponsonby. Neil worked in an office doing something or other - I never quite knew what he did. Even though I lived with Neil for some months, we were never very close, and had not a lot in common. I also gave up the door-to-door salesman's job, as it was totally dependent on commission for any income - no sales - no rent money. My life now went into its most unexciting phase, because I needed to find a job just to survive. Onboard a ship, my next meal or a roof over my head was assured, and it came as something of a nasty shock to find that I needed to actually make an effort to survive. This period also became a lonely part of my existence.

It was a fact-of-life that, when one chose to live ashore in Kiwi, and perhaps hold down a boring 9-5 job, just like every other New Zealander, it was an unwritten law that all contact with the crews of ships was a no-no. You were no longer a part of their world, and you would not be welcome to mingle in the seamen's bars such as Ma Gleason's or the Great Northern Hotel. Somehow, you became an interloper. The same argument applied with regard to the girls who you had previously partied and slept with. You became an outsider, and without realising it - you were suddenly *persona non-grata.*

Together with a half dozen other guys, I got a casual job which entailed painting the steelwork of a paper mill that was under construction to the south of Auckland. The pay was lousy, but at least it was a job. At dawn we were picked up in a mini-bus and taken to the site located in the middle-of-nowhere. It was the first day of employment for all of us. The huge building was at this stage simply a very tall steel skeleton. We could see that steel-erectors, from the safety of wire cages, were in the process of bolting together cross-girders and I-beams as the building rose vertically.

The foreman painter, a bad-tempered Ukrainian called Viktor, issued us with brushes and pots of anti-rust paint and accompanied us up in a rickety elevator to the very top of the building, where the fierce wind whistled around the steel beams. He pointed to the roof-trusses and instructed us to shuffle out onto the one foot wide girders and paint every inch of them "An' don' yugo miss nuthin," he sneered. I looked down. It was easily 150 feet high, and there was no safety net fitted or safety harnesses issued - just a long drop and instant death if one slipped off. Previously, when I had painted a 70 foot high mast aboard ship, at least I was safely encapsulated within a bosuns chair and felt as safe as houses. Here, there was nothing - not even a hard-hat. "Wadya wanna hard-hat for?" said Viktor brusquely in answer to my enquiry, "You'll still be dead when ya hit the ground, won't ya?" My colleagues were all shaking their heads at the prospect of going out onto the girders; so after a short discussion, we told Viktor to stuff his job and he took us all back to Auckland. That was about as much excitement as I could deal with, and I wisely decided that I would endeavour to find a much less dangerous occupation.

I got a decently paid job with New Zealand Railways as a goods wagon checker and spent my days at the city centre railway depot happily sat on a packing crate, whilst ticking off items from my cargo list of goods bound to or from the depot. It was easy work and I was in charge of a gang of four men, mostly Maoris or Fijian's, who would transfer the goods to different loading bays with a handcart. For months on end my life settled down into a predictable format of work, sleep, and eat, and perhaps with an occasional party thrown in. In October 1967 the 6-o-clock swill came to an end, and New Zealand fell in line with Australia, and the pubs stayed open until 10pm. Although the opening hours were now more civilised, it kind of took the fun out of it because, where previously someone would throw a party after the bar closed at six, there were now far less parties.

In late October my sister Linda married a guy called David Parry and they had set up home in North Woolwich. Although I never had a brother, I now had a brother-in-law whom I'd never met.

I would occasionally get a letter from Imelda who was still living in Sydney. However, with her latest letter came some surprising news. She was pregnant! This turn of events made me feel sad at how life had turned out for her, and I felt somewhat guilty because I had not put much effort into making our relationship work.

In April, there was awful news of a shipwreck further south in Wellington Harbour. The ro-ro ferry Wahine was near the end of a rough but routine northbound overnight crossing from Lyttelton. As she neared Wellington in the early morning, she was caught in a fierce storm named Cyclone Giselle. In Wellington the highest wind-speeds ever recorded were logged at 171 mph and the roofs of 98 houses were ripped off.

As the Wahine entered the harbour, the high winds made steering unmanageable and she would not answer her helm. With winds now reaching 99mph she lost control of her engines and foundered after running aground on Barratt Reef. She capsized and sank. Of the 734 people on board, 53 people died from drowning, exposure to the elements, or from injuries sustained in the hurried evacuation and abandonment of the stricken vessel. The news brought a cloud of despondency over the whole of New Zealand, but especially amongst its seafarers.

Out of the blue, Neil announced that he would give up the apartment and return to England. I still missed Imelda, and even though she was pregnant with someone else's child, I decided that I would return to Sydney. Neil and I booked a passage aboard the P&O/Orient liner "Orcades", and in May 1968, as the giant liner slid out of her berth, the band on the quayside played Vera Lynne's, "We'll meet again." As the city of Auckland slipped astern, I asked myself why in hell I was leaving this beautiful country. Deep down I knew that I ought to remain in New Zealand and make my life here, but it was too late and the die was cast. It was the last time I was ever to visit the shores of Aotearoa - The Land of the Long White Cloud.

Kalamazoo

As we berthed at Sydney's Circular Quay, I said my goodbye's to Neil who would be staying onboard the ship all the way back to Southampton. I spotted Imelda waiting for me on the upper floor of the passenger terminal. Her eyes were scanning the ship's decks, searching for my face from among the hundreds of passengers gathered there. I could see from her silhouette the slight swelling of her pregnant tummy. She appeared to be about three months into her pregnancy. I suppressed the desire to wave frantically and instead spent a few minutes studying her face. She looked so beautiful and so serene and so at peace with herself.

However, as soon as I got ashore, I could straightaway tell that something wasn't quite right. Although she came into my arms, she was reticent and held herself back. Very soon the tears began to roll down her cheeks. "Graham, I'm so sorry. I shouldn't have given you the impression that we would be together now that you've come back here. I'm sorry, but I've decided that I'll have my baby adopted, and then I shall try to rebuild my life again. Things didn't work out for us the last time, and there's no reason to think that it would be any better this time around." She looked at me with pleading eyes, silently hoping that I wouldn't try to change her mind. Of course, she was perfectly right. Simply through the lack of effort on my part, I had buggered-up our relationship the last time, and she couldn't put herself at risk of me doing the same thing again. Sadly I nodded in agreement, for I knew in my heart that she was right, and that out there somewhere, was someone who would treat her as she deserved.

As she walked away, I felt such utter sadness because I knew that, due to my thoughtlessness and stupid irresponsibility, I had lost a very special lady. Silent tears rolled down my cheeks.

For a short time I stayed in a cheap hotel in the suburb of Paddington, but moved out after a week or so when I realised that the beds were infested with crabs. It took me another week to get rid of them.

I found a room to rent in North Sydney with a Scottish couple, Kenny and Moira Robinson, who were very kind and made me welcome. They had emigrated just 18-months ago from Dundee. However, Moira was homesick for her native Scotland, so they decided to return home. I therefore needed to find somewhere else to live.

In Kirribilli I rented a room in the home of an English couple, Matt and Pauline West, from London. Pauline had the most drop-dead gorgeous figure imaginable, and although she was at least ten years older than me, I would lay in bed fanaticizing about her. She possessed a long thick mane of curly hair and her womanly curves were ravishing as her breasts stood out proudly, and her long slender legs went on forever. That woman was sex-on-legs. But apart from the fact that she was probably loyal to her handsome husband, there was another insurmountable problem with my unrequited sexual desires. Although she had an extremely lovely figure, she had a face like the back of a bus!

I got a job in the paper cutting room at a nearby printing company - Kalamazoo Printing. The job was very simple in that, as the staff cut the paper to size using powerful guillotines, this resulted in their waste bins getting filled with shredded paper, and I was required to tour the building collecting up the off-cuts, which I would then feed into a paper compactor. The beauty of the job was that many of the guillotine operators were women, and as I pushed my cart around the plant, it gave me ample opportunity to stop and chat. The loneliness of Auckland and any possible resurrection of a relationship with Imelda was temporarily forgotten as I took quite a few of the ladies out on dates.

As time went by, for no good reason, I got homesick and I began to make plans to return to England. Swingin' London, Carnaby Street fashion, psychedelic British rock bands, flower power, and the pub scene were in the news at the time, and the British music scene was topping the charts everywhere. England was the place to be.

Since signing-on the Port Victor in December 1966, I had been away from Silvertown for over 18 months. It was time to head back home. I made contact with the local office of the British National Union of Seamen - the NUS - who would assist me in finding a ship that required crew. They made a note of my name, certification, and contact telephone number, and I went back to Kalamazoo to await events.

11: The Port Montreal

Captain Kensett

In the third week of July I got a call from Tony Ellis, my contact at the NUS. "Graham, there's a ship in port that requires an able seaman. It's the Port Montreal. But she's on a MANZ run. Are you interested?" The MANZ run was an acronym for Montreal, Australia, New Zealand, and would mean that the vessel was on a long voyage of maybe 12 months duration. By this stage I simply wanted to get back home, and would have taken almost any ship available.

However, there was a drawback. "Tony, as you're aware, my last ship was the Port Victor, which I failed to rejoin after being discharged from hospital. Port Line may have a long memory and not want to employ me again," I told him.

"Pop onboard and see what the captain says," he suggested. "They may have forgotten about it."

That afternoon I wangled a couple of hours off work and found the Port Montreal berthed at Pyrmont in Darling Harbour. She was a tidy looking ship of about 8000 tons and looked as if she was well cared for.

I made myself known to the master, Captain Arthur Kensett. The captain was a tall aristocratic looking figure with a receding hairline who looked as if he would perhaps be a harsh disciplinarian. He asked how I came to be living in Australia, and I gave him a heavily edited version of how I was medically discharged from my last ship. I handed over my seaman's discharge book for his perusal. He quickly scanned through the pages - homed in on my last discharge - and asked the very question I had been dreading.

"Why didn't you rejoin the Port Victor after being discharged from hospital?" I had thought this line of enquiry may crop up, so I'd formulated a bullshit story which I hoped would be swallowed. My face adopted what I believed was a most innocent and honest demeanour.

"Well Captain, the Port Victor had sailed away from Australian waters before I was discharged from the hospital, so Port Line released me from any obligation to rejoin her." I hoped that, with the passing of time, he had no way of checking if my story was true. I was keeping my fingers crossed. He looked at me sceptically. "Wait right here while I make a telephone call."

He returned several minutes later with a face that was clearly irritated. He threw my discharge book at me. "Your name's a dirty word at the Port Line office. You've cost this company a lot of money in unused air fares. Now, get off my ship and don't come back."

I returned to work at Kalamazoo with my tail between my legs and resumed my life in the guillotine room. However, just four days later, whilst at work, I had an urgent call from Tony Ellis. "Graham, I've got a ship for you. But you would need to join it right away. It sails this afternoon."

"Hhmm, its short notice, Tony, but I may be able to do it. What's the name of the ship?"

"It's the Port Montreal," he said.

With some exasperation I reminded him, "Tony, I've already told you. Don't you remember? I saw the captain just a few days ago, and he refused to accept me because of the problem with the Port Victor."

"Yes I'm well aware of that," he said.. "However, I've spoken with a chap at the Port Line office just a moment ago, and they are really desperate for an able-seaman. The ship cannot sail with less than the minimum deck crew. Believe me, they will take you."

"Alright Tony," I said uneasily. "Do I just turn up onboard the ship? What if the captain refuses me again?"

"I shall send a car to pick you up. You'll be taken straight to the Port Line office where you'll sign the crew agreement," said Tony. "Then you'll be taken to the ship and sail shortly afterwards. Once you're signed-on, the contract is lawful and the captain cannot do anything about it."

"Yes that's understood," I said. "Thanks a lot, Tony. I appreciate your efforts." We briefly discussed being picked up and I said I'd have to give up my job at Kalamazoo without giving notice. I put down the phone and pondered how I would break the news to Mr Wilson, the plant manager. The germ of an idea began to form in my head. It had worked once before and it could work again.

I went to Mr Wilson's office. There, with a worried look upon my face, I explained that my father was unwell back in England and that I would have to fly home immediately. I was so sorry to leave the company without proper and prior notice, but I would need to be on my way as soon as possible. Mr Wilson was very understanding, and after calculating my due wages, handed over a bundle of cash and I was gone. My father would have turned in his grave.

Moving out of my digs wouldn't be a problem as I had already forewarned my landlady that I would be going at very short notice. I swiftly threw my gear into my suitcase and said a hurried goodbye to Pauline. I withheld the desire to tell her, "Great tits – pity about the face!"

Two hours later, after signing-on at the pay rate of £56 5s 0d per month, the car dropped me at the foot of the Port Montreal's gangway. I could see she already had a tug attached, her main engine was ticking over, her mooring ropes were singled up, and the harbour pilot was onboard. She was ready for departure. I climbed the gangway, where the deck crew were waiting to pull it inboard and stow it ready for sea. The bosun, a gravelly voiced Australian, told me, "Ordinarily, your harbour station will be up forward, but seeing as you're dressed in decent clothes, then perhaps you'd better go up to the wheelhouse and steer the ship out of harbour."

I left my suitcase there and made my way to the bridge. I took my place behind the helm and awaited my steering orders. I was apprehensive in case Captain Kensett began laying-in to me for daring to come back aboard his ship. I was needlessly worrying because, as the ship prepared for departure, the captain stayed outside on the open bridge wing, chatting to the pilot. As we got under way, the pilot, in a loud and strident voice, would shout any helm orders to me, and I would repeat them back to him just as loudly. The captain and the pilot carried on their serious *al fresco* conversation with not a care in the world.

Slowly we edged out of our Pyrmont berth and lined her up to pass beneath Sydney Harbour Bridge. The ship gathered speed as we headed for open waters, and as the breeze increased, the pair came inside the bridge for shelter. The pilot gave me a helm order. "Steady as she goes."
"Aye aye pilot. Steady as she goes," I answered in the proper seamanlike fashion. On hearing an unfamiliar voice, the captain turned to see who it was, and his eyes almost popped out of their sockets when he saw me. His face and neck went an ugly red. "I explicitly told you that you were not to step aboard my ship again," he bellowed.
This wasn't the time or the place for him to begin an argument or altercation, and I could see that the pilot was clearly embarrassed and the other deck officers were attempting to make themselves scarce.
"I'm sorry, Captain," I said calmly as I continued to steer the ship down harbour. "My job was arranged at the Port Line office, and it was they who signed me onto the ship's crew agreement."
He stared daggers and visibly harrumphed, but he knew that legally he was saddled with me. "Well – you have better bloody well behave yourself aboard my ship, young man."
"Yes sir, I will. Thank you very much, sir."

⚓

The Port Montreal was a 7179 gross ton refrigerated cargo ship designed for the European/ Australasian trade, and she had been built in 1954 at Harland & Woollf's Govan yard on the River Clyde. The voyage had commenced from London on 23rd May 1968, and she had already crossed the Atlantic to Montreal and loaded cargo down the eastern seaboard of the USA. She then went through the Panama Canal and across the Pacific to Australia. The ship would be running between dozens of ports from Canada and the USA, and back to Australia. Somehow the NZ part of MANZ was to be missed out – I never found out why.

From Sydney, the ship sailed west to Melbourne, Adelaide and Fremantle as we discharged our cargo which had been loaded in the USA. Over the next few weeks I gradually got to know the deck crew. They were easy to get along with and I instinctively knew we would have a great time together. I had a comfortable single-berth cabin on the port side which looked out onto a shady maindeck passageway with bright white paintwork and teak decking (more holystoning!).

Among the crew were two fellow able-seamen from Whitstable in Kent, the tall good-looking Ian Carter, and Eric "Ernie" Shrubsall, a short muscular guy with a zany sense of humour. Other crew included ordinary seamen, Harry Barker and Kenny Bottoms. Tom Turner was a dark haired DHU who in civilian life was a painter and decorator. It was his first trip to sea. The peggy was John Watson. The bosun was a Tasmanian guy called Keith who liked his drink a little too much; which resulted in the captain having to give him an official warning regarding his behaviour. There were others who I would soon come to know as the voyage progressed. We had a deck crew of nine plus the bosun and the chippie, but we were still one deckhand short.

Retracing our route, we sailed back to the east via Albany, Melbourne and Brisbane to reload a cargo of dairy and meat products for the American markets. The Port Montreal was a happy ship to serve aboard. She had an ill-defined atmosphere about her that made one feel content. Meanwhile I was getting nicely settled in amongst more of my new crewmates. Bob Waters was another nice bloke. He was a very tall, but thin stick-insect from Stoke-on-Trent. Naturally we called him Lofty. The chippie, Kenny Whitfield, was a good-looking Geordie boy who forever had a smile on his face, and in the catering department we had an outrageous steam queen called Lola, whose cabin on the starboard side was always an open house for visitors.

I had received an air-mail letter from home. My sister Linda, who you may remember had married David Parry 10 months ago, had given birth to a boy on 24th August, whom they named David. Blimey, they didn't hang around!

The Millionaire

Six weeks after I had joined the ship, we called into Brisbane to load more dairy and meat produce. One day the chief officer popped into the crew's mess where we were having smoko. "I thought I'd let you know that they'll be a new able seaman joining the ship just after lunch," he informed us. "His name's George Richards and he's a good deal older than you lot of fairies," he said good-naturedly. "He was a Chief Gunnery Instructor in the Royal Navy, and although he hasn't been to sea for some considerable time, he's probably forgotten more seamanship than you lot of overpaid prima donnas' will ever know."

We were loitering around the gangway area after lunch when Kenny spotted him approaching. "Oh my Gaw'd. What the hell's this coming along the pier?" We all looked at the figure making his way towards the gangway. He was an elderly man with a kit-bag over his shoulder and from the way he swayed along the quayside, he looked like a caricature of Popeye the Sailor Man. The chief mate had strangely come to greet the new arrival; an unheard of thing for the mate to do. We all peered curiously as the man made his way up the gangway onto the maindeck. He was short and stocky with skin like tanned leather and a lined face creased like a walnut. He was also as bald as a coot. A huge grin split his face. "G'day. You're the chief officer I presume?"

The mate's face beamed as he shook hands. "I take it you're Mister Richards. Welcome aboard."

"Yes chief. George Richards is the name. Thanks a bunch for the welcome," he said in a broad Australian accent. "Do we have a Pig & Whistle aboard this cow? - 'cause I could sure do with a few beers."

"Er...well," said the chief uncertainly, "it's just about time for the crew to turn-to and start work for the afternoon."

"Awww screw that," said the new arrival. "Man's gotta have coupla beers in this hot sun, ain't he?" He grinned at his new-found crewmates. "C'mon boys. Lead the way to the bar." We left the chief officer with his mouth hanging agape. I liked George immediately.

Our Pig & Whistle, or crew's bar, consisted of just the old recreation room in which the ping-pong table and the dart board had been shoved to one side, and a few plastic chairs were dotted around. As we supped a can of beer, I got chatting to our new shipmate.

"The chief officer has told us that you haven't been to sea in a while, George," I said.

"That's right, mate. My last ship was the Royal Navy battleship HMS Ramillies," he said proudly. "I served aboard her during World War 2."

"So, why have you signed-on the Port Montreal?" I asked.

"Well," he explained, "The wife wanted to go see the grandchildren over in England and spend time with our daughter," he said with his lazy Aussie accent. "She's flown over there, but I fancied just taking a slow-boat-to-china and taking my time about it. So - here I am."

Over the course of the next few days George told me his history. He was born in Bucklesham, Suffolk in 1921 which made him 47 years old. At 17, he had joined the Royal Navy, and by 21 years of age had lost most of his hair in an accidental onboard explosion. It had never grown back. After spending the war aboard the Ramillies, and other assorted battleships, and getting plenty of campaign medals in the process, he had immigrated to Australia with his wife after being demobbed. "Yeah, I was a building contracts manager, and I made a fortune building oil refineries and power plants," he told me. "I was real lucky and made an absolute bundle. I don't need to work anymore 'cause I'm a millionaire." The way George explained his wealth was that he had been a bit of a rogue by ripping-off his employer by accepting back handers in return for contracts.

I looked at him sceptically. "You're telling me that you are a millionaire?"

"Yeah Gra, that's fair dinkum. Straight up."

I looked him square in the eyes. "George, I don't believe a word. I think you're full of bullshit."

"It's true," he maintained. "I own a large manor house outside Sydney, another house in Brisbane and a posh place for the weekend in Surfers Paradise."

"George, you want me to believe that you, who have signed-on this rusty cargo boat as a deck labourer, are actually a millionaire? You gotta be off your rocker to think I'd believe that story."

"Here, look at this photo," he said, taking a photograph from his wallet. The picture showed George, and presumably his wife, standing before some large ornate iron gates; and in the background was a Georgian style mansion. There looked to be plenty of estate parkland.

I studied it closely. "Anyone can stand in front of someone's mansion and have their photo taken," I argued. "I dunno why you persist with this bullshit, George. No one would believe it."

George looked downcast. "I'll prove it to you one day," he said.

Even though I thought that George was a bullshit artist, you just couldn't help but like him. He had a great sense of humour and was always laughing, and the other lads liked him enormously. He was also generous in a slightly strange way. He once gave me a bone handled knife and leather sheath; except that he never just gave anything away; he wanted one shilling for it; a ridiculously modest sum. On another occasion he fished a cowhide wallet from his kitbag. "Here Gra, ya wannit? - Gimme a shilling." All of these unwanted gifts such as a silk tie, a cygnet ring, cufflinks, and a pen, he explained, had been given to him by his extensive family and circle of friends, so he couldn't just give them away – therefore it was - "Gimme a shilling!"

We sailed in mid-September, bound for the Panama Canal. The weather was kind to us; and as the ship cut through the lazy Pacific swells, we worked out on deck in just shorts and t-shirt. I thought that life aboard the Port Montreal was wonderful. With a terrific bunch of guys to work with, and great ports-of-call, she was one of the best ships I had ever served upon. It seemed as if the sun was always shining

George and Ernie suggested converting the recreation room to create a proper crew's bar. The proposal was that we get the chippie to build the bar and shelving; the ship's electrician to fit some snazzy subdued lighting, and Tom Turner to do the decorating. We had a whip-round to pay for some curtains, wallpaper, seating, and linoleum, and arranged with the captain and chief steward to draw cases of beer from the ship's stocks, which would be paid for from the proceeds of the bars profits. Within ten days the rec room had been transformed from a dark and dismal room, into a relaxing retreat where one could unwind with a cold beer after a hard day's work. We called it the Stagger Inn. It should have been the Stagger Out!

⚓

Ernie Shrubsall's favourite rock band was The Jimi Hendrix Experience, and his hero was the band's drummer, Mitch Mitchell. Ernie would attempt to emulate Mitchell's drumming by playing along to Jimi Hendrix tapes whilst having a set of headphones clamped to his ears. There was just one problem. Ernie didn't possess any drum-kit - but simply owned two wooden drumsticks! With these he would bang away at saucepans, oildrum lids, or old biscuit tins – anything he had handy. However, with the Hendrix music playing in his ears, he was quite oblivious to the ear-splitting noise he was making, and it was only us long-suffering crew who could hear it. What a racket! Ernie was saving up to buy a top-of-the-range Premier drum kit when the ship arrived in the United States, but until then, he would have to make-do with just the drumsticks. Watch this space.

The Port Montreal arrived at the Panama Canal in early October. Even though I had now been through the canal four times, it was still a wonderful sight to behold, and a fabulous place in which to sample the delights of the exotic. However, the ship did not stop off anywhere, but simply transited through the canal and proceeded through the Caribbean to our first US port-of-call - Charleston, South Carolina.

Whilst in Charleston the captain and chief officer had their wives fly out to join them. The captain's wife, Norma Kensett, stayed onboard for six and a half months and flew back to the UK with the rest of the crew. I thought it must be rather nice to have one's other half living onboard with you. For the wives it must be the perfect life. Sailing to exotic ports around the world, no housework to take care of, all one's needs taken care of by your own personal steward, all one's meals cooked and served for you, and totally free as a bird to do whatever and whenever you wish. Life couldn't get much better than that.

From Charleston we sailed northwards to Norfolk, Virginia in Chesapeake Bay. Norfolk is the location for the largest naval base in the world. Wherever one looked you could see numerous aircraft carriers, battleships, cruisers, destroyers, auxiliaries and every kind of naval vessel.

Our next port was on the opposite side of Chesapeake Bay at Newport News. The city was well known as a centre for shipbuilding, and many naval ships were being built there when we visited. The city lies on the James River upon which is moored hundreds of surplus ships, in what is known as the Mothballed Fleet. These included old liberty ships, heavy lift vessels, troop transports, tankers, auxiliary ships and every type of craft imaginable. We could see lines of these grey-painted superfluous vessels moored forlornly side by side in fleets that extended for a couple of miles. These once great ships just lay there forsaken and abandoned to their fate - which was to await a call from their owners, the United States Government, who may one day require their services. Otherwise they slowly rusted or became so redundant as to be obsolete. If that were so, then there was only one place for them to go – the breakers yard.

The seasons were changing. It was now October and the weather got chillier the further north we travelled. Our next destination was Saint John, New Brunswick in Canada. The port of Saint John is located on the Bay of Fundy, whose claim to fame is that it has the highest tidal range in the world, with the tide rising and falling up to 55 feet.

One afternoon, after the mate had given us a job n' finish, I was going ashore with Bob Waters to have a look at the town and to perhaps indulge in some clothes shopping. On the quayside we bumped into a young Canadian guy who asked if we wanted a ride into town. We gratefully accepted and he introduced himself as Larry. His car was a classic 57 Chevrolet 4-door hardtop with the 4.6 litre V-8 engine. The car had lots of chrome and the rear wings sported tailfins and had been lovingly looked after.

As we settled ourselves into the upholstered leather rear seats, it subconsciously crossed my mind that our young driver didn't look the type who restored classic cars or spent his Sunday mornings polishing his pride and joy on the front drive. Our unshaven driver was in his mid 20's with black slicked back hair and a cigarette dangled from his lips. The way in which he spoke out of the side of his mouth reminded me of the young Marlon Brando. As he slid behind the wheel he said, "Stand by for the ride of your life." As he gunned the engine, Bob looked apprehensive and gripped the front seat, and before we had even moved, I silently questioned if we had made the right decision to accept a lift from this complete stranger.

My fears were immediately realised when he took off with the rear wheels screeching and blue smoke billowing from the tyres. The powerful car gained speed so quickly that our bodies were pressed back into the seats due to the g-force. We approached an intersection with a *STOP* sign, but he hardly slowed down. He skidded around the corner almost sideways and left a trail of rubber and blue smoke in our wake. He hit the brake, and the car began to fishtail and headed for the wrong side of the street towards a row of shops. People on the sidewalk stared in horror as the Chevy came tearing towards them. Larry wrenched the wheel and the car regained the correct side of the road. As he stamped his foot hard onto the gas pedal, the auto transmission dropped into a lower gear and the car took off at high speed along the dead straight road leading into the town. I looked over at Bob. His face had drained of colour and his knuckles were white. I shouted at the driver. "Hey Larry, wadya doing? Slow down for f*ck's sake!" But my shout went unanswered. I noticed Larry briefly glower at me in his rear-view mirror, but he got his eyes back on the road as the car reached over 100mph. He didn't bother to slacken his speed as we approached a bend a quarter mile away. I honestly thought he would slow down, but he kept his foot hard down on the pedal. As the car reached the corner, we mounted a grassy bank and the Chevy took off. The car was literally airborne! Even though we were probably flying for no longer than two or three seconds it seemed to take forever. We landed with a huge thump and were thrown around in the back seats like rag dolls. As the car shot back onto the carriageway, our demonic driver lost the rear end, and with its tyres squealing, it slid around in a complete 180 degree turn. He recovered by dropping the gears down manually and screeching around in a tight circle to face the correct way into town. Larry slowed only slightly as the Chevy blitzed through the built-up downtown streets. Ahead I saw a policeman on traffic duty as he waved cars through an intersection. Larry didn't give a hoot as he tore through the junction oblivious to the traffic cop's signals. I saw the look of surprise and disbelief on the cop's face as we shot past him and he blew his whistle for us to stop. Two blocks further on, Larry slowed down and glided to a stop outside a liquor store. "There you go, boys. Hope you enjoyed the ride. Welcome to St John."

Hymns on Mont Royal

After a brief one day stopover at Halifax, Nova Scotia, the ship's next stop was to be Montreal. It took the best part of two and a half days to sail up past Nova Scotia, through the Gulf of St Lawrence, and into the St Lawrence River. The Port Montreal was due to stay in her namesake city for only five days.

I dropped into the seamen's mission one evening and got chatting to a girl who was working in the snack bar there. Her name was Maxine, and she was very pretty with innocent brown eyes and angelic features. Because the Mission to Seamen was a Christian agency, one of whose roles was to offer sailors religious comfort; it was quite natural that any girls who frequented the place would be of a religious disposition. I have always been a devout agnostic myself, but I don't have a problem with those who dabble with the bible and like to sing the odd hymn or two. I had never been out with a mission girl before, but we got on very well, and so I asked her if she would like to come out on a date. As I was to find out later; her idea of a date differed wildly from mine.

"How about we meet up on the summit of Mont Royal tomorrow evening?" she said. "There's a chalet at the top. I could bring a picnic, and then we could spend some time up there. Would you like that?"

Mont Royal is the 764 foot high mountain (a mere hill really) which overlooks the city. I liked the sound of that scenario, and I could easily visualise her and I getting snuggled up in a small log chalet on the top of a mountain. I had mental visions of us perhaps sharing a double sleeping bag, and Maxine not trying too hard to fight me for her virtue. My red blood cells were running riot!

"I would like that very much," I answered. "How do I get to the top of the mountain? Do I have to climb all the way?"

She giggled. "Oh no, you can get a bus or a cab most of the way, then just a short walk to the chalet. You can't miss it. I'll see you there at about 7pm." She had a lovely sexy French accent. I spent most of the next day in anticipation of our date. My sexual imagination ran amok as I fantasized about me ravishing her after overcoming her virginal reticence.

In the evening I hopped in a cab, and was somewhat mystified when the cabby dropped me off near the summit. I was not alone. In a steady stream, there were dozens of people going up to Mont Royal, and my thoughts of deflowering the gorgeous Maxine rapidly evaporated as I wondered how many of them would be trying to get inside the chalet. None of them appeared to be carrying sleeping bags!

As I walked up to the summit the situation became clearer. The chalet wasn't a log cabin at all, but a large stone built villa, fully forty yards long with a red tiled roof and bay windows. I later found out that the Kondiaronk Belvedere Chalet, to give it its proper name, could be hired out for ceremonies, corporate events, and gala evenings; and the building could hold up to 700 guests.

Nearby was a huge illuminated sign of the cross that reared skywards for about 100 feet. Bright white electric lights were strategically placed every few feet up both sides of the cross so that it stood out plainly for miles around the city. It must have had an attractive magnetic quality, because it seemed to be where most people were heading.

I found Maxine sitting on some steps; and when I attempted to kiss her, she offered her cheek to kiss in the French fashion. Things weren't looking very romantic.

"Shall we go inside the chalet?" I asked.

"It's not open. The chalet closes at 4pm," she said matter-of-factly. She led me over to the terrace, and we looked down on the panoramic view of the City of Montreal – named after Mont Royal - the mountain on which we now stood. The view was breathtaking, with the whole of the city, with its brightly lit streets and landmarks, visible for miles around. We sat down at some nearby tables and she brought out a small picnic. All notions of a liaison; or of even feeling Maxine's tits, were rapidly going onto the back-burner. After eating some French sausage and salad she said, "Shall we join the other people underneath the cross?"

The other people? Who did she mean? We walked towards the huge cross, where there were hundreds gathered. Suddenly an organ started up and they all began singing hymns. Someone handed out hymn books and Maxine joined in with the singing. She was quite loud and vocal. I wasn't sure what I should do, but I silently mouthed a few words as if I was enjoying myself and had been singing hymns for years on end. A few minutes later a minister began reciting prayers, and Maxine followed the rest of the congregation in bowing their heads in prayer. She leaned over and whispered to me, "Are you a Catholic or a Protestant?"

"Neither," I answered. "I worship at Saint Watneys!"

⚓

The ship now began to make her way southwards, still discharging cargo from Australia as we went. First stop was Boston, Massachusetts, for just a three day stopover. There's not a lot to say about Boston. It's just another big city.

On our voyage to New York we took the shorter route by using the Cape Cod Canal, and so reduced our steaming distance by some 135 miles. As the ship transited slowly through the waterway, the scenery was beautiful and varied with lovely clapboard houses whose gardens came right down to the canalside. With the autumn season upon us, the trees were changing colour to dappled shades of golden brown and yellow and ochre and I stared in wonder as the vibrant scenery was reflected off the smooth waters to produce a mirror image. This was nature at its best.

I was glad to see that almost every one of the houses along our route were proud to fly the Stars and Stripes from a flagpole in their garden. In most of the countries I had visited; in Australia, New Zealand, Canada, the USA, and even Greece, the citizens took pride in their country and in their national flag, and the average resident thought it was patriotic to display their nation's colours upon their front lawn. I thought it a great pity that the average Briton would think it kind of naff or inappropriate to publicly display the Union Jack from the front lawn of their homes. In fact they had to ask their council planners for planning permission to even erect a flagpole. I made a mental note to hang a patriotic national flag from my bedroom window when I eventually returned home to Silvertown; and if the

284

sad bastards at West Ham Council (Planning Department) wanted to argue about it – then they would have a fight on their hands. Having mentally beaten the council planners to a pulp and carried out my civic duty, I went to the bar and had a beer.

On arrival in New York we went into dry-dock at Todd's Shipyard in Brooklyn to have the algae and barnacles blasted off the ship's hull. Brooklyn is a tough part of the city, and New York's finest from the local police precinct came aboard to warn the crew about the dangers of going ashore unaccompanied. If we went ashore alone, they said, then we would very likely get mugged. We took their advice and went ashore mob-handed. Ian Carter, Ernie Shrubsall and I went into Manhattan, where, on 42nd Street, one could go into a blood-bank shop and sell a pint of one's blood and receive $10. I sold a pint, and with the cash bought myself a Wrangler jean jacket and jeans.

On 5th Avenue we went inside the Empire State Building and took the express elevator up to the 86th floor observatory. The lift went up so rapidly, it felt as if one left one's stomach behind; but the wonderful views, with panoramic vistas of the whole of New York City and across to New Jersey and Long Island were magnificent. We walked around Times Square and Greenwich Village and had a steak meal in a restaurant. The steak was the thickest I had ever seen.

The next day Ernie, who had been saving hard, went back into town and purchased his life's dream – a Premier drum kit. It was a very comprehensive kit, with bass drum, snare drum, floor tom, high-hat, three different cymbals, and stands and pedals with drumsticks and brushes. It took him all afternoon to set it up in the Stagger Inn where he promised us a musical soiree later. Once again, watch this space.

Two nights running I went to the Electric Circus, a disco in East Village, Manhattan – but it was a disco with a difference! Strobe lights flashed across the huge dance floor as live bands played on stage. Film projectors played erotic movies onto the walls of the cavernous hall, and trapeze artists, flame throwers, and jugglers performed between the live acts. The whole atmospheric scene was one of the drug culture and hallucinogenic mysticism. This was the days of flower power and free-love and some of the gorgeous girls were half naked or dressed in such skimpy costumes that they left little to the imagination. Separate from the dance hall were numerous semi-private rooms where one could relax on sofas or futons and bean bags whilst taking a trip on some exotic substance. When I walked past some of the rooms, couples were unashamedly and blatantly having sex whilst as high as kites. Some of the bands who played at the

Electric Circus later became well known. They included Velvet Underground, The Grateful Dead, The Doors and Sly and the Family Stone.

⚓

Onwards we sailed to Philadelphia. As we sailed up the harbour, our harbour pilot told us a story that sounded amazingly incredible, but he assured us, was the truth – 'So help me God.' Early one morning his pilot boat came alongside an inbound Greek tramp steamer which he was due to assist in berthing in the city's docks. As he climbed onto the deck from the overside pilot ladder, there was no one in attendance to escort him to the wheelhouse. This is most unusual, because whenever a pilot boards a ship, it is customary for a seaman and a junior officer to greet the pilot and escort him up to the wheelhouse. It's simply a common courtesy shown to pilots the world over. He made his own way up to the bridge-deck, and to his surprise found no one at all in the wheelhouse. There was no sign of the captain, or officer-of-the-watch, or indeed any helmsman; but at least the ship's engines were ticking over. The pilot rang the engine telegraph for slow ahead revolutions, and at least got a response from the engine room. He steered the ship upriver, which took some twenty minutes. All the while no one stepped onto the bridge; all was silent. He looked down onto the decks both fore and aft; no was about. He shouted out for the captain; no response. He sounded the ship's foghorn; no one came to investigate. Eventually the ship reached its designated berth and the pilot simply steered the ship right up to the quayside and rang the engine telegraphs for slow astern. Just as the ship was 30 feet off the quay, the Greek seamen came out on deck and tied the ship up, and the captain and officers stepped onto the bridge as if there was no problem whatsoever. "Aha, we've arrived. Well done, Pilot!"

The moral of the story seemed to be: If one spots a Greek vessel approaching – watch out.

⚓

If I didn't know him better I would have said that George Richards was bullshittin' again. His latest story went like this. Whilst he was serving aboard the Royal Navy battleship HMS Nelson during WW2, the ship, which was supporting the Normandy landings in June 1944, hit two mines and was extensively damaged. She was temporarily patched up and sent across the Atlantic Ocean to Philadelphia Naval Yard for permanent repairs. On arrival, many of the crew, who would remain working aboard the ship, needed to be billeted ashore. The local radio station broadcast a request for the citizens of Philadelphia to come forward and house the British sailors in their own homes. Such was the response, that thousands of the city's patriotic people came along and took a sailor home with them. Finally, when almost all the crew had gone ashore, just George and a few senior sailors were left onboard.

Later that evening a man and his wife turned up and took George off to their home. They, together with their two attractive daughters and numerous servants, lived in a sizeable mansion outside the city. George found himself living a life of luxury amongst one of the best known families in Philadelphia. They owned a well-known department store in the city centre, and George had only to ask for anything, and the item would be delivered from the company's stocks. He also mentioned some dalliances of a sexual nature with both of the daughters. He stayed with the family from June 1944 until HMS Nelson completed her repairs in January 1945.

George's story seemed just too good to be true. Who would believe, that from HMS Nelson's huge crew complement of 1350 men, that it would be George who was to be singled out for billeting with a millionaire family? It didn't seem a very likely story.

One afternoon, George and I were riding in a yellow cab through the city and we got into conversation with the elderly Negro cab driver. George asked him about the department store and about his wartime host family; and sure enough the cab driver verified that the store was still very much in business and told us who in the family were still alive and who had died.

The moral of this story seems to be: He who tells a good yarn is not always a bull-shitter.

Whilst the ship was in Philadelphia, new crew members were flown out from England. Our Australian bosun was replaced by a new bosun called Lawrence Connolly. He was laid-back Irishman with a quirky sense of Irish humour, and so easy to get along with. His only eccentricity was that, come rain or shine; he always wore a black beret upon his head. Also flown out was a new able seaman, Brian Holt from Dover. Brian was a handsome blonde Adonis whose deltoids and pectorals bulged, and who sported a 6-pack on his abdomen.

⚓

After discharging general cargo in Philadelphia, the ship returned up the coast to New York to start her cycle of loading cargo for Australia. We would also be calling at Newport News and Savannah before heading for Panama. On 42nd Street I sold another pint of my blood for $10 and headed for the Electric Circus to spend the proceeds.

The time had come for Ernie to give us the benefit of his musical acumen. He had set up his drum kit in a corner of the Stagger Inn and the crew were gathered one evening to hear him play. The bar was packed as the crew eagerly awaited Ernie to begin his soiree. We thought that he would play the music of a rock band aloud; and we would then be able to hear him play along with it. However, this wasn't his plan. He inserted a Jimi Hendrix tape into his tape player, stuffed a set of headphones onto his ears, and began to bash away. Only Ernie could hear the music – we could hear only the God-awful noise that he was making. What a racket he made – it was painful to listen to, and people began to make excuses to leave the room.

Over the next few days Ernie would play his drums at every opportunity, and his proficiency with the drumsticks never improved. Oh what a noise! Eventually we had to take steps to preserve our sanity, and Ernie was told that he would have to remove his drum kit and play them back aft in the ship's steering flat.

The steering flat is a room located at the very stern of the vessel and situated directly above the rudder. As the name suggests, this compartment contains all the machinery associated with steering the ship. When the steering wheel or automatic pilot in the wheelhouse is turned to say starboard, remote sensors send an electronic message to the steering engine in the steering flat. The motor then moves a hydraulic ram which is connected to the quadrant of the rudder stock, and the rudder then moves over to starboard. Usually only small movements of the rudder are required and so the motors give off just an occasional hum to indicate that they are working. Also located in the steering flat is a vertical trunking, perhaps three feet square, with a ladder that reaches down some forty feet or so into the bowels of the engine room via the propeller shaft tunnel.

Hence, the steering flat is normally a quiet place to be; which was just the perfect location to send Ernie and his drum kit. We helped him to set it up, and the crew's accommodation was thankfully a quieter place. Watch this space.

Brian to the Rescue

After leaving Newport News, the ship was steaming southwards bound for Savannah when we ran into a strong gale. It didn't really affect the Port Montreal too much, as she had good sea-keeping qualities and she could easily cope with a gale. During the afternoon, the ship was some 40 miles south-east of Wilmington, North Carolina when our radio officer, Les Taylor, picked up a Mayday signal from an American yacht that was in difficulties in our vicinity. The yacht wasn't structurally damaged and was still quite seaworthy, but her engine had failed. She had been tossed about by extreme weather conditions for the past three days, and the crew, a young family of four, couldn't cope any longer, and needed to be rescued. A

288

US Coastguard aircraft was circling our vessel and appeared to be indicating the direction to the yacht. Captain Kensett answered the Mayday and set course for the casualty.

I was not to take part in the rescue, because over the past few days, I had exhibited flu-like symptoms, and the chief officer thought it best to confine me to the ship's sick bay in case I caused it to spread like wildfire. However, by this time I was feeling much better and was looking forward to rejoining the crew in working on deck.

As the ship came up upon the yacht, I leant out of the sick-bay's porthole to observe events, and I could see that the yacht was rolling violently from side to side. Captain Kensett spoke to the yacht's skipper by radio, who advised that there were four persons onboard; himself, his wife, his son aged 8 and a daughter aged 6. There was also the family's pet dog and two cats onboard. The family hadn't slept for days on end due to the strong gale force winds, and they couldn't cope any longer. They could hardly stay awake. The yacht was taking in water and her engine had failed, and so she was at the mercy of the weather, which had now increased to severe gale force 9. The family needed to be evacuated off the yacht quickly.

Captain Kensett advised that he couldn't hope to tow the yacht to a safe harbour in these atrocious sea conditions, and that if he were to rescue the family, then the yacht would have to be left to founder in the rough seas. The skipper was told that there would be major structural damage to the yacht as it came alongside the Port Montreal, and his family should watch out for snapping rigging and perhaps a falling mast.

Meanwhile the captain organised our crew. It was his intention to allow the yacht to drift down onto our ship's port side and then pluck the family off the deck. To do this, he suggested using our ship's crane located back aft at No.5 cargo hatch, where we had a large wicker basket, perhaps four feet in diameter, which would be attached to the crane's hook and lowered over the side. The family should then jump into the basket and be hauled up on deck to safety. In the meantime, the chief officer, the bosun, and deck crew gathered at No 5 hatch. They checked out the crane and ensured they had all the equipment they would need to hand.

As the Port Montreal came abeam of the yacht, I could see that she was the yawl "Good Hope" of perhaps 60 feet in length. Her crew had rigged a small foresail so that she was able to steer, but she was largely being tossed about like a cork in the rough seas. I could understand how, in these conditions, the crew couldn't manage any longer. They must have been absolutely exhausted; but I was glad to see that all of them were wearing bright orange lifejackets.

Captain Kensett hove-to just 50 yards from the yacht, and she slowly began to drift down upon our ship. If the captain had opted to reverse the plan, and let the ship drift onto the yacht, then there was the danger that the boat would be swamped and be driven underneath our ship, which would result in the certain death of the family. I was able to lean out of the sick-bay porthole and get a grandstand view of the whole rescue as the yacht got closer. I could see that with the huge sea running, one minute it was way above our deck, and the next it was down in the trough of a wave. She rose and fell on the waves so rapidly that I couldn't see how our deck crew could effectively pluck them from the craft with any success.

When it was almost alongside, Ernie, who was the best crane driver onboard, lowered the basket over the side so that it would hopefully be level with the yachts bowsprit. As the yacht made contact with our thick steel sides, there was the sound of tearing metal as its guardrail stanchions were ripped away, and soon afterwards her mast crosstrees made contact with our vessel's guardrails and snapped in two as if it were a dry twig. The situation was looking dangerous as her mast smashed against our ship's side and instantly fractured. The topmast lazily keeled over as if in slow-motion and hung down towards her deck.

The yacht's skipper made his way forward to the bow pulpit carrying the dog and a cat under his arms and attempted to throw the dog into the basket. As he put the cat down, it ran panic-stricken back aft and the dog began to squirm so much he had to release it.

"What the hell are you doing?" shouted the Mate. "We're here to rescue humans, not animals." The hull smashed against our steel sides again and again, which resulted in wide open splits appearing along the length of its glass-fibre shell. The yacht was rising and falling to such an extent that it was rarely level with the basket for more than a second or two, and getting anyone into it would be very dicey indeed. The fierce wind caught the yacht, and it began to slide astern where it would be impossible to rescue anyone. Someone threw a rope so that the skipper could make fast and stop the boat drifting away, but he was exhausted and could only sit on the deck looking weary.

Suddenly Brian Holt clambered over the rail, and as the yacht became level, he jumped onto her deck and landed heavily, just managing to grab a wire halyard to stop himself from falling over the side into the ocean. He had a long length of gantline coiled diagonally across his muscular chest, and I couldn't at that stage guess what it would be used for. I could see that the skipper was worn out and wouldn't have been able to be of any help for much longer.

The Good Hope slid aft and away from the ship; and very soon she was wallowing in the troughs 50 yards off the starboard quarter. She was drifting at a faster rate than our vessel, and Captain Kensett would have a hell of a time getting the ship back into position. However, it became immediately apparent why Brian had taken the coil of rope with him. I could see him tying together any large flat items that he could lay his hands upon; duckboards, sails, mattresses, and even a chair. He tied the coil of rope onto the bulky mass of items, and with a big heave, threw it all over the side and made fast the ropes end. Brian had just made a sea-anchor which would prevent the yacht from drifting away.

Ten minutes later Captain Kensett had manoeuvred the Port Montreal into position, and once again the yacht drifted down upon us. As she smashed into our steel plating; Brian, with a child under each arm, made his way to the bow where Ernie had positioned the basket. With a huge heave he threw the kids, none too gently, inside the wicker basket and Ernie hoisted them up to safety. Minutes later the same procedure was used to get the mother and father up on deck. Miraculously Brian even returned for the animals, and jumped into the basket with them.

We left the craft to sink in its own good time as Captain Kensett set course for Savannah. On arrival, the yacht's crew, after offering their deepest thanks, were landed ashore. After being checked over by paramedics, they were taken to a hotel for some well-earned rest. The Port Montreal was due to load more cargo in Savannah and we remained in port for four days before resuming our southerly course, bound for Panama and back to Australia. Everyone was safe, and Brian Holt was the hero of the hour.

⚓

Weeks later, as the Port Montreal sailed through the balmy smooth swells of the Pacific Ocean, she was a thousand miles away from anywhere, and it was a lovely sunny morning with blue skies. I had gone up to the wheelhouse to look at our progress on the navigation chart. Afterwards I stood out on the wing of the bridge, chatting to our 3rd Mate, Ian MacRae, who was officer-of-the-watch.

Suddenly, from within the wheelhouse, the brass engine telegraphs rang out stridently as the indicator signalled changing from "full ahead" to "stop." Shortly afterwards both main engines died and the ship became silent, except for the wash of her bow wave as she drifted to a stop and lay motionless on the swells.

"What the hell's happening up here?" shouted Captain Kensett as he stormed onto the bridge. "Who gave the order to stop the engine?" Just then the engine room phone rang, and the captain snatched it from its handset.

"What's the problem, Chief?" he asked. Arthur Kensett listened intently as the Chief Engineer, Eddie Corkell, brought him up-to-date on what had occurred that necessitated the engine being shut down.

"Let me know as soon as you're aware of the problem," said Captain Kensett as he recradled the phone. He repeated what little news he had to the 3rd Mate. "The duty engineer stopped the engine because he heard a noisy racket coming from somewhere back aft. Both the chief and 2nd engineer had gone to investigate. That's as much as I know."

Down in the depths of the engine room, Eddie Corkell and the 2nd Engineer, Ron McDonald, trudged along the propeller shaft tunnel towards the source of the noise. The banging noise was getting louder and it seemed to be coming from the end of the shaft tunnel; yet they knew that no machinery was located back there. Both agreed that Bob Patience, their Australian 4th Engineer, had done the right thing in shutting down the engine when he had first heard the awful noise. With the giant Doxford diesel now silent, the vast engine room was deathly quiet, except that the racket was still emanating from somewhere above them. It was a mystery, and the chief scratched his head in curious bewilderment. They reached the trunking that led up to the steering gear. As they began climbing up the trunking, so the cacophony of noise got louder and more strident. They pulled themselves up into the steering flat; and there with his back towards them, and quite oblivious to the problems he had caused, was Ernie bashing away on his Premier drum kit. The chief stepped over and lifted the headphones from Ernie's ears and shook his head in bemusement. Ernie was totally unaware that he had been the cause of the ship being stopped in mid-ocean and he simply gave the engineer a big smile and said, "Hello Chief, how ya doin?" He cocked his head to one side and listened. "It's gone a bit bloody quiet, ain't it?"

Eddie Corkell was very good about it. He could have banned Ernie from playing his drums in the steering flat, but he didn't. He said, "Whenever you want to play your drums, Ernie, then please go tell the duty engineer, okay?"

⚓

The Port Montreal slogged her way uneventfully across the Pacific Ocean and made the long voyage to Brisbane where we would begin to unload our cargo from Canada and the United States. The ship arrived on New Year's Day 1969 after a 21 day passage. The voyage from Panama had seemed so very long and boring, that we couldn't wait to get ashore. Today was a national holiday, so there would be no discharge of cargo today. We hoisted the cargo derricks in readiness for the wharfies starting work tomorrow, after which the chief officer gave the deck crew the rest of the day off.

George was at it again – bullshitting! His latest tall story reminded us that, not only was he a millionaire, and owned three sizeable properties, but that he possessed a large motor yacht, and a 23 year old girlfriend who adored him. "Yeah right, George. Pull the other leg – it's got bells on!" He got quite upset when we didn't believe him. "Just wait," said George. "You'll see."

He had a bright idea. "Hey, how about we have a party in the crew's bar tonight? I'll bring along my girlfriend and a whole lot more girls, and we'll have ourselves a real shindig, eh?"

I shook my head incredulously. "George, that's nonsense. You're an ugly bastard. You don't have a girlfriend. You're living in dreams old man," I said good-naturedly.

"You'll find out tonight," said George confidently and he went off ashore.

I didn't bother going ashore, but spent my afternoon relaxing. In the late afternoon I was on the after-deck when a stylish white motor yacht steamed along the Brisbane River and came to loiter in midstream off our starboard side. Music was playing and several girls wearing swimsuits were lounging about her upper decks drinking cocktails. On the craft's flying-bridge, and wearing his captain's cap at a jaunty angle, was George Richards. He spotted me and shouted, "See ya tonight, sport." He opened up the throttles and roared away.

That evening George had a girl on each arm and several more astern as he approached the gangway. I helped them aboard and was introduced to his girlfriend Rebecca and her sister Miriam and several others. Rebecca was young and gorgeous, and I could tell by the way in which she looked at George that she loved him deeply. She held onto his arm and never let go. Miriam was very pretty and we spent the evening together in conversation. She had beautiful dark eyes and jet black hair. Her eyebrows weren't plucked, but thick and luxuriant and natural, and somehow it added to her attractiveness.

I asked her about George. "Was he really a millionaire? Did he actually own three houses? Did the big motor yacht genuinely belong to George? What was the attraction for her sister Rebecca?"

"Rebecca's known George since she was 19 years old," she said. "She's adored him from that very first day she met him. As for how rich he is; well, I've been to his house outside Brisbane, and also the one at Surfers Paradise on the Gold Coast – and the big boat most certainly does belong to him. So yeah, I suppose he is quite well off." I nodded at this new-found information and explained to Miriam why I had at first distrusted George on the matter of his being wealthy, and why I had thought he was a bull-shitter. "I can't say I blame you," she said candidly. "If someone who spends his days happily getting his hands covered in grease, and climbing ship's masts, had told me he was a millionaire, then I wouldn't have believed him either."

⚓

The ship sailed south to Sydney and berthed at Pyrmont on a Sunday morning. Immediately my thoughts turned to Imelda. It was in March of last year, ten months ago, that she had met me at the cruise terminal, so she would have had her baby by now. She had stated that she intended having it adopted and I wondered if she had given birth to a boy or a girl. It fleetingly crossed my mind to somehow try to search for her; perhaps through maternity hospitals. However, she had made it quite plain that she didn't want me around, and there was no reason to believe that she would have changed her mind. In any event I had another plan.

Paula Curtis' house in the suburb of Balmain was on a quiet leafy street where the majority of houses were wooden structures built on stilts with a three-sided veranda, much like the Queenslander houses that proliferate further north. She wasn't expecting me and I didn't know what I would find. It had been in February 1965, almost four years ago, that I had last seen Paula as she had waved goodbye as the Port Melbourne had departed from Sydney. For all I knew she may have moved, or have a steady boyfriend, or even a husband by now. We had not even tried to keep in touch, because I had cautioned her that I had no idea whatsoever when I would return.

I knocked on the door and stood back, leaning on the veranda balustrade. She would now be 32 years old, and I hadn't any preconceived ideas with regard to if she had changed a great deal. I was sure that we both had. I heard someone moving about inside, and suddenly the door opened, and there she was. "Hello Paula," I said uncertainly. "I hope you don't mind me just calling on you like this." With a furrowed brow she stared as if trying to recall a long lost memory, but then it all clicked into place and her face lit up with that same broad smile that I remembered from that first meeting at the State Library of NSW. "Well, hello stranger," she said. "What a lovely surprise on a Sunday afternoon. Come on inside." We stepped into her house, and because such a long time had passed, neither of us knew quite what to do, but I took the bull by the horns and took her into my arms. She wrapped her arms around my neck and snuggled in close, and from that moment I knew that we would be lovers again.

As we embraced, we kissed with a longing desire borne of many years separation and our tongues searched and explored hungrily. She had changed very little, except for perhaps a few more laughter lines around her eyes, and I was glad to see that her bottom was still delectable.

From somewhere around my feet a tabby tom-cat gave a miaow and rubbed himself against me. It seems my old friend Snooks had also remembered me as he purred loudly in welcome. We looked down and laughed and both bent to stroke him. She brought cold beers from the fridge, and as the hot Australian summer sunshine blazed down, all three of us sat out in a swing chair on the shady veranda. We spent the next hour or so with her cradled in my arms as we caught up on what had occurred in our respective lives. Paula was still employed at the library and loved her job, and had even been promoted to Senior Curator. I brought her up-to-date on my worldwide travels and adventures, but tactfully omitted any naughty bits; and especially any mention of other girlfriends. She diplomatically didn't enquire about my love-life, and I refrained from asking about hers.

As we talked, I realised that I had missed her very much indeed, and my longing couldn't hold back any more. Without warning, I picked her up and carried her into the bedroom, pulled the sheets back, and laid her in the bed. I quickly undressed her and threw off my clothes, and seconds later we were locked in a passionate embrace with a deep kiss that seemed to continue into the next millennium. Our passion held no bounds, and it was wonderful to again have someone special to love and to cherish, albeit that it would last only for the next nine days until the Port Montreal set sail again. Although we were due to return to Sydney in a little over six weeks, the nine idyllic days passed only too quickly, and all of a sudden the ship was slipping astern from her berth and bound for Melbourne.

In Melbourne the discharging of cargo went on unabated for eleven days, during which time I went to see the lovely Chloe at Young & Jackson's excellent hotel on quite a few occasions. In late January our next stop was Adelaide for just two days, where we completed the ship's discharge and began the task of loading the refrigerated cargo holds with dairy products, meat, and wool. In the evening I had a walk around this beautiful "City of Churches" to stretch my legs and to marvel at the ancient preserved buildings and generally take in the ambience of this most underrated capital of South Australia.

The Fremantle Doctor

The town of Fremantle lay at the entrance to the Swan River, and just 12 miles south-west of the City of Perth, the capital of Western Australia. The chief officer gave the deck crew a job n' knock to paint an offside section of the ship's hull with gallons of grey paint. We slung painting stages over the side and began painting the shell plating with lamb's wool rollers as we lowered ourselves down the ship's side. We had two deckies manning each painting stage, so that we finished the job in the shortest possible time. We had finished by midday.

After lunch I decided to stretch my legs around the town, and as I came into the High Street, I could see that Fremantle had scores of well-preserved Georgian and Victorian buildings.

If you want to find your way around a strange town, then your best bet is to find a tourist or information centre and wangle a pamphlet. These will usually have, not only a map of the town, but will tell you some of the history, which can be very useful. Normally they are to be found in prominently displayed racks, and you're invited to help yourself. I managed to find the tourist office; but when I asked the skinny old woman behind the desk for a pamphlet with a town map, she held her hand out expectantly. "That'll be $2 if you please," she said in a gruff voice that could have belonged to an outback sheep shearer.

She could tell by my facial expression that I was astonished. "Well, that's a bit steep," I said testily. "Usually these things are given away for free."

"Well, ya can't get nuthin' for nuthin' these days, can ya? Ya gotta pay yer way," she said, as if I was one of life's spongers, and that I had come inside simply to spoil her day.

"Do you have any free pamphlets at all?" I asked optimistically.

She looked at me as if I was stupid. "Nah, nuthin's for free. Ya gotta pay for it," she barked. As I handed over some coins, several fell on the floor, and as she bent over to retrieve them, I grabbed my opportunity and kicked the old crone squarely up the arse. Well, I didn't actually do that, but I certainly felt like it.

As I walked the full length of the High Street and the roads branching off to the side, I just knew it was going to be a wonderful afternoon. As you may have guessed, I am not a great aficionado of modern glass and concrete monstrosities that grace our cities; but show me some Georgian or Victorian architecture, and I get sentimental bouts of nostalgia. I love to look at these old building that were built by artisans and craftsmen and are full to the brim with vaulted ceilings, bow windows, bell towers, and colonnades. What beauty is there is some slab-sided piece of structural design that was bolted together between tea breaks?

In the hot afternoon sunshine I sat on a park bench and scanned through my costly pamphlet. In 1829, it said, Captain Charles Fremantle, commanding HM frigate "Challenger", arrived here and established a settlement. Soon afterwards, a larger settlement was set-up inland at a place that would come to be named Perth. Convicts were brought out from England to bolster and reinforce the small population, and the prisoners

296

were set to work erecting many of the fine buildings which I found upon my walk. It crossed my mind that it's a pity that we don't make our modern-day inmates work for their bed and board – but I daresay that Health & Safety Regulations and the Human Rights Act would rear their ugly heads.

As I ambled along the High Street, the lovely 19th century heritage buildings, with their cared-for appearance, merged sympathetically with the downtown modern shop fronts. Further along, past the business and commercial sector, at the western end of the High Street, I found the oldest building in Western Australia, called The Round House. It was a circular structure built of granite that was constructed by the prisoners themselves as their gaol. It had eight cells and quarters for the resident jailer and a central courtyard. It must have been very comfortable indeed, because many years later, the Chief Constable and his family used it as his official residence. Of course this Round house gaol was a million miles away from the Round House pub in Silvertown where on any given night of the week the place was full of poofters and homosexuals wearing gaudy cosmetics and frilly dresses. Struth - it don't bear thinkin' about!

That next weekend, when I was off-duty, a few of us went to South Beach and relaxed on the fine white sand. The weather was hot and the swells coming in off the sea weren't too high. It was great fun to swim in the warm waters of the Indian Ocean and just lay on one's back on the warm sand. Strangely, we had two engineer officers with us, Davy Hollis and Dennis Taylor. Normally, the officers and deck crew didn't mix together because of an antiquated class distinction issue, but these lads weren't the stuck-up kind, and we enjoyed each other's company enormously. In the afternoon the wind swung around and a cooling sea-breeze came in from the south-west that provided relief from the hot blazing sun. The wind was known as The Fremantle Doctor.

⚓

Our next stop was the small town of Albany, just inside the Great Australian Bight, where we stayed alongside to unload for a few days. This was my third visit to this most delightful town over the years. On the quayside, painted onto the flat concrete wharf, were ships names, together with the dates they had visited. They were similar to the ones painted onto the granite cliffs in Port Chalmers; but these were altogether much more accomplished artistically.

I fancied myself as something of an artist, and so I had a stab at leaving our own ship's name for posterity on the quayside. I decided to paint a detailed likeness of the Port Montreal, together with a lifebelt with the ship's name and the Port Line house-flag. Each day I would paint in the cool evenings after work, and slowly the artwork took shape. The ship painting, using normal Port Line deck paints, was fully 15 feet long and the lifebelt about six feet in diameter.

Eventually, just prior to departure, I had finished the ship and I was quite pleased with my efforts, and several of our crew had remarked on how accomplished it was. The lifebelt and company house-flag was almost complete, except that I hadn't painted-in the rope grab-lines that are normally attached to a ship's lifebelt. I had managed only to chalk-in where the ropes were to be painted. I had run out of time.

At last the ship was ready for departure. With her engine ticking over, mooring ropes singled up, and the pilot onboard, I was at my harbour station on the fo'castle head. Suddenly the Tannoy loudspeaker squawked. "Able-seaman Mcglone - report to the captain immediately!" My crewmates looked at me in sympathy, wondering what I had done wrong. I rushed up to the bridge, where I found Captain Kensett gazing down onto the quay. He said, "Young man, you've made a very good job of painting on the quayside. I'm very pleased with your hard work, but the grab-lines on the lifebelt require finishing off. How long do you think it would take you to paint them?"

"I think I could paint then in about 20 minutes, Sir," I said, feeling quite proud.

"Very well then," said the captain. "We'll hold up the ship. You get ashore and try your best to finish it off, okay?"

I quickly drew some paint and fine brushes from the lamp-trimmer's store, and with the captain and the whole crew watching me, I raced ashore and put the finishing touches to the lifebelt grab-lines. Later that day Captain Kensett said to me. "I had my doubts about you when you first came aboard, but you've done well. Keep up the good work." I was chuffed to bits!

⚓

The Port Montreal continued her voyage eastwards and returned to Melbourne, where for six days the wharfies loaded lamb, butter, cheese, and wool, and slowly her hull sank deeper into the water as many thousands of tons were stowed in her cargo holds.

We headed for Sydney, and arrived in the early hours of Saturday on the first day of March. We were scheduled to be here for just three days. The ship berthed in Pyrmont just along the road from Monty's Bar – which was rather handy! With barely concealed anticipation I was looking forward to seeing Paula and picking up where we had left off, so after lunch I made my way out to Balmain.

My persistent knock on her door went unanswered, until a few moments later when the next-door-neighbour, a man dressed in shorts and singlet, shouted across the fence. "G'day mate. If you're lookin' for Paula, she ain't here. She's on holiday and gone up-country for a week or so." He must have noticed my dismay. "Yeah, sorry mate, but she left about two days ago. I'm lookin' after Snooks the cat while she's gone." Paula hadn't known exactly when I would be returning, so I couldn't blame her for not being here. I thanked him, and after leaving her a short note, made my way despondently back to the ship. Well, that was that and I didn't suppose I would see her again, as the Port Montreal would have just two more ports-of-call up in Queensland and then head across the Pacific Ocean to Panama and the USA.

After my initial doubts with regard to George Richards' financial affluence, I thought that I might be invited to go spend a night or two at his alleged mansion – the one outside whose ornate gates he had been photographed. But when I broached the subject, George simply said, "The house has been closed up. No one's there."

That same evening George and I went to Kings Cross, the Sydney district that is chock-a-block with restaurants, nightclubs, strip-clubs, adult bookstores, and bars. As we ambled along Darlinghurst Road, George pointed towards a large grand hotel that belonged to a multi-national chain and said, "I used to be the general manager of that hotel."

"You've gotta be kiddin' me?" I said sceptically. "Are you bullshittin' again, George?"

"You can be so bloody hurtful at times, Gra. I'm offended," he said in mock indignation.

"You've got to admit, George," I said, as we walked up the steps into the sumptuous hotel lobby, "it does seem unlikely, doesn't it?"

"Nope, it's the God's-honest truth, Gra. I worked here about ten years ago."

We were at the reception desk, and George asked the receptionist if the manager was available. A few moments later a smart looking man in his early thirties came into the lobby. He was wearing a hotel name-tag which said "Manager." His eyes opened wide in surprise when he spotted George. "Mister Richards, how nice to see you again," he said cordially as they shook hands. "It must be over ten years ago since you were here in the hot-seat, isn't it?"

"Yeah, it must be," said George. "You were just a junior manager then, weren't you?"

"That's right. Things have changed here since you were manager," he said. "What are you doing in this neck of the woods?"

"Simply passin' through," said George in his strong Aussie accent. "Just a tourist now, Bob."

George introduced me and told him about life aboard the Port Montreal. Bob the manager was awestruck at the tales of adventure on the high-seas and George's extensive travels.

"Hey, why don't you and your friend stay the night here, George?" suggested Bob. "Have a nice dinner in the restaurant? We've got a cabaret show tonight. All on the house, okay?" We jumped at the chance, and Bob went behind the desk, whispered to the receptionist, and returned with two room keys. He accompanied us through to the restaurant and had a word with the maitre d'hôtel, and after saying cheerio, we were seated and given menus. As we ate a lavish meal I said, "George, I'm sorry for doubting you about being the manager. I apologise."

"That's all right, Gra," he said magnanimously. "Forget about it, mate."

An hour later we were in the show-bar enjoying a cabaret from a front row table laden with free drinks. George spotted two young girls in their early twenties sitting at a nearby table and suggested that we ask them to join us. Even though he had the lovely Rebecca, I decided to rag him a little. "George, you're almost fifty years old, you're ugly, and you're as bald as a badger," I reminded him unkindly. "What makes you think that they would be attracted to your ugly mug?"

He chuckled loudly. "Watch and learn, sunshine." He went over to the girls and engaged them in conversation. A few minutes later they accompanied him back to our table. He made introductions. They were called Lucy and Elena and they were very attractive. The blonde Lucy sat close to George and seemed totally engrossed with whatever he was saying to her. She gazed into his eyes and absorbed every word. I shall never call him an ugly bugger again.

Elena was originally from Greece, and like Lucy, was an artist. They were staying at the hotel so as to attend an art college interview the next day with regard to starting a three-year course. Elena was very pretty with long black hair and black eyes and thick natural eyebrows. When she spoke, she had a soft Balkan accent which I found incredibly sexy. She reminded me of Valentina. We seemed to have plenty in common and we talked for ages. I looked over at George and Lucy. They were in deep conversation and had eyes only for each other. Lucy took Elena with her to go to the powder room; no doubt for a girlie chat. Meanwhile George whispered, "How are you gettin' on with Elena? Will she wanna stay the night with you, mate? I hope so 'cause Lucy's shackin' up with me tonight."

I was astonished that George could manage to pull a young girl of just twenty or so, and get her to agree to go to bed with him, but then nothing about George Richards should astonish me now. He must have had

Irish blood in him because he certainly had some blarney, and when he spoke, with his voice's rich timbre, he could make reading a gas bill sound like poetry.

The four of us made our way to George's room and drank some beer from the mini-bar. My room was through a connecting door, and after a suitable interval, I whispered to Elena that perhaps we should leave George and Lucy alone. I took her hand and led her into my suite.

⚓

As the ship loaded the last of her cargo of lamb and dairy products, a large strange item of deck freight was lifted onboard. It was a heavy steel box fully twenty feet long and eight feet wide. At one end were sealable double doors through which to load its cargo. As we lashed the box securely to deck-cleats, the chief officer came along to look it over. "What's this big box used for, Mister Mate?" I asked.

"It's called a cargo container," he said. "It gets loaded at the factory by the exporter, and gets unloaded at its destination by the importer. Other than lifting it ashore with a crane, the dockers never get to touch the cargo inside. Take a good look. You'll be seeing a lot more of these containers."

Three days later, the Port Montreal let go her ropes and departed for the run northwards to visit the quiet harbour of Port Alma in Queensland. We then headed for Brisbane where, during a six-day stay, we finalised the loading of our cargo for America. Of course George's lady Rebecca came aboard, and a happy time was had by all when I resurrected my relationship with her sister Miriam.

At last we headed for Panama, from where we would head northwards and again call at ports up the eastern seaboard of the United States. However, this visit to the USA would be a little different, and we now had something extra to look forward to. Somewhere in the USA, at a port still to be advised, a new crew would relieve us and we would fly home.

The voyage across the Pacific was uneventful except for one thing. One bright morning, I was standing upon the port bridge wing chatting with the 3rd Mate, Ian MacRae. As we talked, he was facing aft and I was facing forward. Suddenly and without any forewarning, he ducked down as if something was about to hit him and said, "Jeezus, what the hell was that?"

At the same instant I saw something dark flash past my peripheral vision and disappear over the horizon. Within a millisecond it had vanished.

I said, "What the hell was that, Ian? Did something just whizz by?" He looked bewildered as he tried to work out what it was that he had seen.

"It appeared to be something long and round, shaped just like a cigar. It was flying so fast, I only saw it for less than half a second. Did you see it?"

"I can't with any certainty tell you what I saw," I said. "It just went so quickly."

There had been hardly any noise, but just an almost imperceptible "whooshing" sound - and then it had disappeared. Whatever it was, it appeared to be at a height just above the ship - about 70 feet. Had it been a supersonic aircraft, then the noise would have been so deafening, it would have blown our eardrums out; and in any event our ship was a thousand miles from any airport. "Do you think we ought to tell the captain?" I asked.

Ian shook his head. "You've got to be joking. What would we tell him? We cannot describe what we saw. We don't know what we saw. No one else seems to have seen it, otherwise they would have run up here to the bridge and reported it to me. Best leave it at that, shall we?"

I related to Ian the story of the UFO that I had seen when on look-out duty aboard the Port Melbourne three years ago. He nodded in understanding as if it made some sort of sense from this whole mystery.

Flying Home

At Panama the ship stayed overnight at Balboa, and several of us went ashore to an electronics store to buy a tape recorder. These were not the small cheap type with a screechy playback, but Japanese state-of-the-art Aiki reel-to-reel stereo tape recorders with separate speakers. They may now seem outdated, especially as some models were fitted with 8-track tape players, but back in 1969 they were the very latest cutting-edge electronics on the market. I cannot remember what it cost, but I'm fairly certain that it was the equivalent of a month's wages. I bought tapes of the latest albums of The Who, Cream, The Beatles, and The Moody Blues, and in my off-duty time I would clamp some headphones to my ears, and with the beautiful music wafting around inside my head, I'd be in heaven.

⚓

After transiting the Panama Canal and offloading cargo at Charleston and Wilmington, we were now tied up in Philadelphia. The date was 24th April 1969. The great day had arrived. This was as far as we were going. Everyone was excited, because after breakfast, we were paid off and awaiting the arrival of the coach that would bring our relief crew who had flown in from the UK just that morning. We were going home.

The Port Montreal had been a good ship to sail in. She had been my home, and in many ways I was sorry to be leaving her. I had been aboard her for almost nine months; and in that time we'd had 33 ports-of-call as she loaded and discharged her cargoes. Although I knew that she was simply a ship made of steel and wood and plastic, it still broke my heart to be leaving her. Somewhat like a magnet, some ships have that attractive quality that makes one want to remain with her. But sadly, it was time to leave.

We were coached to the giant Roosevelt Hotel in the city centre and allotted suites of rooms from where we would await until it was time to depart for our late night flight home. The deck department's suite was equipped with a huge colour television, the first colour set I had ever seen. In the late afternoon, our ship's local agent came by and told us to make our way down to the hotel restaurant, where we would be fed on the company's account. "But hey guys, don't go ordering any alcohol, okay?"

In the restaurant we were greeted by our friendly waitress, Tammy, a little cutie who had a not unattractive 'Southern Belle' accent and who reminded me of a young Dolly Parton. "Hi guys, just take a seat and I'll be right there with menus." About ten of us sat at a huge circular table festooned with flower displays and subdued lighting and enough cutlery to keep the Sheffield factories employed for months. Nearby, the stewards and stokers sat at similar tables and they were equally as impressed.
"Hey, you boys are on an expense account, ain't ya?" said Tammy. "So how would you like some nice thick juicy ribeye steaks - or the soft-shell crab is really good. You guys have whatever ya little ol' heart's desires, okay?" I had never eaten so luxuriously or extravagantly in all my life, and seeing as Port Line was picking up the tab, we made pigs of ourselves. We even talked Tammy into supplying beer and invoicing the company for food.

On our evening coach ride to the airport, I spotted a house that was decked out with the Stars & Stripes draped from the balcony. Balloons were pinned to the front door, and streamers hung across the whole house. A gaily hand-painted sign on the front lawn proclaimed, "Welcome home Chuck. You gave the Viet-Cong pure hell. We're proud of you, son." I turned to George. "If my mother dares to put up a sign like that, I'm going to be mortified."
He chuckled. "You've only been gone a couple of years, Gra. That's not even long enough to change your bed sheets, is it mate?"

Our overnight flight home was aboard a Caledonian Airways Bristol Britannia turbo prop aircraft, and we landed at Gatwick the next morning. As we waited in the baggage reclaim area for our suitcases to be disgorged onto the luggage carousel, it was time yet again to say goodbye to some special shipmates. We had been a good crew together. We had worked well as a slick team and I knew that I would miss them, and always remember them, even though we would probably never meet again.

My sister Glynis had hired a taxi to meet me at the airport. It was great to see her, and as we hugged each other tightly, I realised just how much my little sis had grown up since I'd left, and how much I had missed her. In a month's time she would be 20 years old.

As the cab dropped us off outside our house in Wythes Road, I was relieved to see that my mum hadn't draped the house with the Union Jack, and there were no balloons or streamers, and no big welcome home sign. However, pinned to the front door was a discreet postcard which said, "Welcome home Gra – we've missed you." I couldn't stop myself from laughing.

My mum was waiting for me in the lounge, and as I gave her a big hug, she had tears in her eyes. "Don't go away for so long next time, Gra," she whispered. "I've missed you, son."

We stood like that for ages. A son quietly comforting his mother. I had been away from home for 2 years, 4 months, and 3 days.

12: The Beaverfir

Bound for Canada - 1ˢᵗ voyage

My mum had changed a little. She was now 55 years old and had a few more grey hairs and had put on a little weight. We had all grown older – but in different ways. My stepdad Albert took time off from his busy job to sit and listen to the multitude of story's which I had to tell; and as I told them another tale of fun on the high seas, I looked across at my mum; she couldn't stop grinning. It was so good to be home.

"How's Linda?" I asked mum. Linda had been married to David Parry for just eighteen months and they rented a house in North Woolwich. "Things aren't very good Gra," said mum sadly. "He's a bully and he knocks her about." The brother-in-law whom I had been looking forward to befriending was not to be.

Linda came along that evening to welcome me home and to show off her new baby, David, who was just eight months old. I bounced the little fella on my knee for a while and brought out gifts for the kids. My niece Toni was now five years old, but even though she didn't recognise me, she was pleased as punch with the new dolly I'd brought home from America. Linda didn't volunteer any information about her new husband, except to say that he couldn't make it tonight because he was busy. I left things like that and didn't bring up the subject of her husband again as I knew she'd be embarrassed. The marriage didn't last much longer and she quite rightly divorced him.

As I wandered around the streets of Silvertown, I knew without a doubt that it had changed irretrievably for the worse. Even though it had always been an industrial town with lots of hustle and bustle and noise, most residents had taken pride in their little patch of garden or the front entrance. Brass doorsteps had been polished, windows were cleaned, and housewives would wash down the porch and their bit of pavement. But now, as I looked around me, its grimy buildings and dirty litter-strewn streets looked awful. As part of the East End redevelopment, the Greater London Council had demolished many Victorian era houses and replaced them with anonymous tower blocks, where families who were once familiar with their next-door-neighbours, felt abandoned and alone in these aerial monuments to bad town planning. Consequently many people took the opportunity to leave Silvertown and North Woolwich, and moved out to the new towns springing up in Essex. In their place, new people had moved in; coloured and Asian families who had different and diverse cultures to the original residents. The magic and the camaraderie of Silvertown had gone forever.

I must have salt water running through my veins, because I had been at home for less than five weeks when I desperately needed to feel the sea beneath my feet again. Some unknown magnetic quality was drawing me back and I wanted to experience again that euphoric feeling of setting sail towards far horizons on a new voyage of discovery. I felt like a heroin addict who needed his fix. Perhaps a lack of funds had something to do with my decision as well.

I went to see Reggie the Rat at the federation office. Nothing had changed. Out-of-work sailors still congregated outside the office smoking cigarettes. The blackboard still listed ships sailing to far flung places, and Reggie remained safely behind his steel-barred counter. I'm pretty sure that he even wore the same shirt! Strangely, most of the jobs on the board were touting for crew to join ships that were bound for Australia or New Zealand, which I thought it best to disregard. My mum would have had kittens!

"What else have you got, Reggie?" I asked. "I don't want any long voyages to the other side of the world. Have you got any ships departing on a short trip?"

"How about a nice trip to Canada?" asked Reggie in response to my enquiry. He extracted a job card from his Rollerdex and read it out aloud. "It's the Beaverfir, a Canadian Pacific ship that runs to the Great Lakes. Six week trips; how's that?"

"That sounds promising. I'll pop aboard and look her over first."

"Please yourself," said Reggie. "She's berthed at E shed in the Royal Victoria Dock. Let me know what you decide."

The Beaverfir looked a tidy ship. She was fairly small, about 4,500 tons, but there was a certain something about her that attracted me. She had just four cargo hatches and her engines were located back aft, as was the accommodation. She was painted all white and her funnel bore the chequered motif of the Canadian Pacific Steamship Company. I walked aboard, and in the crew's messroom I found an able-seaman having his smoko. I introduced myself and told him that I was thinking of joining the crew. In answer to my enquiries, he told me that she was a "good feeder," that there was plenty of overtime to be had, and the bosun was so laid-back - he was almost horizontal. Even the captain was a nice bloke, said my informant who introduced himself as Jonesy, and seemed like a nice bloke himself. Jonesy was from South London. He was in his late thirties with a pock-marked face and thinning hair; but he had a cheeky grin and I liked him instantly. There was just one drawback, he said; the ship was a little old-fashioned in that the accommodation for the deck crew was double berthed and I would have to share.

He walked around the ship with me and we looked at the cabins and met the Chief Cook – the most important man aboard any vessel. Jonesy took me to see the chief mate, a stout middle-aged Ulsterman with a thick accent. The mate told me that the ship would be leaving shortly for a quick dry-docking in Rotterdam, then return to London to load cargo for Canada. On the spur of the moment I asked him if I could join the crew. He inspected my discharge book and asked a few pertinent questions about my previous employment. Seemingly satisfied, he shook my hand and said, "Welcome aboard." That same day I reported back to Reggie the Rat and went home to re-pack my suitcase. I said goodbye to my family. "See you in a week's time," I shouted as I walked out the door. I piled my kit into the back of a cab and went to join the Beaverfir. I had myself a new home. On 2nd June 1969 we sailed for Rotterdam.

⚓

My cabin was located way back aft on the port side; which meant that in any rough weather, the propeller would come clear out of the water and the vibrations would make the cabin shake violently. The room was a generous size with two brass portholes, a set of bunk beds, a pair of varnished wardrobes, a desk with a mirror and a comfortable chair to relax in. The walls, or bulkheads, were lined with pleasant magnolia laminated sheets and the room had decent furnishings with a fitted carpet and bright curtains.

Unfortunately my cabinmate was a quiet faceless individual in his forties who, if you passed him on the street, would be instantly forgettable. His name was Ronnie, and he kept himself to himself and spoke little to the other crew members. The only other thing notable about Ronnie was that whatever the weather he always wore a flat cap. A few of the deck crew were Outer Hebrideans, but the rest were from the southern counties. Dave Perry was an able-seaman of about my own age and we hit it off straight away and became go-ashore buddies. Dave was a tall good-looking dark haired guy from Devon with a pronounced West Country accent and a great sense of humour. As opposed to the large crews of 65 or more onboard the older vessels upon which I had served, the Beaverfir employed just thirty seven crew and had no need for a multitude of stewards as we carried no passengers. She didn't even have a deck boy.

The bosun was a great guy called John Glancy. He was short and skinny and liked his booze, but he was superb seaman, and he got on well with all the deck crew. An unusual thing about the Beaverfir was that we possessed a ship's tabby cat called Minx that was fully house-trained and preferred to sleep in the bosun's cabin. None of my previous vessels had animals living onboard, although some Royal Navy ships were partial to

307

carrying a ship's mascot. I heard of a minesweeper serving in the Persian Gulf whose crew had a hairy billy-goat that sported nasty-looking curly horns. One day, after a section of the crew got roaring drunk, they assembled pots of paint and brushes and decided to paint the goat every colour of the rainbow. Our Minxy never left the ship, but would patrol the decks and accommodation searching for mice or rats. He must have been a successful hunter, because I never saw any rodents at all aboard our ship.

⚓

On our first night at the shipyard, most of the crew went ashore to sample the delights of Rotterdam – perhaps they would try to pull one of the virginal dancing partners at the Mission to Seaman? Two of the younger deck crew, who presumably couldn't hold their grog, were picked up by the Rotterdam Police and tossed in jail for the night. The police returned them to the ship in the morning and our captain had to cough up the money to pay their fines, which of course was deducted from their wages.

The dry-dock in Rotterdam was a strange piece of engineering. Ships didn't go into a normal graving dock, which was then pumped out, but instead we floated over a massive ship-lift, which then winched us up high-and-dry clear of the water.

Late in the evening, with most of the crew ashore, I was alone in the crew's messroom when Jonesy came in. "How would you like to earn yourself some extra cash, Gra?" I nodded. Even though I was unsure how I would earn it, I could tell that Jonesy was up to no good, but what the hell?

"Follow me up to the fo'castle head," said Jonesy, and led the way. As we walked along the pitch-black foredeck he whispered, "I want you just to operate the anchor windlass – nothing else. Another thing, they'll be someone else up on the fo'castle, and you don't need to know who that person is. Just stay where I tell you to, understood?" I nodded.

The fo'castle was a dark and forbidding place, and Jonesy had me stand-by the winch controls at the after end and await his orders to operate it. He then went further forward to the stem. As he flashed his torch over the ship's side, I could see that there was another person with him. However, it was so dark I couldn't see who it was, but I could hear some muffled conversation as they spoke.

Jonesy asked me to start the windlass and pay out some of the anchor cable. I set the control to 'lower,' and the winch began lowering out the heavy anchor cable, each link of which weighed 40 lbs. As the minutes ticked by, I estimated that I had payed-out two shackles of cable – that's 180 feet in length. Most ships carry seven shackles of anchor cable in each of its massive cable lockers. Therefore, we should still have more than enough to anchor the ship if need be.

Without Jonesy or the unknown man being aware, I looked over the ship's side and could plainly see what was happening. Down in the bottom of the dock was an open-back truck, and the ship's anchor chain was coiling itself into the truck as I lowered it. We were flogging off the anchor cable! Jonesy called me to stop lowering, and down in the dock I could hear the truck driver disconnecting the cable at the joining shackle, and then the sound of him driving away.

"Okay Gra, we're all finished here," said Jonesy. "You can go back to the messroom now. I'll square you up with some money later on." He then walked forward to the bow to rejoin the dark figure of the mystery man, and I was no wiser to knowing who he was.

I made my way back down the dark foredeck towards the accommodation block, whilst Jonesy and Mister Anonymous remained on the fo'castle and chatted in low voices. On an impulse I slid behind a cargo hatch and waited in the shadows for them to walk aft. Near the accommodation entrance, a dim light shone down upon the deck, and I figured that I would be able to see the other man as they passed beneath it. I heard them whispering as they came aft; and as they walked under the light my eyes almost popped out of their sockets in surprise. The gentleman who walked aft with Jonesy; the man who had just flogged off the ship's cable, was a very senior ship's officer. Later that day I found an envelope on my pillow. Inside the envelope, in used banknotes, was cash equal to one months' wages.

Back in London the Beaverfir began loading general industrial cargo for Montreal and Toronto, and being just a mile from Silvertown, I was at home every night with my family. My mum couldn't quite grasp why, after being away from home for almost two and a half years, I was keen to be back at sea. I tried to explain that I needed to again experience that delicious sensation one gets as one sails towards a new adventure in a new and foreign country. It was a sensation that was difficult to explain to a landlubber. I'm quite sure that working Monday to Friday in a Silvertown factory would have come nowhere near that feeling.

We sailed from London on the 11th June, returned briefly to Rotterdam for more cargo, and then proceeded westwards along the English Channel, bound for Canada. The sea conditions sailing across the Atlantic were very favourable, and with the long smooth swells and blue skies, it was a delight to be out on the ocean. The Beaverfir was a lovely little ship, and she was easy enough to work on deck. In contrast to other ships that I had sailed upon, the food was fabulous. Some company's kept their crews on short rations, and in rare cases doled out the minimum food provisions, as stipulated by the Board of Trade regulations, which a crew member could legally receive. Aboard the 'bad feeders,' each crewman would be given a half pound of loose tea, two pounds of sugar, tins of sweetened condensed milk etc per week. These provisions the seaman had to stow away in his cabin locker, and eke out his rations to last the week. Likewise, the crewman would be fed on the minimum rations that the Merchant Shipping Act allowed each seafarer. Life could be very hard aboard such ships, and a three month voyage would seem like three years. However, the Beaverfir was a 'good feeder.' Right from the get-go the chief cook had said that, within reason, we could have whatever we wanted to eat. If we wanted a thick sirloin steak, then just ask.

As the vessel trudged at 15 knots across the Atlantic and neared the coast of Labrador, we headed for the Belle Isle Straits off the coast of Newfoundland, which would lead us into the Gulf of St Lawrence and on up to Montreal. One morning I came up onto the bridge at 04:00 hours to carry out a lookout duty. As the dawn sun tried to push its way above the horizon, I could make out several large indistinct shapes on all sides of the ship. They were enormous icebergs. I could see that they were far bigger, perhaps twenty times larger than our vessel. As the daybreak came, and the sun's rays shone onto the icebergs, I could see that they were coloured a very pale blue. They were majestically beautiful.

I reported the sightings to the officer-of-the-watch. He studied them through his binoculars and told me that, although they were the full-sized variety, of which only 10% showed above the surface of the ocean, these were not the dangerous bergs. The ones to keep a sharp lookout for were growlers or bergy-bits. Growlers may rise just three feet out of the water, but underwater they may be as big as a double-decker bus. Because they are hard to see, they can be a danger to shipping as they will do a lot of damage if a ship ploughs into one. Bergy-bits are small bergs, but larger than growlers. They rise maybe ten feet from the water and are difficult to see at night or in rough seas.

The icebergs originate from the glaciers on the western coast of Greenland. As the temperature rises and the ice begins to melt, they break off or calve from the glaciers and drift slowly southwards on the wind and the tide. Eventually, as the sea temperature rises in the April – July iceberg season, bits break off them as they drift even further south, until they melt completely.

North Atlantic icebergs usually range in size from just 3 feet above sea level up to a huge 250 feet and can weigh up to 225,000 tons. The highest ever recorded was spotted by a USCG icebreaker in 1958, and was reported to be 550 feet high, making it the height of a 55-storey building.

310

Nonetheless, these are tiny when compared with the flat-topped tabular icebergs that regularly drift in the South Atlantic off Antarctica. In 1956 a chunk of ice broke off from the Ross Ice Shelf and began to drift westwards. It was 12,000 sq mi in area and measured 208 mi by 60 mi. That's larger than Belgium! However, the danger lies in the North Atlantic where the shipping density is greatest and the icebergs could potentially cause havoc. In April 1912 the RMS Titanic ploughed into an iceberg and sank with the loss of 1523 lives. Prior to this time, there was no system in place to track icebergs; and so the International Ice Patrol was formed which provided guard ships to observe them. Nowadays the bergs may be tracked with the use of satellites.

Three days later the Beaverfir berthed at the Old Port in Montreal. It was six months since I had last been in the city and had climbed expectantly up to Mont Royal on a spiritual date with the lovely Maxine. On the first night in harbour, Jonesy asked me to help open up the steel hatch lid to No. 1 cargo hold. He said that an item of cargo was required to be withdrawn from the hold; and because he was in possession of two documents called a manifest and cargo plan, and we were in plain sight of the bridge and officers' cabins, I naturally thought that this was official business. Oh how wrong I was!

We opened up the hold and Jonesy, wielding a flashlight and the aforesaid cargo plan, climbed inside. A few minutes later he climbed out breathing heavily and clasping a large heavy cardboard box, and I lent a hand to pull it out. We stowed the box in a dark corner of the bosun's store and closed the hatch back up again. "Thanks Gra, you can go off to bed now if you want."

The St Lawrence Seaway

We were in the port for only four days during which time we unloaded the cargo of industrial items that we had brought from the UK. On the third day in Montreal it was my 23rd birthday, so to celebrate the occasion Dave Perry and I visited Joe Beef's Tavern for a marvellous booze-up. The next day, on a perfectly beautiful calm evening, we embarked a pilot and let go our mooring ropes and headed for Toronto.

The St Lawrence Seaway, a joint USA/Canadian venture, was a hugely successful feat of engineering. When it was opened for business in 1959, it created a means of navigation between all of the Great Lakes and the Atlantic Ocean. The 189-mile stretch of the Seaway between Montreal and Lake Ontario was one of the most challenging in terms of construction..

En route our ship would pass through seven locks and be lifted 246 feet above sea level. Soon after departure, the Beaverfir slid her bow into St

Lambert Lock and we started our climb up over the Gatineau Hills. As the transit progressed, we passed through Sainte Catherine Lock, then two separate locks at Beauharnois. The huge locks, each 766 feet by 80 feet could accommodate the largest 'Lakers,' the bulk carriers that ply the Great Lakes between the USA and Canada. The rate at which any ship was raised up in the locks was awesome, as it would be filled with 24 million gallons of water within 10 minutes.

Some of the locks had a seated spectator gallery where families could come for a day out to watch the ships as they transited through the seaway. Even though the crew were simply carrying out our regular duties of mooring and letting go the ship, it felt rather strange to be observed by the crowd; as if one were there to perform. Very often we would be waved and whistled at and photographed – and on one memorable occasion - even applauded.

⚓

It was 3am as we approached the US controlled Snell Lock at Massena NY that the problem began. My cabinmate Ronnie was steering the ship, and nobody had realised that he'd already drank a half bottle of spirits and he was very drunk. Both the pilot and the captain were outside upon the wing of the bridge and helm orders were being relayed to Ronnie at the helm.

"Steady as she goes," shouted the pilot, and Ronnie repeated the order and attempted to steer a steady course.

"Wheel amidships," ordered the pilot and Ronnie's alcohol befuddled brain managed to again repeat the order and turn the helm in the right direction. The ship was now running parallel with the lock training wall at a speed of five knots, and would soon be going astern so as to moor up prior to entering the lock.

"Hard a starboard," yelled the pilot, and Ronnie spun the wheel to the right.

"Midships the wheel," ordered the pilot, but Ronnie was blotto and nothing in the world could make him understand. He slumped across the helm and his eyes closed in a drunken stupor. The Beaverfir's rudder was still hard over to starboard and her bow swung rapidly around to the right towards the pier. The pilot and the captain both sensed something amiss and screamed, "Hard a port," so as to apply opposite rudder to stop the swing. At the same time they ran into the wheelhouse to find Ronnie draped across the wheel. They attempted to drag him off and spin the helm in the opposite direction, but it was far too late. With a grinding crash, the starboard bow struck the pier, and one could hear some very serious and expensive damage being done as a sharp obstacle down near the waterline sheared through the ship's shell plating and opened her up like a can of sardines. Eventually the ship was stopped and we tied up to the pier.

The steel plating on the bow, just 18 inches above the waterline, was ripped open in a gash 15 feet long and one foot wide. It soon became apparent that our vessel could progress no further until the damage had been temporarily repaired. If we were allowed to enter the lock and the ship sank, then the whole of the seaway system would come to a grinding halt.

The captain, chief officer, John Glancy, Jonesy and myself together with seaway officials and a Lloyds insurance surveyor, stood on the quay to assess the damage – which was considerable. We needed to work out how we could repair the ship so that she was seaworthy, albeit temporarily. Jonesy voiced a superb idea. "Back in Montreal," he said, "we unloaded some bags of quick drying cement fondu, and some of them split open. How about we stuff the gash full with any old rubbish, rope fenders, pillows, or even a mattress? Then we sweep up the loose cement, mix it with some sand, and make up a mortar mix and render over the damage. It should harden off within a few hours, and then we can be on our way."
"Good idea," said the captain. The seaway authorities agreed. We borrowed a shallow punt and set to work. Within a few hours we had stuffed the hole with rubbish, rendered a cement mix over the gash, and left it to cure. The next morning, after a brief inspection by the Lloyds surveyor, we let go and continued on our way to Toronto. A ship repair yard had been contracted to carry out permanent repairs on arrival. As for Ronnie, I'm sure that the captain thought of a suitable punishment – a double DR probably.

Once the ship had passed through Eisenhower and Iroquois Locks, we came out into an area called The Thousand Islands at the entrance to Lake Ontario. Thousand Islands were truly beautiful. At a sedate speed, the ship passed close by hundreds of small private islands, on each of which was built a luxurious and stately house. As the American/Canadian border ran down through the middle of the lake, all of them flew either the Stars & Stripes or the Maple Leaf flags of their country. All the islands of course had their own pier, and very often we would see a luxury motor cruiser alongside. Around these parts millionaires were a dime a dozen.

⚓

In my cabin I found another envelope on my pillow and inside was some cash. I had no idea what the money was for, but rightly supposed it may have come from Jonesy. I went along to his cabin.
"Did you leave that cash on my pillow?" I enquired.
"Yeah, thanks very much for your help, mate," he said.
"But what's it for? I thought that getting that carton from the cargo hold was all legal and above board."

"Er – well not quite. In fact – to tell you the truth – I stole it," he openly admitted.

"Bloody hell, Jonesy, I wish you'd told me, rather than keep me in the dark."

"If I had, then you may not have helped, and I couldn't have done it by myself, could I?"

"What was in the box?" I enquired.

"Furs from eastern Europe," he confessed. "Sable and Mink pelts from Russia. They were consigned to a fur trader in Montreal."

"Jeezus. How the hell did you know what to nick and where to find it?" I asked.

His face split into a crafty grin. "Someone let me have a copy of the manifest and cargo stowage plan. It was easy."

"Blimey, who gave you that?" I asked, not really expecting an answer.

Jonesy simply tapped the side of his nose, signifying - mind your own business. However, there was only one way that he could have got his hands on those documents, and that was by a deck officer giving them to him.

"So, how did you sell the furs," I asked. "Who'd you flog them to?"

There was that crafty grin again. "I sold 'em to the fur trader who they were addressed to," he said, as if it was the most natural thing in the world to do.

"You did what?" I said incredulously. "You stole his furs, and then you had the bloody cheek to sell them back to him? Blimey Jonesy, you were taking a chance, weren't you? He could have called in the gendarmes."

"Why should he?" he said matter-of-factly. "He got his furs at a fraction of the price, and then claimed the insurance money for non-delivery of his consignment. Everybody's happy – except the insurance company of course."

Nicking cargo was a favourite pastime for many crews. Some of them, such as the guys who manned the ships on the west coast of America run, targeted the substantial consignments of Scotch whisky which were carried in their cargo holds. Even though the hatch entrance was padlocked, the wily and scheming crew would easily circumvent the security measures and were gloriously pissed for most of the trip.

I am ashamed to admit (well, just a little bit!) that I helped myself to my fair share of stolen cargo over the years. In Marseilles I climbed down into the hold so as to liberate bottles of export wine and some Marino wool blankets. On another occasion we were carrying a chilled cargo of delicious crayfish tails from New Zealand back to the UK. The deck crew found a surreptitious route to skirt around the security padlocks and get into the tween deck stowage space and we feasted on these delicacies for weeks afterwards.

Another yarn I heard concerned a vessel on a run to Malaysia. Amongst the cargo, the crew noticed a consignment addressed to The Sultan of Johore, which was stowed securely under lock and key. Even though they hadn't a clue what the cases contained, the crew naturally wanted to get their grubby thieving hands on it and immediately set to work on a plan to liberate the aforementioned sultan's packages. They found a way into the cargo space and broke open one of the cases. Inside they found bars of Cussen's Imperial Leather soap. The sultan apparently favoured this expensive brand of gentleman's toiletries. It was not much practical use to the crew, as it didn't really have any market value; however the deck crowd smelled wonderful for months afterwards.

I'm sure that these relatively small losses of ship's cargo were accounted for by the cargo insurance underwriters at Lloyds of London and simply written off as pilferage or breakages.

However, for audacious criminality, look no further than the passenger liner RMS Capetown Castle (27,002 grt) owned by the Union Castle Line. In January 1965 the ship was on a regular scheduled run between Southampton and South Africa. Apart from a substantial number of passengers, she carried general cargo and mail on the outward voyage and refrigerated fruit and mail on the homeward leg. However, she also carried another important cargo – gold bullion bars from the gold mines of the Transvaal, which were destined for the vaults of the Bank of England.

The gold was normally stored in a secure stowage space in a forward hold, but on that particular trip the gold cargo was greater than normal, and a special compartment had been constructed to hold the excess; located next to the normal vaults in the same forward hold.

During the passage from Cape Town, a couple of the crew had discovered that ventilation shafts into this temporary area had not been blocked off. Via the shafts they entered the cages and stole ten boxes of the gold bullion, which were stowed two ingots to each box. Gold was priced at $35US an ounce, and were valued at about £100,000. They would have been worth many times that amount today. The loss was discovered on arrival in Southampton, when the gold began to get unloaded. Police swarmed onboard and everyone was searched, but to no avail.

The ship was searched numerous times before once again sailing for South Africa. Scotland Yard figured it was an inside job and that whoever nicked it had left the bullion hidden onboard. However, they had no clues or suspects. Over the following months a rigorous watch was kept by undercover police officers, who sailed aboard the ship as bona fide crew-members. They were rewarded when the thieves made their move and tried to flog a few bars in Durban. The remainder of the gold was discovered concreted into the base of a sand filled container on deck and was ultimately recovered and returned to the bank. Two seamen were eventually sentenced to ten years in jail.

Toronto was not only a beautiful city, but slightly trailed behind Montreal as the second largest city in Canada. In the mid-1970s it would overtake Montreal to take the title as Canada's largest city. Dear to my heart, it hadn't allowed its ancient buildings to be pulled down or desecrated, and it still had many old Victorian and Edwardian heritage buildings in a distinctive bay-and-gable design in the district called Old Toronto. There were - and I'm happy to report, still are - many other residential enclaves spread across the city which express an individual character from that of the modern skyscrapers of the city centre.

A ship repair yard had been contracted to carry out the necessary repairs to the Beaverfir's steelwork and they soon had a workboat alongside the bow, where workmen were cutting out the damaged steel plates with oxy-acetylene torches. They welded on new patches that would be a more permanent repair in place of the temporary job we had done back at Snell Lock.

Dave Perry and I went ashore and had a few beers at a pavement cafe on Yonge Street, the city's main thoroughfare. Two girls were sitting at an adjacent table and we got talking to them. I was soon paired up with a delicious creature called Olivia, and they offered to show us the sights of Toronto. As we walked around the city she pointed out the tourist landmarks, and soon we were arm-in-arm, and Dave and his girl likewise had their arms wrapped around each other. As we walked along Bay Street by the University of Toronto, I stopped in mid-walk and kissed her hard on the lips, which left her rather breathless. She was slim with jet black hair and dark liquid eyes which crinkled at the corners whenever she laughed, which was fairly often. We asked if they would like to come back to the ship with us, and very soon we were showing them around the Beaverfir. We had dinner onboard and a few beers in the crew's bar. Dave disappeared with his girl to his cabin and so I took Olivia along to my cabin to show her what my bunk felt like to cuddle up into.

I had a marvellous time in Toronto. The next day was a Sunday, so I was free and not required on duty. Olivia picked me up in her sports car and we went horse riding. She rode as if she'd been born in a saddle, whereas I had never ridden a horse in my life, and although I managed to stay onboard the horse, perhaps we'd better move on to another subject entirely. That night she was back onboard and snuggling into my bunk again. After an idyllic eight days, the ship retraced her route back along the St Lawrence Seaway to Montreal, where we spent just two days topping off our cargo before heading back home across the Atlantic Ocean.

Back in 1961, at a meeting of the US congress, President John F Kennedy had read out a mission statement in which he said, "I believe that this nation should commit itself to achieving the goal before the decade is out, of landing a man on the moon and returning him safely to Earth." This was the beginning of the space race, as Russia and the United States of America vied for supremacy in outer space.

On the previous Wednesday 16th July, a US Saturn rocket, with three astronauts onboard, had blasted off the launch-pad at Cape Canaveral in Florida. This was Apollo 11, and they were bound for the moon.

On Sunday 20th July, as the Beaverfir was on the last leg of her transatlantic voyage, we were steaming eastwards along the English Channel towards London. We had no TV set onboard, but everyone was glued to the broadcast coming over the radio. We listened as the live downlinks coming from the astronauts were re-broadcast by Mission Control at Houston, Texas. Onboard the lunar lander Eagle was the commander, Neil Armstrong, and lunar module pilot Buzz Aldrin. Remaining aboard the command module was pilot Michael Collins. At about 20:15 UTC, as we steamed past the Isle of Wight, we heard the faraway tinny voice of Armstrong coming from 240,000 miles away as he spoke to Gene Kranz, the colourful NASA flight director based at Houston. Kranz, who became something of a celebrity because of his trademark flat-top crew cut, and the vivid waistcoats he always wore as he sat at his console, had been talking to Armstrong. "Landing on the Sea of Tranquillity – is go!" We aboard the ship, and millions of people worldwide, waited expectantly as the lunar lander detached from the command module and began its descent to the moon's surface. This was a very dangerous part of the mission because, if the descent rate wasn't exact, then the craft would crash and disintegrate. Some minutes later we heard Aldrin call up Kranz with the words, "Houston, the Eagle has landed." They had done it!

More minutes went by. Those people ashore, who could view the live broadcast on TV, saw the indistinct and grainy pictures as Armstrong, dressed in his cumbersome space-suit and helmet, descended the ladder and placed his foot on the surface of the moon and ambled slowly about the

317

rocky surface. We all heard those iconic words when Neil Armstrong said, "That's one small step for man – one giant leap for mankind."

The astronauts remained on the moon for just 21 hours, during which time they collected moon-rock samples to bring back to Earth. At last they returned to the command module for the long trip back to planet Earth. Days later, millions more watched as the space vehicle re-entered the Earth's atmosphere, the craft's skin burning white hot with the friction, and everyone breathed a sigh of relief as the multiple parachutes opened and the spacecraft safely splashed down into the Pacific Ocean. It had been wonderful to listen as such groundbreaking history was being made.

We berthed in London the day after the historic event and tied up in the Royal Victoria Dock.

Petra - 2nd voyage

It seemed rather strange that, after the normal period of three months which it usually took to unload and reload my previous ships on the Australasia run, it came as something of a shock to find that our small ship could do the same thing in just nine days. However, the rolls of heavy newsprint paper were quickly discharged and the loading of UK manufactured industrial machinery continued apace.

On 30th July, following a short leave of just eight days, the Beaverfir set sail, bound for the French port of Le Havre to finalise loading, before again setting out across the ocean to Canada. The passage across the Atlantic was uneventful except that we had ourselves a new captain. The Beaverfir was Captain Tom Parker's first command, and he would have previously been the chief officer on other ships in the Canadian Pacific fleet. He was an extremely nice chap and not at all stand-offish and distant as many masters could be. We in fact had something in common in that we drank at the same pub whenever we were visiting Southsea in Hampshire, and so we would pass the time on bridge duties by reliving past booze-ups at the Southsea watering holes. Readers may recall that the pubs of Southsea figured very much in the stories of The Crown Prince and the Isle of Wight Ferries.

After the debacle of crashing the ship at Snell Lock, I also had a new cabinmate. His name was Hugh Wilson and he came from the planet of Zog – or at least he lived on a totally different planet to the rest of the crew. He was a chunky man in his early forties with an unsmiling taciturn face, and to make matters worse, Wilson talked to himself. He didn't just mutter under his breath, but he held a serious two-way conversation, during the course of which, his face would be full of articulation as he nodded, grimaced, or lifted his eyebrows in surprise – in fact he had a full repertoire of facial expressions. I suspect that he told many saucy jokes to that other person who inhabited some deep inner recess of his brain, because he would suddenly throw back his head and let out a loud guffaw of laughter, and hold his side as if he was in stitches. A sad man indeed, and I felt sorry for him, and for whatever demons were inside his head, but I sure as hell didn't want to share a cabin with him.

Beaverfir (Canadian Pacific) 4467 gross tons

After eight days ploughing across the Atlantic, we slowed down off the lighthouse at Father Point (Pointe-aux-Pere) at Rimouski, and embarked two French-Canadian pilots for the long passage up the St Lawrence River past Quebec City to Montreal.

As we sailed westwards along the St Lawrence, I was looking forward to returning to Toronto and resurrecting my relationship with the lovely Olivia. We had exchanged a single airmail letter, and in the one she sent, she said how much she missed me, and how she was so looking forward to visiting my cabin again – nudge nudge, wink wink!

⚓

On Sunday 10th August, we berthed in Montreal; where we were due to spend five days unloading our cargo. I phoned Olivia in Toronto to tell her the ship's itinerary and time of arrival. Her voice had seemed far away and distant when we briefly spoke; which I put down to a bad line. However, there were other reasons brewing in the pot.

That evening, Dave Perry and I had a few drinks in a dockside bar where we got into conversation with the barman. He told us that his previous occupation had been as a boxer where he fought under the name of Kid – something or other. He had been quite successful in his pugilistic career, and had won a majority of his fights – many of which he won as the result of knock-outs. I seem to remember that he fought in the welterweight division. There were certainly enough muscles bulging from beneath his t-shirt.

On the eve of a big fight, he told us, two swarthy muscular men had paid him a visit. They suggested that it may be a good idea if he lost the upcoming fight, as there would be some serious money being wagered on his opponent to win. Our barman must have been a very brave fellow, had a few marbles missing or been downright stupid, because once in the boxing ring, he took his opponent apart and floored him after just two rounds.

The next day the swarthy gentlemen paid him a second visit, and it wasn't a social call. They were most displeased that they and their associates had lost a whole bundle of money. Kid Whatshisname pulled up his t-shirt to show us the entry and exit wounds where they had shot him in the stomach for his stupidity. He informed us that in Montreal there was a quite large and powerful family of Mafia who controlled every facet of organised crime in the city. The moral of this sorry tale must surely be: Don't fuck with the Mafia!

⚓

Later that evening, Dave Perry and I made our way to the La Ronde amusement park on Ile Ste Helene which straddles the St Lawrence River. In 1967 the island was the location of the Expo 67 World's Fair, and many remnants of the exhibition, the Habitat housing complex, and the US Biospheres, were still in place.

We went for a ride on the giant Ferris wheel and then moved on to the dodgem cars; and it was whilst we were whizzing around the circuit that we spotted two girls. The attractive Mademoiselles were driving their dodgem sedately around the track, and I decided to liven things up a bit, so I rammed them up the back end and sent them into a spin. They looked somewhat alarmed, but Dave and I simply laughed and rammed them again. They realised it was just a game and began to enjoy themselves.. When the ride had ended, we strode over and said hello. The shorter of the two was a slightly chubby girl with large breasts and shoulder length blonde hair.

However, it was the second girl that grabbed my attention, and I couldn't take my eyes off her. She was about 5ft 7in, with a slim figure and dark brown hair that trailed halfway down her neck. But it was her hazel eyes and her cheeky grin that drew my interest. The combination of the two, together with her slightly upturned nose sent out a message that, here was a girl who liked to live life to the full and have fun. She seemed somewhat like a tomboy. I was attracted immediately; and with the way that my eyes were riveted to her, I damn well let her know it. Dave and I introduced ourselves, and they did likewise. The 5 foot-nothing blonde was called Gloria, and my girl (I had already decided that she would be my girl), was called Petra. I thought it was a lovely name.

"Sorry about my lousy driving, but I just couldn't resist touching your rear end." She giggled at my *double entendre*.

"Where are you guys from?" asked Petra curiously.

"Dave and I are sailors," I informed her. "We've come from London aboard a cargo ship. Have you ever been onboard a ship before?" They shook their heads. "Would you like to come aboard our ship?" I asked. "We've got a crew's bar onboard, so we could have a few drinks. Would that be okay?" Gloria was nodding her head, and I could see that she was keen on Dave by her body-language and the way in which she leaned against him. I raised a questioning eyebrow at Petra. She smiled back. "Yeah, okay then. That sounds like fun." We walked along the pathway towards the cab rank and I naturally fell in alongside Petra. Glancing behind me, I noticed that Dave was already holding Gloria's hand, and so I also took Petra's hand in mine. She didn't resist. As we chatted, I found that she was almost 21 years old, and would in fact have her birthday during the coming week, but more importantly, she was unattached and didn't presently have a boyfriend. She was easy to talk to and I felt relaxed in her company. By the time we reached the cab rank, my arm was around her waist and I was giving her a kiss.

We took the girls aboard to the crew's bar and sat around chatting and drinking beer. Petra worked at the Royal Edward Chest Hospital as a medical records clerk and lived in an area called Montreal Nord, where she shared an apartment with her brother Tony.

She had been born in Czechoslovakia in 1948, and immigrated to Canada, where she arrived on her first birthday aboard a Cunard liner. Her parents had brought their children up to speak Czech, and for a time it was her first language. She spoke in a soft sensual, and very sexy Canadian accent and she of course also spoke French-Canadian. For a young girl of barely 21 years old, I found her both interesting and knowledgeable on a wide range of subjects, especially when she told me of her father who had been incarcerated at the infamous German concentration camps of Auschwitz, and later at Bergen-Belsen as a political prisoner. After being liberated in 1945, his emaciated body was barely recognisable as a human being. Her father was admitted to hospital, and a year later he had married the nurse who had cared for him and brought him back to health. I thought the story sounded ever so romantic.

After an hour Dave, who had been whispering in Gloria's ear, announced that he was taking her to his cabin. When I took Petra's hand and led her towards my own cabin, she didn't protest, but came into my arms the moment I closed the door behind us. I kissed her again and she allowed my hands to explore the lovely curves of her hips and roam across the smooth orbs of her bottom. I slipped her short jacket off and laid it on the chair and it was quickly followed by her blue jeans and cotton blouse. I put a tape on the Aiki player and we lay in my bunk with the curtains pulled closed so as we could have total privacy. I had already warned her about my Scottish cabin-mate's strange behaviour, but fortunately he was elsewhere and we were not disturbed. We lay in that narrow bunk for the whole night wrapped in each other's arms. My nostrils would flare with the sensual smell of her perfume, and the aroma was wonderful. The next morning was a Monday; I took her ashore early so that she could get home to change before going off to work.

Later that evening she was back onboard, and after having a few drinks in the crew's bar, our lovemaking started all over again. Without a doubt she could certainly be described as adventurous. Fortunately, on this occasion, Wilson never made an appearance and he made himself scarce.

On the Thursday evening the Beaverfir slipped astern from the King Edward Pier and made her way the few miles upstream to enter the St Lawrence Seaway and head for Toronto.

We berthed at Toronto in the early evening and Olivia stood on the quayside looking beautiful as the vessel docked. I ran down the gangway and took her into my arms, but there was no warmth, and she didn't offer up her lips; and right then I knew something was amiss.

"Graham, I'm sorry to have to tell you that I cannot see you anymore," she said. "I've met up again with a guy who I've known for years, and he wants to see me regularly. Let's face it, I would only ever see you every two months or so, and a long-distance relationship isn't going to work, is it?"

She was absolutely correct of course, and I nodded in agreement. It briefly crossed my mind that, with the Seaway being iced-up, and closed to navigation in the winter months, we would have seen each other much less frequently than every two months. I wished her well, gave her a peck on the cheek, and let her go get on with her life. I was secretly relieved that Olivia had found someone else, because I had thought of nothing but Petra ever since leaving Montreal. It crossed my mind that it was just as well that Olivia was out of the picture, because that would have caused serious problems, and I would have to have done something very drastic about that relationship.

⚓

Meanwhile, 270 miles to the south-east, on a dairy farm near the town of Bethel in New York State, there took place an event that would be discussed among music aficionados' for many years to come.

The Woodstock Music Festival was attended by over half a million people who were crammed into a 600 acre field, and it became known as one of the great moments that changed the history of rock n' roll music. Over the four days of the festival, some of the worlds' greatest musicians performed on stage. Among the better known names who took part were; Ravi Shankar, Joan Baez, Carlos Santana, Canned Heat, The Grateful Dead, Credence Clearwater, Sly & the Family Stone, Country Joe & the Fish, Janis Joplin, The Who, Joe Cocker, Blood Sweat & Tears, Ten Years After, Crosby, Stills, Nash, & Young and Jimi Hendrix. Many of these bands were my musical hero's, and I would love to have been taking part in that long weekend of peace and love.

Beaverfir arrived back in Montreal on the Wednesday evening and Dave Perry, Gloria and I met up at Petra's 2nd floor apartment. I swept her into my arms and gave her a long passionate kiss. We planned to stay at the apartment tonight drinking vodka and beers and playing a game of cards.

We were on our second game of gin rummy when there was loud banging on the door, and urgent French voices outside demanded that we open up. "Oh shit, it's the guys who live downstairs," Petra said irritably. "They're Quebec separatists, and they keep harassing me because I speak English. They belong to an extremist political group that wants to separate French speaking Quebec from the rest of Canada. If they get into the apartment, then they'll wreck it." There were more loud thumps on the door and angry French threats. We could hear them kicking the door. Without the slightest trace of fear, Petra instructed us to fill some empty wine bottles with water. "At least, if they break the door down, we'll have something heavy to hit them with," she said with confidence. She went to her

323

wardrobe, and from within extracted a rifle. With the utmost assurance she examined the safety and checked to see that it was loaded. "What the hell are you gonna do with that, Petra?" I asked nervously.

"Don't worry. This is a Remington hunting rifle. Those boys are gonna shit themselves as soon as I point this at 'em."

She calmly drew back the bolt on the door and opened up. The three French-Canadians, all in their early twenties, began to barge into the room, but stopped dead when she brought the rifle barrel up to point at the ringleader's chest. Their eyes opened wide in fear and they raised their hands in surrender as they quickly backed out, with what I could only guess were apologies. "Au revoir," she called, as they headed for the stairs and she re-bolted the door. Petra, looking as cool as a cucumber, took her seat at the table and picked up her hand of cards. "Now, where were we?" Some woman!

The Beaverfir stayed in Montreal for the next eight days and Petra slept onboard every night. We had decided against her apartment in Montreal Nord just in case the separatists started their tricks again. It was company rules that crewmembers should obtain a visitors' pass for each night that their guest was onboard. This was usually obtained from the officer-of-the-watch and was a chit with the guests name and the date written in. However, I had a chat with our Scottish 3rd Mate, Jimmy Donn, and explained that Petra would be a regular visitor, so he gave me an undated chitty that would officially authorize her to come aboard at any time. Those eight days were idyllic. Each night she would come and spend the night aboard the ship, and apart from eating in the crews' messroom, and drinking in the bar, we would be installed in my bunk with the curtains firmly closed. Life was wonderful. All too soon the ship was fully loaded, and it was time for us to head back across the Atlantic bound for London.

The voyage back home was uneventful, and nine days later we tied-up in the Royal Victoria Dock, London. Because the Beaverfir was on a regular run, there were very few crew changes, and so, unlike the other deep-sea ships that I had previously served upon, we didn't have to say goodbye to our shipmates. After a short spot of leave we would again be sailing together for Canada.

I was lucky, because within a half hour I would be back home with my family in Silvertown; whereas some of our crew, including my cabinmate Wilson, came from Scotland or even the Outer Hebrides. There was no way it was worth the train fare for them to travel all that way north, just for a few days at home. Therefore, many of them simply booked a room at the Mission to Seamen and rejoined on sailing day.

The Mission to Seamen was otherwise known as The Flying Angel due to its winged angelic logo (some wags even called it The Flying Tab-nab!) On a typical day, there were so many Hebrideans staying there, that it was known as Stornoway Castle! The rooms in the 10-storey high mission have been described by some as resembling functional prison cells. Some rooms contained just an iron bed, a table and chair, and had bars across the windows. Their single redeeming feature was that the rooms were cheap and were conveniently located on the Victoria Dock Road, Custom House, surrounded my many fine pubs and taverns.

Life back at Silvertown hadn't changed one iota, except that it was nice to be able to lie in bed for a while, instead of turning-to on deck or keeping a bridge lookout as the ship ploughed through the long Atlantic swells. Most days there would be just mum and I at home. Linda was still hanging on in her marriage and had 6-year old Toni and one year old baby David with her. Glynis was at work all day, and Soupy was gainfully employed keeping the Tate Institute spic n' span. I told my family the many stories about my voyage, especially the tale of the barman shot by the Mafia. When I told mum about Petra, she sensed that she was someone special, and not just another transient girlfriend. "Watch out you don't get hurt again, son," she said, as she remembered how my poor heart had been broken when I'd had to leave Valentina all those years ago.

The Great Storm - 3rd Voyage.

After a short leave of just nine days, we set out on my third voyage aboard the Beaverfir. Once again our ship's master was Captain Tom Parker, and on this trip he was accompanied by his wife Irene. After loading further cargo on a two day stopover at Le Havre, we set off for Montreal. After an unexciting voyage across the ocean, we arrived there in early morning on the last day of September.

Petra came aboard straight from her work at the hospital, and it was lovely to see her. I held her at arm's length and was happy to just gaze at her beauty; she looked so pretty. Our moments together mirrored my previous visit, and we stayed aboard most nights drinking in the crew's bar and snuggled-up in my bunk every night.

On our second night in port, we were snuggled romantically together in my bottom bunk, when the door silently opened and Wilson entered the cabin. We of course had the bunk curtains tightly drawn, but nevertheless it was a surprise, because hitherto he had always kept out of our way. Petra looked at me in consternation and whispered urgently, "Is that your cabinmate? Will he be here very long?" I could only shrug my

325

shoulders, as I had no idea if he would be on his way quickly or hang about. I don't think he could have been in any doubt that we were in bed together, because mine and Petra's clothing, including panties and bra, were laying where we had placed them on the chair. I opened the curtains slightly and peeped out. I had left the desk light switched on and the low wattage lamp illuminated the cabin in a soft glow. Wilson picked up the clothes and carefully placed them on the end of his top bunk, then sat down in the chair and faced the wall mirror that was fixed above the desk. Petra whispered in my ear. "What's he doing?" I whispered back. "He's making himself comfortable, I'm afraid."

Wilson stretched out his legs and relaxed as he stared into the mirror. Suddenly his lips began to move and his demeanour became intense as he silently chatted to himself. The man was in his own quirky world. The two personas inside his head exchanged sentences, and his head would nod or shake, depending on whether one of the voices agreed with the other. Sometimes he would hold his belly and silently laugh as if it was a loud guffaw. This went on for some minutes. We simply wanted him to leave, even though it was equally his cabin as well as mine, and he had every right to be there. Eventually I decided to let him know that we were "in residence", and so I coughed loudly, and he got up and departed as suddenly as he had arrived. We never saw anything more of him after that and he kept discreetly out of our way.

After five days unloading, it was time to depart for Toronto; and although we would of course miss being apart, the Beaverfir would return in six days time. It crossed my mind that, apart from Imelda and Paula, she was the only girl with whom I had been with on a regular basis. On all my trips to Australia and New Zealand I had seen nothing of ex girlfriends on subsequent visits to the port. It was as if they had vanished into thin air.

The ship had transited the length of the St Lawrence Seaway and steamed across the expanse of Lake Ontario. In the early hours of the morning, I was putting the crew on the shake for harbour stations as the Beaverfir approached Toronto. I went to call our bosun, John Glancy, but as I switched on his cabin light, I could see that John lay in his bunk with his eyes open wide and staring into space. His mouth was opening and closing time and time again like a goldfish. He was totally mute, and I could get no sense out of him. I didn't like the look of him and I was worried that we may have a serious medical emergency on our hands. Even though I called his name and shook his pillow, his mouth continued to gulp like a goldfish. I called the chief officer and he also looked worried at John's condition. He suggested to Captain Parker that we call for an ambulance to be waiting on the quay for our arrival. Captain Parker asked me if I would accompany John in the ambulance to hospital.

Upon arrival, an ambulance was parked on the quayside with blue lights flashing, and John was put on a stretcher and taken down the gangway with all the crew watching with interest. However, this must have been a private outfit, because before he was allowed into the ambulance the medics wanted a $16 fee. I fished my wallet out and paid the man.

In the hospital emergency room the doctor looked John over and started slapping him quite hard around the face, shouting, "Hey buddy, get up. C'mon, get up and go home." As he slapped John again I said, "Hey doctor, what the hell are you doing? Why are you slapping him?" The doctor said, "There's nothing wrong with him, except that he's as drunk as a skunk. You can take him home now." That was such a surprise. I had no idea that he was simply pissed. With that, John groggily sat up, and a few minutes later we walked out of the hospital and got a cab back to the Beaverfir. Happy days.

That weekend our 2nd Steward Bob Burnham hired a large gas-guzzling car and several of us went for a day's visit to Niagara Falls. The 80 mile journey, via the Queen Elizabeth Highway, was full to the brim with lovely scenery, and we soon ate up the miles and parked in the city centre nearby the waterfalls. Long before we could see the falls, one could hear the roar of the water and see the drizzly mist rising high in the air as we walked to the promenade that leads to the best viewing areas.

My first sight of the waterfalls was awesome. One could stand right beside the Niagara River and watch as almost half a million tons of water every minute tumbled over the precipice into a giant maelstrom far below. The noise as the water cascaded 173 feet onto the rocks was tremendous and it underlined what untold power lay in the fast moving current.

We decided to visit the tunnels going under the falls, so at the visitor information centre I grabbed a free brochure and read up on the history and statistics while we waited in line. Niagara Falls (I read) forms part of the international border between the Canadian province of Ontario and the US state of New York. The twin cities of Niagara Falls straddle across the falls via the Rainbow Bridge, so that there are namesake cities in each country. The falls originate in the Niagara River, which drains Lake Ontario and Lake Erie, and are made up of two distinct waterfalls, the Horseshoe Falls on the Canadian side, and the American Falls on the US side. The city is also a magnet for newlywed couples, and is a customary romantic setting in which to spend one's honeymoon vacation. Looking around me I saw dozens of young couple's arm-in-arm.

At last our group's turn came to go down to the rock face; and after paying our entry fee, we were issued with bright yellow rainwear and gumboots. As we shuffled down the granite steps, we could see that the rock had been hewn out to form a tunnel. Burrowing right beneath the falls, the tunnel turned at a right angle so as to exit with the solid phalanx of water directly in front of us. It was quite unnerving and the noise of all that rushing water made me want to go for a pee.

The falls are also a valuable source of hydroelectric power. In 1961, when the Niagara Falls hydroelectric project first went on-line, it was the largest hydropower facility in the Western world. The Niagara River's flow is diverted via four huge tunnels that arise far upstream from the waterfalls. The water then passes through hydroelectric turbines that supply power to nearby areas of Canada and the United States before returning to the river well past the falls. This water spins turbines that power generators, converting mechanical energy into electrical energy.

I thoroughly enjoyed our visit as it's not too often in one's life when one has an opportunity to witness such a wondrous sight of nature's raw power.

The Beaverfir stayed for only four days in Toronto. After loading a cargo of reels of newsprint, we made our way back through the Seaway to Montreal where we arrived on the afternoon of 10th October

Petra came aboard as soon as we berthed, and we repaired to the crew's bar for a few drinks and to catch up on each other's news. Her life without the periods spent onboard the ship followed regular and ordered patterns and her job at the hospital was uneventful. After the incident with her French neighbours and the Remington rifle, she'd had no more problems with them and they were behaving themselves.

I told her of my developing thoughts of perhaps getting a shoreside job in England, because I reckoned that, with the advent of container ships emerging onto the scene, good jobs were becoming increasingly hard to find. The new far larger container vessels employed just a third of the crew of a conventional cargo vessel and replaced eight 10.000 tonners.
"Where does that leave us, babe? Won't I ever see you again?" she asked.
"Of course you will. Would you like to come over to England once I get settled? Would you want to do that?"
Her face lit up. "Oh yes. Of course I would. That would be wonderful."
"Okay, that sounds like a plan," I said. "But let's see how things pan out, shall we?" There were plenty of details to discuss, such as initially finding an apartment, and she finding some employment. These were exciting times, as each night we would chat about our plans and discuss mundane

domestic things that hitherto, apart from my brief spell with Imelda, I had never given much thought to. Because I hadn't been boozing-up in the clubs and the bars, my savings had accumulated to such a point that on my last leave I had opened a bank account, and a greater part of my wages had been put on high-interest deposit. Over the course of the previous trips I had managed to save quite a sizeable amount; so-much-so that I thought that I may be able to afford a deposit on a house of my own. All these things we talked about as we snuggled up in my bunk night after night and made wonderful passionate love.

⚓

Eventually the time came for the Beaverfir to leave Montreal. We slipped from our berth and headed east along the St Lawrence River bound for Quebec City, where we arrived the next day. The city is the capital of the province of Quebec, and although I had never been here before, I had heard that it was a beautiful place to visit. I was therefore very happy when the chief officer gave the deck crew a job and knock to sugi the boat-deck paintwork. After a quick lunch I strode out to explore the city.

I began my tour by obtaining my usual information pamphlet from the tourist office in Rue Saint Paul, and found that the city's name comes from the Algonquin Indian name which means, "Where the river narrows." Quebec is one of the oldest cities in North America, and so I began to explore by walking around the ramparts of Old Quebec – Vieux Quebec – which my pamphlet informed me were the only remaining fortified city walls that still exist within the Americas. The walls certainly looked thick and solid enough to resist any army intent on defeating the French citizens.

Way back in 1759, the English army of General James Wolfe had attacked the French army under the command of General Marquis de Montcalm. Adjoining the city walls are an open area of parkland called the Plains of Abraham where the armies of Montcalm and Wolfe set about each other. It couldn't rightfully be called a real battle because, although Wolfe had laid siege to Quebec for three months, the actual man-to-man fighting was all over within 30 minutes when Wolfe's soldiers defeated the Frenchies with a single deadly volley of musket fire. It wasn't a good day for either Wolfe or Montcalm because they both caught a bullet from a musket and died of their wounds.

Walking further along the perimeter of the ramparts, I came upon an enormous granite arch called Le Citadelle which is a part of the military installations of Quebec. The star shaped fortifications were built by the British in 1820, and also serve as the official residence of the Governor-General of Canada. Sadly I couldn't go inside to have a look around as it was closed to visitors, but his residence looked suitably imposing from the outside and well worth a look, if only he had been inclined to let me mosey about for a bit. As you can imagine, with all these wonderful old buildings to look at, and a city so steeped in history, I was having a wonderful day. In addition, the weather was calm and the sun even managed to break through the clouds – perfect.

Quebec had originally been founded by Samuel de Champlain in 1608 on the site of an abandoned Iroquois settlement, and he named this region New France. I spent the first hour or so idly window-shopping as I ambled around the pretty streets, although I understood little, because everything was in French, and my command of the language was limited to the French phrase for beer – which funnily enough is bier.

I made my way to the city's main railway and bus station, the Gare du Palais which, with its solid looking two-story structure with curving brickwork, looks somewhat like a French chateau. The frontage has two round towers and the roof is sheathed in copper. Between the two towers are seven tall windows which are surmounted by an ornate clock set into a basalt edifice atop which was the cities coat of arms. I ducked under the covered portico and went inside the busy concourse and found it a delight. The high ceilings had an elaborate design and a complicated frieze ran around the lavish interior. A sign at the entrance told me that the building had been built by the Canadian Pacific Railway Company in 1915. I wiled away 20 minutes by having coffee at the station bar and indulged in one of my favourite pastimes – people-watching.

Sitting twenty feet away from me on comfortable bench seats, were rows of travellers awaiting their trains. One of them, a bald chap in his early thirties, was absorbed in reading the latest news from a large broadsheet newspaper. Without warning, a young fellow sitting opposite him, got up from his seat and knelt down in front of the newspaper reader and seemingly began reading the front page of the chap's newspaper. It seemed such a cheeky and outlandish thing to do, and I watched to see if the reader became aware of what was happening right in front of him, but he was glued to his paper and didn't look up at all. At the time my thoughts were along the lines of, "You cheeky sod. Why don't you go buy your own bloody newspaper?" Other people sitting nearby stared aghast at such a peculiar thing to do, but not one of them said a word and seemingly didn't want to get involved if there was about to be a contretemps. I looked on in baffled amusement.

Suddenly the wild-haired younger fellow, who wore a kaftan and looked much like a hippie, drew a pair of scissors from his pocket and proceeded to carefully cut an item of news from the front page that seemed to interest him, but still the older man was unaware of what was going on around him. The young man got bolder and cut even more pieces from the newspaper, until I thought the reader must surely rumble the fact that his paper was being destroyed before his very eyes; but he continued reading intently. By now the surrounding crowd were unable to take their eyes off the scene; but still no one said a word. It was all very strange behaviour. Things really stepped up a notch when the young guy brought out a box of matches and attempted to set fire to the newspaper. As he struck a match, it fizzled out, and the crowd looked on with horror at such bizarre antics. Still no one moved. Then he struck another match and held it under the bottom of the paper. The newspaper began the burn, with smoke billowing up into Baldy's nostrils, but still he was absorbed in reading. Within seconds the whole newspaper was alight and the older man, suddenly aware of what was occurring, threw the paper to the ground and began stamping on it to put out the flames. The hippie stood with a guilty look upon his face. The older chap was furious and he grabbed the hippie by his hair, and I thought for a minute that he would head-butt the man. But he didn't. He leant over and kissed him on the cheek. I thought, "What the hell's going on?", but without further ado both men bowed to the crowd, and walked away together arm-in-arm.

What I had just witnessed, I later found, was a piece of travelling theatre put on for the benefit of the unsuspecting hordes of bored and weary rail commuters awaiting their trains. However, it was also a sad reflection that in this day and age, no one would speak up when such bizarre conduct was happening before their very eyes. But it was magnificent stuff and it made my day.

My next and last stop was the Chateau Frontenac, a very large grand hotel that sits atop a bluff that overlooks the St Lawrence River, and that had caught my eye on previous occasions when the Beaverfir had sailed past on her way to Montreal. The hotel was truly enormous, and by far the grandest of grand hotels I had ever set foot inside. It had castle-like architecture where turrets proliferated across the whole expanse of the building. Much like the Gare de Palais, the vast area of its crenulated roof was sheathed in copper.

One of the things I like about any large hotel is the fact that they keep open house, and any reasonably dressed bum - like myself - can wander around within; and for the price of a cup of overpriced coffee, can take advantage of the luxuriousness and the ambiance and to rub shoulders with the rich folk who can actually afford to stay there.

It was evening now, and as I walked past the dining room, I peeked in and saw guests having an early dinner. The tables were lavishly set with real orchids and soft lighting, and enough cutlery to sink a battleship. Most of the men were dressed in smart lounge suits or tuxedos with the ladies clad in elegant evening wear. An army of waiters were in attendance, ready to obey their guest's merest whim. Nearby, looking every bit like a Regimental Sergeant Major stood the *maitre d'hôtel,* whose existence in life was to ensure that everything ran smoothly and without fuss. As I stood there gawping at all that wealth and opulence in the room, it crossed my mind that the cheapest meal on the menu would probably set me back two months wages. I decided to give it a miss.

I made my way to the St Laurent Bar where I ordered my overpriced coffee and enjoyed the ambience and wondered if I would ever be able to afford to stay in such a grand hotel as this. Over in one corner, a pianist played George Gershwin's Rhapsody in Blue upon a highly polished grand piano. I spotted a hotel information pamphlet in a rack and started to read up on the history of the place.

The hotel had been built by the Canadian Pacific Railway Company in 1893 to serve their rich travellers who would be taking the train to distant parts of Canada. It listed some of the Hollywood stars and other celebrities who had in the past been guests, and it read somewhat like a Who's Who of public figures. In 1943 the hotel had hosted the Quebec Conference at which Winston Churchill, Franklin D Roosevelt and the Canadian Prime Minister, William Mackenzie King, had met to discuss and plan their strategy for World War 2; and especially for D-Day. As I sipped my coffee, it crossed my mind that I may actually be sitting in that very same chair that Winston's bum had sat in. With that stupid thought running around inside my head, I finished my coffee and headed back onboard the good ship Beaverfir.

⚓

The ship was four days into our transatlantic voyage back to England when the storm hit us. It had begun its existence as just a small blip of a weather depression a thousand miles back towards the west. It had quickly intensified as it fed off the rising warm air currents of eastern Canada and quickly developed into a deep depression. Rapidly it had transformed from a benign regular weather pattern into a malevolent monster. The winds ahead of its path, which until that time had been a light to moderate breeze, increased in strength and travelled madly into an anti-clockwise vortex that covered a huge area of the ocean, perhaps two hundred miles wide. The isobars of the barometric pressure packed tightly together as the storm went active and careered easterly across the Atlantic Ocean. The storm was travelling at a forward speed of 25 knots, and with the up-to-date weather forecasts available via radio, we aboard the Beaverfir had known that it was headed towards us.

Up on the bridge, the 3rd mate had been checking the barometer readings every half hour, and he didn't like what he saw. The barometer was dropping like a brick, and that could mean just one thing. Rotten weather was coming our way and it would catch us up within about four hours. There was nothing at all that could be done about it, and we would simply have to ride out the storm. Already the sky was darkening with threatening grey clouds on the western horizon and the waves had begun to increase in height. Captain Parker had already ordered the duty watch to rig rope life-lines along the decks so that, if there was an absolute need for men to go outside when the storm arrived, they would at least have something secure to cling onto.

Captain Parker had felt the rising seas beneath his feet and came up onto the bridge where Jimmy Donn was plotting an estimated position onto the navigation chart. The captain glanced over his shoulder and nodded in agreement at the fix. The Beaverfir was in position latitude 52N and longitude 37W, which is roughly halfway across the Atlantic between Newfoundland and the United Kingdom. She was presently maintaining an easterly course at full cruising speed of 15 knots. He glanced at the barometer readings which had been entered into the daily log and he was frankly astonished. The pressure had dropped by some ten millibars within the past three hours, and as he tapped the glass on the barometer, it dropped another millibar. That was an enormous and rapid decrease in barometric pressure, and indicated that very severe weather was imminent. The needle on the wind speed indicator had in the past half hour, crept up from 30 knots to 45 knots, so the present weather conditions were already categorised as a severe gale. The wind outside was howling as it shrieked through the ship's rigging and she was rolling from side to side. However, this wasn't just an unexceptional gale, a commonplace enough event in the world of shipping. He was quite certain that the approaching storm would be far worse in intensity and a portent of what was to come. As the storm hurtled towards the British Isles, then it would no doubt diminish in strength and peter out, but right now it was dangerous and packing one hell of a punch.

Tom Parker made himself comfortable in a padded chair in a corner of the wheelhouse and waited for the storm to strike. It was simply a matter of time before it caught the ship up. At 34 years of age he had been at sea for some 18 years. He had begun his sea-going career as a lowly deck cadet, and very slowly had moved up the promotion ladder until this, the Beaverfir, was his first command. Although he had held his Master Mariner's certificate for some years, he'd had to await a command vacancy, and now the coveted position was his. He was proud that he had been appointed at such a young age; one of the youngest ship's masters within the Canadian Pacific fleet.

His mind went over the mental check list of orders he had given prior to the storm's arrival. He had now been the Beaverfir's captain for a little under three months, and although during his many years at sea he had experienced countless storms, this was his first whilst in command. The safety of the ship and its crew were a paramount priority, and apart from rigging the life-lines, he'd sent the bosun and a team of men from stem to stern to double check that anything that could come adrift was securely stowed. Likewise the Chief Engineer, Ossie Woodhouse, had seen to it that his machinery spaces were secure. The whole crew had been forewarned, and the chief cook especially had been advised that sea conditions may deteriorate to a state whereby no meals could be cooked. Of equal importance was the ship's cargo, and he'd ordered that the chief officer tour the cargo holds to ensure that it was all stowed securely and that nothing could come adrift. If anything heavy did become loose below decks, then it could cause either structural damage, or perhaps affect the ship's stability, which in turn affected the safety of the ship. The two problems went hand-in-hand.

Satisfied that he had thought of all precautions, there was just one last thing to consider. As the storm was chasing the ship, then the winds and the waves would come from a westerly direction. This meant that the waves would be under her stern, and if they were to be very large and heavy seas, then they would tend to carry the ship before them in an uncontrollable roller-coaster ride which could make steering very difficult and have dire consequences. Therefore the vessel would at some stage need to be turned around so that she was facing the brutal weather, and although she would pound straight into the storm's waves, he would at least have a modicum of control and she would be easier to handle. However, if that happened, then the ship would make no forward speed, and would remain almost stationary and become what was known as "hove-to." The trick would be when to make the turn. Captain Parker after all had a schedule to maintain. Turn too early and the ship would make no progress towards her destination in London. Turn too late, when the seas were enormous, and the manoeuvre was then fraught with danger. It was a sticky problem.

Within the hour the seas began piling up into ugly white crested waves fully 30 feet to their summit; and several waves, already the height of the foredeck, swept aboard and raced along the decks in a wild cacophony of white spume. Captain Parker gauged that the time had come to turn the ship around and head into the brunt of the waves. From the bridge telephone he called all departments to forewarn them.

The captain scanned the seas, observing the timing and sequence between the troughs. He needed to get his timing absolutely spot-on to avoid any damaging seas slamming into the ship's side and causing her to lurch far over onto her beam ends. He slowed the ship down to "dead slow ahead" – a speed of just four knots – and watched the waves for a suitable opportunity. By now it was impossible to sleep below decks, and other off-watch deck officers had come up to the bridge to witness the heavy weather. "Standby" shouted the captain as he prepared to make the turn. He saw his chance in what seemed a succession of slightly smaller waves and made his decision. "Helm, hard to starboard – engine full ahead please," he ordered with a calmness that he hoped would permeate to all those around him. The single engine powered up to its maximum revolutions, and with the rudder now hard over, her bow begun moving to the right. Halfway through the turn, she slid down into a deep trough, and the succeeding wave smashed into her side with the power of a thousand uncontrollable tons and attempted to push her over onto her side. The Beaverfir gave a lurch and continued to roll far over onto her port side until it seemed that if she went any further, then she would roll right over and be lost. When the ship had reached the furthest arc of her roll, she hung there for long seconds, seemingly wanting to topple over even further onto her beam-ends. Then she rolled violently back the opposite way, her engine racing as the propeller came clear of the water. From down below in the accommodation, those on the bridge could hear the noise as small unsecured items, an untended stack of crockery and several coffee mugs, smashed into hundreds of pieces. Gradually she righted herself and lurched in the opposite direction onto her starboard side. The noise as she did so, from the detritus rolling around below decks, and from the wind whistling through the ship's rigging, made a hellish shrieking noise that brought a tinge of fear to everyone in the wheelhouse. However, her bow was coming around rapidly now so as to face into the waves, and she needed to be slowed down again, otherwise she would cause untold damage to the forepart of the ship. "Engine slow ahead," ordered the captain, and the Beaverfir slowed her forward speed, but with just enough wash past her rudder to maintain steerage way. We had safely made the turn.

I awoke in my bunk and felt the ship's see-sawing movement and the vibrations as the propeller came out of the water. It raced at high speed, before the engine governor cut in to limit the revolutions. I looked at my wristwatch. It said 10:35. I had just another hour to lie in my bunk before getting an early lunch and starting my duty watch at midday.

By mid-afternoon it was my turn at the helm, and to take over from my watch-mate Dave. As I stepped into the wheelhouse, I looked out of the forward windows and gasped. Roaring towards us was a gigantic wave easily as massive as a 5-storey apartment block. My eyes widened in fear as this unstoppable behemoth with an ugly white-capped crest - perhaps a thousand feet in length - came racing towards us. The Beaverfir's bow dipped down into the trough, and she took off, sliding down the slope of the wave before slamming into the underside, where her stem ploughed into solid green seas. Eventually - like a terrier shaking water off its fur - she'd shake the water free of her decks, and come back upright, her steel frames creaking in protest as she rolled. I looked up and the apartment block towered above us with an all-powerful malevolence. The ship's bow, with hundreds of tons of white water smashing around her fo'castle, dragged herself skywards as she climbed up the near vertical wave. As our bow reached the top, a large crested roller smashed against the starboard plating with the force of a dozen locomotives, causing the ship to be slapped sideways as if we were but a mere nuisance that was to be swept aside and not hinder the waves progress. The apex of the wave swept underneath the hull and the bow dipped yet again to begin her nightmare ride down the underside of the trough. It felt like dropping several floors in an out-of-control express elevator. All the while I could hear the steel plating and metal girders that made up the ship's structure, creaking and groaning with the stresses being put upon them by the heavy seas. The solid expanse of those big waves looked massive compared against the diminutive 4467 gross ton Beaverfir. Down in the wave's troughs she looked so small and vulnerable and hardly able to fight against the might of the big rollers. I said, "Jeezus Dave that was a huge one. I've never seen waves so big."

"They're mostly all that size, mate. Sometimes they're even bigger," he said morosely. Dave gave me a course to steer and warned that she was difficult to keep on course. I took over, and Dave went below to wedge himself into a corner of the messroom where he wouldn't be tossed around and injured. Captain Parker had jammed himself into the seat in the starboard corner of the wheelhouse. He swivelled his head around. "Don't try to steer a course, helmsman. Just keep her bow headed into the waves, okay?"

"Aye aye, Sir," I answered. This was much easier than attempting to steer by compass, as I could gauge any variation in the direction of a wave and adjust my rudder accordingly.

Over the course of the next few hours the wind speed had risen dramatically to gusts of 50 knots. The windspeed by mid-afternoon was a steady 68 knots with gusts of 75 knots which, by reference to the Beaufort Scale, was a full blown hurricane. Furthermore, the wave height, which had until now had been very large, become monstrous. The captain remarked that they were the largest seas he had ever encountered in his sea-going career.

As the Beaverfir ploughed through wave after gigantic wave, my confidence grew in our little ship, and in her ability to fight the weather and win the battle like David and Goliath. I knew then that we would make it through the storm and reach home safely. The captain must have also felt the confidence, because he rose from his chair and chatted with the 2nd mate who had been similarly jammed into a corner elsewhere and holding on for grim death. The captain opened the sliding door that led out onto the open wing of the bridge and they both stepped outside. A blast of fresh air came into the fetid wheelhouse that had been closed up tight for hour after hour, and outside fine sea-water spray spewed onto the open decks. I watched the animated faces of the two officers as they chatted. The jerky and unpredictable movements of the ship had now been overcome, and I could see their confidence growing by the minute as the ship coped with the enormous waves that were thrown against her. They made their way around to the back of the bridge where they were now out of sight, and I was alone in the wheelhouse.

Minutes later, a series of waves had taken the ship's bow off course, and I was using maximum helm so as to try to bring her back onto the required heading. Unaccountably she wouldn't respond, and as the bow dropped even further off course, the ship was in danger of broaching sideways onto the waves. I needed more power on the engine to enable her to be brought back on course. "Captain, the ship's off course Sir," I shouted. There was no reply. Maybe they had gone to take shelter from the fierce winds. Perhaps they hadn't heard me above the howling of the wind. "Captain," I screamed as the ship went even further off the heading. Still there was no answer. I was at my wit's end because I urgently needed more power. I left the wheel and ran to the door and peered outside. No one was in sight, but I couldn't leave the helm unmanned to go searching for the skipper and officer-of-the-watch. I raced back to the wheel, and just as I did, so I looked up in horror as I saw a colossal wave bearing down on the ship. Most of the waves within the past hour could be categorised as huge, but this far outweighed anything we had seen until now. The top of the monstrous wave was a menacing overhanging crest that tumbled end-over-end in a cataclysmic nosedive. It towered above me with an impression of immense destructive capability. With white roaring crests – unstoppable and impregnable – it resembled legions of fearless Roman cavalrymen, as the wave rode headlong at the ship. Following close behind were more towering pinnacles of white-topped mountainous seas. Like hordes of unconquerable storm-troopers, intent upon our destruction, they steam-rollered towards the Beaverfir. I estimated the biggest wave must have been damn near 50 feet from peak to trough. I had never been so afraid in all my life. My mouth was so dry I couldn't speak and I had trouble breathing. It towered over our small vessel like a menacing Valkyrie.

There was nothing for it. I rang the brass engine telegraph to "full ahead" and got an instant response of clanging bells as the duty engineer down in the bowels of the machinery space piled on the power. The ship shuddered as the propeller spun faster and faster, and at last her bow begun to come back to the proper heading. Just before that colossal wave struck the ship, the captain and OOW came racing into the wheelhouse. "What's going on?" demanded Captain Parker. "Was it you who rang full ahead?" "Yes Sir. I needed more power and neither of you were here." He nodded and patted me on the shoulder. "Okay, well done. Carry-on." He reduced speed back to slow ahead. Just then the mountainous wave struck the bow with a resounding boom, and hundreds of tons of white water was dumped onto the foredeck and cascaded back over the side. The sound of the wind had increased in strength and it shrieked around the mast and rigging like a wailing banshee. Time and time again Beaverfir lifted her blunt snout and crashed down into the seas, where a solid phalanx of green water and spray would come over the bow and run aft in a raging river of white water.

Captain Parker was apprehensive. The deck forward was filling with immeasurable tons of water, causing her to lean way over onto her port side, hanging there interminably as she continued her roll almost onto her side. Eventually the water would spew out over the side, but the captain was anxious with regard to the vessel's stability. He'd never experienced anywhere near this sort of oceanic weather on his previous voyages.

When many tons of water are slopping about onboard a ship, they cause a vast reduction in the vessel's centre of gravity, called the GM. This reduction of GM can make the ship unstable, and she will theoretically, tend to tip over onto her side. This dangerous reduction in stability is further exacerbated by the free-surface effect of the water. Parker equated free-surface to the slopping motion one feels when attempting to carry a bowl full of water across a room. No matter how much one tries, the water gets out of equilibrium and sloshes all over the sides of the bowl due to its lack of stability caused by the free-surface of the overflowing water. In this case the ship was the bowl, and the water came aboard in a never-ending supply. The point at which Beaverfir would become unstable was all subject to a complicated mathematical formula to which Captain Parker hadn't been concerned with since his days at nautical college. On the bridge, they could only watch as she eventually spewed the sea-water back out over the side through her large well-deck openings. The captain breathed a sigh of relief

338

and lifted his eyes to heaven in thanks to some unknown but very welcome intervention.

The captain's wife, Irene Parker, briefly came up to the wheelhouse from the relative comfort of the Master's suite, where she had wedged herself into a corner for fear of being thrown around in this wild weather. She brought up a tray of tea and sandwiches, for which we were all very grateful. She stood beside her husband, not able to do very much constructively, but simply to let him know that she was safe and doing her bit.

Eventually I was relieved by the next helmsman and I went below for some rest. It had been hard work concentrating on the wave patterns and gauging what helm to apply so as to counter her tendency to sheer off to port. The physical exertion of constantly turning the wheel for an hour had taken it out of me. I counted myself lucky. Our captain, even though he hadn't slept in 24 hours, would stay up on the bridge for hour after hour until the hurricane abated. He was magnificent. Throughout the night the stormy weather went on and on without any let-up, and the nervous tension was showing on my crewmates' tired faces. As the bow rose and fell and crashed into the troughs of wave after wave, it seemed like a never ending onslaught, and our little ship seemed so tiny and insignificant and helpless on this vast ocean.

By the following afternoon, we had been hove-to for 26 hours, and the strain was showing amongst the crew. The galley staff hadn't been able to cook any hot meals because of the danger of using hot fat or boiling hot water, so instead chef had knocked up some sandwiches. But even so, everyone was tired and just wanted to be on our way and making some progress towards London.

Within the hour our prayers had been answered as we felt the ship's movement ease up and the propeller was no longer coming clear of the water. Shortly afterwards, the Tannoy system announced that we would shortly be turning the ship to the eastward. We were on our way home. Hooray!

That was probably the most horrendous weather conditions I'd ever experiences in my sea-going career. Over the coming years there were many more storms which, with the passing of time, one tends to relegate as a minor inconvenience and to focus on the nicer aspects of one's voyages.

I've spoken with many ex seafarers regarding sailing through storms and hurricanes and each of them had horrendous tales to tell of terrifying weather. I heard stories of ships being slammed by huge waves in the North Pacific Ocean and almost tipped over beyond the point of no return. Others suffered cargo shifting, causing the vessel to take on a dangerous list, and everyone witnessed monstrous rogue waves which threatened to overwhelm and sink the ship.

Time and time again some of these incidents occurred around infamous hot-spots which are known for treacherous weather. Chief among them was the Bay of Biscay, the North Sea, the Atlantic Grand Banks, the South China Sea, the Cook Strait and the Southern Ocean. Numerous incidents regarding stormy weather have occurred in every part of the planet.

Every so often I would ask myself why in hell I've enjoyed my nautical career, and I cannot for the life of me come up with a valid and sensible answer. Once the salt water gets into your veins, you'll be bitten by the bug, and they'll be no escape from the need to go earn your living on the sea. I've spoken with many ex seamen about why we enjoyed that lifestyle, and received a whole raft of different responses. They ranged from enjoying sunny weather in the tropics to the close friendship and camaraderie of their shipmates. Others said it was because every day was different and for some it was the sense of achievement in delivering a ship and its cargo safely to its destination. For me it was simply a way of life. Occasionally I would try working ashore in a mundane job, but the sea always drew me back. If it were possible to turn the clock back, then many of the ex seamen I've spoken to would return to the sea without a seconds thought – but only if they could man the merchant ships of the 1960s. They would have no interest whatsoever in crewing the modern container ships which spend little time in port.

Five days later the Beaverfir docked at Silvertown and we signed-off articles and went on leave. The voyage had taken just six weeks, but it had been full to the brim with adventure. I had spent two idyllic interludes with Petra in Montreal, and had a fabulous time. A little less welcome was having to share a cabin with Wilson, the comical episode of John Glancy's imitation of a goldfish, and of course that tremendous storm. The visit to Niagara Falls had been wonderful as well as informative and likewise the stopover in Quebec was sublime. In what other job, I wondered, could I have experienced all these things within the space of just six weeks?

Life back at home remained unfalteringly unchanged as the family went about their jobs and their everyday life. Once again mum and I sat sharing a bottle of stout and laughing and exchanging stories and incidents that had occurred whilst I had been away on my travels. Petra sent a letter telling me that she loved me and missed me, and quite selfishly I couldn't wait to sail across the ocean again to see her.

⚓

A big surprise during my leave was that John Sheppard, who I hadn't seen or heard from since sailing away on the Port Victor nearly three years previously, phoned to ask how I was faring. He was presently living in Portsmouth, and had recently bought a house in the city's North End district. He was employed onboard some HM Government dredgers that mainly operated within the harbour. "It's a great life, Gra, I'm not bouncing around on bloody great waves anymore, but I'm back at home every night," he informed me. I told him that I was due to sail to Canada in a week's time, and he suggested that I might like join him for a few days during the course of my leave.

I got the train down the next day and he met me at the station. He hadn't changed much, and still had the smiling eyes and the ready grin and lots of big ideas. We went for a few pints at the White Swan and exchanged news. We had lots to tell. The romance with the lovely Jenny hadn't lasted long, and he had gone back to sea on a Tate & Lyle's Sugar Line vessel to the Caribbean and various other ships around the world. The dredgers upon which he was employed, mainly dredged alongside the docks and quays where the warships berthed in Portsmouth Dockyard. However, the dredger was presently away at a shipyard refit so, even though the crews still had to clock-in for work, there was little work to be done. "Why don't you come into the dockyard with me tomorrow? You can see what the job entails, and then if you wanna give it a try, you could apply for a job. They're crying out for seamen." John told me that the majority of the crews had no proper Merchant Navy training, and most had never even sailed outside Portsmouth Harbour; so because I held a proper MN seaman's certificate, I would have no problem in being taken-on.

Truth be told, I was already thinking along the lines of seeking a shore-based job, and Petra and I had discussed these matters when I had last seen her in Montreal. The following voyage would be the Beaverfir's last trip to the Canadian Great Lakes before the winter ice made navigation impossible. In winter her voyages would call at the ice-free port of Saint John in New Brunswick and back to Europe, so I wouldn't get to see her at all until the ice melted and the St Lawrence opened up again sometime in March. We had talked about her joining me in England, but I firstly needed to get a shoreside job. This could be just what I was looking for. As far as the Merchant Navy was concerned, the writing was on the wall for all to see. With the advent of bigger and bigger container ships with far smaller crews, jobs aboard British ships were becoming harder to find. Many of the vessels of, for example, Port Line Ltd, were too old and uneconomical to compete and were being sent for scrapping. It was time to move on and find something new.

The next day I accompanied John into Portsmouth Dockyard. With their ship in refit, the dredger crews had no designated place to assemble, and so we made our way to a large strange shelter that the men had built from pallets, bales of hay, and tarpaulins. Inside this cubby hole were tables and benches, and it was all rather cosy. Even though the guys had been given some mundane job to do, and were supposed to be gainfully employed to keep themselves busy, they straight away started up a game of gin rummy. One bloke was posted to keep a lookout for any unannounced visit by the bosses. We were into our fifth game and I was winning – hell, I wasn't even supposed to be there! – when the lookout shouted, "Watch out. Boss man's coming." As the management guy walked around one side of the shelter in search of his merry men, twenty men all shuffled around to the other side so that they were always out of sight of him. He scratched his head in bafflement and went on his way and the card game resumed. The rest of the day carried on in much the same way. I thought, "This ain't such a bad job."

The next day I made my way to the dredging office and applied for a post; and with my far superior Merchant Navy certification I was welcomed with open arms. Of course I still had another voyage to do on the Beaverfir, and so it was arranged that I would begin work with the Ministry of Public Building & Works (dredging division) in two months time.

Cold as Brass Monkeys – 4th Voyage

Nine days later, the Beaverfir departed from the Royal Docks bound again for Montreal. But firstly there was a two-day stopover in Le Havre to take-on more cargo. Our passage across the Atlantic was uneventful, except that the temperature dropped considerably the nearer we got to Canada, and by the time we arrived in Montreal in mid-November, it was freezing. I had never been so cold in my life. However, before we had left England, Jonesy had given me some good advice, although I thought it rather weird at the time. "Beg or borrow a few pairs of your sister's tights," he had suggested. "It'll act as a thermal layer and help to keep the cold out."

We arrived in Montreal late on the evening of 18th November. It was far too late to meet up with Petra. The next morning the temperature had plummeted and I noticed that, so as to keep warm and be able to carry-on with the task of unloading our cargo, the stevedores wore one-piece suits that had electric coils sown into the fabric, and that were powered by a battery pack. They were in essence wearing an electric blanket. Even the cars were equipped with a cable that plugged into the vehicle's engine block so as to keep it from freezing up overnight.

The next evening Petra came aboard and we wasted no time in getting acquainted again. My former cabinmate Wilson - the Man in the Mirror - had gone to pastures new, and I had the cabin to myself. We made the most of it. When we weren't making love, we talked about her joining me in England and I told her about the dredger job. Also, unlike the voyages to Australasia, where I spent copious amounts of money on booze and easy women, I had saved a fair bit of money from these voyages aboard the Beaverfir and I intended putting it to good use. John had put down a deposit and bought a 3-bedroom property, and I intended also to invest my hard-earned money into bricks and mortar. Initially though, I would be renting a room in John's house while I got myself settled in the new job, and so we discussed a timetable as to when she would join me. The ship stayed just three days in port, and sadly we would not, as usual, be calling in to Montreal on the way home, so this would be the last time I would be seeing Petra for many months. We made the most of it by almost wearing out the bed-springs!

On the Friday evening we set sail for Toronto and Hamilton. Our passage along the St Lawrence Seaway was bitterly cold, with temperatures nose-diving to many degrees below freezing. To go out on deck whenever we needed to moor the ship was a pain-in-the-butt. Numerous layers of clothing needed to be worn. I wore a vest, two shirts, woolly jumper, two coats, two pairs jeans, thick woollen socks, stout boots, a balaclava, ear muffs, gloves, and of course my sister's tights. Even so, I was still freezing – as cold as brass monkeys. It was so cold that the captain ordered that we should spend no more than 15 minutes out on the open decks. Everything was covered in ice and it was difficult to carry out the simplest of tasks. Due to wearing many layers of clothing, one particular chore which proved tricky was to go for a pee. As the Beaverfir loitered in Iroquois lock, I desperately needed to rush to the toilet. With frozen fingers I attempted to unzip my two pairs of jeans so as to locate my 'old chap' who was hiding somewhere deep in the recesses of my underpants. Finally I found him – shrivelled up like a button mushroom! I prised him loose and gave him a quick inspection. The poor fellow looked like a pale blue acorn. Without doubt Canada is a beautiful country, but in winter it can be akin to living in a deep-freeze.

The rest of our visit on the Great lakes was completely uneventful, as it was far too cold to want to venture ashore, and we mainly played cards in the warm and cosy crew's messroom. The ship stayed just three days in Toronto, once again loading rolls of print paper, then moved along the coast to Hamilton. After four days in Hamilton, we began our transit back along the St Lawrence Seaway, and again it was bitterly cold as the deck crew tied

343

the ship up as we entered each of the seven lock systems. As the Beaverfir exited the last lock at Saint Lambert, we were back on the St Lawrence River. Engine revolutions were increased and we sped eastwards, leaving Montreal astern.

The next morning we berthed in Quebec City, where we were due to stay for two days to load the last of our cargo. I remembered the fabulous visit to the city on our last voyage, but the weather remained so numbingly bitter cold that I stayed onboard.

At last, in early December, the ship set out for the transatlantic voyage to England. We hit some lumpy weather on the way across "The Pond", but nowhere near as bad as the terrifying crossing of our previous voyage. Our grand little ship took the waves in her stride and we were soon out of the gale and racing for home.

Beaverfir berthed in the Royal Docks on 14th December 1969, and soon after paying-off, I was packed and ready to be on my way back home to Silvertown. I had already informed the chief officer that, sadly I wouldn't be returning for another voyage, and so this was where it was time to say goodbye to some good shipmates. I shook hands with John Glancy our bosun, Jonesy, Captain Tom Parker, George Hendrie our chef, Jimmy Donn the 3rd mate, and with Dave Perry and many others. I also gave Minxy the ship's cat his last stroke before walking down the gangway and having a last look at my ship.

Perhaps most of all I was sad to be leaving the Beaverfir. The old girl had been my home for almost six months, and I had got attached to her in the way that only a ship can tug at one's heartstrings. In reality you know that, even though she's just made of steel plates and rivets and plastic and wood; that somewhere deep inside her, she has a beating heart. Some ships have that quality to endure and to draw you back to them, but this I knew was my final goodbye. As my taxi pulled away from the gangway, I looked back one last time and remembered the wonderful times I had enjoyed aboard her.

13: The Demise of the British Merchant Navy

Rapidly Downhill

The time had come for the Merchant Navy and I to part company. This didn't mean that I would no longer go to sea or be employed in a nautical occupation; it's just that I would no longer be sailing around the world or going deep-sea. I had noticed the gradual reduction in available jobs during 1969, and by 1970, the situation had worsened considerably. The British Merchant Navy had begun to spiral into a mere shadow of its former self. There are many reasons why the Merchant Navy went downhill and out-of-business.

When I started my sea-going career in the early 1960s, Great Britain had a very healthy shipping industry and one of the largest mercantile marine fleets in the world. New ships were being built, and Britain's shipbuilding industry was contracted to build the new tonnage. But the situation quickly changed.

The seamen's strike of 1966 didn't benefit anyone, especially the seamen's union, the seamen themselves or the British ship-owners. The seamen were on strike for six weeks, during which time ships were stuck unmanned in the docks; which then prevented other ships from docking and getting unloaded. Importers and exporters could not buy and sell their goods and couldn't rely on British ships to carry their freight, so when the strike finished in July 1966, many of them switched to foreign tonnage to carry their cargo. That was a big loss for British shipping.

On 5th June 1967, after belligerent acts to-and-fro between the states of Syria, Egypt and Jordan against the American equipped state of Israel, the Israeli's launched a pre-emptive air strike against their enemy's air forces and air bases. And so started what became known as The 6-day War. The Egyptians blockaded and mined the Suez Canal, which not only trapped ships within the Bitter Lakes, but effectively closed the canal to all traffic until 1975. With no direct sea route to any countries east of Suez, all shipping had to take the longer route around South Africa's Cape of Good Hope, consequently using far more fuel and taking much longer. This was another hammer-blow to shipping worldwide.

The reasons for the 1973/1974 oil crisis are complex; not least of which was the United States providing military and economic support for the Arab nation's sworn enemy – Israel. The USA had also re-supplied arms to Israel during the Yom Kippur War, which caused a major blow to the global status of the Arab nations. They needed a way in which to strike a blow against the Americans, and to reassert their importance on the international political stage, so they chose to hit them economically. Therefore, the Organisation of Arab Oil Producing Exporting Countries (OAPEC), put in place an oil embargo which lasted from October 73 until March 74, and the price of a barrel of oil was raised 70%. One of the major running costs of any ship is the cost of fuel oil, and due to the price hike, many ships became uneconomical to maintain. Therefore many were sold or were sent for scrap. This brought the death of British shipping ever closer.

However, by far the largest nail in the coffin for shipping companies was the advent of containerisation. The new large container ships were very fast indeed - 22/25 knots - which cut down on the typical passage time of a conventional 16 knot general cargo vessel on a London to Melbourne run from 29 days to 19 days. Before this advance, conventional cargo ships typically stayed in Australian waters for a period of three months whilst stevedores discharged and re-loaded the ship by manual methods. Cranes with slings unloaded crates onto pallets, and cargo was literally manhandled. Dockers then manoeuvred the crates into the cargo holds, and forklift trucks moved the pallets to warehouses. Damage and delays were frequent and militant trade unions were forever bringing the dockers out on strike. Containerisation changed all that forever.

With a container vessel, the containers are ISO size, and the boxes are simply lifted on or off a truck to a ship using large specialised cranes. Because the container is loaded and unloaded at the factory or plant where the goods are manufactured, stevedores are not required to handle the cargo inside - which cuts out pilferage, the cargo remains dry, the produce can be palletised, and refrigerated containers can be temperature controlled. Containerisation reduces ship to consignee time, and it lowers transport costs, but far more importantly, the vessel's turnaround time is drastically reduced.

By the mid-1960s the writing was on the wall; and so as to move forward and to stay in business, the shipping companies had to modernise. New ships had to be built, and thousands of steel containers would be required. They couldn't afford to do this by themselves as the huge expense would be far too costly. The shipping companies therefore had to amalgamate into large consortiums that could afford to finance the new equipment.

The new British consortiums that were brought into existence were each made up of several shipping groups. The main contenders were ACT (Associated Container Transport) This comprised Ben Line, Blue Star Line, Cunard/Port Line, Ellerman Line and Harrison Line.

Another consortium was OCL (Overseas Containers Limited). It was created by joining forces with Clan Line Ltd, Union Castle, Furness Withy, P&O and Blue Funnel Line. In the United States the ACL consortium (Atlantic Container Lines) and others were being brought into operation to achieve containerisation within their own trading spheres.

Containership ACT 2 - 24,821 gross tons

By the late 1960s the first generation of container vessels were being launched. These vessels were very large and extremely fast. At about 25,000 tons (quickly superseded by 45,000 tonners) they could each carry as much cargo as previously carried by eight general cargo ships. To put things into perspective, the first three ACT container vessels replaced 18 (yes18!) conventional cargo ships, and reduced a typical round trip voyage to Australasia from 162 days (23 weeks) to 70 days (10 weeks). The crew complement reduced drastically from an average of 60 aboard a conventional cargo ship, to 20 crewmen; later reduced even further to 15. The older Port Victor/Port Pirie type cargo ships carried about 65+ crew, the smaller Port Montreal a little less – call it an average of 60 crew. So – some simple mathematics – 18 conventional ships with 60 crew = 1080 men's wages. Three container ships with 20 crew = NO CONTEST!

It is interesting to note that, of the first six ships of the new ACT consortium, most were built in Germany. German builders were also mainly contracted to build the six ships of the new OCL group. Subsequent vessels were mostly built in Japan and many British yards went out of business. Large swathes of shipbuilding cities on the Clyde, the Tyne, in Belfast, Humberside, Barrow-in-Furness, and Sunderland became derelict wastelands with thousands of people unemployed.

The early container vessels carried 20 foot long containers, which became the normal industry measurement when referring to container ship capacity. Therefore TEU (twenty foot equivalent units) means that if a vessel is designated as 2000 TEU, then it can carry 2000 twenty footers or it may carry a mixed cargo of 20 foot or 40 foot containers. The latest container ships are truly enormous. In fact I don't think the word enormous does justice to their size.

As an example, and so as to gauge the difference in size and economics, here are some statistics that may put the efficiency of modern cruise liners, container ships, and oil tankers into perspective.

Name	TEU	gross tons	length	crew	speed	pax
Queen Mary	n/a	81,237	1019	1101	28.5	2139
Queen Mary 2	n/a	149,215	1132	1253	30	3056

Queen Mary 2 carries just 14% more crew than the old Queen Mary, yet carries 43% more fare paying passengers.

Port Pirie	n/a	10,535	529	65	16	12
ACT 2	1334	24,821	713	20	22	nil
Emma Maersk	14,770	170,974	1302	13	25.5	nil

Consider this - just three of the 1st generation ACT container vessels replaced 18 conventional cargo ships. The giant Emma Maersk has 11 times the capacity of the older ACT container vessels, and with a crew of just 13 men.

Hollywood	17,720 dwt	548	60	13	nil
Seawise Giant	657,019 dwt	1504	20	16	nil

Note how the oil tanker Seawise Giant can carry 37 times more cargo than the Hollywood, yet carries only one third of her crew.

As an example of the swingeing cuts being made to the Merchant Navy fleets; in 1965 Port Line Ltd had 35 conventional cargo ships in their fleet. Between 1965 and 1970 they sold or scrapped seven ships. Between 1970 and 1975 they sold or scrapped 15 ships, and by the early 1980s the

Port Line house-flag had been hauled down for the last time. The company, which had began trading in 1914, had ceased to exist. However, the Port Line story wasn't an isolated case. Throughout the mercantile fleets, hundreds of shipping companies were being rapidly decimated by modernisation, and many companies went to the wall. The container ship had replaced them all.

The cost-cutting crew reductions weren't the sole reason for the demise of the British crews. After containerisation, very few British sailors wanted to stay in the Merchant Navy. There are several reasons for this. Previously the crews had enjoyed the lifestyle of sailing to exotic locations and visiting pubs and clubs and having fun with a variety of young ladies thrown in for good measure. Usually a voyage to Australasia would typically encompass a stay in Australasian waters of about three months. Nowadays, on that very same voyage, the crew would be lucky to be able to get ashore at all, because the turnaround time is so short. A vessel may now be in port for as little as 12 hours, with no time to enjoy oneself. Back in the days of traditional cargo ships, they would berth close to the city centre. Nowadays the modern container terminal is sited many miles out of town, which makes a run ashore even more difficult when on a quick turnaround schedule. Furthermore, the reduction in crew meant that crews were working harder with fewer men available.

The modern ship's crew are at their busiest when a container ship enters harbour, because the crew must disengage the container security lashings that secure the boxes in place. If there are several hundred containers to offload, then that is a very labour intensive task. It leaves no time at all for a run ashore. For the engineering staff, the ship's time alongside, when the engines are shut down, is when they must carry out their maintenance.

Together with the lack of shore leave, a further reason for a lack of willingness for a life at sea, is that living aboard a container ship can now be a very lonely existence. With a typical crew of 15 – and at any one time a third of those are on watch – there can often be no one around to talk to. Even though the accommodation is generously proportioned and of a high standard, many crews were suffering from depression due to long working hours and no shore leave. As a further cost-cutting exercise, many companies flagged-out their vessels and registered them in low-cost Panamanian, Liberian or other flags of convenience countries, which enabled them to employ foreign crews on a much reduced wage.

Containerisation affected the ports equally as much as it affected the ships and the shipping business. The ancient docks that were created

349

around general cargo shipping shared many common characteristics. Most docks were upon tidal rivers, and they had enclosed basins with restricted lock access. The locations of these docks meant that they were unsuitable for the handling of these high volume containerised cargoes. Liverpool, London Royal Docks, the upriver Millwall and West India Docks and Surrey Commercial are examples of operational dock systems which were incompatible for container ships. Most had warehouses for the storage and handling of general cargoes, but there was inadequate acreage of land available to handle and store containers, and road access was limited. However, another nail in the coffin for the docks, were that the entrance locks were physically too narrow to allow the new container vessels to enter. The largest vessel ever to berth in London's Royal Docks was the RMS Mauritania in 1939. It managed to slide into the entrance lock with mere feet to spare on each side of its 89 foot beam. The new container vessels, with a width of over 100 feet, were far too large

As containerisation took over, and the conventional vessels were sold or went for scrap, the docks were largely abandoned and turned over to other uses or re-development. London's Royal Docks, for example, has been reborn as London City Airport and the ExCel exhibition and conference centre. West India Docks has been redeveloped into the high-rise office buildings that we know today as Canary Wharf.

New container terminals were built at Tilbury, Southampton, Felixstowe, Liverpool, and a score of other ports that had adequate available land, and that were more suitable for container operations. The new terminals required a very small workforce, so apart from the crews who manned the ships, the biggest losers were the dock workers themselves, who in the past had manually handled the cargoes with slings and billhooks and forklift trucks. At a stroke they were all unemployed. All this had a knock-on effect on the local community. Local companies, who had formerly provided services to the shipping industry, went out of business. Silvertown became a run-down derelict ghost town, and by the early 1980s no ships were loaded or discharged anymore and the docks instead became a place to cheaply lay-up unused tonnage.

Up until now we have dealt mainly with the demise of thousands of cargo vessels. However, other types of vessels were also seriously affected. The passenger liner was a case in point. In the late-1950s the Boeing 707 came onto the scene, and by the mid-1960s, together with aircraft like the Douglas DC-8, they had taken much of the transatlantic passenger trade from the liners. It made economic sense for the traveller to fly to the United States in seven hours, rather than perhaps endure a winter Atlantic crossing, albeit aboard a luxurious Cunarder. By 1965 on some crossings, the Queen

Mary carried more crew than passengers, and the new jet aircraft rapidly sounded the death knell for the transatlantic liners.

Liners on other routes also found difficult trading conditions. During the 1960s many of the countries and colonies of the British Empire that were served by passenger liners gained their independence and no longer required the sizeable ex-pat contingent to work and govern them. Examples were the Indian sub-continent served by ships of the P & O and British India fleets, and the South and East African countries served by vessels of the Union Castle Line.

Some of the passenger ships were modernised with air-conditioning and changed into cruise liners, as opposed to being on scheduled liner voyages. Nevertheless, the rise in the price of fuel oil in 1973 put paid to a countless number of the ships and many were sold, mainly to Greek interests, or were scrapped.

The assisted passage scheme for emigration to Australia came to an end and so, with no more 'Ten-pound poms' to transport, this made the passenger shipping trades so much more difficult to earn a profitable income.

The Ministry of Defence made the decision to transport Britain's troops to and from her far flung outposts by aircraft, rather than employ dedicated troop ships, and so came to an end the centuries old tradition of moving her armies via giant liners.

The gigantic Boeing 747 jumbo jet came on-line in 1970 and took even more trade, not only from the ever dwindling transatlantic liners, but from scheduled liners worldwide.

As already explained, some vessels were refitted into one-class tourist cruise liners and ran cruises from British ports such as Southampton and Tilbury. For some time these cruises were fairly successful, and gave a much needed shot-in-the-arm for the cruise industry. In spite of this, one drawback was that, to reach any cruise destination in perhaps the Mediterranean or the Canary Islands, a ship would need to steam for almost three days before it arrived at a sunny tourist location, often having to brave the infamous Bay of Biscay with its unpredictable weather. During this era of the early 1970s the British worker had more money in his pocket and could afford a decent holiday. These tourists, who had previously been content with a week or two at a UK seaside resort, now wanted to travel abroad; but instead of taking passage onboard a cruise liner, they opted for a new type of holiday – the package tour. Other types of aircraft that made package tours possible, and that also seriously affected the cruise ships, came onto the scene. The BAC-1-11, the Boeing 727 and the Sud-Aviation Caravelle were medium to short haul jet airliners that took holidaymakers to their sunny holiday spot within a few hours, and this negated the need to take a long voyage to the sun.

Even the fishing industry was affected. The downfall of mainstream shipping coincided with another hammer-blow to our fishermen - namely The Icelandic Cod War. In the 1960s we had a vibrant fishing industry, and many large freezer-factory trawlers were built in British shipyards so as to take advantage of the plethora of fish species to be found around the coast of Iceland. However, in 1972 the Icelandic government, seeing their waters overfished, decided to impose a fish quota by unilaterally declaring an Exclusive Economic Zone and extending the fishing limits out beyond Iceland's territorial waters. This led to conflicts between Icelandic gunboats and the trawlers, which resulted is some net-cutting and ramming incidents. The Royal Navy got involved so as to deter harassment, and for a time there were direct confrontations between the opposing navies. However, the British government caved-in when the Icelanders threatened to close down the important NATO air base at Keflavik, and our fishing vessels suddenly found themselves up shit creek without a paddle. The end result was that many fishermen became unemployed and sought jobs within the mainstream shipping industry, which had the effect of more men chasing fewer jobs.

⚓

The time had come for me to leave deep-sea employment and seek a career in a far more secure environment. Consequently I sought a suitable post in the UK where I could progress and perhaps get promotion. Therefore, the Beaverfir was to be my last ship that traded overseas. However, I couldn't just give up my sea-going career completely. I loved the nautical life too much for that. There was just one more obstacle to be overcome – Petra!

By early 1970 I had joined the Ministry of Public Buildings & Works dredging fleet and was renting a room at John Sheppard's house. Petra and I had been corresponding regularly and I was making plans for her to fly over and join me in Portsmouth. I was looking to purchase a house of my own, and seeking a suitable job for her when she arrived. Our life together was looking good, and my view of the world was through rose tinted glasses. One day a letter arrived with a Canadian stamp on the envelope and I opened it with eager anticipation. However, the contents contained a bombshell.

Dear Graham,

It's been months since we've seen each other. I really did plan on coming to see you. I've even gone to the airline to book my flight. Unfortunately, I have to cancel. I'm sorry to have to tell you this in a letter.

I have searched my feelings, and I find that to move to England would be so far away from my family and I would miss them so much. England is so distant from Montreal, and to leave them would seem so final. I'm afraid it's a case of cold feet. I know that you intend to remain in England, and as we live so far apart, I can't see how we can maintain a long-distance relationship.

I hope you have a good life full of laughter and love. I know you'll easily find someone who won't break your heart. I'll never forget you or our time on the Beaverfir. Those are memories I'll cherish for the rest of my life. You made me feel so good about myself; so desirable and loved. You're a very special human being, and because of that you will remain in my heart forever.

Until we meet again, in this life or the next, Petra

So, that was that. Our relationship wasn't to be, and there was nothing that I could do about it. For a very long time I became downhearted, and so took refuge in becoming a bookworm and listening to music. To forget my despondency I threw myself into my work and in making plans to buy a house.

⚓

Well, there we are at the end of my tale. That special era of the 1960s held some of my happiest memories. Nowadays I have a comfortable life with a nice home, a decent car and money in the bank. If you were to ask me if I would swap all of these things, and exchange them to go back to working aboard a rusty cargo ship, spend weeks on end sailing across empty oceans, be away for months at a time, working long hours and have to endure stormy weather; I would give it ten seconds thought and my answer would be.......you bet I would!

The Silvertown kid – Bibliography

Thanks to Wikipedia for checking a plethora of facts.
Happy Valley facts – www.campoalegresex.com
Port – To –Port Distances – www.searates.com
St Lawrence Seaway facts –
www.greatlakes-seaway.com/en/seaway/vital/index.html

Photographs of Saville Road floods - Mauritania - Dominion Monarch in dry dock – Tate & Lyle sugar refinery – Aerial view of Royal Docks by kind permission of Jenni Munro-Collins & Richard Durack at Newham archive local studies.
Photographs of Port Pirie, Port Melbourne, Port St Lawrence, Somerset, Sussex, Argentina Star, Icenic, Port Victor, Port Montreal, Beaverfir, Glenorchy, and container ship ACT 2, by kind permission of Iain Lovie (Napier, New Zealand) – photograph(s) from the collection of Iain Lovie
Aerial photo Port Melbourne – by kind permission of Rueben Goossens www.ssmaritime.com
Photos of Southsea & Camber Queen by kind permission of Ian Boyle www.simplonpc.co.uk
Photographs of TS Vindicatrix and Monty's Bar by kind permission of Jim Lloyd.
Photograph of Chloe by kind permission of Megan Herring, Functions Manager, Young & Jackson Hotel.

Printed in Great Britain
by Amazon

86216738R00210